WOMEN'S READING IN BRITAIN
1750–1835

The growth of female reading audiences from the mid eighteenth century to the early Victorian era represents both a vital episode in women's history and a highly significant factor in shaping the literary production of the period. This book offers for the first time a broad overview and detailed analysis of this growing readership, its representation in literature, and the extent of its influence. It examines both historical women readers, including Laetitia Pilkington, Elizabeth Carter, Frances Burney and Jane Austen, and a wide range of texts in which the figure of the woman reader is important, from Gothic (and other) novels to conduct books and educational works, letters, journals and memoirs, political and economic works, and texts on history and science. Jacqueline Pearson's study offers illuminating insights which help to make sense of the ambivalent and contradictory attitudes of the age to the key figure of the woman reader.

Jacqueline Pearson is Senior Lecturer in English Literature at the University of Manchester. Her previous publications include *The Prostituted Muse: Images of Women and Women Dramatists, 1642–1737* (1988) and *Tragedy and Tragicomedy in the Plays of John Webster* (1980) and many articles and essays on drama, fiction, women's writing and reading.

Lit - Other

£17-50

(cheapest
online
£25-00)

WOMEN'S READING
IN BRITAIN
1750–1835

A dangerous recreation

JACQUELINE PEARSON

CAMBRIDGE
UNIVERSITY PRESS

PUBLISHED BY THE PRESS SYNDICATE OF THE UNIVERSITY OF CAMBRIDGE
The Pitt Building, Trumpington Street, Cambridge CB2 1RP, United Kimgdom

CAMBRIDGE UNIVERSITY PRESS
The Edinburgh Building, Cambridge, CB2 2RU, UK http://www.cup.cam.ac.uk
40 West 20th Street, New York, NY 10011-4211, USA http://www.cup.org
10 Stamford Road, Oakleigh, Melbourne 3166, Australia

First published 1999

Printed in the United Kingdom at the University Press, Cambridge

Typeset in Baskerville 11/12.5pt [VN]

A catalogue record for this book is available from the British Library

Library of Congress Cataloguing in Publication data
Pearson, Jacqueline, 1949–
Women's reading in Britain, 1750–1835: a dangerous recreation / Jacqueline Pearson.
p.   cm.
Includes bibliographical references and index.
ISBN 0 521 58439 6 (hardback)
1. English prose literature – 18th century – History and criticism.
2. Women – Great Britain – Books and reading – History – 18th century.
3. English prose literature – 19th century – History and criticism.
4. Women – Great Britain – Books and reading – History – 19th century.
5. Women and literature – Great Britain – History – 18th century.
6. Women and literature – Great Britain – History – 19th century.
7. Authors and readers – Great Britain – History – 18th century.
8. Authors and readers – Great Britain – History – 19th century.
9. Literature – Appreciation – Great Britain – History.
10. Books and reading in literature.
I. Title.
PR756.W65P43 1999
828'.608099287 – dc 21   98-38078 CIP

ISBN 0 521 58439 6

For my mother,
Elizabeth Pearson,
my sister,
Jonquil Yates,
and my nieces,
Claire and Alex Yates
three generations of women readers

Contents

Preface   ix

Introduction   1

1   Pygmalionesses and the pencil under the petticoat:
    Richardson, Johnson and Byron   22

2   What should girls and women read?   42

3   The pleasures and perils of reading   87

3   Pleasures and perils of reading: some case histories   122

5   Where and how should women read?   152

6   Preparing for equality: class, gender, reading   176

7   A dangerous recreation: women and novel-reading   196

Conclusion   219
Notes   221
Select bibliography   260
Index   285

Preface

Between 1750 and the mid 1830s literacy among women increased and women became increasingly significant in the literary marketplace: indeed, it has been argued that by the end of the eighteenth century the majority of reading audiences were female. Moreover, women's reading became central to a range of discourses, not all of which are obviously concerned with gender or literacy. Everywhere one looks in the literature of the period, one sees women reading. The discourses of women's reading are voluminous and paradoxically both repetitive and deeply contradictory. This book explores these phenomena both as a way of clarifying our understanding of women's cultural position in the late eighteenth and early nineteenth centuries, and as a way of better comprehending the authors, male as well as female, who wrote with this audience in mind. I take it for granted that writing on reading, both non-fictional and fictional, is 'ideologically freighted':[1] studying these writings displays more fully than anything else I know the contradictions in contemporary gender ideologies and the complex relationships of contestation but also complicity between women generally thought to represent very different political positions. Writing cultural history requires juggling large numbers of balls at once, but I have consciously attempted to balance broad generalisations and specific close readings (of, among others, works by Charlotte Lennox, Ann Radcliffe, Charlotte Dacre, Hannah More, Jane Austen and Sarah Green). While, especially in chapter 2, I deal with women's reading of a wide range of material, the book focuses especially on the issue of fiction-reading, since this issue recurs so compulsively and anxiously in contemporary texts.

I have adopted a method in some respects as influenced by the postmodern women's novel as by conventional academic discourse: rather than presenting a single linear argument I spiral around some key issues, returning to them in different contexts: the elision of sexuality and textuality, the dangers of novel-reading, reading and its various relationships to domesticity, family, and community, the temptations of resisting reading. The introduction outlines more fully the problems I am dealing with and the methodologies I adopt. Chapter 1 examines male writers' attitudes to their female readers, and their reading of female writers, citing especially Richardson, Johnson and Byron. Chapter 2 examines women's reading genre by genre, including religious reading, conduct books, history, travels, science and imaginative literature, and demonstrates both the anxiety of commentators about virtually all reading for women, and how women could read even the most legitimate texts resistingly. Chapter 3 looks in more detail at the pleasures and perils characteristically associated with women's reading, and chapter 4 further develops some key themes by four case histories of women readers, Laetitia Pilkington, Frances Burney d'Arblay, Elizabeth Carter and Jane Austen. Chapter 5 explores the gendering of library use in the period, and the differences between reading silently and reading aloud; chapter 6 focuses on the impact of class (and, very briefly, of 'race') on the gendering of reading. Finally, chapter 7 examines in more detail the issue of women's novel-reading, focusing on four novels which apparently attack it, Charlotte Lennox's *The Female Quixote*, Eaton Stannard Barrett's *The Heroine*, Austen's *Northanger Abbey*, and Sarah Green's *Scotch Novel Reading*.

This has been a long-term project and I owe more debts than I can easily acknowledge or pay, to students, colleagues and friends. I must, however, not forget to thank Paul Dawson, David Thame, and Kathryn Sutherland, or to acknowledge my special debt, as always, to Glenys Davies. I am grateful also to the British Academy Humanities Research Board, who financed a semester's leave, and to the University of Manchester Research Support Fund.

Introduction

It is observed by Bacon, that 'reading makes a full man, conversation a ready man, and writing an exact man'.

So Samuel Johnson (mis)quoted in 1753.[1] But what kind of *woman* did reading make? From the 1750s to the 1830s culture, elite and popular, was preoccupied with such questions to an extraordinary degree. The reading woman became not only historical reality but also sign, with a bewildering range of significations. The period's most important debates, about authority, gender and sexuality, the economics and morality of consumption, national identity and stability, class and revolution, use the sign of the reading woman: and she might function as either positive or negative term. In British accounts of the French Revolution, conservatives registered support for traditional values by hagiographical accounts of Marie Antoinette reading with her children, or anxieties about social change through the image of a maidservant who dares to sit reading in the presence of her mistress. Those sympathetic to its aims depicted the importance of books for the emancipation of women 'bastilled . . . for life' in unjust social institutions, or used the difficulty of access to literature to symbolise the oppression of labouring-class women.[2] Women's reading became 'a site on which one may see a variety of cultural and sexual anxieties displayed',[3] even anxieties which do not seem primarily concerned with either gender or literacy.

'Literacy was a part of the agenda for modernity, the city, and the Enlightenment', and reading became 'politicized as never before'.[4] The polyvalence of the image of the reading woman is, however, striking. On the one hand, 'reading was felt to be a potentially seditious employment for women': on the other, it is women's 'most rational employment', the 'spirit's oil without which, its own friction against itself would wear it out', its function not only intellectually fulfilling and psychologically

1

therapeutic but also moral, a protection against 'dissipation', whose 'true use' is to make women 'wiser and better'. Richard Newton's 'A Bachelor's Litany' (1795) asks to be saved from

> A Wife who when Stockings and shirts want repair,
> sits reading a novel all day in her chair,

but also from 'a Wife who in reading could ne'er find delight': reading both symbolises and opposes domestic values.[5] Thus the same commentator might display contradictory attitudes to the reading of the same books: Anna Letitia Barbauld defended recreational reading on the grounds that the imagination like the body needed exercise, but also attacked it as 'an indolent way of passing the time'. This polyvalence was one reason why contemporary writing continually returns to women's reading, not only in education and conduct works but also in what Nancy Armstrong calls the 'scene of reading' in fiction.[6]

'[T]he rise of the domestic woman' in the late eighteenth and early nineteenth centuries was a 'major event in political history', and the entrenchment of 'domestic ideology' shaped the feminine role and female subject in fundamental ways, with women becoming 'the symbols and the guarantors of a secure, middle-class virtue'.[7] In this domestic world, literary consumption seemed 'inherently ambiguous', disturbingly both 'radical and reactionary'. Books provided women with 'a way of remaining in the home . . . and yet communicating . . . with the world outside': this duality threatened subversion of an ideology of separate spheres. Some literary forms particularly aimed at women, like conduct books, letters, magazines and novels, implicitly renegotiated the distinction between public and private, creating a world, and a format, which was 'domestic yet public', their reading constituting 'an event somewhere between the private and the social'.[8] For some commentators, female reading was dangerous because it could distract from domestic duties or transgress the limits of a private sphere: good women must show 'self-denial' and resist the 'pure pleasure' of reading to 'take up the . . . needle'.[9]

Some progressive intellectuals tried to resist the conceptualisation of reading as guilty pleasure by representing it as itself domestic, even a metaphor for domesticity. In one *Lady's Magazine* story the hero dreads a wife who does not read and thus cannot appreciate 'domestic pleasures', and a number of idealised heroines, like Gertrude Ashurst in *Fatal Obedience* or Maria Edgeworth's Belinda, display their 'taste for domestic pleasures' specifically through their 'taste for reading'.[10] In Edgeworth's

Letters for Literary Ladies (1795), the 'pleasures of reading' are contrasted with the more dangerous pleasures young men find outside the home, and are figured as specifically 'domestic', the text's central term in its argument about women's education. The first writer, an opponent of female education, fears that reading will teach a girl to despise 'domestic life', though his more liberal correspondent argues that reading preserves rather than compromises 'domestic virtue', which requires the exercise of reason rather than 'ignorance'. Reading which teaches women 'only to *feel*' is dangerous, as the story of Julia demonstrates, but Caroline's wiser reading teaches her to '*think*' and thus to be happy in 'domestic life'. The second letter ends with a utopian vision of marriage as a relationship of 'equals', and of a stable society based on a network of domesticities, each dependent on a literate wife and mother.[11]

The demands of domestic ideology were absolute and replaced any other code of instructions about female reading, or so some women imply. The Duchess of Devonshire excuses herself for reading *Les liaisons dangereuses* and Rousseau's *Confessions*, both with an English reputation for immorality, not only because they were fashionable and so essential to effective social life, but also because her husband had read them and marked them for her, so her reading of an apparently transgressive text is actually dutifully compliant to domestic ideology. Frances Boscawen shared reading with her admiral husband even when they were physically apart, and this service to domestic ideology liberated her to read a number of suspect texts, such as Mandeville's sceptical *The Fable of the Bees*, Smollett's robust *Roderick Random*, and, most remarkably, Diderot's erotic tale *Les bijoux indiscrets*:

> But my dear, what a book! I am ashamed of it! I have read it right through, and because I would not conceal from you the worst actions of my life, I send it to you, to show you what a wicked book has engrossed your chaste wife these last two days. But it is you, my dear love, who have caused this vulgarity, for if I had not sought your amusement, I should not have amused myself with such an improper book.

Later, in widowhood, without the alibi of domestic ideology, her reading becomes more conservative, and she even apologises for reading such moral novels as Moore's *Mordaunt* and Jane West's *The Infidel Father*.[12]

Reading could serve as a metonym for civilisation, for without a 'thorough Knowledge of Books', a 'Disadvantage in Morals' is inevitable. Sir William Weller Pepys defends Hannah More's project for educating poor children by asking, 'If you had lost your way in a wood and saw two men at a distance . . . the one with a gun, and the other with a book, to which of them would you address yourself?'.[13] But treatments of reading tend to be blatantly gendered. In Pepys' rhetoric, even in a context where the subject is a woman's involvement in the campaign for literacy, it is *male* reading which is evoked to represent civilised values. Reading, indeed, tends to be depicted as shaping the male subject in a range of positive ways. Isaac D'Israeli's *Curiosities of Literature* shows Newton reading when struck by the apple, Joshua Reynolds inspired to become an artist by reading 'Richardson's Treatise', and how Cowley 'became a poet' by reading *The Faerie Queene*.[14] In *Frankenstein*, 'the destinies of the explorer Robert Walton, the scientist Frankenstein, and the unnamed creature are determined by their reading'. The same does not seem to be true of Elizabeth, Justine, or even Safie, whose reading lessons prove so enabling for the monster, who attempts to recreate himself through scraps of androcentric culture – a volume of Plutarch's *Lives*, *The Sorrows of Young Werther*, and *Paradise Lost*, providing so richly ambiguous a language for self-hood.[15]

Enlightenment educationalists argued that '*Reading* is as needful for one Sex as the other', but also accepted it would have different roles in the lives of men and women: as Mary Wortley Montagu formulated it, reading was necessary for the 'Reputation of Men' but only for 'the Amusement of Women'.[16] It was, moreover, conceptualised differently according to gender. While men's reading was shown to facilitate intellectual development, women's tended to be located in the female body, represented as a physical not an intellectual act. Consequently it was believed to have a direct effect not only on female morals but also on the female body, girls being urged to limit their 'reading' because it was an enemy to 'health and beauty', likely to 'hurt [the] eyes' or 'spoil [the] shape' of the woman reader. Immoderate reading caused fainting and even dangerous changes in pulse rate.[17]

Reading empowered the male: 'He that loves reading . . . has but to desire' and he will acquire knowledge and power.[18] But female desire was more problematic, and the literature of the period is full of women and girls who long to read but are forbidden to do so or are restricted in their reading: Susan Sibbald, Laetitia-Matilda Hawkins' Rosanne and Gertrude, and Mary Hays' Emma Courtney were forbidden access to family libraries, parents tried to prevent Laetitia Pilkington and Frances Sheridan from even learning to read, Sarah Fielding's Cynthia is thought lazy when she reads. Domestic duties, especially sewing, frequently interrupt reading, as for Dorothy Wordsworth, made to sew 'an old shirt' when she wanted to read the *Iliad*.[19] Even when they acquired literacy, books and time to read, reading often leads women and girls astray. Their reading provides thumb-nail sketches of fictional female characters, sharpening contrasts between sensible and foolish, virtuous and vicious. This is a favourite technique of Maria Edgeworth. In 'Mademoiselle Panache', to take only one example, Helen Temple reads *Gaudentio di Lucca*, a utopian novel advocating 'the patriarchal theory of government', monogamy and domestic values, then attributed to Bishop Berkeley and known for its 'refined understanding', which she has borrowed from the private library of respectable Mr Mountague. Lady Augusta on the other hand reads 'one of the very worst books in the French language' from the circulating library,[20] so transgressing proprieties of reading, nationalism and female privacy.

In the age's literary discourses, misreading tends to be gendered as feminine, as in the work of Gibbon or David Hume, Boswell's life of Johnson, or D'Israeli's works on literature. Women show 'false taste' in reading, 'skip over' prefaces to get to a 'picturesque scene, or a tender letter', thus defying the authority of the author, or behave still more transgressively. D'Israeli accuses Catherine Macaulay of tearing pages from a manuscript she was reading in the British Museum: 'when . . . she came across anything tending to favour the Stuarts or discredit the Whigs, she would destroy the offending page'.[21] D'Israeli attacks women readers both for excessive and for insufficient zeal: while Macaulay mutilates manuscripts, Anna Letitia Barbauld is facetiously praised for not 'wasting the bloom of life in the dust of libraries' before publishing her (by implication worthless) history of the Jacobean court. A correspondent to the *Lady's Magazine* in 1795 protested that *she* 'do[es] not always read superficially', and urged women to read Mary Wollstonecraft instead of D'Israeli.[22] Even women writers internalised the association of bad reading practices with the feminine: Mary Berry attributes her habits of 'desultory and . . . improper reading' to a series of inadequate or absent mother-figures, and persistently figures too boring, too much, or the wrong kind of reading as feminine.[23]

Some of the contradictions surrounding women's reading are encapsulated in two very short tales from the *Lady's Magazine*, 'Passion subdued by Reason. A Fragment' of 1795 and Maria Graves' 'The Generous Lover' of 1781. In the former, Matilda is about to elope with Florio, but

in this state of mind, she chanced to take up a volume of our great English moralist, and, opening on a number of the Rambler, in which . . . he has inculcated the necessity of bringing our passions . . . under the guidance of reason; she read till the ebullitions of her enthusiasm began to subside, and her understanding again recovered its usual influence. She awoke as from a dream . . .

While for some reader-response theorists, reading is a 'trance-like state' which 'effaces personal identity', for Matilda it offers an insight into what is allegedly real and rescue from the 'dream' of sexual desire. This conversion experience enables her to reconcile reason and passion, and convert Florio's 'licentious passion' to 'esteem, reverence, and constant love'. 'The Generous Lover' also centres on an act of female reading but deals with it in a very different way. Amelia, who is 'passionately fond of reading novels (a species of amusement highly pernicious to youth of both sexes)', acquires from her reading unrealistic desires, chief of which is 'a titled husband'. As a result, she becomes vulnerable to the proposals of a libertine lord and elopes with him, pausing en route only to go 'to the library' and to take from it 'one of her favourite novels'.[24]

Both tales, in their moralistic eighteenth-century idiom, demonstrate a Derridean belief that 'Reading is transformational'.[25] In one sense this is perfectly simple. The period tended to think in terms of a binary opposition between 'good' and 'bad' books:[26] Matilda reads good books, the moral essays of Johnson, while Amelia reads bad books, novels. Nonetheless, even these short tales hint at complexities surrounding these oppositions and the figure of the female reader. Both demonstrate not only how fiction constructs an implied, ideal reader but also how it controls the historic reader. In 'Passion subdued by Reason', the reader is presented with a utopian pattern for the reading experience, which legitimises her reading and associates it with both pleasure and virtue as long as she remains compliant to male authority. 'The Generous Lover' seems more repressive, generating anxiety about the very process in which the reader is at that moment involved. However even this tale allows more freedom to the female reader than initially appears. When Amelia's aristocratic lover abandons her, she does not die of a broken heart or commit herself to a celibate future; instead she is allowed a happy marriage to a former wooer, now 'generous' enough to renew his courtship. Misreading need not incur lifelong embitterment. The young female reader needs to discriminate what she reads, not to stop reading, and the *Lady's Magazine* markets itself as an aid in this crucial act.

Many contemporary texts draw simplistic distinctions between 'good' and 'bad' books, but what makes the study of women's reading so difficult and so fascinating is that these distinctions are not as absolute, as universally accepted, or as simple as they appear. 'Bad' women, self-apologists and scandal-writers, could easily appropriate the cachet of 'good' books as camouflage, or even as ways of challenging the distinction between good and bad models of femininity: so Laetitia Pilkington depicts herself reading sermons, Teresia Constantia Phillips praises Sarah Fielding's didactic *The Governess*, and Mary Robinson presents herself enjoying the moral poems of Barbauld.[27] Conversely, some 'good' women ignored or resisted received codes of reading propriety: Anna Larpent on the same day in 1792 read 'piety and radical politics', Paine's *Rights of Man* and Sarah Trimmer's *Sacred History*.[28]

In a Sausurrean sense, indeed, women's reading has no innate meaning but takes significance from contrasting terms. It is equated with virtue and reason if it is contrasted with transgressive sexuality (as in 'Passion subdued by Reason' or Regina Maria Roche's *The Children of the Abbey*[29]), or with frivolous activities like maypole dancing or card-playing, as in the frontispieces for the *Lady's Magazine* for 1791 and 1780. On the other hand, reading might equal idleness or vanity if contrasted with the efficient running of a household (Mrs Classic in 'The Governess'), with putting one's clothes away tidily after use (as in Elizabeth Hamilton's *The Cottagers of Glenburnie*), or with proper performance of religious duties.[30] Reading can thus figure either sense or sensibility, producing some curious ambiguities.

Reading figures the virtue of a number of heroines, especially before the 1790s. In *Hortensia: or, the Distressed Wife* (1769) the lady author implies the virtue of the long-suffering protagonist by making her 'particularly fond of reading' (I, p. 8) and concerned to educate her children as keen readers (II, pp. 72–3). In Susan Keir's *Interesting Memoirs* (1785) all the virtuous heroines – Adelaide, Louisa Seymour and Lady Granville (I, p. 116, II, p. 244; I, p. 205; II, p. 262) – are remarkably literate. This filters down to periodical fiction, and a number of *Lady's Magazine* heroines have 'digested books', which demonstrates their virtue: Sophia Belmont, for instance, is 'more like a heavenly being than an inhabitant of this earth. She has read a great deal'.[31] Actual reading need not be specified; the act of reading is enough to define a woman as virtuous. Women writers, especially when they were relatively uncommon, found it useful to legitimise their own access to literacy and provide comforting self-images for the female reader, whose activity is presented not as time-wasting self-indulgence but as the result of, indeed identical to, virtue.

But this association of literacy with female virtue is only one side of the story. Between 1752, when Charlotte Lennox published *The Female Quixote*, and 1824 when Sarah Green wrote *Scotch Novel Reading*, a number of novels, tales, poems and educational works centre on full-scale critical analyses of female reading practices, becoming especially common from the 1790s. Indeed, the endangering of the heroine by unwise reading – which may mean politically radical or religiously sceptical works, but will most often mean novels – became 'one of the most hackneyed situations in the novel of this period'.[32] It seems there was hardly any crime, sin or personal catastrophe that injudicious reading was not held to cause directly or indirectly – from murder, suicide, rape, and violent revolution, through prostitution, adultery and divorce, to pride, vanity, and slapdash housewifery.[33] In particular, criticism of women's reading became highly sexualised, sexual transgression being repeatedly figured by unwise reading.

If early works briefly use reading as a sign of virtue, the full-length nineteenth-century accounts often distinguish specifically between good and bad books and reading practices. Reading becomes a central moral metaphor. In Susan Ferrier's *Marriage* (1818),[34] each central character has chosen a 'book of life' (p. 430), which defines her or his nature and moral status. For the superficial doctor, this is a cookery book: 'A good recipe for a pudding is worth all that your Shenstones . . . ever wrote' (p. 428). The irresponsible Juliana and her daughter Adelaide have chosen 'French and German' novels (pp. 115, 237), and Adelaide's adultery with Lord Lindore begins with shared reading of 'Rousseau and Goethe' (p. 475). Adelaide's semi-literate aunts understandably believe 'reading's a very dangerous thing' (p. 188). However the virtuous Mary, Adelaide's twin and opposite, loves poetry, especially Wordsworth (p. 487), and is committed to 'THE BOOK', the Bible (p. 195). Her love for Col. Lennox grows on the solid foundation of good shared reading, so will succeed when Adelaide's fails.

GENDER, READING, READERS

It is daunting to write at all about women, reading and readers, partly because such excellent work has already been done in these fields (especially by Kate Flint, Roger Chartier, James Raven and Ina Ferris[35]), but also because each of these key terms is now acknowledged to be problematic. As Sara Mills writes, 'the very category "woman" is difficult to maintain', since it erases important differences between cultures and historical moments, and assumes unanimity between groups and individuals whose interests might be dissimilar.[36] Kristeva and Irigaray have destabilised traditional notions of gender, criticising essentialist assumptions and viewing gender as the product not of biology but of social construction: 'as soon as she desires . . . as soon as she speaks . . . the woman is a man'.[37] Eighteenth-century radicals would have agreed with these insights even if this terminology was not available to them; Catherine Macaulay argues that traditional femininity is constructed not innate, the result only of 'situation and education'.[38]

If the category 'woman' has no guaranteed stability, and if femininity is manufactured rather than innate, it becomes all the more important to trace the meaning of such terms in as nuanced and historically informed a way as possible. This is especially necessary for the eighteenth century, the point in Foucault's model of the history of sexuality when 'specific mechanisms of knowledge and power centring on sex' were first formed; the dawn, in Roy Porter's words, of the 'codification of sexuality'.[39] The period was marked by a strong desire to classify and categorise, to affirm clear boundaries: it is the age of the rise of scientific taxononomies and the growth of dictionaries and encyclopedias. This desire to categorise extended to gender and the conceptualisation of gender roles. Physiological and psychological texts emphasise allegedly innate differences between the sexes, as does the 'reorganisation of gender roles'[40] in the middle classes, where male and female lifestyles became increasingly different and these differences were canonised in conduct texts. Women writers were increasingly ghettoised into feminised genres specialising in sensibility. A 'new sense of a female market' became increasingly commercially important, leading to changes in publishing in fields like science and history and to the introduction of 'more finely printed novels' to appeal to a 'young, female, and leisured audience'.[41]

Yet this trend toward defining the sexes through binary oppositions was necessitated, perhaps even generated, by powerfully opposing forces. Even scientific taxonomies – of Linnean botany for instance – show '[t]ensions about defining gender boundaries' which expose 'gender anxieties', even a 'category crisis', behind the age's belief in allegedly natural and absolute gender distinctions.[42] Gay and lesbian subcultures developed and, perhaps for the first time, a homosexual identity became available.[43] Such modifications of gender roles as society allowed were all to the disadvantage of the female sex. Many feminists complained about male encroachment on traditional women's jobs, like hairdressing, haberdashery and selling women's clothes,[44] and the 'medicalization of sex'[45] even saw the replacement of midwives by male *accoucheurs*. Reading provides one area in this period of category crisis where its various conceptualisations of the category 'woman' are especially rich and their contradictions unusually accessible.

The term 'reader' is no more transparent than 'woman'. Elizabeth Freund lists some incarnations of the reader in recent criticism, 'the mock reader (Gibson), the implied reader (Booth, Iser), the model reader (Eco), the super-reader (Riffaterre), the inscribed or encoded reader (Brooke-Rose), the naratee (Prince), the ideal reader (Culler), the literant (Holland), the actual reader (Jauss), the informed reader or the interpretive community (Fish)'. One might add to this list, especially for my purposes, the resisting reader (Fetterley), the oppositional reader (Chambers) and the conscripted reader (Stewart).[46] This book will be most concerned with actual readers (whom I shall usually call 'historical readers', to emphasise the obvious but vital fact that historical moment will colour all questions of reading), with implied readers (as Iser calls the hypothetical reader to whom the text is directed), and with resisting readers of all kinds, who read against the grain of the text and disrupt the authority of the author for their own purposes. I shall be especially concerned with the 'intradiegetic reader, or the reader within the narrative',[47] a figure ubiquitous in the literature of the period: the *mise-en-abyme*, as Lucien Dällenbach has taught us to call the technique by which reading *within* the text figures and directs the reading *of* the text, is a frequent device.[48]

I will consider readers within the narrative alongside, and on a par with, historical readers, although I am aware of the dangers of such a procedure. Some accounts of reading and writing in the eighteenth and nineteenth centuries have too easily accepted contemporary stereotypes which developed in the service of vested interests, without checking them against the historical record. More recent work sometimes confirms but often challenges the stereotypes: Jan Fergus's research on booksellers' records confirms that most readers of Minerva Press sensation fiction were women, but decisively overturns the stereotype that men and women of the servant class read little but novels.[49] Depiction of fictional readers in contemporary novels can, of course, 'only indicate very crudely the *actual* readers': but, as Jonathan Barry has argued, readers-within-the-text can nonetheless 'tell us a great deal about the writers' and publishers' attitudes to their readers and attempts to educate their readers into fitting certain models'.[50] Such insight into the construction of the reader is as important as (though not identical with) the evidence provided by historical readers. Chapters 2, 3 and 7 deal primarily with embedded readers within literary texts, chapters 4, 5 and 6 with historical readers, although virtually all, like chapter 1, balance the two.

'No history of literature can be complete unless it takes account of the readers as well as of the writers', but the 'record of what any individual has read is almost always incomplete'. Readers are 'enigmatic' figures, not just 'passive receptacles for texts' but 'consumers who are actively reinterpreting and redefining messages',[51] and there are many problems, empirical as well as theoretical, in studying them. For one thing, reliable literacy rates are unavailable, partly because the concept of literacy has been shown to be more slippery than it once seemed. The traditional test, the ability to sign one's name, would fail to discover a number of fluent readers in the lower classes, for reading was taught separately from, and anterior to, writing. It has been suggested that 'Almost all' men from the middle classes and above 'were literate', though only half of labouring men, while women 'were proportionally less literate', only about 40 per cent in 1750 being literate.[52] In 1790 Edmund Burke estimated that there were 80,000 readers in England, about 1.3 per cent of a population of six million. Such statistics, however, are not only untrustworthy but avoid my central points of interest, for the ability to read is not the same as the habit of reading, or the ability to procure books. The distinction between literacy and illiteracy was more fluid than today, and a range of ' "Bridging" processes, such as reading out loud' were important, especially to women.[53] Literacy rates were rising, especially in the lower classes, though this was probably not a consistent process. In 1800, about 200,000 poor children attended Sunday schools where they were taught to read: by 1830, this had risen to 1,400,000.[54]

The evidence from print runs helps to chart the habit of reading rather than simply the ability to read. James Raven comments on the smallness of most runs in the mid eighteenth century, the vast majority of which were smaller than 2,000, with the average for a novel only about 800, some as small as 500.[55] Elizabeth Griffith in 1786 writes of the typical novel having a run of about 1,000, though her point is that a high proportion were taken by circulating libraries, and therefore had a multiple readership.[56] The first edition of Frances Burney's *Cecilia* (1783) ran to 2,000, and her last novel, *The Wanderer*, sold 3,600 copies in six months and was expected to sell at least 8,000, proof of her unusual popularity.[57]

Books were a relatively expensive commodity throughout the period, and readership may have been 'constrained more by the price of books than by standards of literacy'. James Raven suggests that an annual income of £50 might have been the minimum which allowed the buying of books, and that in 1780 about 150,000 households came into this category.[58] Women, less likely to have an independent income, probably found the price of books especially inhibiting: Mary Brunton recommends Froissart's *Chronicle* to a friend, but realises she will be unable to buy it for it is 'beyond the reach of ordinary purses', and the young Susan Sibbald, without the money to buy books, is reduced to copying whole volumes in longhand in order to share her favourite reading with a friend.[59] The circulation of cheap or free printed material suggests a much larger pool of potential readers. Smollett's *History of England*, published in sixpenny weekly numbers, had a circulation of about 10,000; James Harrison's *Novelist's Magazine*, which serialised classic novels from 1785, issued editions of more than 12,000; the *Lady's Magazine* and the *Gentleman's Magazine* had monthly circulations of over 15,000; Burke's *Reflections on the Revolution in France* sold 30,000 copies and the cheap second part of Paine's *Rights of Man* (1792) perhaps half a million; in the first year of issue Hannah More's Cheap Repository Tracts allegedly reached an audience of over 2 million (about a quarter of the whole population of England); and the British and Foreign Bible Society issued $2\frac{1}{2}$ million Bibles between 1804 and 1819. The circulation of newspapers more than doubled between 1753 and 1792, showing at the later date an overall circulation of over 15 million.[60] However, such figures, while suggestive, are hardly conclusive: distribution is not synonymous with consumption, and we cannot know how many individuals read popular circulating library books, or what proportion of the targetted audience read More's tracts or their free Bibles.

While literacy itself is a problematic term and the habit of literacy still harder to quantify, women readers are paradoxically both the most visible in the literature and the most invisible in the historical record. It is difficult to muster detailed information, especially for the earliest part of the period and the lowest classes. A few women from privileged or literary families – Mary Shelley, Mary Russell Mitford, Clarissa Trant, Anna Larpent and a few others – kept detailed records of their reading, but such evidence tends to cluster in the later period, and is rarely available for women below the professional classes. Mitford read 22 books (55 volumes in all) in January 1806, including poetry and travels but predominantly fiction; Clarissa Trant read 28 books in 1827, including German and French literature, history and travels, and religious works; and Anna Larpent read over 440 titles in the ten years from 1773, including novels in English and French, plays, history, travel, sermons and poetry.[61] Such statistics cast light on fictional readers, like Harriet Fitzpatrick in *Tom Jones* who read 'half a thousand' books in three months, Mrs Dough who claimed to read 'five or six volumes in a day!', and Emma Courtney who read ten to fourteen novels a week.[62]

Even autobiographical accounts, however, may not be the transparent historical record they seem. The temptation to suppress facts, even to tell outright lies, was sometimes strong. Frances Burney was nervous about her reading, and seems not always to tell the literal truth about it.[63] Anne Lister was also economical with the truth about her reading. As a lesbian in early nineteenth-century provincial society she had necessarily learned habits of evasion, no doubt exacerbated by the tension between her conservative gender and class politics and her own gender transgressions. In July 1820, visiting friends, she is asked if she has read Byron's *Don Juan*, but 'would not own it', since it was an 'improper' book and the appearance of respectability was important to her: she clearly had done so, though, and by March of the next year can participate in a discussion of its first two books. Lister and her female friends repeatedly use reading as an indirect means of discussing sexuality. In Paris in 1824, as she and Maria Barlow embark on an affair, the two reveal their awareness of lesbianism through references to reading, 'the Latin parts of the works of Sir William Jones', Paul's Epistle to the Romans, and a 'little book', *Voyage a Plombières*, 'where is the story of one woman intriguing with another'. Moreover, as Emma Donoghue has demonstrated, Lister uses Juvenal's Sixth Satire, with its overt lesbian theme, 'to test women she suspected were lesbians'. Byron's poems also constitute a term in this lesbian code: Lister discusses them with Miss Brown (who likes Byron's poetry 'perhaps too well') and with Sarah Ponsonby (one of the Ladies of Llangollen, who is 'ashamed' to admit she has read the first canto of *Don Juan*, and is 'afraid' to read *Cain*), and plans to give Maria Barlow 'Lord Byron's works' as a parting gift.[64]

It is difficult to study women's reading because of tendencies to distort historical record, or to use reading in coded ways. Moreover, even women who kept journals or expressed literary views in letters rarely bothered to keep detailed accounts of purely recreational reading.

Novels especially tended to be viewed as at best ephemeral, at worst immoral, especially in reading communities like Evangelicals. Faith Gray, dutiful member of a devout evangelical York family, self-accusingly notes in a review of the year 1768 a 'strange mixture of Morality, History and Novels in my reading', but although she itemises some of the morality and history she is uninformative about the novels, and the same aporia occurs in the journal of her granddaughter Margaret Gray, who in the winter of 1825–6 records religious and historical reading in detail, and only adds that for 'ornamental reading, one has always both time and inclination'.[65]

A further problem is the temptation to oversimplify, to present as monolithic a mass of readers with different needs, attitudes and horizons of expectation. We are dealing not with a single community of women readers, but with an almost infinite number of reading communities divided on lines not only of gender but of class, age, date, region, nationality, political and religious affiliations, education, and so on, and by purely personal taste. The voices that are heard loudest will be, inevitably, those of published women writers of the professional class and above. But even this relatively homogeneous group shows a wide range of attitudes. Lichfield poet Anna Seward read poetry enthusiastically but was less interested in history and fiction, the Burney family read history but were critical of fiction, the Edgeworths (at least during the lifetime of patriarch Richard Lovell Edgeworth) read all kinds of informative literature but little fiction, while the Austens devoured novels shamelessly. In order to write about that mythical creature the woman reader it will sometimes be strategic to flatten these differences between reading communities, though I hope not to lose sight of the fact that class, nationality and age combine with gender to make a complex map of reading.

THE FEMINISATION OF THE READING PUBLIC

In the late eighteenth and early nineteenth centuries it was often argued that the participation of women in literature, as writers and as readers, indicated the superiority of modern British culture. One of Johnson's biographers approvingly describes an increase in female literacy in the 1750s,[66] the *Lady's Magazine* for 1777 comments that 'the practise of reading' is now 'more general than ever', a fictional gentleman in the mid 1790s writes that 'women of literature are much more numerous now than they were a few years ago', and thirty years later a commentator contrasts England with France because in England 'not only men, but men, women and children read'.[67] In the late eighteenth century, manners 'were widely perceived as being recast in a more feminine mould', and this naturally affected the literary world. And yet this vital issue was treated with notable ambiguity. As late as the nineteenth century women were still being urged that reading was incompatible with 'discharging the various duties of a wife and daughter, a mother and friend',[68] though they were simultaneously warned that they had 'more need of Reading' than men to compensate for their less rational natures: while men 'are the creatures of circumstance and example', women, confined to a private sphere, have a particular reliance on 'Reading'.[69]

Being an effective woman reader required the agility of a tightrope-walker. Literate women had to avoid the stigma of the learned lady, whose reputation was bad throughout the period: when accused of being a 'great reader', a heroine generally protests, and only foolish or malicious characters make such accusations. But a virtuous woman or girl must not fail to read, either, or this might endanger her, as it does the 'illiterate' Hannah Primrose in Inchbald's *Nature and Art* (1796). For a woman to write or read badly was at least by the nineteenth century 'disgraceful'.[70] Contemporary comment, however, is less concerned about women or girls who do not read than with those who read the wrong books, in the wrong ways and the wrong places.

From the 1750s, many texts show an acute awareness of female readers and the problems they raised. In some cases this is central and direct, as in education manuals and literary histories like Wollstonecraft's *The Female Reader* (1789) or Clara Reeve's *The Progress of Romance* (1785), or in conduct works, some of which, like Lady Sarah Pennington's *An Unfortunate Mother's Advice to her Absent Daughters* (1761), or Henry Kett's *Emily, a Moral Tale* (1809), contain full-scale bibliographies for girls and young women. But women's reading takes a prominent role in many genres, including fiction. Some novels include 'extensive discussion' of women's reading of specific texts – of *The Sorrows of Young Werther* in Helen Maria Williams' *Julia* (1790), of *Paradise Lost* in Hannah More's *Coelebs in Search of a Wife* (1808), of Frances Burney's *Evelina* in Eliza Taylor's *Education; or, Elizabeth, Her Lover and Husband* (1817).[71] Others deal more generally with issues of women's reading: some education novels, like More's *Coelebs* or Laetitia-Matilda Hawkins' *The Countess and Gertrude; or, Modes of Discipline* (1811), seem little more than a string of loosely connected scenes of reading. Even in less didactic works, like novels by Burney, Charlotte Smith, Ann Radcliffe, Susan Ferrier, Wollstonecraft, Charlotte Dacre, and many others, women's '[r]eading is a major theme'.[72]

Female reading figures both solitary and selfish pleasure and rationality and self-suppression; as such it reveals the contradictions in contemporary gender-ideologies. Female readers were kept in a state of anxiety about how much to read, what to read, where and when to read. Even liberals believed it was necessary to control access to literature for women, especially young women, and more repressive commentators argued that women's intellectual inferiority should confine them to a non-literary world where their only 'book' should be the 'hearts' of men.[73] Women readers, however, developed a range of strategies to evade these proscriptions or apparently to accept while covertly resisting them, and, as we shall see in chapter 2, could read even the safest texts subversively.

There are important reasons for working towards a fuller understanding of women's reading in this period. The female reading public was, commercially and culturally, of enormous significance: presses like Lane's Minerva, which specialised in popular fiction, seem to have published with a largely female audience in view.[74] Indeed it seems likely that, because of improving female education and changing patterns of leisure in the middle classes, 'the majority of the reading public, for all genres, was female'.[75] Gentry-class women were thought to be especially suited to 'Reading' because their 'almost intire Vacation from Business' allowed them 'more spare time upon their hands . . . than men': Gibbon certainly believed that 'women in general read much more than men' (though he also thought their reading practices flawed and un-methodical).[76] This majority reading public has never been fully studied, yet further knowledge of them will not only contribute to women's history but may change the way we view the canonical male writers of this period.

Possibly because of this feminisation of the reading public, anxieties centring on the figure of the woman reader grew more acute as the period progressed. As Kate Flint reminds us, Freud argued that 'books and papers are female symbols', and Byron certainly saw literature as a dangerously emasculating realm, which conditioned his view both of women readers and of his own work.[77] Reading was seen as 'passive' (and hence feminised), compared to the 'active art of writing',[78] and whereas writing was taught as a vocational skill by male experts, reading tended to be taught within the home by the mother or at an elementary dame school, thereby adding another layer of feminisation.

It has been said that 'Writing is the act of saying *I*', a 'projection of the person who writes into the public domain of discourse'.[79] In these terms, one might suppose that reading might be 'the act of erasing I' in order to submit to the authority of an author, or a confinement to a private domain. As such it might seem a safe activity for a woman. And yet, as eighteenth-century commentators knew as well as we do, reading is by no means necessarily such a passive, self-abnegating act. Rather than erasing I, reading might reassert it by privileging personal pleasure, and rather than confining within a domestic sphere, it might open up a wider community of ideas. One classic model involves the lordly Author-ity addressing the passive, humble reader, forever dependent upon him and inferior to him, object of lecturing, mockery, and 'victim-ization'.[80] But, Iser notwithstanding, the eighteenth-century reader was as likely to be resisting as 'docile', and could be 'fundamentally creative rather than passive'. Indeed, in some radical writers '[p]ower and authority' are seen as 'the property not of the author, but of the reader'.[81] The reader brings opinions of her own to the text, and is not always prepared to accept the authority of the author. We read 'eagerly a book which supports our favourite opinions' and 'suffer our minds placidly to reflect [its] images', while the writer with opposite views is read with 'coolness', and we simply become 'more confirmed in our own opinion'.[82] The reader reads actively and in one sense is omnipotent, with the ultimate sanction of simply closing the book: of a book she dislikes, Hannah More remarks that 'it is in the reader's power to make it as short as he pleases',[83] and despite this gendering of the reader as male, the reading female shares the same power.

Readers can use a range of resisting strategies to unsettle the authority of the author and appropriate the text for their own purposes. A resisting reader might choose to identify not with the hero but with the villain, and thus refuse the author's implied moral. Sir Edward Denham in Austen's *Sanditon*, and a number of villains in periodical fiction, read *Clarissa* to identify with Lovelace rather than the heroine.[84] Women equally exercised the power of resisting reading. Anna Seward reading Maria Edgeworth's *Leonora* identified with the glamorous novel-reading villainess rather than the domestic heroine, to the author's annoyance:[85] Austen resisted the moral pressure of Burney's *Camilla* by killing off the moralistic Dr Marchmont, the cause of much of the heroine's suffering, in marginal annotations to her copy.[86] These processes of resistance resemble Harold Bloom's view of the development of literature from one 'strong' writer to another through fruitful misreadings, and they are as available to female as to male readers.[87]

Obviously both men and women, boys and girls, read in this period, but the issue in fiction, reviews, and educational works is dominated by *women's* reading. A number of texts begin by making general points about reading but there is then a rapid silent slippage from reading in general to women's reading in particular, which marks the special anxieties surrounding the growth of women's literacy. In 'The Generous Lover', novels are defined as dangerous for both sexes, but the story goes on to concentrate on their danger to female readers. A review of 1753 by William Whitehead begins by criticising the 'extreme indecency' of modern novels, and the dangers they pose to 'our young men and women', but within a page is worrying only about the reading of 'young ladies':[88] another review of 1761 by Owen Ruffhead which begins by attacking novels as appealing only to the 'giddy and licentious of both sexes' slips into an attack on *women's* reading practices and a gendering of the ideal 'serious and solid' reader as male, as opposed to the 'fair customers' of the circulating library.[89] Regardless of historical reality, poor reading practices are gendered as female, good as male.

Not only gender but age was relevant in defining appropriate reading. It is understandable that some adult works should be thought unsuitable for the young, or that women should read in different ways at different stages of their lives. Maria Josepha Holroyd in her teens was 'enchanted with the "All for Love"', of de Staël's *Delphine*, which in mature years she viewed more critically (if still with enjoyment, although her husband was 'disgusted' by it).[90] Nonetheless, it is unusual to find educationalists admitting that the rules for adult women could reasonably be different from those for girls. Edgeworth's bad teacher Mademoiselle Panache argues that she was right to censor Augusta's reading when she was a child, but that as an adult 'she is at liberty' to choose her own books (p. 396): but the whole thrust of the tale discredits this. The implication is often that women are children of a larger growth, and such formulations as 'fair customers' elide the distinction between vulnerable young girls and mature women. Catherine Macaulay's *Letters on Education* (1790) is unusual in its resistance to the stereotypical gendering of reading: she tends to distinguish not between books suitable for male and female readers, but those suitable for the young of both sexes and for adults. She admires some works, like Pope's 'Abelard and Eloisa', or Burney's

Cecilia, but thinks them unsuitable for the young because they 'may fill a young person's mind with too vast an idea of the power of love' (I, pp. 131, 147). Macaulay's gender-free formulations ('a young person') are very different from the hierarchical and gendered treatment of readers in the reviews quoted in the previous paragraph.

Gender routinely intervenes to define not only readers but texts. Genres which emphasised 'imagination' were gendered as feminine, those requiring 'severe application' as masculine.[91] In effect this means the gendering as feminine of novels, romances, and some lyric poems, while men read 'better books',[92] epic, satire, classical literature, history and science. In Peacock's *Nightmare Abbey* when a parcel of new books arrives, 'Marionetta inspected the novel and Mr Listless the poem',[93] and this seems to be regarded as natural. However, the evidence suggests that in real life male and female reading practices were less different than some commentators implied. Dr Johnson in youth loved romance reading and as an adult enjoyed Burney's feminocentric novels, and Gothic novels found an appreciative male audience.[94] Even the *Lady's Magazine* had a band of regular male readers, judging from their comments and contributions. These facts tend to be suppressed in the interests of a rearguard battle to preserve established literary forms from contamination from the new, especially the novel, and a desire to preserve male hegemony over a print culture in which female writers and readers were becoming increasingly central.

If literary genres were gendered, so were elements within them. Indecency and violence were thought unsuitable for women. Keats and Byron used overtly sexual description as a way of repelling female readers, and Byron figured as female and identified with a female readership the new prudery which he felt compromised the reception of his work. Conversely William Godwin urged Charles Lamb to tone down his 'shocking' description of the blinding of Polyphemus in *The Adventures of Ulysses* not because this was unsuitable for children but because it would result in 'excluding the female sex from among your readers', and so be commercially disastrous.[95]

This study deals with women's reading, especially, though not exclusively, of and in fiction, since the novel was the form most rigorously censored and policed, ideologies of reading met their fiercest challenge from the novel, and the novel tended to be gendered as feminine. Elizabeth Bergen Brophy demonstrates that novels were frequently alluded to in women's journals and letters of the period, and that 'women not only read but discussed them as models for conduct' to a much greater degree than other genres.[96] Moreover, empirical research demonstrates that, in our time at least, men and women 'read lyric poetry similarly, narrative fiction differently'.[97] There is some evidence that in the eighteenth and nineteenth centuries too the sexes read the same texts in different ways. Reading Latin and Greek literature, for instance, must have felt very different to elite-class men, for whom it was the central element in a prolonged formal education, and to women, who must often have felt interlopers in a high-status masculine space.[98] It has been suggested that in this period Milton was read by women as 'revolutionary, even in his representation of women', by men as a 'spokesman for orthodoxy' (though if this is so, male radicals like Blake and Shelley would have to be seen as reading as women).[99] All the evidence casts doubt on 'models of readership which stress passive uniformity'.[100]

Novels in particular may have generated different meanings for their male and female readers. Catherine Talbot records a social reading of *Sir Charles Grandison* where the men 'have no patience with Harriet's vanity and talkativeness', whereas Talbot and her female friends were 'ardent enthusiasts' for the heroine, Talbot nostalgically describing her youth as 'those Harriet Byron years'.[101] Maria Edgeworth thought John Moore's novel *Zeluco* 'the best philosophical romance of the age', a moral tale fit for young female readers and proving that not only 'trifling, silly people were novel-readers', while Byron uses it as part of a very different agenda, identifying against the grain of the text with the eponymous villain.[102]

The historical moment is also a key element conditioning how a text is read. Some stereotypes – the novel-reading female servant, the novel as an accessory to seduction – and some injunctions – to read history rather than fiction, to read socially rather than solitarily – remain remarkably constant from the 1750s to the 1830s: in other respects, as I shall show, different parts of the period had different anxieties and different solutions to the problems raised by women's reading. The perennially favourite books survived because they appealed to readers in all phases of the great cultural shifts from Enlightenment to the 'Age of Sensibility' to the Romanticisms of the turn of the century. *Sir Charles Grandison* could be read by late Augustans like Catherine Talbot as a work of rational Christian morality, while Edgeworth's *Ormond* could focus on elements apparently anticipating Romanticism, like the madness of Clementina.[103] Moreover, we must not assume that contemporary readers read texts in ways that have become critical orthodoxy in the twentieth century. Burney's *Camilla* now tends to have a reputation as a dull, over-written work marking a decided loss of artistic energy after the success of *Evelina*: but Jane Austen uses it as a positive model of female authorship as opposed to the more ambiguous model of Ann Radcliffe, and Maria Edgeworth, visiting Tunbridge Wells in 1831, finds *Camilla* 'present every where' and remarks on the 'astonishing power a good author has to give local interest'.[104]

Before exploring in more detail the protocols governing women's reading and its pleasures and perils, it is necessary first to examine some uses of the 'trope of the woman reader'[105] in the work of major male writers, including Fielding, Richardson, Johnson and Byron, and how these writers were read by women (and read their women readers).

CHAPTER I

Pygmalionesses and the pencil under the petticoat: Richardson, Johnson and Byron

A founding text of modern feminist literary theory, Sandra Gilbert and Susan Gubar's *The Madwoman in the Attic*, centres on the 'anxiety of influence' suffered by women writers in a cultural world dominated by men.[1] But how did eighteenth- and nineteenth-century male writers respond to the growing visibility of women writers and commercial importance of women readers, and how were the canonical male writers read by these women?

One of the most striking phenomena of the eighteenth century is the growth of women's involvement in literary culture as writers and as readers,[2] though major changes took place in the nature of this female readership and its reading practices in the course of the period. As early as the 1750s female readership was becoming 'increasingly decorous', and by the early nineteenth century Byron noted a growing prudishness in his audience which he bitterly (though not necessarily accurately) blamed on its female members.[3] Mrs Keith of Ravelstone remembered, as a girl in London perhaps in the 1760s, hearing Aphra Behn's fiction 'read aloud for the amusement of large circles of the first and most creditable in society': in old age she tried to reread it but, affected by the changing cultural climate, found it too embarrassing to continue.[4] Not only sexual explicitness became problematic for women readers: Mary Russell Mitford complains of 'want of elegance' even in the novels of Jane Austen.[5] Texts historically thought appropriate for women were reevaluated because of changing standards of propriety. In 1782 Hester Thrale read the *Spectator* to her daughters, who found hilariously improper 'the Idea of *a Lady* saying her Stomach ach'd, or that something stuck between her Teeth'; Coleridge in 1811 also thought reading the *Spectator* to one's 'wife and daughters' required careful vetting lest it 'offend the delicacy of female ears, and shock feminine susceptibility'.[6]

WOMEN READERS AND MID EIGHTEENTH-CENTURY FICTION

The canonical novelists of the mid century were very aware of the growing importance of women readers and writers, though most references tend to be satirical, or at best humorous. Smollett's *Humphrey Clinker* (1771) expresses anxiety that women's 'delicacy, and knowledge of the human heart' have given them a virtual monopoly over the novel, and revenges this by satirising Lydia Melford, a devotee of the circulating library whose love of 'the Arabian Night's Entertainment, and the Persian Tales' suggests the romantic fantasies that cause her imprudent elopement.[7] Fielding likewise uses Shamela's library as a coded language for her body and her character, its contents obscene texts ('The Third Volume of the *Atalantis*. *Venus in the Cloyster: Or, the Nun in her Smock* . . .'), religious works showing her hypocrisy ('Some Sermon-Books'), and mutilated texts demonstrating the illegitimacy of her claim to elite culture ('*The Whole Duty of Man*, with only the Duty to one's Neighbour, torn out . . . Plays, with . . . Part of the first Act torn off').[8]

While Fielding's reviews 'condemn the behaviour of non-reading female characters' and recommend women writers like Charlotte Lennox, in his novels women readers like Mrs Bennet in *Amelia* (1752), or Harriet Fitzpatrick, Bridget Allworthy, Jenny Jones and Mrs Western in *Tom Jones* (1749), tend to be mocked. Fielding, indeed, identifies both female reading and writing with sexual risk or transgression. Delarivier Manley in *Shamela* and Aphra Behn in *Tom Jones* embody improper reading, and so forceful is this gendering of corrupt literacy that keen female readers are often suspected or convicted of sexual impropriety: Jenny Jones is the foundling's supposed and Bridget Allworthy his actual mother; Harriet Fitzpatrick, consoled in an unhappy marriage by her 'beloved reading', is wrongly believed by her husband to be unfaithful. Even Sophia Western's reading generates misunderstanding or danger, although her choice of books consistently demonstrates taste and virtue: while reading the work of a 'young lady' of a 'good understanding . . . and . . . good heart' (perhaps Sarah Fielding), Sophia is berated by her ignorant aunt.[9] Women's reading, however innocent and however charming the sensibility it reveals, is a problematic area for Fielding.

Fielding's novels polarised readers, who equally praised the realism of *Tom Jones* and, women especially, worried about its moral tendency. Many were enthusiastic about *Amelia* or *Joseph Andrews*: Charlotte Lennox's Henrietta, indeed, regards the latter as the ideal novel, in direct contrast with immoral female-authored texts like Eliza Haywood's, and

Catharine Macaulay also believed it 'may be read with safety, even with improvement by youth'.[10] But *Tom Jones*, because of its robust sexual permissiveness, proved more difficult. Conduct-book writers, like Eugenia de Acton, specifically prohibited it, Richardson castigated female friends for liking a work of such an 'Evil Tendency', Johnson chid Hannah More for reading so 'vicious' and 'corrupt' a novel, and in Goldsmith's *The Vicar of Wakefield* Olivia is rendered vulnerable to seduction by unwise reading encapsulated by *Tom Jones*.[11] But it continued to find female defenders, even unexpected ones like virtuous Elizabeth Carter and vigorously conservative Jane West, and the *Lady's Magazine* repeatedly praised it as not only 'entertaining' but embodying 'a complete body of ethics', although other women's periodicals insisted its 'urbanity and interest' were dangerously compromised by 'levities and impurities', and Mary Brunton praised the 'admirable construction' of the plot but found it inferior in characterisation to Edgeworth, and in morality to Richardson.[12]

In the 1770s and 80s, reading Fielding could suggest true or false female taste and virtue: in Elizabeth Blower's novels, he is enjoyed by virtuous heroines like Cecilia in *George Bateman* (1782) and Miss Hampden in *Maria* (1785), but also by fools like the Taddington sisters:[13] how women read is more important than what they read. By the nineteenth century women faced a double bind: they 'must . . . know what is contained in the writings of Fielding', but must not mistake his 'wit' for 'wisdom'. In women's fiction *Tom Jones* tends to be enjoyed only by inexperienced or transgressive readers, like Edgeworth's Ormond and Austen's John Thorpe.[14] In Susan Ferrier's *The Inheritance* (1824) the moral Mr Lyndsay and Mr Z- rejoice that the work of Fielding is less 'popular' than it was, the 'better taste' of the present age, inimical to 'impure writers' and 'impure readers', rejecting its 'grossness, profanity and licentiousness'. In the moral novels of this period, women who defend Fielding are especially suspect, like Miss Pratt in *The Inheritance* and Brunton's Julia Dawkins.[15] What appeared just and moral in the 1750s seemed, to the narrower standards of female propriety of the 1820s, simply 'impure'.

READING RICHARDSON

While Fielding used an authoritative authorial voice, Richardson's epistolary method appeared to allow his characters to speak for themselves without authorial intervention, thereby giving the reader a more 'constructive role to play'[16] and establishing a less hierarchical relationship between writer and reader. As Fielding increasingly figured vice or folly, or the inelegant masculinity of a past age, Richardson's novels maintained their status as key texts, appealing to readers of political persuasions from conservative James Fordyce to radical William Godwin, to the end of the period.[17] Of course they had their critics: Mary Wollstonecraft attacked *Clarissa* as morally confused, showing 'strange notions of honour and virtue' by depicting the heroine 'robbed . . . of her honour' by rape. Others found the novels 'prolix to a blameable degree', or 'antediluvian' in their depiction of manners: yet Richardson's 'sublimely pathetic' works still found female advocates who attacked the 'indelicate species of delicacy' that was beginning to find the 'pure christianity' of *Clarissa* risqué, and as late as 1820 Charlotte Grove regarded *Sir Charles Grandison* as her '*favorite* book'.[18]

Some mid-century novelists offer power to the reader: in Sterne's *Tristram Shandy* (1759–67) a blank page is left for the reader's own picture of the action.[19] Richardson extends these powers explicitly to women readers, who seem to have enjoyed the 'authorising' they experienced in reading his novels.[20] His concern for women readers can be seen in two ways: his representation of female characters through details of their reading, and his consultation with real female readers.

Reading is significant in the representation of both Pamela and Clarissa. Pamela's literacy, so satirised by Fielding, helps to render her a fit wife for her elite-class husband and a good mother to their seven children, whose education is based on her reading of '*Locke's* Treatise of Education'. In *Sir Charles Grandison* (1754) women's reading is a central issue. The heroine Harriet Byron is a 'young woman of reading' (I, p. 70), including the Bible, Swift, *Paradise Lost*, Dryden, her 'favourite' poet Young, and Richardson's own *Clarissa*. This literacy and the moral character it implies render her a fit bride for the idealised hero, one of whose first gifts to her after marriage is the keys to his library.[21] Other female characters are also characterised through reading in a way that is rarely true of men. Richardson's work implicitly legitimises the activity of his own female readers, though he accepts his age's distinctions between good and bad reading. In *Grandison*, romances are attacked as an 'unnatural kind of writing', a 'dangerous elegance' (VII, pp. 398, 400), fortunately now ousted by the morally and aesthetically superior *Spectator*, and Pamela also dislikes romances for their improbability and immorality, and cures a female friend of a silly love of 'Poetry and romance'. Both episodes allow Richardson to distinguish his own 'History of Life and Manners' from 'a mere Novel or Romance'.[22]

Even more important are the ways Richardson encouraged his readers to become active participants in the construction of meaning in his novels, using active verbs – carving, judging, debating – to describe reading.[23] Female readers and writers were especially important in the development of his novels. He is sympathetic to the rise of the woman writer, arguing with ponderous playfulness that the 'pen is almost as pretty an implement in a woman's fingers, as a needle'. As a printer he published the work of many women including Susanna Centlivre, Eliza Haywood, Sarah Fielding, Charlotte Lennox, Elizabeth Carter, Mary Barber, Mary Leapor, and Elizabeth Rowe, and he collected unpublished work by women including the poems of Mehetabel Wesley. He even incorporates women's writing into his novels, including Elizabeth Carter's 'Ode to Wisdom' in *Clarissa*, and material from letters by Lady Bradshaigh and other female correspondents into *Sir Charles Grandison*,[24] so the traditional distinctions between writer and reader, male authority and female passivity, are renegotiated. Richardson, hailed in Duncombe's *Feminiad* as 'the sex's friend', consulted female correspondents and listened to their views in the later stages of composition and revision of *Clarissa* and at every stage of the planning and writing of *Grandison*, entering into 'prolonged debates' with them on a number of key issues.[25]

Women readers wrote the Richardsonian text. In the case of *Grandison*, they are allowed to feel powerful, but were generally compliant to his plans, while with *Clarissa* they often made their presence felt as resisting and rebellious readers, which caused Richardson 'frustration' and prompted an attempt to reassert his own authority and control readers more firmly.[26]

Some women readers felt deep interest and empowerment over their involvement in *Grandison*. In 1750–1 when the novel was in the planning stage Richardson wrote to one woman friend that his female correspondents had to 'help to *make*' the protagonist, and to another that his hero 'owes the existence he has to you'.[27] Catherine Talbot and Elizabeth Carter envisaged themselves as 'two Pygmalionesses'[28] forming the work and its hero. In this extraordinary image of gender reversal, Sir Charles figures as the beautiful female statue, the female readers as male creator, and the actual male author as the goddess Aphrodite breathing life into their creation. Such images of reversed gender play about Richardson's conceptualisation of his own writerly activity: as a bourgeois he felt, perhaps, feminised in relation to his gentry-class correspondents. In letters to Lady Bradshaigh he figures himself as 'a poor old woman, who, having no bellows . . . endeavours to blow up into a faint blaze a little handful of sticks', begging his correspondent to provide a 'waxen taper' to fire his 'extinguished' imagination.[29]

In the case of *Grandison*, Richardson left some latitude to the imagination of readers: a 'Letter to a Lady' draws attention to the fact that Clementina's future is left open, that she may or may not marry at the end of the year: 'Do you think, Madam, I have not been very complaisant to my Readers to leave them the decision of this important article?' There is, though, unease as well as playfulness in Richardson's acknowledgement of the unruly and individualistic readerly imagination: 'some of my correspondents rejoice that Clementina is not married in the book; hoping that she will never marry; while others express their satisfaction in the time given her, and doubt not but she will' (vii, p. 468). In 1754, Richardson considered adding a further volume tracing the post-publication history of its characters, suggesting that the novelist should function only as editor, to 'pick and choose, alter, connect and accommodate' writing by his correspondents, who would each adopt a persona from the novel and write in character. Although Richardson mentions correspondents of both sexes, the plan centred on women: Lady Bradshaigh was to write as Charlotte Grandison, Elizabeth Carter as Mrs Shirley, Susanna Highmore as Harriet Byron, and Hester Mulso Chapone as Clementina.[30] This unique experiment was a logical extension of Richardson's conception of the reader: the writer often appears, as he writes in another context, a 'passive man', while the reader is active, 'every one putting him and herself into the character they read'.[31] This bold revision of reader–writer relations, however, finally came to nothing, although a letter by Bradshaigh as Charlotte survives; Richardson appears more reluctant than he thought to cede absolute control to readers, and perhaps his correspondents were reluctant to risk female propriety by actually becoming authors.

Although *Grandison* generated discussion, it did not arouse such rebellious readings as *Clarissa*. By adopting an epistolary mode with little apparent authorial intervention, Richardson risked 'hermeneutic anarchy'. Many women delighted in the freedom this offered to 'the Readers Judgment', but some went too far for the author's comfort, finding Clarissa less perfect and Lovelace less devilish than he wanted, like 'a young Lady' who is too sympathetic to Lovelace, prompting

Richardson to revise to make his anti-hero 'still more and more odious'.
The 1751 edition adds new footnotes which demonstrate growing resentment of female misreaders, 'a hardened view of gender in reading', and
a decreased 'readiness to let women read for themselves'.[32]

Despite consulting female readers during the composition of *Clarissa*,
Richardson rarely accepted their advice on substantive issues of plotting. (The same is true of *Grandison*, where he invites Lady Bradshaigh to
choose from a number of possible endings, while warning her that the
'Catastrophe, whatever it be, is decided'.[33]) There was much female
resistance – 'infinite trouble and opposition' – to the tragic trajectory of
Clarissa, which Richardson was wholly unwilling to accommodate, insisting that his was the 'only natural' conclusion.[34] Bradshaigh pleaded
for a happy ending, at first wanting an unraped Clarissa and a reformed
Lovelace to marry, later more modestly asking for the rape to fail and
Lovelace to be wounded in the duel but survive to repent. Her sister
Lady Echlin even wrote a new ending for the novel roughly along these
lines.[35] This has been read as the resistance of naive readers to the
demanding moral subtlety of the author,[36] but it is likely that Richardson's female readers having been offered power were reluctant to
renounce it, especially when this involved sacrificing an important
female role-model. Richardson, while authorising active reading, at the
same time felt hurt and angry at the strength of readerly resistance,
blaming himself for the decision to publish in parts, which allowed too
much freedom to readers, and 'left everyone at liberty to form a
catastrophe of their own'.[37] Although in theory supporting an active
model of female readership, Richardson is human enough in practice to
resent opposition to his authorial intentions.

Richardson's novels also offered female readers an empowering
authorisation for displays of extreme emotion. Susanna Highmore and
her parents were so moved by *Clarissa* that they 'each read to
[them]selves and in separate Apartments wept'. Lady Bradshaigh reacted to the death of Clarissa as to that of a beloved friend: 'Would you
have me weep incessantly? . . . I long to read it – and yet I dare not . . .
in Agonies would I lay down the Book, take it up again, walk about the
Room, let fall a Flood of Tears, wipe my Eyes, read again . . . throw
away the Book crying out . . . I cannot go on . . .' At one point she even
had a male friend read it first and break the news gently, and her
husband, alarmed at her emotions, begs her to 'read no more'.[38] Bradshaigh's emotional response is a symptom of resisting reading, a form of
self-assertion which gains the sympathetic attention of husband and

friends and seeks to dissuade the author from what she considers a fundamental aesthetic and moral error.

Richardson's novels issued 'the compelling invitation . . . to read as a woman', and gave women opportunities for extraordinary readerly power, or, even more appealingly, an only lightly coded language for their own 'painful and hidden experience'. This helps to account for the novels' intense long-term popularity. Although Anne Grant was told in 1778 that 'Nobody reads Clarissa now',[39] she is rightly sceptical, for the evidence suggests that Richardson was read throughout the period, especially by women, and writers continued to expect readers to pick up allusions. Geraldine Verney in Smith's *Desmond* (1792) compares the novel's villains to Lovelace and Sir Hargrave Pollexfen (II, p. 293), and Lord Danesforte in *Ethelinde* (1789) is also 'a modern Lovelace' (II, p. 193). Many *Lady's Magazine* pieces praise Richardson or create character through short-hand references to his novels – 'another Miss Byron', 'this modern Miss Byron'.[40] Women identified with Richardsonian characters, compared their friends to them, or judged acquaintances by their response to them. Hannah More playfully compared herself to Harriet Byron for 'telling my own praises', Elizabeth Montagu noted 'a resemblance of character' between Clarissa and Elizabeth Carter, and Anne Grant used response to *Clarissa* as a 'criterion by which I . . . judge . . . any one's character and taste'.[41] Even Mary Wortley Montagu, although she thought the novels 'miserable stuff' likely to do 'more general mischief than the Works of Lord Rochester', in old age 'was such an old Fool as to weep over Clarissa Harlowe like any milk maid of sixteen', since she recognised in the novel 'a near resemblance of [her] Maiden Days'.[42]

WOMEN WRITERS, WOMEN READERS AND THE LIVES OF JOHNSON

Samuel Johnson, 'bred a Bookseller',[43] built his life around reading and writing books, and in biographical anecdotes books represent the hardest and softest sides of his complex character: in a quarrel with bookseller Thomas Osborne he felled his adversary literally with a folio, and books bearing her name were his most poignant and treasured memorials of his wife.[44] His early reading had an immense impact: as a child reading *Hamlet* he was terrified by the ghost, and youthful religious doubts were overcome by reading.[45] He did not choose exclusively the literature of 'high' culture, and his literary views were characteristically 'anti-elitist . . . populist, reader-centred, even democratic': he was fond, for instance, of 'reading romances of chivalry', a taste he shared with his wife.[46] Women initiated him into the world of literacy – his mother, her maid Catherine who read him stories of George and the Dragon, Mrs Oliver who kept a dame school. His relationships with his mother and wife are most tellingly defined by images of shared reading: he told Hester Thrale, for instance, that his wife 'read comedy better than any body he ever heard'.[47]

Boswell, determined to claim Johnson for high masculine culture and dissociate him from its feminine rivals, presents his attitude to his mother's reading as negative, while Thrale presents it as positive. Boswell's Johnson is bored when compelled by his mother to read *The Whole Duty of Man*, while Thrale's Johnson remembers his mother teaching him to read with 'tenderness and gratitude'.[48] That the truth lies somewhere between is suggested by Johnson's most private autobiographical writing where, surely thinking of his own marriage as well as his parents', he speculates that if his 'mother had been more literate', the marriage would have been happier. Female literacy figures a utopian domestic happiness never achieved by Johnson or his father.[49]

Johnson's work foregrounds issues of reading and writing. His periodicals aimed to 'inculcate . . . the necessity of reading', which for him was an act not of dry rationalism but of 'passion', a model which could accommodate women as they were seen in contemporary gender-ideologies more easily than more rigorously intellectual accounts.[50] His periodical writing, moreover, repeatedly focuses on women writers and readers and their special problems: the impoverished middle-class Zosima and the servant Betty Brown have difficulty in finding work because potential employers unjustly associate female literacy with vanity and sloth, and Cornelia's relatives disapprove of female reading.[51] He was appreciative and supportive of a number of women writers. Elizabeth Carter, Hester Chapone and Catherine Talbot contributed to his *Rambler*, he wrote poems in praise of Carter, and included quotations from a number of women writers in his *Dictionary*. He was a 'patron' of literary women: Isobel Grundy lists more than twenty he helped. He even worked in a semi-collaborative way with some women writers: he wrote a number of dedications and book-proposals for Charlotte Lennox, appears in fictionalised form in *The Female Quixote*, and may even have contributed the decisive penultimate chapter of that novel.[52] He was well aware of the growing importance of women readers, claiming that 'all our ladies read now', an 'improvement' beneficial to society.[53]

Johnson was not the 'misogynist' or 'male supremacist'[54] sometimes presented by commentators from Boswell onwards: but his view of women writers and readers could be ambivalent. In his vocabulary of images women's reading could figure utopian domesticity, but also a revolt against domesticity: Myrtilla, introduced to reading by the more sophisticated Flavia, neglects her domestic tasks and despises her aunt for lacking 'knowledge of books'.[55] A similar ambivalence characterises his treatment of women writers. 'Of the female mind, he conceived a higher opinion than many men', but he also claimed that 'Publick practice of any art . . . is very indelicate in a female.'[56] He criticised an education that confined women to domesticity, but also praised women writers for not losing touch with their domestic duties, singling out Elizabeth Carter not only for her translation of Epictetus but also for her ability to 'make a pudding . . . and work a handkerchief'.[57] In a favourite image, he figured the new generation of women writers as 'Amazons of the pen', an ambivalent image which both appreciates their heroic defiance of 'masculine tyranny' and displays anxiety at their transgression of their 'due sphere'.[58]

Boswell's *Life of Johnson* (1791) is obsessively interested in his attitudes to literary women, writing his relations with them in edgy, sometimes disconcertingly sexualised, terms, and organising his observations of Johnson around an image-cluster in which women readers and writers are identified with falsehood, forgery, crime, and illicit sexuality. Ridicule of Catherine Macaulay leads on one occasion to a discussion of bribery in public life (pp. 608–9), on another to an attack on writers who pass off the works of others as their own (p. 749); criticism of Montagu and Thrale precipitates a discussion of literary forgeries (pp. 750–1). Boswell routinely genders poor writing as feminine, whatever the sex of the author, and associates it with female unchastity: a discussion of the adultery of Lady Diana Beauclerk leads into criticism of Hawkesworth's travel writing for an alleged lack of originality (pp. 536–7). Poor reading is also gendered as feminine: a woman's failure to read an allegorical picture correctly is contextualised by accounts of the untruthfulness of some books including Thrale's *Anecdotes*, a wife who 'fraudulently' appropriates her husband's fortune, and Johnson's humanity to a sick prostitute (pp. 1311–13).

Boswell's Johnson persistently makes 'the female a metaphor for the misreader' and figures the good writer and reader as masculine, a 'man', to use one of Johnson's favourite words, who 'writes from his own mind' (p. 612). This recapitulates Johnson's practice elsewhere: the *Lives of the*

Poets includes no female poets, the ironic definition of the poet in *Rasselas* is vigorously masculine, and his accounts of writers routinely assume the primacy of the masculine: 'An author partakes of the common condition of humanity: he is born and married like another man.' In one periodical essay, writers are 'men who think with vigour', while women readers are characterised as 'young and . . . ignorant'.[59] Boswell emphasises Johnson's gendering of literary creativity and consumption. 'Manly' texts for Boswell are 'not works of mere amusement', but serious 'literature' (p. 44), and virtually all worthwhile female writing is in actuality originated, or at least polished, by the male: Hannah Glasse's popular cookery book is attributed to Dr Hill, Johnson himself 'revised' with 'his own genius' the poems of Mary Masters and Anna Williams (pp. 1254, 372), and Frances Burney's popular novels only entitle her to a place among Johnson's 'imitators' (p. 1371). For Boswell women's reading too tends to be seen as inaccurate and transgressive, as Elizabeth Montagu is accused of having read less than she claims, and of a rebellious reading of Gibbon, whose work she has bound 'without the last two . . . chapters': it is symbolically appropriate that this anecdote follows shortly after an account of a tragedy about a castrated king (pp. 910, 906).

If Johnson was a patron of women writers and concerned but ambivalent about women's writing and reading, his work was a vital resource in the reading of women, an author whom all agreed was not only entertaining but instructive. Often Johnson is evoked as a conservative embodiment of traditional morality whose textual intervention saves vulnerable young women like Matilda in 'Passion Subdued by Reason' and the young Lady Davenant in Edgeworth's *Helen*, or whom women readers neglect at their peril. The vulnerability to seduction of the heroine of Jane West's conservative *A Tale of the Times* (1799) is signalled by her disillusionment with her 'favourite author' Johnson and the 'moral . . . romance' of *Rasselas* (ii, pp. 181, 179). But as Claudia Johnson has pointed out, there were different ways of reading Johnson, who could be read as an embodiment of conservative values, but whose instinctive 'sympathy with the underdog' could look 'rebellious', and thus appeal to progressives like Catherine Macaulay and Mary Hays. Even Mary Wollstonecraft uses Johnson, not only as a 'rhetorical device to add authority', but also in appreciation of his 'populist' views, even reading him as 'sympathetic to the condition of women'. At the turn of the century Johnson could thus be read as 'a kind of Romantic hero' or as an embodiment of repression, a 'lover of discipline and system, averse to those rights which man inherently possesses',[60] his views on women as either misogynist or liberal.

WOMEN READING, READING WOMEN: THE ROMANTIC PERIOD

In the Romantic period women writers became more numerous and women readers more influential, and so caused increasingly acute anxieties to their male contemporaries. Some of the most fruitful recent reassessments of Romanticism have read it as the reassertion of a specifically masculine literary authority after a brief period of cultural domination by women.[61] Romanticism's 'celebration . . . of passionate feeling' and its tenet that 'everything that passes in [the] . . . minds' of the poets was 'of paramount importance', seemed calculated to exclude women, trained in an ideology of self-suppression, and many contemporary women responded 'very negatively'.[62] Anne K. Mellor has convincingly argued that despite the construction of romanticism in the academy through the works of six canonical male writers, this is a distortion because it neglects the 'numerous women writers who produced at least half of the literature published in England between 1780 and 1830'.[63] Some had high contemporary reputations, like Felicia Hemans and Joanna Baillie, and many were commercially successful. In 1798 William Lane, founder of the Minerva Press, listed ten 'particular and favourite authors' on the Minerva list: all were women.[64]

Domestic ideology worked to distance women from Romanticism: the virtuous heroine of *The Countess and Gertrude*, for instance, cannot reconcile Burns the poet, the 'artless child of nature', with Burns the '*shocking bad husband*' (III, p. 256). In his 1830 memoir of Byron, Thomas Moore defends the poet by arguing that poetic genius and 'domestic life' are simply incompatible, and that the poet cannot be judged by its trivial standards.[65] This functions as another strategy for excluding women from literary culture. Felicia Hemans opposed Moore's formulation, as she had to if she were to maintain her own right to poetic creativity, recruiting the patriarchal authority of Wordsworth to articulate a more female-friendly model for poetry. Her account of a visit to the poet shows him rooted in domesticity, '*paternal*', the 'true *Poet of Home*', and quotes his counter-Moore arguments that poets like Byron fail in domestic life 'not because they *possess* genius, but because they do not possess genius *enough*', for true genius is acutely sensitive to 'the beauty of domestic ties'.[66] By appropriating male authority to redefine poetic creativity in a way which is gender-neutral or positively privileges the feminine, Hemans rendered possible her own poetic vocation which Moore's opposition of poetry and domesticity menaced.

Some female readers, then, resisted the masculine sublime of Byron: others enjoyed the frisson of transgression offered by his poems of unspeakable sins and amoral heroes, and his poems were read even in religious and respectable families like Ruskin's. Davidoff and Hall emphasise Byron's popularity and cite such anomalies as Jane Ransom Biddell, pious reader of Hannah More, who admired Byron's work so much she named her son Manfred. The 'search for individual auton-omy and liberty' which Byron's heroes dramatise was appealling to an upwardly mobile middle-class readership, especially its female mem-bers,[67] who responded to his poems with pleasure but also guilt and ambivalence. One of Susan Ferrier's moralistic characters expresses this ambivalence by envisaging a utopian future when the 'profane and licentious' elements in the poet's work will wither away, leaving what is 'fine' for 'lovers of virtue'. (Elsewhere in Ferrier's work a love of Byron indicates immoral characters, and is identified with conspicuous con-sumption, embodied in a 'beautiful copy . . . bound in red morocco – rather too fine for reading'.[68]) Anne Grant admired Byron's 'very beautiful' poems but could justify reading them only by persuading herself that they constituted a useful negative role-model teaching 'the evils of . . . perverted genius'; young Felicia Hemans was fascinated by Byron, wearing a brooch containing a lock of his hair, but gave this up when she learned of his 'Mephistopheles-like character'. Hemans 'shrank from any thing like coarseness of thought', and if 'any passage in one of her most favourite writers offended her delicacy, the leaf was torn out without remorse', even if this left a 'pause and chasm' in a favourite book.[69] Hemans' respectability as a writer depended on rigorous self-policing as a reader: better a literary aporia than a fractured reputation.

Women in Romanticism are most visible even today on the margins of male Romanticism – Wordsworth's sister, Coleridge's daughter, Shelley's wife – servicing that Romanticism. They acted as channels, sometimes in the most literal ways, for male creativity. Byron, whose handwriting was notoriously indecipherable, provided his publisher with legible copy through the intervention of a stream of female amanu-enses, Teresa Guiccioli, Claire Clairmont, Lady Byron and Mary Shel-ley. Sara Coleridge edited her father's works, becoming an 'unacknow-ledged collaborator' and practically inventing Coleridge the philosopher: Mary Shelley was also the first editor of her husband's collected works. Such apparently compliant acts of service were not, however, always what they seemed. Mary Shelley read the poems of her husband and Byron critically, even rebelliously, and sought to edit out or tone down obscenity, personal satire, political radicalism and religious scepticism. Byron often accepted her alterations, and sometimes offered her a choice between alternative versions, which he generally allowed to stand.[70] What looks like readerly compliance to the authority of the male author might actually be a subversive revision of masculine individualism.

The first generation of Romantic poets was less affected by anxieties about female rivals than later generations. Still, even Wordsworth's preface to the *Lyrical Ballads*, the manifesto of English Romanticism, is strictly gendered: his definition of the poet as 'a man speaking to men'[71] immediately erases his primary audience of sister and wife, the majority female reading public, and the numerous contemporary women poets. Wordsworth read some women poets with pleasure, but again in rigidly gendered ways. He appreciated Anne Finch, Countess of Winchilsea, and had some of her poems copied into an album for Lady Lowther, 'misrepresenting' the poet by reading her in terms of an anachronistic ideology of domesticity and suppressing the more witty and rebellious poems. He praised Hemans primarily for her piety and her 'modest and humble' qualities, judging her as a woman first, a poet second. In Wordsworth's household even Hemans felt the need to resist, at least playfully, the cult of domesticity, arguing, for instance, that jewellery might make a better wedding present for a young woman than a kitchen implement.[72] Hemans needed a model of the poet which was compatible with domestic ideology: but she also needed to extract herself from a domestic ideology which defined her place as in the kitchen. The female Romantic had to be a walker of fine lines.

In the second generation of Romantics, anxieties about reading and being read by women became deeply entrenched. Scott begins *Waverley* with 'an elaborate suppression of prior', mostly female, 'narrative models', distancing himself from Radcliffean Gothic or the sentimental fiction of Lady Morgan and associating his work instead with masculine authority-figures imaged as a 'knight with his white shield'. This recuperation of the novel as a male-dominated form rooted in the authority of history transformed its status, rescuing it, in the eyes of at least one twentieth-century male scholar, from the 'danger of becoming the preserve of the woman writer and the woman reader', and giving it instead 'a new masculinity', which for this critic seems synonymous with universality.[73] While Scott was anxious about women writers and read them resistingly, Keats feared the power of women readers, showing an 'active disdain' for them, insisting that 'he does not want ladies to read his poetry: that he writes for men': he even copied 'exceptionable' poems into his portfolio, and planned more sexually explicit versions of his poems, with the deliberate object of making his work 'unfit for ladies'. Keats imaged the act of poetic receptivity and creation as female, and a terror of the dissolution of his masculinity translated into angry resentment of female readers.[74]

BYRON READING WOMEN, WOMEN READING BYRON

Of the canonical Romantics, Byron's reading of women writers and views on women readers is most fully documented, obsessively articulated, and ambivalent. He 'professedly despised the society of women, yet female adulation became the most captivating charm to his heart'.[75] He veers between seeing himself self-pityingly as a 'martyr' to women, 'sacrificed *to* them and *by* them', and self-dramatisingly as an oppressor of women, a Zeluco, Othello or Falkner pursuing a female Caleb Williams; between seeing women as morally better than men and as amoral 'Children'; and between advocating a return to the ancient Greek seclusion of women and issuing a 'radical onslaught' on the confinement of women within domestic ideology.[76] These ambivalences find their sharpest articulation in his treatment of female reading, female writing, and the gendering of literary creativity.

Byron recognised the need to appeal to the large and influential new audience of women readers – 'Who does not write to please the women?'[77] – and in 1807 he asked his bookseller which of his poems 'Ladies have bought' (I, p. 125). Yet his poems and letters generally show contempt for women readers. Like Keats he insists he 'will not make 'Ladies books'' (VI, p. 106), and in a youthful letter writes that his present mistress has 'only two faults, unpardonable in a woman – she can read and write' (I, p. 161). He praises the unspoiled illiteracy of lower-class and Turkish women, who do not rival or criticise male literary authority – 'They cannot read, and so don't lisp in criticism.'[78] In the misogynist utopia in his *Ravenna Journal* (1821), women will be kept at home, their reading confined to 'piety and cookery', with poetry and politics specifically banned (VIII, p. 15).

Byron sees women as incompetent readers for two opposite and, one might have supposed, incompatible reasons. He imagines them always in search of sexually arousing material: he imagines them 'disappointed' because *Hours of Idleness* contained 'nothing indecent' (I, p. 125). But they are also contradictorily made to figure a trend in modern literature he dislikes and fears, a prudish reaction against sexual explicitness. Byron's publisher and male friends were disturbed by the growing explicitness and cynicism of *Don Juan*: Byron berates John Murray for excessive caution, and curses the 'damned prudery' of John Cam Hobhouse (VI, p. 103). And yet he also personifies this cultural shift as feminine. *Don Juan*, he argues, is '*too true*' for 'the women', who 'hate every thing which strips off the tinsel of *Sentiment*' (VII, p. 202). These arguments appear increasingly in his later letters, which create a world of sentimental, hypocritical female readers unable to cope with the harsh and rigorous truth of the male vision, and which defensively position the poet within a sexually explicit, masculine tradition legitimising his work.[79] Although this gendering of literacy is rhetorically useful to Byron he knows it is not literally, historically true: one minute he is saying that he 'never knew a woman who did not hate' the indecent *Memoirs of the Count Grammont* (VII, p. 202), the next he is quoting Madame de Staël's approval of them.[80]

Byron is always alert to the presence of women readers. In *English Bards and Scotch Reviewers*, he saves some of his sharpest barbs for 'ladies' who patronise working-class male poets: the low-status poet deserves the low-status reader, both characterised by an unmasculine 'softness'.[81] This association of female and low-class readers recurs in his insistence that he will not write 'al dilettar le femine e la plebe' (VI, p. 106).

Like Keats's, Byron's anxiety about female readers may spring from a fear that literature, especially poetry, had a feminising, emasculating power: real men are 'agents and leaders', the age's 'preference of *writers* to *agents*' symptomatic of 'effeminacy, degeneracy and weakness': at this point his journal immediately goes on to associate himself with more manly activities, personified by the prizefighter 'Gentleman' Jackson (II, pp. 217, 220–1). Because of this anxiety, Byron tries to create more masculine images for poetic creativity, sometimes imaging composition as an 'ejaculatory' act, sometimes rejecting conventional rhetoric of female muses and a feminised Nature. *Childe Harold's Pilgrimage* begins with an apparent invocation to the muse, but it is in fact an announcement that the muse will not be invoked: her shrine at Delphi is 'long deserted', and female literary hegemony is over. Some poems begin with specifically masculine images of creativity which displace the female muse, like the painter Lawrence in *Hints from Horace* and the poet Samuel Rogers in *The Giaour*.[82]

Byron struggles to gender as masculine artistic creativity and the poet, but these laboriously maintained images are fragile. Preparing his Drury Lane address he is angry that the theatre manager is determined to '*castrate*' his lines, and compares himself with the 'Hottentot' who is enabled to run at great speed but only with the sacrifice of '*one* testicle' (II, pp. 212, 211). Elsewhere he describes his poems as 'disjecti membra poetae' ('membra' is a Latin euphemism for the penis), or compares the mutilated body of his poetry to that of 'the Levite's Concubine', who in Judges 19: 22ff dies as a result of gang-rape and is dismembered. Fear of castration, feminisation and rape haunt Byron's images for poetry and poetic identity. He frequently depicts himself, powerless and emasculated, beset by monstrously powerful females reading his texts or himself. So Lady Oxford figures as '*Armida*', the enchantress who reduces Rinaldo to her slave (II, p. 251). Byron even imagines himself as a character in a work authored by a powerful woman writer, trapped passively in a feminised textuality from which he cannot escape, like a 'hero of Madame Scudery or Mrs Clarke', dominated by women like Lord Delacour in Edgeworth's *Belinda* (II, p. 194). Perhaps his disgust at Caroline Lamb's publication of *Glenarvon*, in which he features as the eponymous anti-hero, was so intense partly because it literalised this fear of becoming textualised and manipulated by a powerful female author.[83]

Books and reading played a central part in Byron's love affairs. Frances Webster smuggled love-letters to him 'in a music book – or any book' (IV, p. 29), he wrote a love-letter to Teresa Guiccioli in her copy of de Staël's *Corinne* (I, p. 8), and in the early stages of his courtship of his future wife they read each other's poems. Books and reading also marked the end of relationships or critical moments in them. At the end of their affair Caroline Lamb wrote 'Remember me' on the flyleaf of one of his favourite books, Beckford's *Vathek*, and one element in the Byrons' final separation was her breaking into his writing desk and finding some letters to a married woman and a 'book . . . that did not do much credit to my taste in literature' (Medwin thought it Crébillon's indecent *The Sofa*, Hobhouse Sade's *Justine*).[84] In some relationships a book represents transparently his sexual ambivalence. In 1820 he sent Teresa Guiccioli a copy of Benjamin Constant's *Adolphe*, which was 'not a very tactful gift' for his married mistress since it deals wih the 'misery' of extramarital affairs,[85] and Guiccioli was 'very much hurt' by it (VII, p. 163).

Byron was disturbed both by the demands made by female readers and the prominence in his cultural world of rival women writers. Pen and pencil often serve as lightly veiled euphemisms for the penis, their appropriation by female writers the source of anxiety or disturbing comedy (as with Lady Bluebottle in *The Blues: a Literary Eclogue*, whose 'hand [is] on the pen'[86]). Sometimes Byron simply eradicates women writers from his literary landscape: his 'Gradus ad Parnassum' depicts a pyramid of poets, with Scott at the apex, descending through Rogers, Moore, Campbell, Southey, Wordsworth and Coleridge to 'The Many'. No individual female poet is even named (III, p. 220): they belong by definition to the *hoi polloi* of literature.

Byron read many women writers and early in life admired some, including Elizabeth Inchbald (III, p. 236) and Maria Edgeworth. By 1813 he has read *Belinda* (II, p. 194), *The Modern Griselda* (II, p. 199), *Ennui* and *The Absentee* with enough admiration to 'fear' meeting the author and to ask his publisher to send him *Patronage* (III, pp. 48, 44, 204). He came to dislike her politics and to complain that her work showed 'no more heart than a post',[87] but he continued to appreciate grudgingly her 'intellect and prudence' (VIII, p. 30). Frances Burney was another early enthusiasm. In 1813 he is 'almost . . . sick' to get an advance copy of *The Wanderer* (III, p. 204), and in 1812, in company with his future wife and others, conversation turned to 'the best English Novels': he predictably nominated Godwin's radical *Caleb Williams*, and everyone agreed on *The Vicar of Wakefield*, but, surprisingly, Byron also argued for 'Miss Burney's Novels'.[88] This liking, though, depended on his belief in her subservience to the patriarchal culture of a previous generation, a writer whose work 'Dr Johnson superintended [and] revised' (II, pp. 143, 146). He disliked *The Wanderer* which did not show proper subservience to a male-dominated literary world, as he disliked other assertive women writers, like Anna Seward, who provokes a diatribe about literary 'Bitches' (II, pp. 132).

Byron's anxiety about writing women is marked in his ironic recognition that his publisher's two most popular books are *Childe Harold's Pilgrimage* and Mrs Rundell's *Domestic Cookery*: 'Such is fame . . . to divide purchasers with Hannah Glasse or Hannah More.'[89] Two models of popular female authorship, the writer on housewifery and the writer of moral and conduct works, impinge threateningly on his high-culture, masculine poetic project, and the public is too undiscriminating to distinguish between them.

Like Johnson whom he admired, Byron imaged inferior literary work as feminine. His version of literary history identifies women with the low tastes and crass commercialism of the mass market: Susanna Centlivre, for instance, is accused of writing popular 'balderdash' which drove the superior comedies of Congreve (VII, p. 61; VIII, p. 57) from the stage. All kinds of literary sins are imaged as feminine, from prudish and insensitive criticism to 'Stupidity' and plagiarism (VI, p. 256; VII, p. 61; VIII, pp. 166, 215). Hobhouse's *Miscellany* becomes the '*Miss-sell-any*', a pun which revealingly combines femaleness with sordid commercialism, and again female sexuality is identified with dishonest and inflated language in a repeated pun on 'cant' and 'cunt'.[90]

Byron's view of women writers became more jaundiced as his relationships with the women in his life deteriorated, and the years 1817–20 in particular produce some extraordinary outbursts against literary women. By 1814 he had decided that he 'hate[d]' *The Wanderer* and *Patronage*, although he had been so eager to read them, and from this point his contempt for 'feminine trash' is entrenched, his treatment of women authors teetering between obscene diatribe and a contemptuous insistence on their unimportance. Thus he soothes a male friend's anger at Lady Morgan with 'authoresses . . . can do no great harm': though later, in calmer mood, he adjudges her book on Italy to be 'really *excellent*' (VI, pp. 12–13; VIII, p. 186).

As Byron increasingly genders creativity as masculine and contrasts favourite masculine authors – Pope, Moore, Scott, Crabbe – with 'feminine trash', his images of the female writer become surrealistically, obscenely, concerned with their physical sexuality, and the female author becomes increasingly imaged as an unsexed or hermaphrodite figure whose monstrous body figures literary transgressiveness. Caroline Lamb, author of *Glenarvon*, becomes a 'monster . . . that *has no sex*' (V, p. 93), and even de Staël whose work he admired is adjudged 'Epicene' (III, p. 66). In 1816 he admired Felicia Hemans, praising *The Restoration of the Works of Art in Italy* as 'a good poem – very' (V, p. 108), but by 1820 he associates her with a whole corrupt literary culture, prudish, 'stiltified & apostrophic' (VII, p. 113), and sees her as a literary hermaphrodite, 'Mrs Hewoman's', 'your feminine *He-man*' (VII, pp. 158, 183). He does not exactly 'despise' her, he tells Murray, 'but if [she] knit blue stockings instead of wearing them it would be better' (VII, p. 182). The literary woman is a monster, since she pushes herself into a public marketplace when her proper milieu is the private sphere.

Byron was an 'enthusiastic admirer' of the dramatist Joanna Baillie, thinking her the best tragedian since Otway and Southerne (III, p. 109), but his treatment even of her centres on images of sexual reversal. Voltaire's views on why women cannot write tragedy is quoted: ' "the composition of a tragedy required *testicles*" – If this be true Lord knows what Joanna Baillie does – I suppose she borrows them' (v, p. 203). This is playful, but also libellously suggests plagiarism, promiscuity and transsexuality, again dramatising a sexualised anxiety about successful literary creativity in a woman.

The most extreme version of making the female writer sexually monstrous occurs in an outburst against Maria Edgeworth. His attitude to Edgeworth was always ambivalent. Even as late as 1821 he admired her, but for her modesty rather than her literary gifts: 'One would never have guessed she could write *her name*' (viii, p. 30). He attacked Richard Lovell Edgeworth as 'a bore', but found his novelist-daughter a 'pleasant reserved old woman'. However, as he begins to think of her as a writer, he becomes increasingly angry about the monstrous coexistence of literary success and female sexuality. She must have a '*pencil* under her petticoat': like Joanna Baillie, or de Staël with her pen behind her ear, she becomes a hermaphrodite by the act of writing. This phallic 'pencil' operates 'undisturbed' in the 'vicinity of that anatomical part of female humanity', and gives Byron an opportunity to attack Edgeworth's alleged prudishness and sexlessness. 'That sort of women seem to think themselves perfect because they can't get covered': but sexually active women are no better, and both are dehumanised as in Byron's invective they become cows and bitches (vii, p. 218). This curious passage, which begins with a casually patronising account of a social encounter with a pleasant old woman, exposes surreal horrors behind her mild exterior, as the woman writer becomes not only sexually monstrous but also bestial.

CHAPTER 2

What should girls and women read?

When Dr Johnson visited Frances Sheridan and found her daughter 'attentively employed in reading his "Ramblers"', Sheridan was more anxious than proud, and 'hastened to assure' him that the girl was allowed only 'unexceptionable' books, and that she was 'very careful to keep from her all such books as are not calculated, by their moral tendency, for the perusal of youth'. Johnson disagreed: ' "Then you are a fool, madam! . . . Turn your daughter loose into your library; if she is well inclined, she will choose only nutritious food; if otherwise, all your precautions will avail nothing to prevent her following the natural bent of her inclinations." '[1] Sheridan is more typical of the age than Johnson, and this was even more marked by 1824, when her granddaughter Alicia Lefanu described Johnson's opinion as 'injudicious and dangerous', for 'the practice of indiscriminate reading' would obviously teach the child 'immoral precepts'.[2] Although this narrative does not *seem* to be gendered – age, not gender, seems the criterion of suitability – gender was surely a significant unspoken element. Contemporary comments are always more anxious about female than male reading, and accounts of girls' reading, including the family history of the Sheridans and Lefanus, repeatedly emphasise the need for restriction.[3]

However much commentators differed in detail, virtually all thought women's reading mattered, for society as well as individuals. In 1814 Laetitia-Matilda Hawkins denied 'that books produce no effects', certain that reading 'censurable' books 'can do . . . harm'. Moreover, reading had to be policed because it was a crucial element in the 'creation of femininity'.[4] Anxieties clustered especially around the power of reading to affect the emotions. Supporters of sentiment argued that imaginative reading had positive functions to 'humanise the heart', though rationalists viewed it more negatively, fearing it might develop 'the heart prematurely' and lower 'the tone of the mind'.[5] The rhetoric of texts on reading depends on generating oppositions between heart and mind, good and bad books and reading practices.

Most education and conduct works address women's reading, sometimes generally, sometimes specifically, with bibliographies or even, like Wollstonecraft's *The Female Reader*, substantial extracts, of suitable books. Women writers are generally more concerned than men to provide detailed accounts of acceptable reading. Indeed, the two most popular conduct writers, James Fordyce and John Gregory, avoid specific recommendations. Gregory 'is at the greatest loss what to advise you in regard to books', spending more time on dress, behaviour and conversation; Fordyce contents himself with forbidding novels (except Richardson), and warning women that their chief 'business' is not to read books but 'to read Men, in order to make yourselves agreeable and useful'.[6]

While sceptical, politically radical or erotic works were routinely banned, and novel-reading disturbed many comentators, extreme inconsistencies are found about which individual texts are acceptable. Ideological packages which with hindsight appear coherent and inevitable did not necessarily seem so to contemporaries. A correspondent to the *Lady's Magazine* in 1800 praises modern authors for combining 'imagination' and 'judgement', but then self-contradictorily recommends both the 'unexceptionable lessons of morality' of Godwin's novels and Sophia King's anti-Godwinian *Waldorf*. Real women blithely refused to fit the moralists' categories of good reader/bad reader. Respectable Maria Josepha Holroyd, later Lady Stanley, read and enjoyed both conservative Hannah More and radical Mary Wollstonecraft, and her tastes encompassed conduct and educational works and moral novels, but also riskier Gothic and sentimental fiction, and even outright transgressive French and German novels, especially Rousseau.[7] The rhetoric of the moralists is just that and, as always, real life was richer and stranger than their prescriptions allowed.

My argument in this chapter is twofold; first, it is almost literally true that all genres of reading, however apparently safe, upset some commentator in this period; secondly, almost all genres, however apparently harmless, could be read rebelliously and resistingly rather than compliantly. I shall work from the most legitimate kinds of reading to the most problematic.

BIBLICAL AND RELIGIOUS READING

Even biblical and devotional reading were not always considered safe for female readers. Conservative educationalists tended to argue that 'a girl's reading is to be concentrated as far as possible on the Bible stories', and even the most repressive allowed women to read 'devotion and housewifery', if nothing else.[8] '[A]ll good little girls read the Bible', and the idealised women of the moralists, Ellen and Anna Stanley in Elizabeth Sandham's *The Twin Sisters: or, the Effects of Education* (1788–9), Lucilla Stanley in More's *Coelebs in Search of a Wife*, Hawkins' Gertrude, Ferrier's Mary Douglas, or Lady *** in 'On the Education of the Female Sex', all read the Bible, sermons and other religious works.[9] Such reading is clearly transformational: in Hawkins' *Rosanne* (1814) and Charlotte Anley's *Miriam; or, the Power of Truth* (1826) a freethinking and Jewish heroine respectively are converted and convert non-Christian fathers by reading 'that precious book' the Gospels. For conduct writers like Sarah Green or Gregory, 'the Scriptures' came first in any programme of female reading.[10] Gregory not only recommends religious reading to his daughters, he also figures religion as a feminised discourse since it appeals, in a word he persistently genders as feminine, 'to the heart': women should therefore avoid strenuously intellectual works or controversy (p. 17) and confine themselves to religious texts whose 'softness and sensibility' (p. 24) identify them with the female reader.

However, although religious reading was widely recommended, radicals and conservatives alike believed that tact had to be exercised in using it in the education of girls. Wollstonecraft warned against teaching girls to read from the Bible, lest it become a 'task' rather than a religious experience, and Catherine Macaulay goes further, arguing that both sexes should avoid childhood religious reading, which will 'naturally give rise to doubts' in a pre-adult.[11] Early reading makes scripture 'too familiar' and 'disagreeable'. Julia Delmond in Elizabeth Hamilton's *Memoirs of Modern Philosophers* turns to novels because her education, too strictly confined to religious reading, makes Sunday a time of 'bondage and dismay', Mary Berry loathed the Psalms when made to read them, and Frances Burney knew a girl who became an 'infidel' when forced Bible-reading made her 'sick to death of it'. Compulsory religious reading could easily backfire, and readers be 'alienated or embarrassed by . . . didactic insistence': in Edgeworth's 'Vivian', Lady Glistonbury educates her daughter from Toplady's Sermons, Wesley's Diary and *Pilgrim's Progress*, but her 'ignorance and . . . rigidity' make virtue 'repulsive'. Even good books can be dangerous, encouraging not virtue but 'affectation'.[12]

Reading comparative religion might shake one's faith (as for the Lambs' young Mohammedan), controversy 'entangle' women readers in an 'endless maze of opinions', and the literature of proselytising sects like Methodists was thought especially dangerous (as for Edgeworth's Lady Glistonbury or Lady Delacour). Another danger was 'Books of flaming devotion' which 'kindle the heart' but 'confuse the head': even religious reading might lead to 'corruption' if it allows 'the softer passions to mix too strongly with . . . zeal for religion'.[13] Again the rhetorical opposition of heart and head indicates the contradictions of contemporary gender-ideologies: for Gregory, women should cultivate the 'heart', while for the commentators just quoted, the heart has to be restrained.

Even the Bible might not be safe for young female readers. Frances Burney D'Arblay, for whom reading and writing were problematic acts, thought 'Many would be my doubts as to the old Testament for a Girl', for the 'Translators' have failed to exclude 'improper' expressions. A boy can be allowed the 'risks and dangers' of access to 'the Scripture at large', but a girl should be restricted to edited summaries, those of Sarah Trimmer being especially recommended.[14] Matthew Lewis in *The Monk* shows the dangers of such views as part of a wider, self-interested, anti-censorship programme. The 'prudent' Elvira allows her daughter only a bowdlerised Bible, believing it full of 'indecent expressions' which encourage 'ideas the worst calculated for a female breast', awaken 'sleeping passions', and inculcate the 'first rudiments of vice'. By implication, Lewis defends his own blatantly transgressive text as having informative functions for the virtuous female reader: had she been allowed wider reading, Antonia might have acquired enough wordly wisdom to suspect Ambrosio.[15]

The view that girls' access to biblical texts should be limited met opposition from moralists too. Lady Sarah Pennington advises against the use of digests which encourage the reader to acquire 'a mere Shadow of Piety', instead recommending 'the whole scripture'. Hester Thrale insisted her daughters read 'the Bible from beginning to end', a *Lady's Magazine* article urges girls to 'learn . . . religion from the Bible, not from the vain comments of man', and Hannah More also advocated reading 'the *Bible itself*. The devout Stanley twins in Sandham's *The Twin Sisters* are contrasted with the worldly Arnold sisters, who do not read the Bible, though they sometimes look at 'Mrs TRIMMER's history of it', a text which is praised as a supplement to, not a substitute for, the Bible.[16]

Since the Bible (in sanitised versions) and devotional reading (if neither too intellectual nor emotional) were so insistently offered to women readers, it is unsurprising that some showed resentment or resistance, or at least an ability to appropriate such texts for their own purposes. Charlotte Lennox's Harriot Stuart repels the advances of a 'young chaplain' who woos her with poetry and plays by mockingly recommending religious reading, 'the study of Tillotson and Barrow' (II, p. 25). The aunt of Harriet Elderton in Elizabeth Blower's *George Bateman* punishes a hypocritical clergyman by flinging at him 'a large quarto book of divinity-tracts . . . which she had just been reading' (I, p. 146). Jane Austen associates Blair's Sermons with hypocritical or ineffectual readers, like the heroine's aunt in 'Catherine, or the Bower', or Mary Crawford in *Mansfield Park*. In *The Countess and Gertrude*, the Toms sisters use the Bible only to 'smooth a cambric hankerchief' or 'absorb the humidity of a bit of lace', and Hawkins tells of an actress whose aunt tries to arrange her marriage to a man of sober habits by displaying her sewing, 'with "the Practice of Piety" conspicuous in her work-basket' (I, pp. 57, 16).

Each text, moreover, constructs not only its ideal reader but also its resisting reader. Lady Byron 'never read a work *for* [Christianity] without a disposition to infidelity, nor a work *against* without a disposition to belief'. Even women who in their waking lives read devotional reading compliantly might show unconscious rebellion. In 1822 Maria Edgeworth's sister Elizabeth dreamed 'she went to call upon a lady, and found her reading a pious tract called, "The Penitent Poodle!"':[17] only the sleeping mind dare satirise religious reading and its domination of the lives of women readers.

CONDUCT BOOKS

The importance of conduct books in women's lives and literature is beginning to be recognised. Nancy Armstrong sees them as 'colonizers of [the] household', reinforcing domestic ideology and articulating a 'specific understanding of the relationship between reading, sexuality, and social control'. However, readers were not only shaped by but also resisted these mechanisms of control, a process as important in the history of culture as their repressive functions.[18]

Among the most popular conduct books were Fordyce's *Sermons to Young Women* (1765) and Gregory's *A Father's Legacy to his Daughters* (1778), which frame the lengthy bibliography of Henry Kett's didactic novel *Emily* (II, pp. 190, 195), and conduct books appear in practically all lists of approved female reading. Fordyce is recommended by Sarah Green, Catherine Talbot, Burney, Clara Reeve and innumerable others. He was a favourite of the *Lady's Magazine*, hailed as a 'paternal friend' who had 'sav'd' by his good advice 'thousands of our sex' (7, 1776, p. 272): his work is among very few by male authors admitted to Leonora's gynocentric library (9, 1778, p. 32). Even Mary Wollstonecraft, so critical of Fordyce and Gregory in *A Vindication of the Rights of Woman*, recommends at least Gregory in the earlier *The Female Reader* (1789).[19]

Conduct texts were at the forefront of the contemporary reconceptualisation of domesticity, embodying 'bourgeois and patriarchal' ideologies in opposition to a bankrupt courtly culture. They offer a 'grammar' of female subjectivity, constructing a 'new kind of woman', a 'domestic woman' whose image naturalised female 'propriety', modesty and self-denial. Conduct texts addressed to women increased dramatically in popularity in the course of the eighteenth century: an important cultural shift is indicated by the fact that while most seventeenth-century conduct books address 'the male of the dominant class', by the eighteenth and nineteenth it had become a gynocentric genre.[20] The 'most successful conduct texts were in constant circulation', and even sixteenth- and seventeenth-century texts were reissued, texts which depicted a different world but whose images of female silence and obedience remained the same: the result is to reinforce 'the assumption that femininity is an unchanging, "natural" condition'.[21]

Conduct books were popular although they offered a repressive, even 'gloomy', picture of women's 'history' as 'trials and sorrows'. Not only was their prognosis grim, but their specific injunctions demonstrate disconcerting aporias and contradictions. While they seem to offer a consensus opinion on behaviour, the vigour with which they attack some practices – novel reading, for instance – implies a culture in which they are prevalent and even accepted. Even Wollstonecraft's *Thoughts on the Education of Daughters* paradoxically advises young women to base their lives on 'sincerity', but that their feelings 'ought not to be displayed'. Gregory's *Father's Legacy* is full of contradictions: young women should be silent in company but able to complain if insulted 'with a becoming spirit'; their dancing should show 'spirit' but also 'delicacy'; they can take part in conversation without speaking a word.[22] The 'female body', although at the centre of conduct book discourse, is 'never represented', and indeed the whole conduct-book image of the ideal woman is 'internally contradictory'.[23] Marriage is depicted as both necessary and, since men and women are in an 'insidious state of warfare', deeply problematic; femininity is 'natural' and innate, yet a constant struggle is needed to maintain it.[24]

These contradictions revealed faultlines that could be worked on by resisting readers. Conduct texts, including Hester Chapone's popular *Letters on the Improvement of the Mind*, are prominent among the 'mopeish old books' that tomboy Joyce in Burney's *The Woman-Hater* fantasises about burning. In *The Rivals* (1775), Lydia Languish leaves Fordyce's *Sermons* open – at 'Sobriety' – to distract attention from the novels she really reads: the repressive text is ironically used to conceal and facilitate the very behaviour it forbids. Lady Delacour in *Belinda* mocks 'Fordyce's Sermons for Young Women', particularly its injunctions 'against novel reading' (pp. 265, 64): it is also the book that Mr Collins in *Pride and Prejudice* reads aloud on his first visit to the Bennet sisters. Austen resisted conduct works, for 'pictures of perfection' made her 'sick and wicked': she satirises their repressive discourse by allowing her flamboyant villainess Lady Susan to simulate it; she also mocks Gregory.[25]

Even Susan Ferrier, who supports traditional protocols of female reading and behaviour, can only use Fordyce satirically. In *Marriage* it is virtually the only book known to the semi-literate aunts (pp. 65, 188, 203), and in *Destiny* (1831) Edith's insensitive aunt sends her copies 'three several times'. The frequency with which Ferrier returns to Fordyce indicates the depth of her resentment. In *Marriage* he represents illiteracy and failure to think for oneself, and in *Destiny* also a tendency to live in the past, for Edith's aunt is 'at least forty years behind the rest of the world in her ideas'.[26] Neither Austen, Edgeworth nor Ferrier believes that reading Fordyce will construct the ideal domestic woman: the strongest attack on correct reading in *Pride and Prejudice* is Austen's revelation that it constructs only the pedantic, ignorant Mary, who 'read[s] great books, and make[s] extracts' (p. 55).

Some readers argued that conduct books would do more harm than good, discouraging young women by offering a model of behaviour achievable only by 'angels'. The *Lady's Magazine* in 1810 criticised Hannah More as 'ridiculously exact and severe on . . . trifles', restricting behaviour until 'there is not a bit of human nature left'. Anna Seward similarly found Thomas Gisborne's conduct books 'too strict', suggesting they 'might have been more generally useful upon a less rigid plan of admonition, especially the volume dedicated to females'. Others thought such books positively misleading: 'There is no peculiar Heaven for little girls: the virtues and vices are of no sex.' Finally, a few politicised writers identified a hidden agenda in conduct books and protested against it. Wollstonecraft's *Vindication of the Rights of Woman* offers critiques of Fordyce and Gregory, criticising Gregory for elevating 'starched rules of decorum' over rational behaviour, thus rendering women 'artificial, weak characters', and Fordyce for an 'affected style' whose 'lover-like phrases of pumped up passion' produce 'the portrait of a house slave'. Both are accused of denying 'nature': a vigorous contest is going on over this favourite word of Gregory's.[27]

INFORMATIVE READING

While many commentators were anxious about imaginative reading, informative reading, especially history, geography, travel-writing, manuals on household skills, literary criticism and some kinds of science, was generally allowed. The idealised girls of conduct texts, Kett's Emily, Hawkins' Gertrude and the exemplary Louisa of John Bennett's *Letters to a Young Lady* (1789), read 'natural history, botany, history, geography and religion'. Even this was not, however, unproblematic. While a girl should not be ignorant, she should not be too well-informed either: the period's paranoia about the learned lady, associated in stereotypes with dirt, neglect of domestic skills, vanity and sexual immorality, put pressure on real learned women. Elizabeth Carter was famous for her puddings and did needlework during conversation, and was consequently praised for a lack of 'affected consequence', which demonstrated that 'all this learning has not made her the less reasonable woman'. This formulation 'seems oxymoronic', but eighteenth-century commentators believed that for a woman to be learned and reasonable were very different. Some families thought any amount of learning too much for a girl. Elizabeth Hamilton was brought up by an aunt who, 'suspecting she was growing too fond of books' which might satisfy her 'avidity for information', tried to restrict her reading to 'general amusement', so Hamilton read 'many books by stealth'. She accepted the need 'to avoid any display of superior knowledge' to such a degree that 'she once hid a copy of Lord Kaims's Elements of Criticism under the cushion of a chair, lest she be detected in a study which prejudice and ignorance might pronounce unfeminine'.[28]

HISTORY

The eighteenth century showed the rise of history as a discipline and the first comprehensive philosophical histories of England, notably David Hume's (1754–62). For most rationalist intellectuals history, 'that noblest of studies', took a central role in women's education: British history, to encourage patriotism, and classical history, to allow access to the foundations of Western culture, were specially recommended. Hannah More, Sarah Green and Sarah Pennington placed history high on the agenda, 'fact, and not wit', 'instructions which only truth can give', its 'plain and unornamented' narrative suitable for female readers because it could not 'mislead the judgement or to inflame the passions'. All the evidence is against Bridget Hill's view that in the age of Catherine Macaulay, 'little history was read . . . by women'.[29] Most women who recorded their reading include some history, which also (including biographies, memoirs and letters) features in most lists of recommended books for women and girls. Even Gregory, although generally uninterested in reading, believes history-reading can contain 'no impropriety'. In women's periodicals, like the *Lady's Magazine*, history was a vital ingredient. The February issue for 1772, for instance, begins 'A concise History of England' which praises the 'general utility of History' and the magazine for that year also includes a series of biographies of famous women.[30]

Women's relation to history was, however, problematic. History operated as a 'cultural institution endorsing . . . [traditional] constructions of gender', and the historian's claim to 'neutral mastery' and universality is compromised by his failure to constitute women as 'historical subjects'. Women, 'conventionally ignored by history', were offered history by conservative educationalists as training in compliance to a male-dominated culture and its discursive practices. Although history is recommended as a 'study proper for both sexes', it is implied that boys and girls, men and women, will read it for different reasons. For a boy, the 'study of history' is a preparation for 'active' (i.e. public) life. History-reading prepared a girl, whose 'sphere of action is more narrow and confined', for domestic life, making her 'more a companion for her husband, and brother'. For her, its functions would be primarily 'moral', even 'religious', since it provided 'the study of virtue' rather than 'the study of vice' to be acquired from novels, with which history was persistently contrasted.[31]

The heroine of Jane West's *The Advantages of Education: or, the History of Maria Williams* (1793) is educated by her mother in 'the Morality of History' (I, p. 169), learning from it not only 'patriotism . . . virtue . . . integrity' but also 'Religious principles' (I, pp. 39–41). In fiction, a love of history defines a rational and moral female character, often in opposition to an excessively imaginative and emotional companion who reads novels or poetry. Eleanor Tilney is contrasted with Catherine Morland in *Northanger Abbey*, Rose St Austin with Armida Fitzalban in Maturin's *The Milesian Chief*, Louisa Maybank with Anna Rivers in Eliza Parsons' *The Errors of Education*, Mrs Malden with Bell Stewart in Hamilton's *The Cottagers of Glenburnie*, or Helen Stanley with Cecilia in Edgeworth's *Helen*. All good girls read history, like Fanny Price in *Mansfield Park* who reads 'a daily portion', Hawkins' Gertrude, Caroline in Charlotte Smith's *Rambles Farther*, and Elizabeth Raby in Mary Shelley's *Falkner* (though Shelley stresses that as well as these 'masculine studies' she also learns needlework and 'habits of neatness and order', without which any woman will be 'unhappy' and 'unsexed'). Sometimes the profits of such a study are very literally depicted: Caroline in Edgeworth's 'The Orphans' is able, because of prints she has seen in ' "Rapin's History of England" ', to help her orphan friends by identifying valuable coins.[32]

For a conservative theorist, key words in the justification of female history-reading are 'example', 'model', and 'imitation' – 'virtues to be imitated, and . . . vices to be shunned' – and history is used more as a form of control than intellectual development. When Maria Williams is persuaded it is wrong to go to a 'public masked ball', she stays at home reading the history of Regulus, from which she learns 'to smile in misery and triumph in suffering'. History, by dealing with public issues, keeps the heroine safely private. (This system did not, of course, always work, and Mary Wollstonecraft laments that though her charges read '*cart*-loads of history' they have not, as propaganda promised, developed 'sentiment' or self-control.[33])

The history of famous women was often recommended as a source of *exempla*: Kett recommends Mary Hays' *Female Biography*, and Sarah Green advises girls to read 'the examples of chastity you will find in history, and . . . copy the bright originals'.[34] Kett and Mrs Williams in *The Advantages of Education* recommend, for instance, the history of Lady Jane Grey: but while for Kett, Grey is a role-model of conservative femininity, for Mrs Williams she provides instead an 'awful lesson' against 'carrying to too great an excess that amiable compliance of temper' which traditional ideologies preached to women (1, p. 171). History offered opportunities for complex acts of resisting reading, even for otherwise conservative commentators like West.

The fourth keyword is, of course, 'truth'. History was marketed to female readers as the 'spirit and lively description of the best novels, without their improbabilities'. To a neo-Puritan streak in eighteenth-century thought, the *truth* of history, a term usually used as if unproblematic, gave it moral as well as aesthetic priority. 'Novels . . . exhibit only fictitious characters, acting in fictitious scenes', while the lives of great 'men' give a more 'just [and] vivid picture of life and manners'. Vicesimus Knox thought historians like Plutarch essential for a 'lady's library', recommending 'true histories' over fiction. Moreover, because it offered 'the direct path of truth', history was suitable for all classes as well as both sexes, from the aristocratic Caroline Lennox who read and reread Clarendon and had a 'lifelong taste for Roman history' to the landlady of the Dolphin in 'A Sentimental Journey. By a Lady', whose favourite book is the 'HISTORY OF ENGLAND'.[35]

The Burney family were deeply indoctrinated in the superiority of historical truth: novelists Frances and Sarah Harriet Burney were enthusiastic lifelong readers of history. The young Frances believed she could not be 'pleased without an appearance of truth', and so rated *The Vicar of Wakefield* less highly than Richard and Elizabeth Griffith's allegedly autobiographical *A Series of Genuine Letters between Henry and Frances*, 'doubly pleasing . . . for being genuine'. (That Burney's youthful concept of historical truth is naive is suggested by the more cynical Anna Seward, who mocks the contrast between the 'boasted attachment' of the letters and the real relationship.[36])

Biographies and memoirs, especially by or about women, were particularly offered to female readers. There is a 'natural curiosity in the mind of man' (sic) about true lives, and the female reader needs role-models to teach 'admiration' and 'ambition', but also 'humility'.[37] In Ferrier's *The Inheritance* Lyndsay's battle with Delmour for the heart of Gertrude St Clair is enacted as a conflict over her reading. When she ceases to read with the moral Lyndsay and turns to Delmour's 'French novels', it is clear that he is losing her. To warn her of danger, Lyndsay reads to her from 'the "Life of Col. Hutchinson"', which presents a picture of 'true and faithful love' very different from the 'counterfeit' in the novels (pp. 666–7). Lucy Hutchinson's biography of her husband represents truth and domesticity as opposed to an aristocratic culture of seduction, and Gertrude will guarantee her happy ending by choosing biography and Lyndsay rather than the novel and Delmour.

Some women, conservative and radical, were aware that history was not unmediated fact but was constructed in the light of predetermined political agendas. Conservatives protested attempts to use history as a coded language for other political views: Jane West and Hannah More warn against histories with revolutionary or sceptical agendas like those of Voltaire and Gibbon, which More warns are interwoven with 'irreligion', urging that women should read only authors of 'sound Christian principles'. Radical women used the very legitimacy of history-reading to question women's political position: Charlotte Smith argues that because all educated women 'are expected to acquire some knowledge of history', it implied their right to have opinions not only on 'what *has passed*' but also to have an active voice in 'what is passing'.[38]

Since women were traditionally 'hidden from history',[39] history-reading could constitute a rebellious, even a feminist, act. Clione in the *Lady's Magazine* complains of the neglect of women's education and the low intellectual quality of books 'addressed to the ladies', which are 'only fit for pretty idiots' (perhaps she has conduct books in mind). The solution to this conspiracy to keep women in 'eternal ignorance' is 'to seize by violence, and appropriate to ourselves the knowledge designed for imperious man' (10, 1779, pp. 373–4), and this intellectual conscious-ness-raising begins with a *History of Modern Europe*.

Rebellious women readers could, then, demand the right to read history and so develop their intellectual powers: but they could equally profitably deny the authority of history. Catherine Morland in *Northanger Abbey* famously prefers novels, finding in history

nothing that does not either vex or weary me. The quarrels of popes and kings, with wars or pestilences, in every page; the men all so good for nothing, and hardly any women at all. (p. 123)

Catherine is gently mocked for preferring fiction to fact: but similar views are heard from female intellectuals. Refusing to read history might mean refusing authority to its gender- and class-specific discourse. Many women certainly drew attention to the limits of the traditional histories. Austen doubted whether history 'is ever anything much more than a convenient fiction', and Maria Edgeworth emphasised the con-structed nature of the allegedly 'true' narrative, accusing male historians of privileging style rather than substance, and of bias: Johnson's life of Savage, for instance, transforms 'an idle, ungrateful libertine' into 'a man of genius and virtue'.[40]

Catherine Talbot, though generally a keen history-reader, concurs with Morland, finding the lives of great men 'a dangerous study', since they appear to celebrate 'ambition and revenge . . . cruelty and deceit'. Hays' Emma Courtney and Anna Seward criticise history's obsession with 'errors and crimes', and its tendency to define as heroism what was really 'a species of insanity'. Elizabeth Hamilton argues that historians perpetuate false notions of morality, 'extenuate what is reprehensible . . . extol what is undeserving of sober approbation', and Edgeworth warns that 'great caution' should be used in teaching children history, since their 'simple morality' is 'puzzled and shocked' by an 'inconsistent, ambiguous system' in which the historian tries 'to appear moral and sentimental' while actually condoning 'barbarity'. Hamilton even argues that women are more competent readers of history than men, since they can respond more critically to its glamourisation of power.[41]

History, it goes without saying, was generally the history of men, and another tactic of resistance was to protest this bias – Catherine Talbot castigated Thucydides for his erasure of women, and Elizabeth Hamilton implicitly corrects 'the absence of women from the historical record' – or to read the traditional histories as a woman, like Frances Burney reading Plutarch's Lives to find evidence for domestic virtues and 'paternal affection'. In particular, women criticised the failure of traditional histories to give sufficient importance to the 'privacy of domestic life'. Joanna Baillie justified her pseudo-historical dramas from '[o]ur desire to know what men are in the closet as well as the field', a desire 'very imperfectly gratified by real history', and Hamilton traced her own use of semi-historical modes to a desire to explore 'circumstances which it suited not the dignity of history to record'. While Mary Wollstonecraft thought the 'reading of history' no better than 'the perusal of romance' if it focused on 'mere biography', Baillie and Hamilton more subversively used the limitations of history to justify the practice of 'romance . . . and novel writers' and readers.[42]

Some writers sought to rectify history's omission of women: Hays published *Female Biography* in 1803, and the lives of distinguished women regularly featured in periodicals for women and girls. Others simply rejected history, like Hume's friend to whom he loaned Plutarch's *Lives*, 'which she found very amusing till she found out that they were true'. Such readers may be presented satirically for their rejection of history or their failure to distinguish fiction from fact, like a woman who took the fiction of Lee's *The Recess* for historical truth and consequently believed Mary Queen of Scots was an 'abandoned woman',[43] but they might be making a conscious, rebellious, choice.

Eighteenth-century novels frequently labelled themselves histories or memoirs, and women like Hamilton or Sarah Fielding renegotiated their exclusion from history by writing pseudo-historical forms which allowed the incursion of feminised romance into masculine history. Lady Morgan blurred the boundaries between history and the novel: *The Princess, or the Beguine* (1834), planned as a history of Belgium, became a novel, while *The Life and Times of Salvator Rosa* (1824) began as a novel but became a biography. Joanna Baillie's elision of the distinction between historian and novelist, or the *Lady's Magazine* claim that 'Romance is very often more true than a history', criticise a masculine form and legitimise a feminine one, and this could have even more subversive effects, as writers disguised illicit fictional texts as authentic histories. As Elizabeth Hamilton's Hindu rajah is surprised to discover, 'the word *History* had more meanings in the English language, than that which is given to it in the Dictionary'.[44]

GEOGRAPHY, VOYAGES AND TRAVELS

Voyages and travels were 'immensely popular across a very wide social range', generating 'a whole publishing industry'. Reading travels, like history, labels a virtuous female character, like Kett's Emily, Fanny Price, or Hawkins' Gertrude, who reads 'voyages and travels', including John Byron's *Narrative* (1768) and George Anson's *A Voyage round the World* (1748).[45] Travel-writing was a staple of women's periodicals: the *Lady's Magazine* for 1798 begins a serialisation of Macartney's embassy to China and includes descriptions of Peru, Baalbeck and Stockholm. Hannah More and Vicesimus Knox find travel-books 'very necessary', and Sarah Green recommends that a girl spend 'one morning a week' reading geography and travels. Like history, they were widely recommended to women readers: Boswell, indeed, patronisingly places them in opposition to 'Manly' literature. They were thought to provide 'peculiar Pleasure and Improvement' because in them 'no passion is strongly excited except wonder' (apparently regarded as one of very few safe passions).[46]

Much travel-writing subscribed to a 'myth of European superiority'. Fordyce assumes it will 'inspire gratitude for the peculiar blessings of our country' and 'pity for those in ignorance and barbarity', and it teaches Kett's Emily to appreciate being 'a native of a country enlightened by divine truth' (I, p. 86). English civilisation is approvingly compared with its 'other', the uncivilised world outside, and travel-writing thus constitutes 'a hegemonic . . . tradition', a reflection and instrument of English colonialism. Moreover, its agenda was generally 'patriarchal' as well as anglocentric: '[r]epresentations of women' were 'central to the process of constructing a male national identity' in this period. The West 'feminised' and 'eroticised' the East, and travel-writing typically presented a male explorer bringing culture to a land whose uncivilised, natural qualities are imaged as feminine. The 'masculine (man, Empire,

Civilization)' was shown to have 'an unquestioned, God-given right to subdue the feminine (woman, Earth, Nature)'.[47] Still, despite this anglo-centric, androcentric agenda, the ready acceptance of travels as a key element in women's reading is surprising, since they seem to constitute a classic example of reading as escapism. It is hardly coincidental that Fanny Price and Hawkins' Gertrude are unappreciated dependents who might wish to escape the limitations of their lives. Moreover, as with histories, moralists feared hidden agendas of 'infidelity' or libertinism: John Wesley criticised Cook's travels for their acceptance of the sexual promiscuity of Tahiti. The legitimate text might allow transgressive access to the 'primitive', even the erotic, through the 'surrogacy' of reading.[48]

Travel-books by women sometimes used the conventions of the genre not to confirm but to challenge traditional assumptions about gender roles. Mary Wortley Montagu's 'Turkophilism' allowed her to criticise the position of women in English society, celebrate the greater economic freedom of European women, and paradoxically present the harem women of Turkey as more 'free' than their English counterparts. Women, the 'other within', might subversively identify with the 'other without', as readers as well as writers. Montagu's *Letters* and accounts of the sexual freedom of Tahitian women were popular: Elizabeth Montagu and Anna Seward, for instance, read both.[49]

Travel-reading and writing might thus, subversively, criticise an anglocentric, patriarchal status quo. Wollstonecraft used descriptions of the sexual freedom of Tahiti to argue that the removal of 'obstacles to . . . the simple sensations of desire' would produce not immorality but a higher morality purged of jealousy and artifice. Even conservative Elizabeth Montagu read 'Bankes's Voyage', and although she disapproved his religious scepticism she also criticised 'the prudery of the Ladies, who are afraid to own they have read the Voyages', arguing that accounts of the open sexual freedom of 'the Demoiselles of Ottaheité' were less 'dangerous' to young British women than the 'secret' liaisons of their own society.[50] Moreover, as with history, women use their reading of travels to interrogate an androcentric concept of heroism. Elizabeth Montagu felt 'surfeited' with what she thought the pointless explorations of Cook or Bruce: 'of what use is this discovery of the source of the Nile?'.[51]

Finally, reading travels might not only offer escape generally but more specific tactics of resistance. A favourite book in Fanny Price's small library is Lord Macartney's *Journal of the Embassy to China* (1807), in which a key episode is the ambassador's refusal to prostrate himself before the Emperor, thus providing 'an example of someone who successfully said, "No"', and 'prepar[ing] her for her rebellion' against Sir Thomas Bertram. Like history, the 'literature of travel was . . . a powerful enabling presence for the novel', the legitimate text camouflaging and thus facilitating the illicit.[52]

IMAGINATIVE LITERATURE: POETRY AND DRAMA

It is generally supposed, that the imagination of women is particularly active, and leads them astray. Why then do we seek by education to exercise their imagination and feeling, till the understanding, grown rigid by disuse, is unable to exercise itself?

So Mary Wollstonecraft demanded, revealing the contradictions surrounding imaginative reading for women and girls. If, as prevailing opinion believed, women were naturally softer, more sensitive and imaginative than men, poetry might have a special role in the construction of femininity, might indeed be viewed as a feminised medium, having 'some analogy with the sex' since both were 'dressed in the most striking colours'. Hester Chapone recommended poetry to young women to train the 'imagination', which 'when properly cultivated . . . becomes the source of all that is charming in society', and Kett also included poetry, the 'offspring of a fervid imagination', in an ideal female education. Women poets could legitimise their activity by arguing that, since poetry is 'a matter of feeling' rather than 'critical doctrines or theories', they as women could claim equal if not superior expertise.[53]

This praise of imagination, though, locates the danger some commentators found in poetry and drama. Even in the age of Romanticisms, female imagination could seem a site of anxiety, assimilated to insanity and sexuality, or at best an obstacle to women's achievement of full rationality. Too much imagination and poetry might be as dangerous as too little: Hannah More, though herself a writer and reader of poetry, deprecated 'a poetical education for girls', considering poetry a dangerous stimulant to female 'imagination', likely to produce vanity and 'delirium'. The same, however, does not apply to male readers. Poetry 'influence[s] the two sexes in a very disproportionate degree', for while too much poetry is dangerous for a woman, a 'man of taste' can enjoy poetry freely as the 'auxiliar of virtue'.[54]

Because of poetry's association with the ambiguous imagination, fictional women readers might be virtuous heroines or in need of an education in self-restraint. Novels of the 1750s and 1760s by women are full of idealised genteel heroines who display their sensitivity by reading (and writing) poetry: in one novel of 1763 the heroines read Pope, Swift, Dryden, Young, Milton and Shakespeare, and write poems.[55] Gothic heroines are also great readers and writers of poetry. However from the 1770s, with the development of Romanticism, which many women readers found problematic, poetry-reading is as likely to be identified with self-indulgence and undisciplined sensibility. In Burney's *Camilla*, Mrs Berlinton's reading of Akenside and Collins fosters a dangerously romantic sensibility: the ambiguity of Williams' *Julia*, who struggles against her love for her friend's husband, is symbolised by her 'particular sensibility to poetry' (I, p. 13). In Samuel Jackson Pratt's *Shenstone-Green; or, the New Paradise Lost* (1779), Matilda Beauchamp is an over-enthusiastic reader of Shenstone's poems, which leads her to persuade her father to invest his money in a utopian community, with disastrous consequences. As a novel of 1769 tells us, reading Shenstone can counteract 'the uncomfortable selfishness of the present age', but clearly for Pratt in the 1790s this idealism can go too far. An ideal education in sense and sensibility would need to combine poetry with some more factual discipline, so Roche's Madeline Clermont is given 'perfect knowledge of the historian's record, and just conception of the poet's beauty'.[56]

To some extent judgements depend on what poetry is being read. When Mrs Williams in West's *The Advantages of Education* discovers her daughter's 'romantic bias' makes her 'susceptible' to poetry, she has her read an 'Ode on the Consolations for Affliction' rather than the 'Ode to the Imagination' (II, pp. 87, 84), tying poetry to a religious rather than an aesthetic agenda. Religious and descriptive poetry were almost universally acceptable. A *Lady's Magazine* hero recommends to female friends 'Milton, Pope and Young . . . Thomson, particularly in his "Seasons", and . . . Cowper', and this pantheon recurs repeatedly in advice to female readers. Even Lady Pennington, who is sceptical about imaginative literature, allows Pope's *Essay on Man* and Thomson's *Seasons* (and later editions add Young's *Night Thoughts* and other poems).[57]

Cowper was frequently recommended in didactic works, being a favourite of Charlotte Smith's young readers and the Stanley family in *Coelebs*. Reading Milton was only unacceptable to those with ridiculously extreme views (like the Irish evangelicals satirised in Maturin's *Women*), and a taste for *Paradise Lost* became a touchstone for female taste and virtue, as with More's Lucilla Stanley, Kett's Emily, Adeline in

Radcliffe's *The Romance of the Forest*, Clementina in *Sir Charles Grandison*, Elizabeth Raby in Shelley's *Falkner*, and Edith in Ferrier's *Destiny*, who chooses it for Sunday entertainment, while the rest of the family are reading a French play. Women who are ignorant or unappreciative of it, like Miss Silvertop in *The Denial* (1790), are satirised for folly and vulgarity.[58]

Thomson's *The Seasons* is likewise used as a metonym for an acute but morally disciplined sensibility: Radcliffe and her heroines love Thomson, he is recommended in didactic works by Charlotte Smith and Laetitia-Matilda Hawkins, and he provided epigraphs for Jane West's conservative fiction. Williams' Julia finds Thomson 'the most soothing' of poets, and reads *The Seasons* 'to calm [her] mind' (II, p. 201): the fact that he is viewed as an antidote to passion may explain his popularity with educationalists. A shared taste for Thomson often figures and facilitates a virtuous relationship: in a *Lady's Magazine* tale, the hero shows his willingness to marry the heroine despite her inferiority in rank by reading aloud to her 'the book she held', which 'was Thompson's Seasons'. A rejection of Thomson reveals character-flaws from the immaturity of Burney's Camilla who will not stay to listen to a reading of his 'elegant and feeling' poem, to more profound moral faults, as shown by Lady Juliana in Ferrier's *Marriage*.[59]

Romantic poetry was more problematic, with Burns and Byron especially the objects of fascinated disapproval. It is interesting that even after 1800 the poets being recommended are still Milton and those of the early eighteenth century rather than Romantic contemporaries. Wordsworth constitutes a partial exception, and at least after 1800, when his revolutionary past had been forgotten, he assumed some of the mantle of Thomson, a love of his poems defining sensitive but virtuous characters like Ferrier's Mary Douglas or Shelley's Elizabeth Raby.[60]

Even legitimate authors, however, did not have to be read in compliantly moralistic ways. Donna Landry has argued that women readers enjoyed Pope despite his alleged misogyny because they identified their 'female powerlessness' with his 'exclusion' from power because of Catholicism and ill-health, and that this exclusion 'works against his complicity with the gender-ideology of his time', allowing a space for the resisting female reader to read against the grain.[61] Pope's insistence that he was a natural, not an educated, genius who 'Lisp'd in numbers, for the numbers came', offered a useful model for women poets, and this line is actually quoted to describe the poet-heroine Maria Villiers in Frances Brooke's *The Excursion* (1777). For women poets like Judith

Cowper and Mary Chandler, Pope provided a 'gendered and hierarchical concept of poetry' which was in complex ways both inhibiting and enabling, and in servant-poet Mary Leapor's *Crumble-Hall*, a 'Popean intertextuality' uses his style 'in the service of quite other values' both of class and gender.[62] For women novelists Pope was also a constant, ambiguous presence – he is repeatedly invoked, for instance, in *The Excursion* – and some offered resisting readings. Brooke's *The History of Emily Montague* (1769) through its lively heroine Arabella Fermor reassesses Pope's verdict on the heroine of *The Rape of the Lock* (Belinda was based on the historical Arabella Fermor): that Arabella is made to quote Pope wittily allows her both to celebrate and to challenge her creator. Edgeworth's *Belinda* appropriates the name of Pope's protagonist but also challenges Pope's verdict on her and women in general by dividing her into the virtuous heroine and the flawed but fascinating Pope-quoting Lady Delacour.[63]

Drama raised in similar but even more acute form the perils of sensibility. At one extreme, it was argued that 'plays', like 'romances, love-verses, and cards', are 'utter ruin to young women' because they are incompatible with the 'wholly domestic' scope of their lives. Another commentator thinks the 'gross indelicacy' of characters like Monimia, Desdemona and Millwood renders drama entirely unsuitable, although *The Orphan*, *Othello* and *The London Merchant* were generally considered unobjectionable for women.[64]

And yet not only play-reading but play-going was approved even by novel-hating commentators: Sarah Green, for instance, regards the theatre as 'a School of Wisdom and Morality' (a view fiercely resented by some female novelists).[65] In 'A Sentimental Journey. By a Lady', the travellers and their landlady regret the occasional 'abuse' of the drama but consider plays 'not only innocent but absolutely necessary' (*Lady's Magazine* 3, 1772, p. 198). However, the ambivalence surrounding drama is demonstrated by the fact that in novels attending plays often has frightening, disgraceful, or embarrassing consequences. Burney's *Evelina* is embarrassed by the coarseness of Congreve's *Love for Love*, in Edgeworth's *Harrington* the (apparently) Jewish heroine is distressed at a performance of *Merchant of Venice*, and in *Hortensia; or, the Distressed Wife* (1769) the heroine, at the theatre to see Rowe's *The Royal Convert*, discovers her husband with his mistress, and on another trip to the theatre he deliberately tries to facilitate her seduction by a libertine aristocrat.[66] In none of these novels is theatre-going wrong in itself, or the plays seen inherently dangerous, except insofar as a public scene is necessarily dangerous for a woman.

To some extent the same rules governed drama-reading as playgoing. Comedy was equated with dangerous 'Novels and romance' and other literary 'poison', and the 'licentious' comedy of the seventeenth century was banned, with Eugenia de Acton condemning not only Wycherley and Congreve but also Ben Jonson. It was generally assumed that modern comedy showed more 'decency and regularity' and was less objectionable, though even *The School for Scandal* was attacked by Jane West as 'dangerous', while Sarah Green criticised it for ridiculing 'sentimental virtue'.[67] Tragedy is usually allowed since it is rarely 'offensive to delicacy', but will 'soften and ennoble your hearts'. This, however, might be exactly the problem: Wollstonecraft reverses usual protocols by allowing comedy but finding tragedy dangerous because of its false sentiment, and conservative commentators agreed that tragedy's emphasis on the irresistibility of love might 'soften the heart' to a dangerous extent.[68]

Respectable elite-, middle- and even labouring-class women clearly did read plays in significant numbers. Mary Leapor's meagre library contained 'Some Volumes of Plays', and her poem 'The Temple of Love' begins by imagining her falling asleep while reading Rowe's *Jane Shore*; at the other end of the social spectrum Mary Delany frequently discusses her reading of plays. Richardson's and Fielding's virtuous heroines read and go to plays. Pamela attends a performance of Ambrose Philips' tragedy *The Distrest Mother*, and the 'reading ladies' (i, p. 180) of *Sir Charles Grandison* are knowledgeable about drama, quoting from Dryden and Lee's *Oedipus*, Steele's *The Tender Husband*, Buckingham's *The Rehearsal*, and Lee's *Theodosius*. Clarissa knows *Venice Preserv'd* and *Oedipus*, Sophia Western in *Tom Jones* reads Southerne's sentimental tragedy *The Fatal Marriage*, and Amelia Booth 'one of the excellent Farquhar's comedies'.[69]

These last examples, though, point out ambivalence surrounding the image of the play-reading woman. A lively response to drama demonstrates sensibility and even virtue. Clarissa is endowed with 'the dignity and high seriousness of tragedy' by her ability to quote Otway and Dryden, and such images may be, as Susan Staves argues, liberating in their depiction of middle-class women becoming 'consumers of texts originally produced for aristocratic men'.[70] But Clarissa and Sophia are also rendered vulnerable in specifically gendered, and sexual, ways by their exposure to drama. By leaving the domestic sphere for the public space of the theatre, a woman may take a dangerous step, but even reading plays may dangerously risk an erosion of the privacy of the private sphere. Sophia's sympathetic reading of Southerne's suffering heroine seems to generate the attempted rape by Lord Fellamar, and Clarissa's reading of *Venice Preserv'd* emphasises her sexual vulnerability by its implied comparison between her and another victim of rape, Belvidera.

Fielding's Amelia seems to offer an idealised image of compliant female reading. She is an idealised wife whose reading symbolises her dedication to the domestic world which her husband endangers by going out drinking and gambling. But the choice of Farquhar may suggest that she has unadmitted fantasies of resistance, by implying an engagement with images of assertive femininity which she will never overtly espouse. One wonders whether she is reading *The Recruiting Officer*, with its transvestite heroine who is allowed to enact her own 'Manly' nature,[71] or *The Constant Couple* or its sequel *Sir Harry Wildair*, whose rakish hero had recently been successfully played as a breeches role by Peg Woffington, or *The Beaux-Stratagem*, whose heroine Mrs Sullen gains an informal divorce from her neglectful husband. Play-reading may dignify but endanger a heroine of lively sensibilities, but may also allow her to express covert rebellion against the very image of compliant femininity which she is at that moment apparently enacting.

Among dramatists, the reading of Shakespeare was virtually universally sanctioned: in Sarah Green's list of recommended reading he comes after the Bible and Pope's Homer (p. 94). Indeed, reading Shakespeare becomes a useful shorthand term for both virtue and taste, as in Susan Keir's *Interesting Memoirs*, Elizabeth Blower's *George Bateman*, a number of Radcliffe novels, and Ferrier's *Marriage*. Women who dislike Shakespeare, like Mrs Chartres in *Julia* who is 'disappointed' by *Macbeth*, commit an unforgivable crime against taste.[72]

During this period Shakespeare became 'normatively constitutive of British national identity', a 'part of an Englishman's constitution'. The same was true of the English*woman*: Williams' Julia is proud to be a native of 'that blest isle where Shakespeare rose', and as early as the 1720s Theobald remarks how much Shakespeare was 'the Subject of the Ladies reading'. He was a vital resource for women readers, even a point of entry into the world of print culture, for 'women were increasingly involved in the popular dissemination of Shakespeare', especially, like Mary Lamb, Elizabeth Macauley, Caroline Maxwell or Henrietta Bowdler, introducing his work to children or rendering it more suitable to 'family circles' by purging what was 'vulgar, and . . . indelicate'. Shakespeare, a key literary figure who 'looked into nature, not into books', and seemed to specialise in the depiction of 'domestic ties', offered enabling models for women readers and writers.[73]

Women like Hester Thrale, Burney, Wollstonecraft and Elizabeth Montagu knew Shakespeare well and quoted him frequently as part of their claim to a share in English culture. Montagu wrote a 'nationalistic defense' of Shakespeare against Voltaire, which is cited in fiction – in Edgeworth's *Patronage* and 'Emilie de Coulanges', and in Maturin's *Women*[74] – as a blow for England, rationality and female virtue against France, autocracy and female vice. Reading Shakespeare could symbolise virtue and, like Thomson, facilitate virtuous heterosexuality. In Susan Keir's *Interesting Memoirs*, Louisa Seymour and Lord Hastings read Shakespeare, demonstrating the 'equality' (II, p. 147) that enables their succesful marriage. Shakespeare might even give women a covert language for expressing strong emotion which their society demanded was not openly articulated. Louisa inadvertently reveals her love for Hastings by her response to the passage from *Twelfth Night* where Cesario relates the death of 'his' sister from unrequited love (I, p. 165). This 'sister', who 'never told her love', offered simultaneously a model of and a way of circumventing virtuous female silence and self-denial, and many female characters allude to this passage.[75] Such intertextual strategies, however, must be very tactfully managed: otherwise the result is an anti-heroine like Euphemia Dundas in Jane Porter's *Thaddeus of Warsaw* (1803) who pursues the unfortunate hero with aggressive readings from *Romeo and Juliet* (II, p. 179).

Some women protested the cultural centrality of Shakespeare, or found it at best problematic. Implicitly defending her own novelistic practice, Eugenia de Acton argues that Shakespeare's plays show 'more indelicacy than any of the novels . . . of the present day'. Even Hannah More, who argued that Shakespeare's plays offered the female reader both 'entertainment' and 'lessons of a nobler kind', also finds elements which are 'vulgar', 'absurd', and 'indecent', so that the 'nicest selection' is necessary.[76] In an extreme case, evangelical Charlotte Tonna (born 1790) in her Victorian memoirs remembers a youthful crisis when she 'drank a cup of intoxication' under whose influence her brain 'reeled', until 'Reality became insipid', she neglected 'household affairs', and her 'mind became unnerved, [her] judgement perverted'. This dangerous reading is not an indecent novel, but *The Merchant of Venice*, which Henry Kett recommends for sound moral lessons about not 'judging from appearances'. Tonna shows a neo-Puritan attitude to fiction, a strong commitment to domestic ideology, and a virulent case of the Protestant work ethic: but she also shows an incipient if confused feminism, for one of her charges against Shakespeare is teaching her 'a thorough contempt for women'.[77] From the viewpoint of the mid nineteenth century, Shakespeare did not seem so female-friendly.

Women could use their reading of Shakespeare 'to raise a wide range of contemporary concerns', including women's education and role. It could also be used in self-fashioning, though a twentieth-century eye can discern problems in this enterprise. Mary Wollstonecraft in her public works quotes Shakespeare 'chiefly in the voices of male misogyny', and in her private correspondence identifies 'with the voices of Shakespeare's male tragic heroes – never his women': she can find no female models for her sense of alienation.[78] This identification with male models might indicate problems about accepting her femininity in a world where to be female was to be second class, but might equally represent a resisting reading of Shakespeare's androcentric worlds, especially his gendering of tragedy as masculine. Shakespeare's plays certainly offered opportunities for resisting reading. Catharine Macaulay's daughter shared her mother's republican views, and read Shakespeare for her own purposes, confessing that far from being delighted by *King John*, she 'never read the Kings'.[79]

SCIENTIFIC READING

The period marks a delicate balance in the history of science, when it had already entered 'general and polite culture' but not yet become a profession. It was thus uniquely accessible to women, who were 'cultivated as consumers of scientific knowledge'. 'Cultural' science offered opportunities to women, while 'professional' science, constructed by the implementation of Latin terminology and a rhetorical style aimed at '[p]urging the feminine from science', marginalised and excluded them. The self-imaging of scientific writing, as of travel-writing, depicted the analysis by 'a male intelligence' of 'a feminized "Nature"',[80] so that a reading position for a female intelligence was hard to find.

Scientific reading nonetheless featured in many education programmes for women, especially the Edgeworths'. Maria Edgeworth, writing just before the watershed in the professionalisation of science which Shteir places about 1830, rejoices that science was becoming more female-friendly, that 'unintelligible jargon' no longer 'supplies the place of knowledge', finding this 'much in favour of female literature'. The Edgeworths encouraged boys and girls to participate in science: Lucy like Harry reads science and does experiments (though unlike him she has to mend her clothes first). Edgeworth attacks prejudice against women in science, but she and her father still assume that girls will show a bias to the arts, boys to the sciences: Harry is 'excessively fond of mechanics and of all those scientific things', while Lucy is a more competent reader of literature, and also has to spend time 'learning other things, which it is more necessary for a girl to know'.[81]

Despite the gendering of science as masculine, the 'immense proliferation of science books' in the period included many by and for women: 'women's popular science writing' – and reading – 'was a distinctive feature of . . . culture'.[82] As in other genres, women gained legitimate access to male- controlled realms of knowledge by presenting themselves not as co-workers in original discovery but as teachers of children: some insist on their non-expert status by giving their work deliberately informal or pedagogical titles, like sketches, recreations, dialogues or conversations.[83] A number of popular science books were specifically addressed to women readers. The most famous, Fontenelle's *Entretiens sur la pluralité des mondes* (orig. 1686) had a long-term popularity, appreciated by the Countess of Hertford, Mary Wortley Montagu, Mary Delany, Frances Boscawen and Mary Shelley: in *The Invisible Spy* (1755) Eliza Haywood mocks Miss Loyter for being disappointed that a book that begins with 'a gentleman and lady . . . taking their promenade together by moonlight' was not a romance but a scientific work![84]

Science-reading became increasingly acceptable for women as the period progressed. While the first issue of the *Lady's Magazine* (1770) offers a vigorous defense of women's education but doubts the propriety of including science, by 1806 even the elegant *La Belle Assemblée* began a series of 'Familiar Lectures on Useful Sciences', including botany, perspective, and mechanics.[85] Some conduct books recommended science for women: Kett's Emily reads geography, botany, oceanography and astronomy. For intellectuals like Edgeworth and Wollstonecraft, science was important as part of women's claim to equal rationality, and the Bluestockings studied science: Elizabeth Vesey's library contained thirty volumes, with mathematics in the majority but including astronomy, physics, geometry, mechanics and natural history. However the 'constraints' of such reading are also apparent. Some commentators feared scientific reading would inculcate a materialistic, godless view of the universe. Jane West suspected a conspiracy of the 'new philosophy' to infiltrate science-writing with a 'covert intention of per-verting the mind which they pretend to inform'.[86] Advocates of science-reading for women tended to argue that its revelation of the wonders of the natural world supported rather than undermined religious faith. Kett gives science-reading specifically moral and religious functions, 'to excite our gratitude to the benevolent Giver of all things' (1, p. 103): in the *Lady's Magazine* a series beginning in 1800 introduced 'The Moral Zoologist', 'moral' in the sense that it uses science as an aid to the 'contemplation of the great Author of Nature' (31, p. 10); and a poet also sees science as an aid to religion, for 'To study nature is to study GOD' (8, 1777, p. 269).

But to many conservatives science remained problematic for women readers. One eighteenth-century doctor believed excessive reading of 'natural philosophy' could cause female madness and suicide.[87] Some assumed science was beyond women's capacity: a *Lady's Magazine* writer recommends physics but simultaneously argues that science is largely outside women's 'sphere of intelligence', and that they should cultivate 'imagination' rather than intellectuality, and avoid 'abstract studies and difficult researches'. Repressive commentators thought scientific read-ing incompatible with proper female domestication, for 'when the Mistress studies Newton', her 'Children and servants' suffer 'absolute neglect', a proposition embodied in Mrs Classic in 'The Governess'. Even Hester Chapone advises her niece to avoid 'abstruse sciences' and not exchange 'the graces of imagination' for the 'severity' of scholar-ship.[88] Imagination, despite its dangers, was at least more feminine than rigorous intellectual endeavour.

Nonetheless, some science was generally considered suitable for fe-male scrutiny. Edgeworth thought chemistry 'well suited to the talents and situation of women', because it 'can be pursued in retirement' and 'applies immediately to useful and domestic purposes': moreover (and we will recognise the rhetoric used to support the history- or travel-reading) it prevents the 'danger of inflaming the imagination', by keeping the mind 'intent upon realities'.[89] Astronomy attracted women like Mary Delany, Elizabeth Carter, Elizabeth Vesey, Hester Thrale, Hannah More, Kett's Emily, Hays' Emma Courtney and Mary Raymond, Radcliffe's Adeline and Clara La Luc, Hawkins' Gertrude and Austen's Fanny Price.[90] Astronomy might, as Kett hoped, teach the power of God, but it might have more potentially rebellious uses. For Fanny Price, shared astronomical observation is a tentative early step in her relation-ship with Edmund, even a covert way of asserting her own claims against

Mary Crawford. The heavens might even serve as a 'metaphor' for a 'realm beyond the constraints of genteel femininity',[91] as in the poems of Ann and Jane Taylor: the woman reading astronomy might not be so compliant to domestic ideology as Kett sanguinely predicted.

In the period's upsurge of science publishing, natural history sold 'the *best of any books* in England', botany in particular being both 'fashionable' and 'useful', with a proliferation of books aimed at female readers after 1760: Queen Charlotte 'loved Botany', and the 'very first book' that Frances Burney read to the queen was on this subject.[92] As Londa Schiebinger reminds us, Hegel identified women with plants because of their supposed passivity, and botany rapidly developed a reputation as a feminised, 'unmanly' discipline, which by 1830 needed '[d]efeminizing' to reappropriate it for a more rigorous and professional male intellect.[93]

Botany was vital for women in its ability to bridge 'aesthetic, utilitarian and intellectual approaches to nature'. Gardening and herbalism were 'fields in which women had long been active', and gardening is a favourite activity of conduct-text children, like the Stanleys in More's *Coelebs*, the children of Hortensia, West's Maria Williams and girls in Edgeworth's tales. Moreover, 'traditional associations' link 'gardens with women and nature and with femininity, modesty and innocence', and this could be taken as legitimising female involvement in more scientific botanical reading.[94]

'Botanical knowledge', that 'amusing and useful science', was acceptable when it confirmed 'religious principles' and conservative gender ideologies, and it legitimated some women's access to public spheres, as Mary Delany gained fame for flower pictures and Charlotte Smith for flower poems.[95] However, a 'fear of female learnedness was a leitmotif in much eighteenth-century writing about women and science', even in work by women. Smith self-defensively distinguishes the good female botanist Mrs Woodfield from the pedantic Mrs Tansy who disguises her ignorance in 'jargon', and Hortensia in Maria Jacson's *Botanical Dialogues* (1797) criticises a 'ridiculous' female botanist who brings 'disgrace' on herself by vanity and self-display. Like the girl who reads history, the girl who reads botany is often shown as ideally domestic, like Emmeline in Sarah Wilson's *A Visit to Grove Cottage* (1823) who castigates a female friend for disliking William Withering's *Botanical Arrangement* (1776), for 'botany accorded with conventional ideas about women's nature and "natural" roles'.[96]

Botany however also allowed only slightly disguised articulation of 'social theory', and its reading necessarily 'raised questions about

gender and sexuality'. It could thus be recruited as a vehicle for conservative or more radical ideologies. Shteir cites a 1780s poem which
'represented Linnean botany as a panacea for social disorder', so that
systematic botany becomes identical with 'hierarchy, and traditional
authority'.[97] Classifying plants in terms of their reproductive systems,
Linnaeus 'naturalized sex and gender ideologies of his day', offering 'a
conservative gender construction'; he might thus offer unexceptionable
reading even for the Proper Lady. But conservatives did not always
view Linnaeus so positively. From 1760, his taxonomy 'played a central
part in making botany accessible', but by foregrounding sex he ensured
that '[c]ultural tensions about women, gender, sexuality and politics'
clustered around botany, and 'disgusted parents and deterred pupils' by
intruding 'impure ideas'. Withering's popular botany bowdlerised Linnaeus for the 'ladies', and opponents criticised Linnaeus' work for
'shock[ing] female modesty'.[98] The lady in the garden might not be a
modest Flora but a transgressive Eve (to use an image of Richard
Polwhele's).[99] In Barrett's *The Heroine* a lady 'talks botany with the men'
only because she 'thinks science an excuse for indecency', and Erasmus
Darwin's 'The Loves of the Plants', which deals poetically with 'the
Linnean sexualities' was a particular site of conflict, criticised as 'indecent, and . . . profane', the 'degradation of a lovely science', but also
praised for its interplay of science and '*imagination*'.[100]

Some conservatives, especially in the 1790s, were critical of botanical
reading, like John Berkenhout who argued that botany could not be
'consistent with female delicacy' ('Thus is the fair book of knowledge to
be shut with an everlasting seal!', wrote Mary Wollstonecraft, angrily
identifying women's cultural blinding with the blindness of Milton).
Richard Polwhele goes even further by identifying botany not only with
unruly female sexuality but also with revolution. *The Unsex'd Females*,
which attacks Wollstonecraft and other radical women, expresses
amazement that anyone should think 'the study of the sexual system of
plants' compatible with 'female modesty': Polwhele is especially outraged that he has 'several times' actually seen 'boys and girls botanizing
together'. He equates botany not only with immodesty but with freethinking, republicanism, the French Revolution, the wearing of hairpie-
ces, and anything else he considers dangerously unnatural and unfeminine. In order to avoid becoming 'unsex'd', women are advised to
study 'NATURE's law', but this is clearly not the same as nature study, or
even compatible with it.[101]

TRANSLATIONS AND READING IN FOREIGN LANGUAGES

Although girls were sometimes urged to read only the originals, translations being necessarily 'very imperfect', more realistic educationalists
recommended translations. Direct access to foreign languages, especially Latin and Greek, which were still central to elite male culture and
education, was more problematic. 'The classics marked out . . . the
gentleman', and both the class and gender implications are important:
Chesterfield, indeed, defines 'the term *illiterate*' as referring to a 'man
who is ignorant of those two languages'. A woman who read the classics
might display subservience to the great male tradition, but might
equally risk criticism for vanity and pedantry. Classical learning was
only praised if concealed (as by Lucilla Stanley in More's *Coelebs in Search
of a Wife*), marked by 'innocence' and 'humility' (as by Harriot Tren-
tham in *Millenium Hall* or the heroine of a novel of 1763), or visibly
compatible with domesticity and religion (as in the case of Elizabeth
Carter): a female reader who flaunts classical learning will be satirised,
like Mrs Classic in 'The Governess'.[102]

The *Lady's Magazine* story 'The Unexpected Recovery' indicates the
anxieties surrounding female reading of Latin and Greek. Pintoria has
had 'the advantage of a classical education', and learned from it 'a
regard for virtue'. However, this may be dangerous for a woman, for it
has taught her to despise female delicacy, and allow 'liberties' from
men instead of keeping them 'at an awful distance'. Consequently she
lays herself open to the advances of the 'depraved' Adelpho (10, 1779, p.
512). By learning male virtue, Pintoria neglects the vital but entirely
different female virtue. If Latin learning was a key element in the
'system of education and socialization for boys', the classically
educated girl may be mis-socialised across gender boundaries and
become unmarriageable. Hartley Coleridge twitted his intellectual sister that for a woman '*Latin* and *celibacy* go together', and in Mary
Shelley's *Lodore* Fanny Derham, who reads 'Plato, and Cicero, and
Epictetus' is free of 'vanity and affectation', but although she is 'loved
by her own sex', her intellectuality is 'little in accord with masculine
taste', and she will never marry.[103] Although the *Lady's Magazine* encourages female education, it is ambivalent about classically educated
women. Anne Dacier is praised for learning and 'modesty', but a high
proportion of a short article is devoted to criticism of her 'whimsical
and grotesque' character, and accounts of misogynistic remarks made
against her (3, 1772, p. 9).

Mary Wortley Montagu, a keen reader with good self-acquired classical knowledge, still urges that her granddaughter 'conceal whatever learning she attains' as she would hide 'crookedness or lameness', Burney's *Camilla* figures classical reading as deformity in the character of Eugenia, and Hannah More defends Latin learning for some women but also images it as a 'personal defect'. Burney's friend 'Mr Fairly' spoke in 1789 with 'very uncommon liberality on the female powers and intellects', but even he is anxious about women's access to the 'learned languages', recalling his mother's classical reading as a site of conflict in her family, only resolved when her brother 'burnt all her books'.[104]

Given such views, it is easy to understand the young Burney's paranoia about being detected in classical learning. When in 1769 she read Thucydides, she emphasised even in her private diary that she did not read 'the original Greek . . . *I think the precaution necessary!*'; later she was affronted to be interrogated about her knowledge of Greek and Latin. Her accounts of classically educated women show anxiety and hostility, with Burney aligning herself with the men in their criticism of female learning. She relates approvingly Johnson's satirical sketch of Hortensia, who makes herself ridiculous by walking in the park repeating Virgil, and quotes his circle's disapproval of Greek scholar Sophie Streatfield.[105] In the year from which all these examples come, 1778–9, immediately after her own first publication, *Evelina*, Burney was deeply anxious about being judged as a transgressor of the bounds of proper female knowledge, and dramatises her obedience to traditional ideologies by implicitly comparing herself, to their detriment, with still more transgressive readers.

Some women protested their exclusion from a central area of elite culture and insulting stereotypes of the woman who reads the classics. Frances Sheridan's Sidney Biddulph (1761) is reading Horace in Latin when first approached by Mr Arnold, and their different attitudes to female reading predict their unhappy marriage. He would prefer her to confine herself to 'embroidery', while she refuses to 'beg his pardon for understanding Latin'.[106] As the period proceeded the centrality of the classics in male education came under fire with some progressive educationalists arguing that girls, 'fortunately for them', were advantaged by exclusion from an outmoded classical education. As the classics symbolised increasingly less effectively male authority they became less contentious for women readers. The idealised Marchioness de Vallorie in Mary Robinson's *Vancenza* (1792) has 'unaffected virtue' which is undamaged by 'classical knowledge' (I, pp. 11–12), and a *Lady's Magazine* article of 1810 mocks the view that female domestication 'depends upon . . . ignorance of Greek' (41, p. 130). Indeed, it could be argued that 'superficial knowledge' causes vanity, while 'true . . . learning' inspires 'humility': the best cure for female vanity will thus be more, not less, classical learning. Hannah More sanguinely predicts that men 'delight to associate with those . . . who have read the same books', so the ideal match for the clasically educated man is the classically educated woman (though Vicesimus Knox and Mary Shelley were less optimistic).[107]

Translations from classical or modern languages were seen as legitimate, indeed central, texts in the libraries of literate women. Hester Chapone recommends translations of Homer and Virgil, 'which every body reads that reads at all'; her account effortlessly erases the vast majority of female readers, recreational readers and virtually every reader of a class below her own. Hannah More, striving to educate labouring-class poet Ann Yearsley, immediately thinks of supplying her with translations, including 'the most decent of [Ovid's] metamorphoses'.[108]

Some knowledge of Italian was widespread among educated women from Harriet Byron to Sarah Harriet Burney: at the turn of the century it was so fashionable that one commentator thought it would soon replace French. German was less usual: Jane Austen's first biographer believed it 'no more thought of than Hindostanee as part of a lady's education' in Austen's youth, though this is clearly an exaggeration, since it was not only read by gifted linguists like Elizabeth Carter but was fashionable enough to be learned by the bourgeois Dundas sisters in *Thaddeus of Warsaw*.[109]

Central to 'the education of a gentlewoman' was 'a knowledge of the French tongue', for 'there are more agreeable books of female literature in French than in any other language', the letters of Marie de Sevigné and the educational works of Stéphanie de Genlis being especially recommended. (Even these texts, however, might be two-edged, since Sevigné as *salonnière* and Genlis as educator of the royal princes played decided 'political' roles, which undercut their espousal of domestic roles for women. Genlis's affair with Philippe-Egalité also made her an uncomfortable role-model for conservative female readers.[110]) In any case, the centrality of French in female accomplishments could be seen as questionable. Hannah More worried about exposing Protestant girls to Roman Catholic French teachers, and with the French Revolution French literature became increasingly problematic. Moreover, More is scathing about an education in French for lower-class women who barely have 'the knowledge of [their own] native tongue'.[111] That conservative women were increasingly uneasy with the centrality of French in female education is demonstrated by Elizabeth Hamilton, whose naive Brahmin Sheermaal finds the whole practice baffling, and can only assume that England plans a vast espionage movement against France staffed by francophone women (*Letters of a Hindoo Rajah* I, p. 133)!

Reading foreign languages in order to translate was also routinely subject to constraints. Elizabeth Carter's translation of Epictetus (1768) at some points 'gives only the general sense' – an 'allusion to defecation' is, for instance, dropped, as 'scarcely acceptable in our Language'. Elizabeth Helme's popular translation of Le Vaillant's *Travels from the Cape of Good-Hope into the Interior Parts of Africa* (1790) also carried on running self-censorship, making 'some alterations . . . in deference to the sex of the translator', mainly the omission of some 'physiological observations' which 'a lady could not, with propriety, follow'. This meant cutting eight pages, and an illustration, about the 'Hottentot apron' (the allegedly enlarged labiae of some African women). Helme emphasises that she has corrected the 'mere effusions of fancy and vivacity' of a 'French author' to make the text 'accord with the delicacy of a female translator' and 'the temper and genius of English readers'.[112] Both translators accept that because of their sex there are areas that are closed to them, but both turn an apparent restriction into a strength by identifying their femininity with English taste and morality as opposed to the crudity of the pagan Romans or the excessive 'vivacity' of the contemporary French.

If female reading of novels and plays was always cause for concern, their reading in French or German was thought doubly pernicious. Conservatives like More thought German drama condoned adultery and social disorder: in *Mansfield Park* Elizabeth Inchbald's adaptation of Kotzebue, *Lovers' Vows*, images and facilitates the sexual irregularities within the Mansfield circle. 'French novels' were seen as dangerously 'seductive', and that adjective is to be taken literally: in Ferrier's *Marriage* their reading prefigures adultery, and in Edgeworth's fiction a number of women – Miss Hauton in *Patronage*, Lady Augusta in 'Mademoiselle Panache', Olivia in *Leonora* – display their immorality by reading them. In Maturin's *The Wild Irish Boy* (1808), Athanasia Montolieu's reading 'of a Rousseau, of a Gothe [sic]' demonstrates her vulnerability to seduction, and she can only be a true wife when she has '*banished all [her] French books*'.[113]

Indeed, virtually the most dangerous texts in the period's *index librorum prohibitorum* were Rousseau's *Julie, ou la Nouvelle Eloise*, 'the book that all mothers prohibited and all daughters longed to read', and Goethe's *The Sorrows of Young Werther*. In real life, both were read with pleasure by respectable women, like Maria Josepha Holroyd, but they were also important in the self-fashioning of radical or unconventional women, like Charlotte Smith or Anne Lister. Both texts stood at the confluence of a number of key cultural debates particularly about the morality of sensibility and, after 1789, the cultural politics of revolution. Earlier, Rousseau was often praised and recommended: he is in Frances Burney's list of morally acceptable novelists, and in Hayley's *The Triumphs of Temper* (1781), the climax of Serena's visit to the court of Sensibility is the epiphany of Rousseau, whose 'enchanting art' helps 'lend attraction to severest truth'. However in the rhetoric of post-1789 fiction women who read Rousseau and Goethe tend to reveal serious moral weakness. Hawkins' Gertrude is right to refuse to borrow Rousseau's work, for 'every decent person' is 'shocked or disgusted . . . with the "Nouvelle Heloise"'.[114]

Reading *Werther* was accused of encouraging self-indulgent sexuality and transgression of traditional femininity as well as suicide: More stigmatised Wollstonecraft as a 'Female Werter', Anne Grant criticised Charlotte because her 'divided affection' was lacking in 'delicacy', and religious Clarissa Trant refused to read the book. In fiction, its readers will be self-indulgent, immoral, or at best immature women, deceived by a 'flowery and enthusiastic style' into 'sympathising with the extravagant . . . distresses of a madman'. It is a favourite of Olivia in *Leonora*, Lady Isabella in *Castle Rackrent*, and Adelaide in *Marriage*, and in Smith's *Emmeline* Delamere uses a volume to emotionally blackmail the heroine, but she is strong enough to resist the selfish power of male romanticism.[115]

Helen Maria Williams' *Julia*, a rewriting of *Werther*, also incorporates a lengthy discussion of it. Julia and Seymour, the husband of her friend Charlotte, fall in love, though they struggle against their passion. He reveals his feelings over a discussion of *Werther*, Julia arguing that though 'it is well written' its 'principles' are suspect, Seymour denying its 'bad tendency' and praising its realistic depiction of passion (II, pp. 202–3). Williams displays her own ambivalence in this dialogue. The novel declares its intention to 'trace the danger arising from the uncontrouled indulgence of strong affections', which render even the virtuous 'victims of sorrow' (I, p. iii); it mocks sentimental fiction by showing it read only

by foolish characters (II, p. 48); and it ends approvingly quoting Gregory's *Legacy* about the necessity of suffering in silence rather than
indulging in emotion (II, pp. 239–40): yet at the same time it reproduces
as well as critiques *Werther* in its sympathetic depiction of self-destructive
passion. Williams seems to argue simultaneously that *Werther* should and
should not be read, since it both demonstrates the sympathetic sensibility of the heroine and endangers her.

Rousseau's *Julie* produced criticism on an even more extreme scale,
for hostile critics believed it depicted an adulteress sympathetically, and
Rousseau was thought to be advocating political as well as moral
revolution: a Gillray cartoon shows Sensibility crying over a dead dove,
while she holds volumes of Rousseau and has her foot on the severed
head of Louis XVI. Moreover, the 'new kind of reading' Rousseau
encouraged, an intensely 'personal' engagement between reader and
writer, was often considered dangerous for women. It has been argued
that French women readers of Rousseau generally 'interpreted his cult of
domesticity as an empowering discourse', while still being 'ambivalent'
about Rousseau's 'complex and contradictory' treatment of women:
English treatments after 1789 seem generally more hostile, though even
women who explicitly attack Rousseau, like Wollstonecraft and
Edgeworth, may still be influenced by him and echo some of his ideas.[116]
In English fiction female reading of Rousseau is almost synonymous with
seduction: in George Walker's *The Vagabond* (1799) Fenton tries to seduce
Laura with *Julie*, a book 'likely to introduce a desire for dissipation' (II, p.
43), although she recognises its 'sophistical jargon' as the self-serving
arguments of 'a man who kept a milliner' (II, p. 42). In West's *A Tale of the
Times* (1799) Fitzosborne plans his seduction of Geraldine Monteith by
sending her 'to fetch a volume of Rousseau' (III, p. 36), knowing that in
doing so she will find a letter to her husband from his mistress: Rousseau's text is thus doubly associated with illicit sexuality.

Rousseau's novel was itself conflicted: he simultaneously offers it to
make philosophical ideas accessible to women and declares his work
unfit for them; he accompanies it with an *Entretien sur les romans* which
depicts shared reading as an important foundation for domestic life, but
in the novel depicts 'a kind of reading diametrically opposed'.[117] Some
female readers appreciated these 'paradoxes', but often express their
enthusiasm tentatively. Mary Hays acknowledges that although his
work is not 'pure', the 'graces of his style' make him impossible to read
'dispassionately', and Wollstonecraft loved his passion but was critical of
his views on women's education. In *The Wrongs of Woman*, Maria's affair

with Darnford 'takes place literally at the margin of Rousseau's text' which passes between them, but the novel's 'corrupting influence' causes the 'fairy landscapes' of vivid sensibility ultimately to become a depressing recapitulation of Maria's unhappy marriage.[118] While Wollstonecraft struggled to make sense of her ambivalence about Rousseau, conservatives advocated censorship or self-censorship: but this enterprise might be unexpectedly problematic. Hays' Emma Courtney is so fascinated by *Julie* that her anxious father confiscates it: but ironically this act of 'paternal censorship has . . . the opposite effect to that intended', for it prevents Emma reading the last volume, which depicts Julie's 'moral reform'.[119]

Similar ambivalence, but also the usefulness of Goethe and Rousseau for liberal agendas, can be seen in the novels of Sydney Owenson Morgan, where women's reading is a key issue. Her first novel, *St Clair; or, the Heiress of Desmond* (1803), was consciously written 'in imitation of *Werter*',[120] and incorporates a lengthy debate about Rousseau's *Julie*. St Clair falls in love with the brilliant Irishwoman Olivia Desmond, and in their courtship shared reading takes a crucial role: she lends him her annotated *Werther*, which persuades him of 'the congeniality of our tastes' (p. 60), and he gives her a copy of 'the "*Nouvelle Eloise*"' (p. 177). Her fiance Colonel L- attacks both Goethe and Rousseau as immoral, 'dangerous' in their celebration of 'ungovernable passions' (pp. 179, 183), while Olivia and St Clair love this 'sublimity of . . . passion', which they think 'ennobling' (p. 182), able to 'enlarge [the] ideas. . . liberalize [the] mind' and 'strengthen . . . bonds of philanthropy' (pp. 183–4). The conflict between the two men over Olivia and her reading escalates, culminating in a duel in which the colonel is wounded and St Clair killed: Olivia dies of grief. The novel is deeply ambivalent about Goethe and Rousseau. On the one hand, it addresses itself to 'Children of passion and of sentiment' (p. iv), was inspired by Goethe, and represents a passionate engagement with the texts of European Romanticism as a sign of superior intellect and sensibility: but its tragic and moralising conclusion seems to validate the Colonel's view, with its emphasis on the 'fatal delusions' (p. 244) caused by unwise reading. *St Clair* both celebrates and warns against the power of *Werther* and the *Nouvelle Eloise*.

Morgan's *The Wild Irish Girl* (1806) also depicts women's reading of a similar range of books, but what makes its analysis more coherent and compelling is its cooption of the symbolism of reading for a political agenda, that of Irish cultural nationalism. *The Wild Irish Girl* begins with a polarisation of Irish 'barbarity' and English 'civilization' (p. 1),[121] but this distinction is constantly being eroded, as Horatio learns about Ireland and its culture and as barbarism is rewritten in positive terms as the 'picturesque' (p. 2) and civilisation negatively as patriarchal autocracy. Ireland is feminised, with Dublin a feminine city, 'delicate' compared to the masculine 'strength' of London (p. 3). As a result union is optimistically predicted not only between the protagonists Glorvina and Horatio but also between England and Ireland.

To achieve this, *The Wild Irish Girl* makes repeated symbolic use of books and female reading. The narrator, Horatio M-, banished to the family estate in Ireland by his authoritarian father, finds a 'mysterious' locked room which turns out to be a study housing 'books related to the language, history and antiquities of Ireland'. These images embody the novel's anti-colonialist discourse, dramatising Ireland in the possession of foreign absentee landlords. Morgan also emphasises the symbolic connections between Ireland, books and the female body. Horatio at first suspects the locked room is a secret love-nest, and is 'tempted to become [his father's] rival' (p. 27). When Horatio meets the Irish princess Glorvina he is struck by her literacy, for although she is 'wild' she is also highly educated, though without 'pedantry' (p. 56): indeed she argues that 'we are all the beings of education' (p. 110). She is rarely seen without a book, and is identified with books, since she was born in the very room 'where my lord keeps his books' (p. 29). She reads 'the best French, English and Italian poets' (p. 153), and Irish poets including Ossian (p. 107) and Campbell (p. 65).

Horatio woos her by reading to her and giving her presents of books that will teach her to 'know . . . the latent sensibility of her soul'; these include '*La Nouvelle Heloise* de Rousseau . . . the *Paul et Virginie* of St Pierre; the *Werter* of Goethe . . . the *Atila* of Chateaubriand' (p. 140). This curriculum is diametrically opposed to that of traditionalist educationalists not only in its erotic and emotional emphasis, but also in its exclusive choice of French and German works. This unsettling of English cultural hegemony is a major element in the novel's anti-colonialist discourse. English novels, Horatio confesses, 'carry away the prize of morality' but are dull, and 'rarely seize on the imagination through the medium of the heart' (p. 140), his aim in Glorvina's sentimental education.

However, because in the narrative of female reading she had inherited the connection between reading and seduction is so firmly established, with Rousseau a key figure, Morgan cannot ignore it, and at one point she makes Horatio anxious about Glorvina's reading. He is delighted to find her reading his Rousseau, but disturbed to find in the book a letter from another man, placed 'in that page where the character of Wolmar is described'. Horatio is tormented by uncertainty about whether his role is the lover St Preux or the husband Wolmar. That Horatio 'conflates' these roles marks Morgan's 'legitimizing'[122] of passion, which becomes no longer transgressive but an instrument of healthy individuality and nationhood. Fortunately the mysterious rival is Horatio's own father, keen to expiate his oppression of his Irish tenants by marrying Glorvina, and he readily cedes her to his son: patriarchal colonialist authority is replaced by a more egalitarian relationship between the sexes and the nations, with Rousseau and Goethe the instruments of this democratisation. Morgan vindicates female reading, using it to critique English rule in Ireland and offer a utopian vision of the union through shared culture of both individuals and nations.

PHILOSOPHY AND METAPHYSICS

Apart from novels and romances, the most persistent reading ban for women and girls was on certain kinds of philosophy and metaphysics. Hannah More recommends 'Watt's or Duncan's little book of Logic', or 'some parts of Locke's Essay on the Human Understanding', though she regards even these religiously devout works as 'strong meat', only safe after a 'proper course of preparation' in the 'exercise [of] the reasoning faculties': 'French philosophy' should be entirely resisted. The sceptical philosophy of the Enlightenment and the revolutionary 'new philosophy' were regarded with deep suspicion by conservative commentators. In the 1790s in particular, the 'very word "philosophy" . . . acquires particularly volatile implications'. Because religion was itself sometimes regarded as a feminised discourse, even men who did not themselves believe in its objective truth thought it in their interests to keep women religious: friends told Boswell that Helvetius' sceptical *De L'Esprit* was 'a dangerous book for women', and that even if a man 'thought Deism the true religion', he should not 'say so to [his] wife'.[123]

The dangers of metaphysics could be allayed by sensitive treatment. Maria Edgeworth admired Elizabeth Hamilton for making the 'dangerous labyrinth' of metaphysics 'practicable' and 'pleasant', but also 'what is of far more consequence to women, safe'. But elswhere women's reading of metaphysics is rarely treated positively. Vicesimus Knox's Corinna reads 'Voltaire, Rousseau, Bolingbroke and Hume', who 'darken the understanding, and . . . corrupt the heart', and this anti-pantheon, and the topos of female corruptibility, become familiar in conservative writing. These philosophers' 'seducing doctrines' succeed in 'relaxing . . . the fibres of [the female] mind', and again the fiction demonstrates that 'seducing' is to be taken literally as well as metaphorically.[124]

In Smollett's *Roderick Random* (1748), Miss Williams, daughter of an 'eminent merchant', develops an 'aversion for . . . good books', and is encouraged by a female friend to read sceptical philosophy, 'Shaftesbury, Tindall, Hobbs'. When her family discover this she is banished to the country, where she becomes 'addicted . . . to poetry and romance'. As a result of this misreading, she is seduced, impregnated and deserted, and sinks into poverty, prostitution, disease, and 'madness'.[125] Fiction and philosophy are an explosive combination. As Mrs Fielding points out in Hamilton's *Memoirs of Modern Philosophers*, 'a flight into the regions of metaphysicks must . . . be a dangerous excursion' to 'an imagination inflamed by an incessant perusal of the improbable fictions of romance' (III, p. 164).

Such identifications were troubling to women novelists. Frances Burney was 'horror-struck' in 1780 to meet a 'young and agreeable infidel' who has learned scepticism from reading Hume and Bolingbroke. As a female novelist, though, Burney is more ambivalent than Smollett or Knox. Like them, she seeks to control women's reading: but while setting boundaries in one direction, sceptical philosophy, she also allows the opening up of reading possibilities in fiction. She emphasises that this female atheist 'never read novels', which she 'hate[s]', using the episode to legitimise fiction by demonstrating that there are worse dangers for the woman reader than novels.[126]

From the 1790s the focus of attack shifted from the sceptical philosophy of the Enlightenment to the 'new philosophy' of Paine and Godwin with its utopian agenda and revolutionary potential. Conservatives subscribed to a conspiracy theory, arguing that its advocates smuggled the new philosophy into apparently innocent genres, including history, travel, science and religious works. A whole subgenre of anti-Godwinian and anti-Wollstonecraftian fiction and polemic arose, its aims specifically didactic: Elizabeth Hamilton was pleased to receive a letter from a young woman who had recognised elements of herself in the absurd Bridgetina Botherim in *Memoirs of Modern Philosophers*, and had 'instantly abjured the follies and absurdities which created the resemblance'.[127]

Godwin inspired satirical portraits like Mr Subtile in Isaac D'Israeli's *Vaurien* (1797), Hardi Lok in Sophia King's *Waldorf: or, the Dangers of Philosophy* (1798), the great Stupeo in Walker's *The Vagabond* (1799), and

Mr Glib in *Memoirs of Modern Philosophers*. Godwin was believed to advocate social levelling and the dismantling of monogamy and the nuclear family, and in fiction such ideology inevitably leads to violence and often to madness and suicide. In *Waldorf* the new philosophy is like 'a dagger in the hand of a madman' (I, p. 94), its reading resulting in the protagonist's suicide: in *The Vagabond* the hero's corruption by radical philosophy leads to a series of crimes, apparently including seduction, duelling and matricide. More's Mr Fantom, a disciple of Paine (p. 3), is too busy with visionary schemes for universal improvement to be of practical help to individuals, and his doctrine teaches his servant to disregard private property, as a result of which he is hanged for theft.[128]

Women, depicted in traditional ideologies as intellectually weaker than men, and constructed as the guardians of the family which Godwinian ideas allegedly endangered, were thought particularly vulnerable to the new philosophy. The 'gross vices of men' promulgated by it were thought 'peculiarly disgusting' in women, who were urged by conservative commentators to avoid 'unnatural practices' (including, in one case, skating!) and accept that 'the family is the great scene of female action, and of female pleasure'.[129] Conservative attacks on the new philosophy tend to focus on the disastrous consequences of *female* reading, usually figured as specifically sexual. In Maturin's *The Wild Irish Boy* Miss Percival, a devotee of 'Godwin's Political Justice' and *The Rights of Woman* (I, pp. 210, 263), has an illegitimate child. In Charles Lucas's *The Infernal Quixote: a Tale of the Day* (1801), Lord Marauder seduces Emily Bellaire by giving her books, 'particular passages of which he often marked, and sometimes pointedly read'. These include Voltaire, Rousseau, and, most devastatingly to Emily's virtue, 'Mrs Wollstonecraft's Rights of Women' (I, p. 135).

Wollstonecraft became in some circles synonymous with the new philosophy's attack on domestic ideology, traditional femininity and female chastity. In 1799 the *Lady's Monthly Museum* published a letter allegedly from a mother about the corruption of her daughters by Wollstonecraft's work. A 'young lady' loans them 'Mrs G[odwin]'s Vindication of the Rights of Women' (sic) and other 'books on the same subject' (as in many accounts of female misreading, the donor, author and recipients of the dangerous books are all female). As a result, the girls' 'heads were . . . turned': Harriet loses 'all that softness so amiable in a woman', Martha 'applies herself to books', especially transgressive classical learning, Clara goes to anatomy lectures 'disguised in . . . boy's clothes' and takes up dissection, displaying unfeminine 'cruelty', and

Lucy unites the worst qualities of both sexes, male 'roughness' and 'feminine weakness'. Wollstonecraft is blamed for all kinds of transgressive behaviour, and reading her seems inevitably to make women 'odious and ridiculous' (3, 1799, pp. 433-5).

More often Wollstonecraft's writings and example are seen to cause not only gender but sexual transgression. After the publication of Godwin's *Memoirs and Posthumous Works* in 1798, a number of bitter critical portraits appeared in conservative fiction, like Watson's *The Vagabond* and Robert Bisset's *Modern Literature* (1804): Watson's portrait of the adulterous Mary Cloudley actually uses, and acknowledges in footnotes, Godwin's *Memoirs*. In such accounts Wollstonecraft appears as virtually a prostitute, a *'lewd woman'* 'polluted . . . by the *last crime of woman'*, while at the same time being, one would have thought contradictorily, *'unsex'd'* by her literary and political activity. Such attacks were intended to make Wollstonecraft's work unreadable by respectable women, so that even for sympathetic female readers she offered only a 'problematic legacy'.[130]

Yet it seems that the original reception of her works was generally favourable, and even after Godwin's *Memoirs* she was praised and defended, not only by other radicals. Possibly we can posit a groundswell of popular opinion more sympathetic to her than conservative rhetoric allowed. The *Lady's Magazine* serialised *Thoughts on the Education of Daughters*, published a letter praising her and wishing 'she were better understood', and in 1798 even printed extracts from the notorious posthumous works: in 1805 an article, 'Defence of Mrs W. Godwin', admitted her faults but praised her 'talents' and 'virtue', and attacked the 'prejudice' of 'inhuman and unchristian' critics.[131] Even the more conservative *La Belle Assemblée* praised her 'energetic and original' work, her 'clear and never-exaggerated ideas', and her respect for female friendship (1, 1806, p. 533). Even some conservative writers agreed with her: Elizabeth Hamilton in *Letters on the Elementary Principles of Education* rejects More's claim that undutifulness in children is caused by the spread of radical philosophy, and echoes Wollstonecraft's view that modesty should not be regarded as 'a *sexual* virtue'.[132]

The danger to women of reading radical texts is repeatedly imaged as sexual transgression leading to illness, breakdown and death. Elinor Joddrel in Burney's *The Wanderer* learns sexual assertiveness from philosophy-reading, and when she is rejected by the man she loves attempts suicide. Even a brief contact with Wollstonecraftian ideas may have an infectious power. Lady Delacour in *Belinda* is manipulated into fighting a duel, in male disguise, by the Wollstonecraftian Harriot Freke. In the course of this she suffers an injury which, she believes, causes breast cancer. Transgression of a feminine role causes her femininity to be perceived as a site of disease: when she reinvents herself as good wife and mother she discovers she is not suffering from cancer at all (pp. 216, 54–8).

Much women's writing is painfully ambivalent about Wollstonecraft. Conservatives may admire her abilities even when they think them misused; liberals and radicals are nervous about her reputation even while they admire her work. Anne Grant admires her 'boldness', 'masculine energy', 'powers of feeling, and . . . rectitude of intention', but still considers her work 'dangerous'. A long discussion of the *Vindication of the Rights of Woman* accuses Wollstonecraft of 'self-contradiction', and compares her to 'a line in an old song, "One foot on sea and one on shore, / To one thing constant never"'. The intertextuality reveals confused feelings below the decorous surface, for the quotation is actually from *Much Ado about Nothing*, and its condemnation of inconstancy is applied specifically to men in their dealings with women. Grant disagrees with Wollstonecraft's radical critique of gender roles; yet she also remembers male inconstancy at the very moment of convicting Wollstonecraft of unfeminine boldness.[133] In novels a number of disciples of Wollstonecraft meet tragic or ludicrous fates. Some, like Bridgetina Botherim in *Memoirs of Modern Philosophers* or Harriot Freke in *Belinda*, are used simply for satire, but some are more complex. In *The Wanderer*, for instance, the heroine suffers specifically because of her female vulnerability and the lack of job opportunities for women in English society; and yet the Wollstonecraftian Elinor Joddrel is condemned for her politicised critique of the status quo. Conservatives like Grant and Burney were more ambivalent about the Wollstonecraftian project than they knew.

Even more complex is Amelia Opie's *Adeline Mowbray* (1804), a novel about reading the life of Wollstonecraft and the work of Godwin. Opie, in youth a member of Godwin's circle, reappraised her career in this book, which depicts two generations of women endangered by misreading. Adeline's mother becomes obsessed by 'abstruse systems of morals and metaphysics', which she buys from 'her aunt's bookseller' (p. 2: again female control of the buying and distribution of literature has disastrous consequences).[134] Adeline acts upon her mother's theories, accepting the anti-marriage arguments of Glenmurray (Godwin), whose book she carries everywhere in her muff (p. 37). She enters a free association with him, although he urges marriage; at his early death she is left unsupported, and the result is, eventually, her death. Such a summary makes it sound a typically repressive fiction, but it is not so simple, for Opie's novel seems 'decidedly unenthusiastic about the forms [it] appear[s] to advocate'.[135] Its conservatism is undercut by its depiction of Adeline's free union as happy in every way but its economic consequences, while most of the novel's traditional marriages are deeply flawed: while the surface criticises Godwinian marriage-politics, subtextually it presents a complimentary portrait of Godwin and a wistful depiction of the possibilities of a free union. Its treatment of Wollstonecraft is similarly two-edged. Adeline offers a monitory but respectful portrait of Wollstonecraft, deserted by Imlay, left to support a child alone, her first published work devoted to 'instructing children' (p. 176). But Wollstonecraft is imaged not only as the doomed Adeline but also as the strong Quaker woman Mrs Pemberton (who has journeyed to Lisbon to tend a dying friend, like Wollstonecraft). Opie thus offers two contrasting versions of Wollstonecraft, one optimistic, one pessimistic, reading resistingly both the texts of Godwinism and of conservatism.

NOVELS

If the reading of philosophy, classical literature and botany became sexualised, this was even more exaggerated in the case of novels. Even keen readers like Anna Larpent felt anxious about novels' 'too seducing, too trivial, too dangerous' power. Anne Lister dreaded 'the stimulus, the fearful rousing, of novel reading', identified novel-reading with her lesbian sexuality, 'my former feelings', and was afraid novels encouraged 'romance', in this case a clear euphemism for sexual desire: she prescribed 'perpetual exertions' as the only effective antidote. In fiction and didactic writing a female imagination, 'inflamed with the rhapsodies of novels', is sexually vulnerable, and the 'seduction narrative' recurs compulsively in anti-novel discourses (often, paradoxically, taking the form of novels). In a periodical of 1753 a clergyman's novel-reading daughter is seduced by a dragoon who has learned novel-jargon of 'sublime honour, spotless virtue, and refined sentiment': Emily Atkins in Mackenzie's *The Man of Feeling* (1771) reads 'novels' and this 'course of reading' prepares her for seduction: in 1762 Elizabeth Montagu attributed the seduction of a society beauty to her love of 'French novels'.[136]

Most commentators were anxious about novel-reading. Defenders of elite androcentric culture, feminists arguing for the equal rationality of women, and moralists 'in opposition to consumerism' all condemned novels as 'horrid trash', 'utterly unfit' for young women because their indulgence in 'passion and pleasure' leads to corruption of 'both the head and the heart'. Conduct books, including those of Fordyce, Gregory, Gisborne, Pennington, Green, Chapone, More, West, Hamilton and de Acton, focus their treatments of female reading on forbidding or problematising novels.[137] Even Laetitia-Matilda Hawkins' *The Countess and Gertrude*, which shows the heroine's virtue growing as a direct result of reading, excludes the novel as a 'wretched taste' causing 'diseased hearts' (II, pp. 169, 186). Novels were dangerous because they wasted 'thousands of hours' in 'misapplication of time', because they were addictive and a dangerous 'habit is formed', because they caused 'discontent with the uniformity of common life', and an 'insatiable craving for novelty' which leaves the reader 'disgusted with every thing serious or solid'. In particular, novels were dangerous because they taught 'false expectations' (to use a phrase which recurs repeatedly in anti-novel discourses), and because they encouraged identification with fictional heroines which could have dangerous side-effects.[138]

Even – indeed, especially – the novels most praised for high ideals and high moral tone might be the most dangerous in teaching false expectations. Knox's Fulvia and Goldsmith's Lady Betty Tempest read novels and become 'too tender, too susceptible, too pure, too elevated, to live in this world', and another lady learns from reading *Sir Charles Grandison* such impossibly high standards no real man can live up to them and she dies an old maid. Even the best novels are dangerous because they encourage 'expectations . . . which can never be realized', for the 'romantic passion, which young people are taught from novels and romances, to believe absolutely necessary in married life . . . seldom exists'. Novels appear to offer 'comfort' but actually cause only 'disappointment'.[139] Moreover, reading novels is claimed to refine the sentiments but 'actually diminishes, instead of increasing, the sensibility of the heart', replacing 'active benevolence' with self-indulgent feeling.[140]

In popular physiology and psychology, the female intellect was viewed as, like the female body, soft and fragile, with female ego-boundaries dangerously permeable – 'Matter too soft a lasting mark to bear'. As a result, women were deemed vulnerable to excessively identificatory reading practices – 'this identifying propensity' – which might endanger their fragile sense of rational selfhood. D'Israeli quotes Mme

Roland's account of reading narrative poetry and fiction so intently that she identified fully with the characters: 'I sought for nothing around me; I was them.' This suspension of self seems to D'Israeli a specifically female reading practice, and its dangers become apparent in texts which emphasise the female reader's uncritical identification with novel heroines:[141] Euphemia Dundas in Jane Porter's *Thaddeus of Warsaw* models herself on the heroines of fiction and pursues her tutor Thaddeus until she discovers a prototype, Burney's *Camilla*, which at least keeps her 'silent' (III, p. 48), and Julia Dawkins in Brunton's *Self-control* has, like Pope's typical woman, 'no character of her own', and is always imitating the 'heroine whom the last novel inclined her to personate' (p. 64).

One surprising aspect of the discourse on novels is the relative unanimity, and ambivalence, of women of very different political views. Wollstonecraft condemned novels as signs of a 'frivolous mind' which 'make women the creatures of sensation', but she read novels for pleasure and argued that 'any kind of reading', even the 'muddy source' of 'knowledge' provided by novels was better than none. Hannah More, her political opposite, also argued that 'Reading . . . has . . . its moral uses, independent of the nature of the study itself', and that the 'less brilliant girl' needs 'the allurement of lighter books', and allowed that some novels, 'accurate histories of life and manners', could safely be read by girls.[142]

However, while anti-novel comment dominated the battle on paper, it had clearly lost the real war. Some argued that the paranoia over novel-reading was much ado about nothing: 'What harm is there in . . . novels and romances? A bad book is soon thrown aside; no-one is obliged to read it.' A correspondent to the *Lady's Monthly Museum* even argued for the 'good Effects of reading bad Novels', since 'sense may be acquired from studying nonsense', though he had to explain in a subsequent issue that he was not defending '*immoral* novels' but only '*stupid*' ones. Others urged that at worst novels offered 'entertainment', and an 'innocent' escape from the 'anxieties' of real life,[143] and at best a 'thorough knowledge of human nature', 'noble sentiments', 'a useful and impressive moral lesson', 'moral truth, and . . . virtue'. It was also argued that novel-reading kept women from worse pastimes, 'cards, scandal, and the toilet'.[144] Moreover, it might have important educational functions, and not reading novels could prove a crippling handicap. Eugenia in Burney's *Camilla* does not suspect her fortune-hunting suitor because she has read epic poems and not novels, and the classic texts of male culture have little to offer women; Calantha in Lamb's *Glenarvon* is also at a disadvantage with her wooer because 'even the more innocent fictions of romance had been withheld from her'; and Erasmus Darwin tells the story of a lady 'who was persuaded by her guardian to marry a disagreeable and selfish man', and who regretted that she had been 'prohibited from reading novels', for if she had 'I should have chosen better.'[145]

Charlotte Smith shows 'ambiguity' about novel-reading, but also defends it implicitly and explicitly. Her heroines read novels without harm, and indeed often with remarkably fortunate consequences. Smith frequently uses the conventional trope of the foolish woman misled by fiction, like Miss Cassado, Clarenthia Ludford, Miss Ashwood, Augusta Delamere and Miss Goldthorp, though these are always minor characters, never the heroine, whose reading is always more competent. A number of Smith's idealised female teachers have been novel-readers, like Mrs Talbot in *Conversations, Introducing Poetry* and Mrs Woodfield in *Rural Walks*: in youth both read 'a great number of novels', so that the former became 'extremely romantic', and the latter learned 'false views of life', but these effects were clearly not permanent, and if anything they make the women better and more understanding teachers.[146]

Smith's worst characters are not misreaders but women who do not read and try to limit the reading of daughters or female acquaintances, like Mrs Lennard, Lady Newenden, Mrs Crewkerne, Mrs Lessington and the mother of Geraldine and Fanny in *Desmond* (1792). At the heart of this 'radical' novel,[147] indeed, is an explicit 'defence of novel-reading' (II, p. 175), with Geraldine denying that 'novel reading can . . . corrupt the imagination, or enervate the heart'. Realist fiction has important educational functions, and even 'absurd' novels may 'do no good', but can 'do no harm' (II, pp. 166, 173). Far from becoming 'romantic' (II, p. 174), Geraldine is warned against rather than encouraged to imitate novel staples like 'suicide', 'conjugal infidelity', and defiance of parental authority (II, p. 146).

Despite her ambivalences, Smith opposes arguments that novels are innately corrupting. She recommends the 'admirable novels of Evelina and Cecilia', *Clarissa* and *Sir Charles Grandison*, and despite reservations (interestingly about its probability rather than its morality) also allows girls to read *Tom Jones*; but her defence of the novel goes further.[148] She has two key arguments. First, not women but conventional women's education is to blame if readers are corrupted by novels. Novels are 'almost the only reading that young women of fashion are taught to engage in', and such readers need novels to provide 'some few ideas, that are not either fallacious, or absurd': novels 'may awaken a wish for useful knowledge', or at least offer basic information to a reader who would never look at 'books of Geography or Natural History'.[149] The solution is not less reading, but more. Secondly, novels are conventionally attacked for improbability, their place 'quite out of common life', while Smith repeatedly implies that real life is stranger than the Age of Reason was prepared to admit. Rosalie Lessington, criticised by her mother for reading novels and romances, finds herself in a romance where she is not, after all, the daughter of that mother. Smith uncovers the reality of fiction and the 'Romance of Real Life',[150] blurring the boundaries between fictional and non-fictional discourses to legitimise women's reading and writing.

CONCLUSIONS

Women's reading of fiction, poetry and plays was criticised, science and the classics risked transgressive access to knowledge, history and travel-writing while generally allowed posed their own problems, and even the Bible troubled female delicacy. It might be argued that such injunctions were not gendered but were offered to all inexperienced readers: Vicesimus Knox recommends very similar books, especially history and travels, for boys and girls.[151] But it would be surprising to find a boy restricted in his reading of science, drama, poetry, the classics and the Old Testament, and there seems a particular urgency in attempts to police women's reading. Women commentators complained that the age's mechanisms of discipline and control aimed not at the typical reader but at the extremely vulnerable, uneducated and immature, at the 'ignorant, the silly, and the weak', and so deprived the vast majority of female readers of harmless and enjoyable books: the girl so 'unfortunately combustible' as to be corrupted by reading botany or the Old Testament was an invention of the conservative press.[152] Nonetheless, this imaginary girl was crucial to the rhetoric of repression throughout the period.

What worried conservative commentators was less the inherent nature of texts than their hidden agendas. Botany meant sexuality, astronomy evasion of traditional femininity, classical literature usurpation of male prerogatives, poetry a disruptive imagination, metaphysics revolution, the novel seduction. For the conservative thinker, even the most respectable reading contained hidden dangers, and to some extent this is borne out by the gleeful way in which women readers used legitimate texts for their own purposes. In my next chapter I shall examine in more detail the pleasures and perils reading offered to women.

CHAPTER 3

The pleasures and perils of reading

Many women enjoyed reading as 'pure pleasure', 'cheap', but 'an unspeakable benefit', capable of 'softening the cruellest Accidents . . . there is no Remedy so easy as Books', but pleasure itself could also be a problematic area. Anne Grant loved books, but felt guilty about literary pleasure: she enjoyed Byron's poems but worried about their morality, and was 'fully convinced of the bad tendency' of the works of Peter Pindar exactly because of 'the amusement I derive from them'. Reading might corrupt the woman reader or distract her from household concerns, but the very pleasure which was its major advantage might be equally its chief moral problem.[1]

One reason for this lies in the period's constant elision of textuality and sexuality, especially in the case of women, whose reading is repeatedly figured as a sexual act or seen to reveal their sexual nature. In Mary Hays' clandestine courtship with John Eccles, her coded signal to him that she was alone was to 'lay a book against the window'.[2] Reading could, in fiction and real life, figure and facilitate a virtuous relationship: Maria Josepha Holroyd was drawn to her soldier-husband by shared literary tastes, with 'Madame Roland's works' representing 'classical ground in our history',[3] and in Inchbald's *Nature and Art* (1796) the virtuous relationship of Rebecca and Henry is cemented by shared reading, for Henry 'never read a book from which he received improvement, that he did not carry . . . to Rebecca', in contrast with William's seduction of the 'illiterate' Hannah (I, pp. 132, 180).

Good reading facilitates virtuous heterosexuality, bad reading is metaphorically 'seducing' and can lead to actual seduction. However, it is not simply that good reading develops good sexuality, bad reading bad. A recurrent theme in Mary Robinson's *Memoirs* is how men seek power over women through books. Mr Robinson wins, with disastrous consequences, her mother's consent to marry Mary by pandering to the mother's 'fondness for books of a moral and religious character' and by giving Mary 'elegantly bound editions': later Lord Lyttelton tries to seduce her by giving her Anna Letitia Barbauld's poems which she 'read . . . with rapture'.[4] Clearly neither Hervey's *Meditations* nor Barbauld's poems are dangerous in themselves, but both can dangerously reveal women's capacity for 'rapture' and be used as dangerous instruments of male power and desire. Virtuous women are constructed by good reading, but this reading may by failing to warn them of sexual danger imperil rather than protect them. Robinson renegotiates the distinction between good and bad books, and so defends her own work, and by implication her reputation.

In this chapter I examine the pleasures and perils with which women's reading was associated. Indeed, although it has seemed convenient for discussion to separate the two, it should be emphasised that this is strategic rather than actual, for it is precisely the fact that reading is pleasurable that struck some commentators as dangerous. I shall begin with a range of genres, focusing eventually on the Gothic fiction of Ann Radcliffe and Charlotte Dacre, texts which foreground the role of readers within the text and raise important issues about how they should themselves be read. I will begin, though, with an analysis of one of the books in which the coexistence of pleasure and danger in women's reading becomes most urgent and explicit: Hannah More's *Coelebs in Search of a Wife* (1808).

PERILS AND PLEASURES: *COELEBS IN SEARCH OF A WIFE*

Hannah More is a key figure in the history of women's literacy who reveals very clearly the contradictions surrounding these issues. A passionate opponent of the French Revolution, she was also, like her Mrs Jones, a 'moral revolutionary whose mission is reading itself': committed to conservative causes, she nonetheless advocated women's education and spearheaded the movement to educate the poor and could thus be seen as 'progressive rather than . . . traditionalist':[5] stressing in her writing that woman's place was in the home she nonetheless colonised for herself a public space: condemning the dangers of novel-reading, she nonetheless cast this condemnation in the form of a novel. *Coelebs* encapsulates these contradictions in dramatising the troubling coexistence of pleasure and danger in female literacy. It can be seen as a vindication of women's reading, since its hero approves of female reading and the idealised heroine is highly literate and her reading is a definite aid to her domesticity. But More also advocates the censorship of female reading, and this ambiguous text suggests ways of containing the dangers of female pleasure, not least the pleasure of textuality itself.

Coelebs begins and ends with critical analyses of female reading practices, which frame its moral discourse. It begins with the narrator Charles's criticism of resisting readings of Milton's Eve. The 'ladies' misread when they judge the poet a 'domestic tyrant' and think his insistence on Eve's subservience to domestic ideology 'derogatory to the dignity of the sex'. Charles approves Milton's Eve as the model of the 'delicately attentive wife' (XI, p. 2), and the wife he seeks is an unfallen Eve, whom he finds in Lucilla Stanley. Their relationship is established towards the end over another discussion of Eve, whom she reads, correctly in Charles's terms, as 'the most beautiful model of the delicacy, propriety, grace and elegance of the female character': their shared reading practices demonstrate the 'full . . . sympathy' of the lovers (XII, pp. 288, 289). The novel is highly allusive with *Paradise Lost* the crucial intertext, read not as castigating woman's desire for knowledge, but as teaching the 'most indispensable . . . branch of female knowledge', domestic ideology (XI, p. 2). Lucilla's 'knowledge' can be 'detected' although not 'displayed': 'it was easy to trace her knowledge of the best authors, though she quoted none . . . This . . . is the true learning of a lady' (XII, p. 290). Eve's transgressive thirst for knowledge is corrected, and the ideal wife, literate but modest, achieves the pleasures of reading without any of the dangers.

The ideal woman in More's novel is a reader, but a reader compliant to both domestic ideology and the authority of the author. The good author is typically imaged as male (Milton, Cowper, Southey), while bad authorship tends to be represented by female models, like Lady Melbury or Charlotte Dacre. Lucilla is the 'creature of . . . books', and not only books but 'the best books' (XI, pp. 239, 181). But it is not enough to read, not even to read the best books: the manner in which they are read is equally important. There is nothing wrong with Lucilla's knowledge of Latin, for this is 'less likely to make her vain' than accomplishments that can be more readily displayed in company (XII, p. 233). However it is also thought proper and attractive that when it is discovered she 'blushed excessively' and 'slid out of the room' (XII, p. 231). The ideal woman is a modest, even a secret, reader. In many of the novel's literary discussions, women are present but respectfully observe 'the most profound silence': embodying a notorious injunction from Gregory's *Legacy*,[6] Lucilla proves that 'silence' – a quality persistently associated with her – can be 'intelligent' (XI, p. 323). Good (female) reading is concealed reading. Lucilla 'reads her Bible' (XII, p. 45), but even this must not be done assertively. When Charles finds her reading at the sickbed of a poor old woman she tries 'to conceal the Bible, by drawing her hat over it' (XII, p. 283), and when Lord Stanley catches her and Mrs Carlton reading a religious work, they 'strove to hide the book' (XII, p. 79). Even Charles, the 'Paladin of the reading ladies', is charmed by her modesty (XII, p. 151).

Women have a difficult path to negotiate: they may have 'knowledge' but must not flaunt it, though they must be responsive to literature and not display 'want of sense, of feeling, or of good breeding'. A lady must not be capable only of domestic tasks, a 'vulgar, ungentlewoman-like, illiterate housewife' (XI, p. 324; XII, p. 166), but equally she must not neglect domestic duties to read, or boast about her reading, or read books which are dangerously pleasurable, like novels and German plays. In order to demonstrate these protocols, *Coelebs* surrounds its idealised heroine the 'reading lady' (XII, p. 101) with a whole gallery of female misreaders.

It is wrong not to read, like Mrs Stanhope who is too illiterate to educate her children and whose 'aversion' to her husband's library has made him sink into 'idleness' (XI, pp. 125–6). But too much reading, or the wrong reading, is equally dangerous to domestic happiness. A young girl learns from her reading that 'love and poetry' are the 'great . . . concerns of human life': her chosen lover deserts her, and she falls victim to 'a mistaken education and an undisciplined mind' (XII, pp. 245, 248). Lady Melbury is a poet and a reader of 'fascinating' German novels, who boasts of her sensibility yet shows so little real sensitivity that her failure to pay her bills causes the ruin of the tradeswoman who supplies her with artificial flowers (XI, pp. 140–59). Lady Denham keeps a religious book ostentatiously open in her room, the opposite of Lucilla's concealed reading, but only uses it to store a list of guests she has invited to a benefit for an Italian singer (XI, pp. 118–19). Two foolish sisters embody the worst elements in women's reading with their love of sentimental or sexually explicit novels, poems and plays:

Tears of Sensibility, and Rosa Matilda, and Sympathy of Souls, and Too Civil by Half, and the Sorrows of Werter, and the Stranger, and the Orphans of Snowdon [and] Perfidy Punished, and Jemmy and Jenny Jessamy, and the Fortunate Footman, and the Illustrious Chambermaid . . . (XI, p. 34).[7]

In contrast, the women who 'bless, dignify, and truly adorn society' are not writers, ostentatious readers, or themselves textualised: 'the poet does not celebrate them; the novelist does not dedicate to them', but they 'produce much happiness at home' (XI, pp. 132, 131). Reading is acceptable as a source not of pleasure but of service. Mrs Carlton 'frequently sat up late, reading such books as might qualify her for the education of her child', and her commitment converts her erring husband, and they cement their relationship by reading together (XI, pp. 256–7). Lady Melbury also finally improves her family life by reading. Converted by reading 'a translation from a Roman classic' (perhaps Elizabeth Carter's *Epictetus*?), she marks her rebirth by rejecting 'a large cargo of new French novels and German plays' in favour of the Bible. Her relationship with her husband is revitalised: 'we read together; we became lovers and companions' (XII, pp. 399, 412, 407, 412). As in many More tales, 'literacy itself proves the key to moral conversion and economic renewal'.[8]

More in *Coelebs* does not quite neglect the pleasures of reading, and indeed criticises Lady Aston's nervousness over the very word 'pleasure' in the context of reading. Mr Stanley argues that it is best to allow young readers controlled access to 'the most unexceptionable parts' of secular authors, since any other approach will excite curiosity and the desire for pleasure (XI, pp. 220–1). Young readers need and can safely be allowed some 'pleasure' (XI, p. 221) to instil a love of books and draw them to informative and religious reading. The Stanley daughters may hear Cowper's 'John Gilpin' to inspire them to progress to the more strenuous moral reading of *The Task* (XI, pp. 396–7). Reading pleasure, though, is legitimate only as the instrument of a higher good, so novels, romances, German plays and some poems, which are vehicles only of pleasure, are banned.

However, even More's cautious defense of reading pleasure cannot avoid its potential danger. While 'lighter books' might attract the young woman and lead her to more solid reading, they might equally offer a dangerous 'stimulant' which must 'be not only continued but heightened'. Bigger and bigger fixes will become necessary, until the girl succumbs to the ultimate substance abuse, 'novels'. The young female reader needs 'encouragement' less than 'restraint', and so the very 'tediousness' of some writers of informative works is actually an advantage, since it will not tempt the young woman to pleasure but will allow her to develop the 'discipline' of self-sacrifice which is to be crucial to her role within domestic ideology (XI, pp. 380–2).

Coelebs legitimises reading for women, figures it as domestic harmony, and even permits pleasure as part of the reading experience. But there is a high price to pay. Reading must not only be confined to good books but must be concealed, compliant, and devoted to an ideology of service. Women must be sensitive to literature, but not too sensitive: they may gain knowledge and pleasure but not too much. So hard is the balancing act involved that, to paraphrase *Rasselas*, it is hard to imagine that any female can ever be a good reader. More emancipates her female audience to read without being mocked for pedantry or confined to trivial books for ladies: but this emancipation is possible only as long as the female reader accepts firmly delineated boundaries.

THE PLEASURES OF READING

Reading was most legitimate for women when it figured the pleasures of domesticity: in Elizabeth Helme's *St Margaret's Cave: or, the Nun's Story* (1801), the heroine demonstrates her virtue by her favourite pastimes of 'sewing, and reading' (III, p. 82). Women, assigned special duties of entertaining and smoothing over social difficulties, found books useful aids. When Trelawny first met Shelley, the poet was distant, Trelawny ill at ease, but Shelley's hostess Jane Williams turned a social disaster into triumph by asking Shelley about the book he was carrying and inviting him to read to them. Reading helped evade boredom and loneliness: Mary Wortley Montagu, 'a Rake in Reading', relieved her lonely old age in Italy by eagerly awaited parcels of books from her daughter, devouring novels compulsively while despising them. Women also used literature, especially novels, as 'travelling books' or light holiday or convalescent reading. Reading might function quite simply as escapism, so that Claire Clairmont, lonely and depressed, 'lay on the sofa reading endless French novels'.[9]

In a crisis reading could calm and distract the mind and relieve the pain of neglect or grief. Anne Grant's letters often recommend books she has found sustaining in bereavement to suffering friends. Reading 'soothe[s] . . . the anguish of [the] wounded mind' for many women, real and fictional. Wollstonecraft's *Maria* and the heroine of Mary Robinson's *The Natural Daughter* read to escape the horror of incarceration in an asylum, Frances Thynne Seymour finds that even 'real calamities' can be 'lulled' by reading, Janet Schaw and her cousin, sailing from Scotland to the Caribbean, try to keep calm in a terrifying storm by reading Lord Kaims ('like philosophers not Christians'), Pamela is somewhat comforted in her kidnapping by her access to her 'master's library'. Gothic heroines, however acute their suffering, rarely lack books: Smith's *Emmeline*, having 'an hour or two on her hands', immediately sends 'to enquire for a book'.[10]

After the breakdown of her marriage in 1752, Sarah Scott read voraciously and eclectically, 'the history of Florence and Lord Bacon's Essays, and the Old Plays, Christianity not founded on argument, Randolph's answer to it . . . and some of David Simple's Life . . . an account of the Government of Venice, Montaigne's Essays . . .'. In her crisis over her second marriage, Hester Thrale, feeling neglected and misunderstood by family and friends, turned to books, quoting with approval Johnson's dictum that reading was literally a matter of life and death, even able to prevent suicide: her own favoured means of escape was not 'Romances & Novels' but classical history. Most poignantly Mary Wollstonecraft, usually a fierce critic of escapist reading for women, wrote to Godwin in advanced pregnancy, 'I wish I had a novel, or some book of sheer amusement, to excite curiosity, and while away the time – Have you any thing of the kind?'.[11]

But reading is not only pleasurable because it allows escape from grief, loneliness, boredom and frustration: it might also provide an indirect, even an only half conscious, language for appeal, complaint or rebellion. The Shelley circle has left a particularly rich range of examples. In 1816, left alone in Bath by her husband, Mary Shelley records reading 'the Solitary wanderer', Charlotte Smith's *Letters of a Solitary Wanderer* (1799), a collection of interlocking tales in which a number of suffering women relate their stories. It is the single occasion her comprehensive reading-diary mentions this book, which she seems to choose at this point to express a resentful, self-pitying protest against her desertion. Reading could offer a range of self-expressive, self-defensive strategies, as practised by the governess Miss Jervis in Shelley's *Falkner*, who maintains a proper distance between herself and her employer by travelling 'in a corner of the carriage, with a book in her hand . . . never speaking' (p. 40). When in 1818 Claire Clairmont rejected Peacock's marriage proposal, she stayed in her bedroom reading while he dined with the Shelleys. Again, in accordance with his radical ideology of marriage Shelley left his best friend Hogg and his wife Harriet alone together, but Harriet, who did not share her husband's views, kept Hogg at arm's length by 'read[ing] to him relentlessly', especially solid informative works like Robertson's histories which it was impossible to 'divert into anything personal'. And self-defence could pass over into outright rebellion: Wollstonecraft writes of women's reading allowing an 'Indirect' articulation of resentment and anger.[12]

In Gothic fiction, books and reading are frequently used by heroines for self-protective purposes. In Isabella Kelly's *The Abbey of St Asaph* (1795) Elinor Douglas finds consolation for a life of poverty in 'books, music, and the pencil' (I, p. 6), and in *The Romance of the Pyrenees* Victoria conceals her distress by pretending absorption in a book (a transparently false effort, since the book turns out to be in Greek, which she does not understand).[13] However, the attempt to use books and reading to moderate or conceal strong emotions frequently backfires. Regina Maria Roche's *The Children of the Abbey* (1796) is ingenious in its repeated use of reading as a covert language for the emotions of the heroine. Amanda meets Lord Mortimer, whom she will love, in his library, so that their love seems legitimised by its origins in a controlled literary sensibility. She protects herself from revealing an apparently impossible love by repeatedly using books as camouflage, simulating reading to 'avoid the appearance of sitting in expectation of his coming' (I, pp. 95–6). As she becomes more deeply involved, however, books no longer conceal but expose her emotions: her 'feelings could no longer be repressed' and she makes a mess of reading aloud, and on two much-imitated occasions, reveals her emotion by dropping a book (II, pp. 45, 166).[14] The almost automatic association of female reading with sexuality, even as in this case a virtuous sexuality, underlines the dangers inseparable from the pleasures of reading.

As such episodes suggest, reading has a potential to offer coded messages by which women could communicate desires otherwise unspeakable. In Richard Graves' *Eugenius, or Anecdotes of the Golden Vale* (1785), Flora reads Otway's powerful sentimental tragedy *The Orphan*, and when Eugenius takes the book from her it opens 'of itself' (II, p. 51) at a passage she has marked. A good woman cannot speak her love directly, but 'Otway does it for her.'[15]

In fiction, women's reading often frames, even seems to precipitate, dramatic catastrophes, pleasurable or dangerous. The contrast between the tranquility of the reading woman and the dramatic events that explode around her is, as we shall see, narratively appealing for writers from Fielding to Burney. At its extreme, there is even a superstitious sense that reading has a magical, 'uncanny' quality, suggested by the period's fascination with the *Sortes Virgilianae*, in which a book is opened at random and read for its prophetic message for the (usually female) reader. Lady Delacour in *Belinda* uses the *sortes* on 'Marmontel's Tales' and finds a warning about her husband (pp. 162–3); tragic women, like Maturin's Armida Fitzalban or Zaira Dalmatiani, find accounts in

Virgil of the desertion and suicide of Dido which predict their own fates. Hester Thrale, though, trying it in 1783 as she agonised over whether to marry Gabriel Piozzi, found the encouraging quotation 'Oh Decus Italiae'.[16]

Reading can frame scenes of legitimate erotic relations or protect against illicit eroticism, producing almost magical escapes from danger or misunderstanding. In Roche's *The Nocturnal Visit* (1800) Jacintha, alone in the house on the night of a terrifying storm, reads Thomson's 'pathetic play of Tancred and Sigismunda' (I, p. 132), when her lover Egbert Oswald seeks shelter, and they are able to resolve misunderstandings caused by her wicked stepmother. Right reading can even protect against seduction or rape. In Elizabeth Blower's *George Bateman: a Novel* (1782), Cecilia goes to collect a book 'of chaste and refined sentiments' (II, p. 196) which she has inadvertently left in the parlour, and is thus able to overhear Lord Leftoff plotting her seduction, and escape.

The reading of Charlotte Smith's characters seems particularly capable of generating miraculous rescue from their complex and apparently insoluble problems. In *Montalbert* (1795) Rosalie is visiting the circulating library when her long-lost husband fortuitously reappears, though their reconciliation is only complete when she also becomes a writer and lets him 'read her narrative' (III, p. 256). Ethelinde seems able to generate surprising reunions and rescues through her reading. Thwarted in her desire to take from the circulating library volume two of Mackenzie's *Julia de Roubigné* (a revision of Rousseau in which a jealous husband kills an innocent wife), she borrows instead another 'simple and natural story, Fatal Obedience, or the History of Mr Freeland' (V, pp. 115–16). In this anonymous novel, the 'angelic' (*Fatal Obedience* II, p. 232) heroine obeys her father and marries an unworthy husband, and as a result dies of want after her father's death and the suicide of her husband. Both texts issue warnings against oppressive uses of power by fathers and husbands, and excessive compliance by heroines. As a result of this education in resistance, Ethelinde's reading assumes the ability to reconstruct patriarchal relations. As she reads out of doors, she is approached by a stranger, who has seen her in the library, and who turns out to be her brother's missing father-in-law, whose wealth will ensure the survival of the impoverished family. Later, believing her beloved Montgomery is dead, she retires to a cave in Grasmere, where 'a book lay before her on the oak table, and a few flowers . . .' (V, p. 259): in this Romantic setting she is discovered by

Montgomery, almost miraculously returned from the dead. In such episodes women's reading is not only legitimised but given quasi-magical power to precipitate the happy ending.

FEMALE READING AND THE PLEASURES OF COMMUNITY

The most legitimate pleasures offered women by reading were those of domesticity, family and community, and reading was 'idealised as the basis for the formation of community'.[17] Nineteenth-century women writers, like Maria Edgeworth or Hannah More, repeatedly depict wives reading with husbands, mothers with children, daughters with parents, as a means of figuring literacy as domesticity; or friends reading together might form quasi-domestic communities like the 'socially conservative' conversational circle which Betty A. Schellenberg finds a vital mode of social organisation in eighteenth-century novels.[18] However, if reading could figure and facilitate community, it could construct not only traditional domestic communities but other extended or non-traditional communities, whose significance could be subversive or even consciously revolutionary.

Women might construct female communities, actual or notional, through shared reading, communities which again might be traditional or not. The former mirror, and position themselves on the margins of, the nuclear family. In Sarah Green's *Mental Improvement for a Young Lady* (1793), the duties of the young woman repeatedly involve a community of female readers, with young Charlotte praised for picking up a book dropped by her grandmother or encouraged to help another old lady by copying out a manuscript poem (p. 21). A community of female readers may be a pair of friends reading together, like Catherine Morland and Isabella Thorpe in *Northanger Abbey*, Sapphira and Alicia in 'The Mistaken Lover', whose 'mornings were spent in reading' together, or Harriot Stapleton and Sophia Manton in 'Exalted Friendship', who are '[e]ntertained with the same books'; or it may consist of more extended groups, like the Bluestockings or the reading-community of women's magazines. Women fostered this sense of community by giving or lending each other books: Elizabeth Montagu provided her less affluent sister Sarah Scott with books, and Florina in a *Lady's Magazine* poem, who writes of 'books' as her 'greatest joy', asks a friend to lend her a book.[19]

Community could be created not only among women readers but also between female writer and female reader, a repeated motif in the

Lady's Magazine. Harmonia, who is 'particularly fond of reading the productions of her own sex', asks the magazine to resume its series on women writers. Pratilia falls asleep over the *Spectator* account of Leonora's library and dreams she visits it, updated for the 1770s, finding that Leonora has 'discarded . . . all [her] male authors', and now has a comprehensive library of women writers past and present, from the 'unrivalled lustre' of Catherine Macaulay to novelists like Charlotte Lennox and Sarah Fielding and literary foremothers like Margaret Cavendish. Revising Addison's original, the author transforms a satire on female vanity into a utopian vision of female power and pleasure centred on literary production and consumption.[20] The evidence suggests that women 'liked to read what women had written',[21] and the *Lady's Magazine* fostered this sense of community by eliding the roles of writer and reader, encouraging readers to contribute poems, letters and fiction, so that a hierarchical distinction between readers and writers is replaced by a looser and less hierarchical community of literary women and men.

While some writers figured reading as service to domestic ideology, for others it might facilitate radical revisions of traditional ideology. In Sarah Scott's *Millenium Hall* (1762) the utopian separatist community, and especially Miss Mancel and Mrs Morgan, are bound together by shared reading. Miss Mancel's guardian makes them a gift of books, but this gift exploits the ambiguity of female reading, for what seems the confirmation of family bonds is actually a coded first step towards seduction (pp. 90, 101). In a world where paternal and marital relations are invariably exploitative, the two are happiest in a world of women, where shared reading can be enjoyed free of sinister overtones. Scott was clearly anxious that her novel should not be read as a challenge to women's role within domestic ideology, and she emphasises the charitable role of women within what is in effect an extended family, and emphasises that they are neither man-haters nor opposed to marriage (pp. 163–6). Nonetheless, the shared female reading of Millenium Hall, or the Ladies of Llangollen, or the heroine and her friend in the *Lady's Magazine* story 'Matilda; or, the Female Recluse',[22] might encourage potentially revolutionary revisions of the nuclear family, and sometimes that revolutionary potential was actualised. In Wollstonecraft's *The Wrongs of Woman*, the heroine and her gaoler Jemima are 'able to establish . . . common discourse' across the class divide through Jemima's 'extensive reading'. Female friendship[23] is sustained and figured by reading, and provides a space which simulates, but in so doing allows an escape route from, the patriarchal home and its ideology of domesticity.

Some of the clearest evidence of shared reading's construction – and failure to construct – alternative communities in which women played a full and active part comes from Shelley and his circle. Shelley sought to construct around himself a series of communities, largely female, held together by shared reading tastes and practices which he fostered. Despite his advanced views on sex and gender, Shelley tended to cast himself in the role of the male mentor educating the women around him. He dedicated many poems to female friends, and sent volumes of Locke and Southey to Elizabeth Hitchener, and of Scott, Locke, and Edgeworth's *Leonora* to his first love Harriet Grove.[24] He and the unorthodox household of Mary Wollstonecraft Godwin, their children, and Claire Clairmont were engaged in a massive shared reading programme, which the two women recorded in detail.[25] Even during their elopement in Switzerland and Germany in 1814, Shelley read to her: 'the siege of Jerusalem from Tacitus' is read by Lake Lucerne, and as they sail to Mainz he 'read aloud to us Mary Wollstonecraft's Letters from Norway'.[26]

Sharing books and reading formed a key element in this community, but in Shelley's dealing with other women their resistance to his reading programmes is more marked. His engagement to his cousin Harriet Grove, for instance, probably broke down partly because of her resistance to his project to construct her as a radical reader. She enjoyed novels and plays: in 1809–10 she read with pleasure in a family group a number of popular best-sellers (which in this period means largely novels by women), including Lady Morgan's *The Novice of St Dominick*, Agnes Maria Bennett's *The Beggar Girl and her Benefactors*, Edgeworth's *Tales of Fashionable Life*, and Roche's *The Children of the Abbey*, as well as classic novels including *Joseph Andrews*, *Sir Charles Grandison*, and *A Sentimental Journey*.[27] However, she shows no obvious interest in radical politics, or poetry, and even Shelley does not succeed in changing her tastes or reconfiguring her association of reading with domestic ideology.

That he will never do so is clinched by a detail of her reading which the editor of her diary does not recognise. In December 1810, a box of books arrived and the family began to read a novel which they 'liked very much'. This book is 'Modern Philosophy': that is to say, Elizabeth Hamilton's *Memoirs of Modern Philosophers*, whose anti-heroine, 'Miss

Biddy Botherim', who made them laugh 'a good deal' (p. 596), is a devotee of radical Godwinian philosophy, a satirical portrait probably combining elements of Mary Hays and Mary Wollstonecraft. Harriet Grove's resistance to Shelley's philosophy and aesthetics, and her preference for reading in a traditional domestic community, clearly mark the lack of future for their relationship.

Shared reading failed in Shelley's first marriage to Harriet Westbrook in a more spectacular and tragic way. While they were together he encouraged her to read some key Romantic texts (Coleridge, Scott, Southey, Volney's *Les Ruines*), radical politics (*The Rights of Man* and *The Age of Reason*) and radical sexual politics (Wollstonecraft's *Vindication of the Rights of Woman*, and James Lawrence's anti-marriage utopia, *The Empire of the Nairs*).[28] But the failure of shared reading to constitute Harriet as a revolutionary, especially in marriage, soon becomes apparent. She, in any case, had views of her own, and tried to equalise the process of indoctrination. At a crucial stage in their relationship, when she wanted marriage, he a free association, he sent her a copy of Lady Morgan's *The Missionary*. This novel must have appealed to him not only because it seems to question the superiority of Christianity, but also for the exotic Indian heroine, Luxima, who gains the love of the ascetic Hilarion, and teaches him 'that there were, in this world, sources of blameless pleasure, which it were, perhaps, more culpable to neglect than to embrace'. Shelley obviously uses this as a way of persuading Harriet to accept a union without marriage. She, however, also sent him a novel, Amelia Opie's *Adeline Mowbray*,[29] which argues the impracticability of Godwinian marriage-politics within society as it is currently constituted, and, perhaps, rebukes Shelley for his failure to realise the economic and social consequences for women of a relationship without marriage.

When their marriage failed and Shelley fled to the continent with Mary Godwin, the books he had shared with Harriet became a practical problem whose custody needed to be discussed. Interestingly, Shelley wanted to be sent his copy of the posthumous works of Mary Wollstonecraft, while Harriet 'wished to retain' this.[30] It is hard to know whether this is an act of revenge, a determination not to be excluded from a triangle comprising Shelley, Wollstonecraft and Wollstonecraft's daughter, or a desire to preserve some vestige of the marriage by retaining a book which was central to the shared reading on which it was founded. In the case of P. B. and Harriet Shelley, reading utterly failed, at least from the woman's point of view, to constitute a revolutionary community in direct opposition to domestic ideology and patriarchal marriage.

THE PLEASURES OF READING: ANN RADCLIFFE AND FEMALE GOTHIC

Gothic fiction 'played a significant part in late eighteenth-century debates over the moral dangers of reading', and Radcliffe and her followers gave women's reading crucial roles, so that Gothic acquired 'a special potential to deal with the issues of . . . reading as a woman'.[31] In Gothic fiction, reading both aids in characterisation and addresses the genre's central concern with the relation of power and gender. Gothic heroines suffer protracted and appalling trials, but rarely to an extent that leaves them without books, which are always available from local circulating libraries, can be borrowed from the daughter of the landlord of the inn at which they are staying, or are to be found in the mouldering and disused libraries which occur so often in the symbolism of female Gothic.

Radcliffe's novels had a wide popularity, appealing to inexperienced and experienced readers alike. She offered passionate involvement to young women like Catherine Morland and Susan Sibbald (who at the end of an all-night reading of *The Mysteries of Udolpho* was terrified by a mysterious sound, which turned out to be only a servant putting out beer-barrels!).[32] A more sophisticated reader like Hester Thrale might be smugly superior to Gothic, contemptuous of Radcliffe and detesting *Frankenstein*, allying herself with an elite male culture: but other intellectuals like Elizabeth Carter, Maria Edgeworth, Mary Wollstonecraft, Anna Seward and Frances Burney, enjoyed Radcliffe or found in her novels a useful language, not always parodic, for describing their own circumstances.[33] Radcliffe was, moreover, unusual in being a writer of exciting imaginative fiction who was generally judged morally safe for female readers: the *Lady's Magazine* even uses a passage from *The Romance of the Forest* in an article on the education of girls. It is hard to overestimate Radcliffe's influence at the turn of the century, not only on compliant readers like Regina Maria Roche and Isabella Kelly who imitate her closely, but also on resisting readers like Austen, Charlotte Dacre and Wollstonecraft who show strong signs of her influence but also subvert her themes and techniques.[34]

Radcliffe's popularity is partly attributable to her engagement with women's reading and her tactics of providing her female readers with legitimising reflections of their own activity. David H. Richter argues that Gothic is situated at the junction of a 'major shift in response of readers to literature, a shift (in Jauss's terms) from *catharsis* to *aisthesis*', from reading 'for the sake of entry into a verisimilar world' toward 'reading as an escape from the world one inhabits'.[35] Late eighteenth-century ideologies of fiction-reading tend to privilege 'cathartic' over 'aisthetic' texts, for the former might, it was argued, offer useful information and instruction, while aisthetic reading was likely to be dangerously individualistic and hedonistic. It is exactly this 'aisthetic' model of female readership that Radcliffe foregrounds and legitimises.

As an early nineteenth-century reviewer claimed, Radcliffe's 'readers are the virtual heroes and heroines of her story as they read'. Because her heroines love reading, the roles of reader and heroine are elided, creating an 'intimate and insidious relationship' between text and reader. Radcliffe 'brings us into her text', offering us both 'interpretive omniscience' and a 'responsible' commitment to 'narrative law and order',[36] so suggesting that we might share the pleasures of both aisthetic escape and cathartic education. If her narratives ultimately contain and retreat from subversive impulses, subversive possibilities nonetheless remain implicit in their very reading protocols.

Radcliffe's treatment of female reading is remarkably positive. Fondness for reading is a key feature of her characteristic heroine – inexperienced but cultured, capable of intense feeling but also self-restraint, quiveringly sensitive to the beauties of nature and literature but not misled by this into unwise behaviour. Indeed, Radcliffe tends to use reading as a metonym for female virtue, with books instruments of consolation, self-knowledge, and even salvation for her embattled heroines. Radcliffe seems to agree with one of her good fathers, that 'virtue and taste are nearly the same, for virtue is little more than active taste': books, which figure taste, must also figure virtue, and her villains and bad parents tend not to read at all. Such a view effectively 'traps the reader' into collusion with the author, compelled to accept her implicit identification of the novel itself with virtue.[37]

Radcliffe's heroines read histories or other legitimate genres, but are especially fond of poetry: Julia Mazzini in *A Sicilian Romance* (1790) enjoys 'the poetry of Tasso' (I, p. 15), Adeline in *The Romance of the Forest* (1791) reads 'the best English poets', especially Shakespeare and Milton (pp. 82, 261), Emily St Aubert in *The Mysteries of Udolpho* (1794) has learned Latin and English in order to appreciate 'the sublimity of their best poets' (p. 6), and Ellena in *The Italian* also enjoys the 'best . . . poets' (p.

94). The novels frequently quote Shakespeare, Milton, Thomson, Gray, Collins and other poets.[38] As Radcliffe creates a dense intertextuality that legitimises her own access to literacy, her heroines by their reading also claim a place for themselves and their readers within literary culture.

For Radcliffe's heroines, reading is not only assimilated to virtue, it is also assimilated to nature, so naturalising woman's claim to a place in cultural production and consumption. In *A Sicilian Romance*, Julia's book-closet 'looked upon the sea . . . and afforded a prospect of the neighbouring woods' (I, pp. 10–11). In *The Mysteries of Udolpho* descriptions of the idyllic home of La Vallée repeatedly underscore the connections of reading with the natural world: the library 'opened upon a grove' and adjoins a greenhouse, which connects with a room where Emily keeps both her books and 'some favourite birds and plants' (pp. 2–3). In good homes, the distinction between indoors and outdoors dissolves, so it no longer makes sense to insist that a woman's place is in the home. Emily's father is a feminised man, devoted to 'scenes of simple nature, to the pure delights of literature, and to the exercise of domestic virtue' (p. 1). This significant tripartitite identification defines La Vallée as a feminine (indeed, as its name suggests, symbolically yonic) space and contrasts it with the sinister Udolpho ruled by the terrifyingly masculine Montoni (whose name suggests the phallic mountain as opposed to the feminine valley).[39] Radcliffe characters, especially heroines, often read out of doors to enjoy the pleasures of literature and nature simultaneously.[40] Even while La Motte and his family are hiding out in a ruined abbey in *The Romance of the Forest*, Adeline 'would often ramble into the forest' to read (p. 34), and later, under the protection of La Luc, she wanders 'among the sublime scenery . . . with no other companion than a book' (p. 260). Reading is routinely identified with the natural as opposed to the artificial: while Madame Cheron retires to put on her makeup, Emily 'charm[s] her mind by reading' (*Udolpho*, p. 121).

Sometimes Radcliffe presents shared reading as a key element in virtuous heterosexual relations. We know Valancourt will, despite his flaws, prove a fit partner for Emily, for he owns 'volumes of Homer, Horace and Petrarch' (p. 35), and his courtship focuses on reading: he exchanges her book for his annotated Petrarch (p. 58), and during her absence visits La Vallée and reads her books (pp. 593–4). While in *The Mysteries of Udolpho* the sexes can meet on equal terms in reading, in *The Romance of the Forest* it is more or less female-specific. La Motte owns the books Adeline reads but does not seem to read them, and the Marquis tries to seduce her in a decadent love-nest decorated with 'scenes from Ovid . . . the Armida of Tasso . . . Busts of Horace, Ovid, Anacreon, Tibullus and Petronius' (p. 156), but is not seen reading these poets, who appear only as distorted representations within a corrupt scopic economy, like Adeline reduced to objects of the male gaze.

The pleasures of reading in Radcliffe are, most simply, the pleasures of escape. Emily St Aubert tries to 'charm her mind by reading' (p. 121) and temporarily escape her troubles, and Adeline gains from books 'information and amusement', but also escape, 'oblivion of sorrow' (p. 35). A book is a soothing 'opiate', a 'Lethean medicine' which offers 'forgetfulness' (p. 35, 208), and reading, especially poetry, allows the mind to 'abstract itself from its own cares' (p. 114). Attempts to escape are sometimes successful, sometimes not, for in extreme cases even reading is insufficient.[41] The good female reader must not seek to escape from the real world altogether, but for temporary relief the pleasures of escapist reading are gladly accepted. God, the 'Great Author' (p. 284), even offers a legitimising prototype for the novelist's creation of worlds.

In the only episode in *The Italian* where female reading is significant, Ellena, imprisoned in a convent, is brought books by Sister Olivia, and is pleased to find 'the best Italian poets, and a volume or two of Guicciardini's history'. With the aid of 'a volume of Tasso, [she] endeavoured to banish every painful remembrance from her mind' (pp. 94–5). Reading brings escape from grief, fear and loneliness, and Ellena is not condemned for this. Through this image of the lonely, escapist reader Radcliffe legitimises the very reading practices in which it is likely her readers are themselves involved. Frances Burney, a reluctant admirer of Radcliffe, acknowledges her special appropriateness for 'lonely hours and depressed spirits', and Wollstonecraft agrees, urging her sister Everina to read *The Italian* only in her 'own chamber, not to lose the picturesque images with which it abounds'.[12] Despite Catherine Morland's reading of Radcliffe partly for the pleasures of community, Radcliffe was thought by other, especially older, women readers to offer preeminently the pleasures of escape to the lonely reader.

For Radcliffe, women's reading also offers the pleasures of self-legitimation. Books and reading offer a link, often the only remaining link, with the family from which the heroine is separated,[43] and figure the bond between the parent, usually the father, and the female child, a link broken, often by violence, and which must be reformed for the full and safe maturing of the daughter. Revisiting La Vallée after her father's death, Emily is upset by the sight of 'the books, that he had selected for her use, and which they had read together . . . a reading-desk, on which lay a book open, as it had been left by her father' (pp. 94–5). The books make concrete her links with a benevolent paternal culture, lost but to be recovered through her marriage with the literate Valancourt.

In *The Romance of the Forest* reading constitutes a link to a lost paternal culture in a more terrifying way. Hiding in the Abbey from the Marquis de Montalt, a sinister father-figure (and, it is feared for part of the novel, actual father), Adeline finds a manuscript, fragmentary, bloodstained and almost illegible, which is, it transpires, a chilling record of the last days of her own father. Reading in Radcliffe is revelatory, necessary not only for the temporary pleasures of escape, but also for the more permanent pleasures of identity and self-knowledge. Only by reading this link with her lost father can Adeline at last learn who she is and face the future free from the shadows of incest and murder that haunt her relations with false fathers, La Motte and the Marquis.

Reading usually figures a link between father and daughter: in *The Romance of the Forest* the reading of the manuscript forms a crucial pivot between the sinister images of masculinity and paternity of the early part of the novel and the reinvention of both in the purified, feminised family she establishes with Theodore and his sensitive, literate father La Luc. *The Italian* varies this pattern by presenting reading as a crucial link with the maternal, for it is a lost mother who must be rediscovered before the heroine can read herself as wife and mother. Sister Olivia is, it transpires, actually Ellena's mother, the transmission of books between them an important symbol of genetic and social continuity. Radcliffe writes *The Italian* as 'corrective' to Lewis's *The Monk*, and one thing she revises is Elvira's censorship of her daughter's reading.[44] Whereas the mother in *The Monk* withholds reading and so keeps her daughter ignorant and vulnerable, Radcliffe makes the transmission of texts between mother and daughter symbolise the crucial, and redeeming, links between them.

For Radcliffe, then, reading offers the pleasures of entertainment and information, of nature, of escape, and of identity and self-legitimation. And yet there is one curious exception to this which may indicate Radcliffe's reluctant participation in her age's ambivalence about of women's reading. As St Aubert is dying, he charges Emily to destroy unread 'a packet of written papers' (*Udolpho*, p. 78): she attempts to obey but 'involuntarily' reads 'a sentence of dreadful import' (p. 103). This

episode is oddly handled, for although the reader is periodically reminded of it (e.g. pp. 491, 497), we do not discover the secret of the
paternal text until much later, and we never learn exactly what that
dreadful sentence is: our role is thus that of an unfallen Emily, preserving the injunction that she accidentally transgresses. The secret, it will
be recalled, is that Emily's aunt was murdered by her husband's jealous
mistress, and St Aubert wishes to keep this from Emily to save her from
distress. Like Eve, or Bluebeard's wife, Emily transgresses a patriarchal
imperative and suffers for it. It is unclear, however, whether she was
wrong to read the forbidden text. In an exact analogy, she is terrified to
discover a sinister figure beneath the veil, supposedly a murdered female
corpse. And yet if she had examined this figure more closely, 'her
delusion and her fears would have vanished together', since she would
have discovered the figure was 'not human, but formed of wax' (p. 662).
By implication, it could be argued that her distress over the dreadful
sentence is caused not by transgressive but by incomplete reading of the
paternal text. St Aubert's protective injunction paradoxically causes
rather than saves her from pain and fear: censorship of female reading is
at best futile, at worst damaging.

THE PERILS OF READING

Reading, then, offered pleasures ranging from escapism to the discovery
of one's true identity, from domesticity to revolutionary alternatives.
However, each reading pleasure is haunted by a dark double. If reading
promised renewed community or family ties, it could also threaten their
erosion: in particular, reading shared by a mother and daughter is a
repeated site of anxiety, a means of articulating the age's 'matrophobia';[45] if reading could figure the pleasures of virtuous sexuality, it
could also threaten the dangers of corrupt sexuality; and if scenes of
reading can generate happy endings, they can also generate dangers,
especially sexual dangers, for the female reader. I end this chapter with
an examination of a Gothic novelist who, unlike Ann Radcliffe, persistently associates female reading with the collapse of domestic ties, sexual
danger and social dysfunction, Charlotte Dacre.

Sixteenth- and seventeenth-century accounts of women's reading
often identify literacy with serious dangers to the female self, especially
insanity and unchastity, and despite the reconfiguring of reading to fit
positively into the new domestic ideology these elements continue to be
heard. In 1819 Ellen Empson asked Anne Lister 'not to study so much',

fearing that she is 'going mad' from excessive reading, and in clinical writings on female insanity it is sometimes emphasised that the sick woman has 'very superior literary acquirements', in one case 'spouting parts of Shakespeare' in a fit of mania.[46]

Women's anxieties about their reading are revealed by economies with the truth. Claire Clairmont read for pleasure and escape, but even so unconventional a woman felt anxiety about reading pleasure, and in her respectable old age censored her diary to obliterate any record of having read such objectionable texts as the memoirs of courtesan Ninon de l'Enclos and the works of Boccaccio. Censorship and self-censorship could take even more active forms. Mr Rishton read *The Faerie Queene* to Frances Burney and her sisters, 'in which he is extremely delicate, omitting whatever, to the poet's great disgrace, has crept in that is improper for a woman's ear', and Burney applauds this bowdlerisation, accepting as natural that the rules of propriety are different for men and women.[47] Here women's reading is controlled by male assumptions; but acts of censorship can be assertive and even subversive when practised by the female reader herself. Felicia Hemans, as we have seen, practised literal self-censorship, and Sarah Harriet Burney read Ariosto with 'delight', but 'Here and there, he is a bad boy, and as the book is my own, & I do not like indecency, I cut out whole pages that annoy me, & burn them before the Author's face.'[48] Sarah Burney sees her subject position as reader as essentially active, not passive, figuring herself as the mother entitled to castigate the naughty child, and as the executioner inflicting the horrific punishment for high treason, so that Ariosto is figuratively castrated for treason to the sensibility of the female reader. The resisting female reader literally reconfigures the male text.

If reading can figure and facilitate shared community, the female reader might worry that she was unworthy or unable to join that community. Was Catherine Morland afraid she might not be terrified enough by Radcliffe's novels? Lady Louisa Stuart as a girl of fourteen certainly 'had a secret dread [she] should not cry enough' in reading Mackenzie's cult book *The Man of Feeling* 'to gain the credit of proper sensibility'.[49] Even after having achieved literacy, gained access to books and the time and space to read them, even after having chosen the right book, there were still anxieties that one might not be able to read it in the way prescribed by one's community.

While the perils of reading were largely conceived as moral or cultural, some were entirely practical. Before electricity, when night-time reading had to be done by candlelight, it posed actual as well as symbolic risks. In 1804 Lady Glanville, who 'had been reading' late at night, died as a result of her clothes catching fire, and in 1814 Hannah More, 'reaching across the fire-place to a book-shelf', was seriously burned. Some novels, including *Clarissa*, imitate *Gulliver's Travels*, where the fire in the queen's palace in Liliput is caused by 'the carelessness of a maid of honour, who fell asleep while reading a romance'. Female reading, especially of fiction, especially by young or lower-class women, becomes a sign of an 'inflammable mind'.[50]

Reading might cause anxiety because it led to madness, or allowed dangerous pleasure, assertion, or protest, or figured a community for which one might be unworthy, or because it was associated with actual or figurative conflagration. The very intensity with which women desired to read might itself be dangerously self-assertive. Many of Charles and Mary Lamb's stories in *Mrs Leicester's School* foreground female reading. They were 'both great readers', and Charles describes Mary, 'tumbled . . . into a spacious closet of . . . reading', trying to educate herself without guidance. He is fascinated by books and occasionally even skirts the issue of gendered reading, presenting himself as uninterested in 'narrative' and preferring history or belles lettres, while Bridget Elia (i.e. Mary) is a stereotypical female novel-reader who 'must have a story'.[51] Reading is of profound importance to a number of girls at Mrs Leicester's School, sustaining them in loneliness and forging family or community links; and yet it is also a risky, even a transgressive, act, equally capable of eroding those links, as Maria Howe in Charles's 'The Witch Aunt' endangers her only loving relationship by unwise reading which leads her to suspect her aunt of being a witch.

In the most extreme case, Margaret Green in Mary's 'The Young Mahometan' has weak eyes and therefore her mother bans reading as 'a forbidden pleasure' (p. 306).[52] However Margaret desires books with such intensity that, like Bluebeard's wife, she enters a locked and forbidden room associated with desire, which, in this instance, is symbolised by books (p. 307). Here she finds and reads books about Islam which in the Lambs' Eurocentric view are self-evidently 'very wrong' for her (p. 308). This transgressive reading precipitates a psychological crisis followed by physical 'fever' (p. 310), and Margaret is only 'cured' (p. 311) when a male doctor enters the female community, replacing the false authority of the mother and bad books with true patriarchal authority. His cure works by reinscribing Margaret in a proper female subject position by introducing her to legitimate female activities like society and needlework, apparently safe despite her weak eyes (p. 310). Reading appears a solitary, transgressive, even masturbatory act whose impulses need to be redirected into a male-dominated, outward-looking sociality (and, by implication, sexuality). Mary's tale offers highly repressive images of female reading, and it is especially surprising to find her recommending needlework as a facilitator of correct female socialisation when she is elsewhere[53] so critical of it as a pastime for non-professional needlewomen. Her ambivalences about her own roles as female writer and reader are painfully strong.

Unless she reads aloud to entertain an audience, a reading woman clears a space for her own pleasure and potentially neglects her primary duties of caring for others.[54] As a result of its potential to figure transgressive female desire, reading, even of legitimate books, often seems to generate danger. In Edgeworth's *Belinda* the heroine is 'alone, and reading' (p. 212) when she is harassed by her dark double, the Wollstonecraftian Harriet Freke. Belinda's reading is improving and compliant to traditional gender ideologies ('Smith's Theory of Moral Sentiments . . . Moore's Travels . . . Essay on the Inconsistency of Human Wishes', pp. 214–15), but still seems to summon up Freke and her transgressive reading practices, while also giving Belinda the strength to resist the sinister feminism Freke embodies.

Magazine fiction often focuses on reading's power to generate danger. In 'The Fortunate Sequel; or, the Adventures of Ella Worthy', Lady Bab Hardwick, at night in an unfamiliar house, goes 'towards the study in pursuit of a book', but is terrified by the appearance of an old gypsy woman with a knife. This is, however, only one of the house's strange, realistic, statues. Lady Bab's desire to read has, it seems, disordered her sense of the relation between representation and reality. The reading of Gothic fiction, with its privileging of aisthetic reading practices and its encouragement of identification between reader and heroine, might be especially disruptive of a sure sense of the nature of reality and thus endanger the female reader. In 'The Old Woman', Albinia's 'reading a romance, which appeared powerfully to agitate her mind' apparently generates spectral manifestations which trigger a breakdown. (In fact the apparently supernatural events are a trick by a female servant with a grudge.) Only the intervention of (again) the wise male authority of doctor and clergyman rescues her from a female world unable to distinguish reality from representation and cures her 'of her taste for romances'.[55]

An extreme case of the power of reading to generate danger is provided by Charlotte Lennox's last novel. Like all Lennox's novels,

Euphemia (1790) is much concerned with women's reading, which it depicts as having 'positive moral effects', implying that 'reading the right books in moderation is a sign of female virtue'.[56] Nonetheless, it is at the same time associated with family disunity, which adds disquieting ambivalence to an apparently positive account. Maria Harley shows virtuous domesticity by reading to her sick uncle, but this only inspires her step-aunt to practise jealous 'artifices' against her (I, p. 10), and another keen reader, Clara Bellenden, all 'life, soul and sensibility' (I, p. 175), finds her literacy alienates her from her mother and sister, who 'hates reading' (II, p. 201). Reading is least problematic when it figures benevolent English colonialism and civilisation: at a service in a Mohawk chapel 'many of the Indians had their books in their hands', and an English widow in America who educates children and is loved by 'her negroes' is 'never without a book in her hand' (III, pp. 190, 185).

In other contexts female reading tends to have a more equivocal and sinister relation to rationality and civilisation. In the most dramatic example, Euphemia with Clara and other female friends make 'an excursion into the woods' of Albany (III, p. 106), equipped with a picnic, their sewing, and something to read: 'Miss Bellenden produced her netting, Louise her flower-piece, Mrs Benson and I our plain-work, and Clara her book' (III, p. 107), which she reads aloud. This book is Burney's *Cecilia*, a 'very sensible novel' by a 'generally admired' writer. Even the celebrated sense and virtue of Burney's fiction cannot, however, protect Euphemia from a Johnsonian anxiety about 'imagination' and its 'tyrannical power' to 'usurp' over 'reason', which even so worthy a work as *Cecilia* may liberate (III, pp. 107–8). As a result, this reading generates a terrifying incident, an Indian attack. Fortunately little harm is done: three drunken Indians break the china but are pacified by a male friend and given presents by the women. The Indians embody terrifying forces of irrationality and imagination unleashed by reading even the most moral and 'elegant' (III, p. 107) work of fiction, forces which seem both external and internal to feminised culture and the female self.

As we have discovered, the most persistent dangers of female reading are figured as sexual, and possibly the Indians should be read not only as forces of barbarism but specifically as sexual threat. Certainly the breaking of china in eighteenth-century literature may figure the loss of virginity, and Indians function as part of a discourse of sexuality in Burney's *The Woman-Hater*, where Captain Ludlow's adulterous desire for Eleonora Wilmot is symbolically punished by his capture by Indians (III.viii.55–60), in Mary Brunton's *Self-control* (1811), where the heroine, abducted at the instigation of Colonel Hargrave, is led to him through the 'pathless wild' by Indians (p. 413), and in Lennox's earlier *Life of Harriot Stuart*, where the heroine is kidnapped by Indians hired by a presumptuous lover, who actually appears in Indian disguise (I, p. 87).

If *Euphemia* offers a coded language for the (sexual) dangers inseparable from female reading, other novels depict these dangers quite directly and literally, and indeed an association with seduction or rape is one of the most persistent motifs centring on reading throughout the period. As Caroline Gonda puts it, 'the female reader surprised' constituted an 'erotic convention':[57] in Hugh Kelly's *Memoirs of a Magdalen: or, the History of Louisa Mildmay* (1767) the heroine is reading *Clarissa* (the episode where Lovelace 'attempts the sanctity of her chamber') when Sir Harry Hastings attempts to rape and kidnaps her,[58] in *Tom Jones* Lord Fellamar tries to rape the reading Sophia (p. 706), and in *Fatal Obedience* Gertrude Ashurst is 'looking over some books' when she is 'kissed . . . with . . . violence' by Mr Savile (I, p. 66). For women novelists, this motif dramatises profound anxieties about female knowledge and agency. Sarah Scott's Cornelia has been reading late at night when she is carried off by ruffians in the pay of the profligate De Rhée; Frances Sheridan's Sidney Biddulph is 'reading' in her bedroom when Mr Ware tries to rape her; the heroine of Lennox's *Henrietta* is reading when a libertine lord emerges from her closet and makes advances to her; Miss Hampden in Blower's *Maria* is reading in the garden when Lord Newry approaches her with a 'freedom' which is an 'insult'; and even in Roche's *The Nocturnal Visit*, where reading is so powerful in shaping a virtuous heterosexuality, Jacintha is 'deeply engaged in a very interesting story' when Lord Gwytherim attempts to seduce her.[59]

In none of these women's novels is the heroine's reading specified: but even apparently innocent reading endangers the female reader, whose deep involvement in a world of imagination makes her vulnerable to male (conventionally figured as aristocratic) stories of rape and seduction. However, in none of these novels by women is the rape or seduction actually successful. The authors are, as it were, caught between two opposite paradigms of reading, which is seen simultaneously as protecting and endangering. Especially in the 1790s and 1800s, such dramatisation of the dangers of reading crystallised around the novel, which came to be seen as the agent of seduction in the most literal ways. As early as 1765 James Fordyce saw most female novel-readers as spiritual prostitutes, and by the 1790s this metaphor was taken literally by many conservative commentators. A magazine-article of 1797 stigmatised novel-reading as 'a Cause of Female Depravity', in 1806 Edward Barry placed novel-reading among 'incentives to seduction' and the *Edinburgh Review* considered female novel-readers 'upon the borders of prostitution', in Adam Sibbit's *Thoughts on the Frequency of Divorces* (1800) novels, particularly *Werther* and the 'profane lessons of the *Monk*', are blamed for the collapse of family life, and *The Evils of Adultery and Prostitution* (1792) causatively links an 'increase' in adultery and prostitution to novel-reading.[60]

Associations between reading and sexual danger are found throughout the period: an early novel, Sarah Scott's *The History of Cornelia* (1750), shows the connection particularly clearly. After her mother's death, Cornelia is educated by her father, who spends hours with her 'reading' books which encourage 'virtue founded on reason, true religion, and benevolence' rather than 'sentiments', until 'there was scarcely a good author among the Greeks, Romans or moderns, with whom she was not acquainted' (pp. 3, 8, 3–4). When her father dies, she is brought up by her uncle Octavio, who develops an incestuous passion for her and tries to further this by controlling her reading, in particular seeking to 'soften' her by getting her to read 'plays, romances and poetry' (p. 8). When he finds her weeping over the 'imaginary distresses' (p. 9) of a fictional character he assumes that the work of softening is complete and declares his passion. She however rejects him with 'Fear and astonishment', and flees from his house (p. 10). Her later career sometimes recapitulates this sense of the danger of women's reading, but reading also consoles her in loneliness and danger (e.g. p. 57), and reading a good text, in this case Cornelia's own 'thoughts on several subjects' (p. 72) converts De Rhée's mistress and aids Cornelia's escape from his power. After the traumas of reading repeatedly embodied in the text, Cornelia at last settles down with Bernardo, who is remarkably fond of 'reading' (p. 242), and who for the first time since the death of her father reestablishes the link between masculinity and good reading practices which makes a happy domesticity possible.

In the episode where Cornelia's uncle attempts to seduce her, Scott retells stories of seduction from Delarivier Manley's *Secret Memoirs . . . from the New Atalantis* (1709), especially that of Charlot, seduced by a guardian who uses reading as his instrument.[61] Such Restoration texts identify reading directly with sexual transgression, and show women helpless before the combination of paternal authority, androcentric literature, and their own sexuality. Scott rewrites Manley's text for the mid eighteenth-century female reader in an entirely more moral and optimistic way. This reader is reassured about her own reading, for in *Cornelia* reading forms virtuous exogamous bonds which displace the risks of rape and incest. What is dangerous is not female reading but corrupt male uses of it, and if good books are read, even the risk of 'plays, romances and poetry' is controllable (p. 8); the female reader is not, as in Manley, inevitably and helplessly doomed to sexual defeat but is an active moral agent. Indeed, even the worst books can be read virtuously, for Cornelia is not corrupted by reading romances, and Scott is able to read even such a dangerous text as the *New Atalantis* morally.

It is not true that 'heroines do not read novels except as a prelude to seduction', but the association is strong. The reading especially of young or lower-class women is persistently sexualised. Boarding-school girls obtain novels 'clandestinely' and read them in bed, young women hide novels among clothes or underwear, so that novel-reading becomes identified with the female body and a dangerous sexuality.[62] Fanny Hill sometimes equips herself with a book as part of her scene-setting with her own body; when she prepares to seduce an innocent 'country lad', she signals her interest by 'throwing down a book I had in my hands'.[63]

READING THE MOTHER: THE DARK SIDE OF DOMESTIC IDEOLOGY

If Enlightenment female intellectuals tried to reconceptualise women's reading as a vital aid to domestic ideology rather than a potantial hazard to it, this was only partially successful, since, as we have seen, even virtuous women experienced reading and its pleasures as problematic, associated with anxieties about confinement, absence or transgression. In Lawrence Stone's histories of divorce from the seventeenth to the nineteenth centuries, reading is often a contributory factor in marital breakdown, as in the marriage of the Botelers (he was 'enraged' by her persistent reading of *The Whole Duty of Man* and 'one day he seized and burnt it') or of the Marchioness of Westmeath (who complained of her husband's 'sexual immorality', the most appalling symptom of which was his giving her a rude French book to read).[64]

The relationship between female reading and the domestic becomes more problematic in the context of women's ambiguous links with the mother. In numerous examples – Laetitia Pilkington, Mary Berry and Dorothy Wordsworth for example – restriction on reading is imposed not only by domestic ideology in general but quite specifically by the mother or substitute mother.[65] Women writers, who had much to gain

from identification and 'complicity' with the father who is the entrance
to the world of culture, often show fear of becoming their mother's
'double and extension' and hence of being silenced in a world where the
word of the father signifies power.[66] Repeatedly in novels, memoirs and
conduct texts good habits of reading are attributed to the father (as in
Scott's *Cornelia* or Kett's *Emily*), bad to the mother. The 'vices of men
often proceed from the bad education which their mothers have given
them', and this is still truer of women, while good education is achieved
from the 'father's direction'. Worst of all, as a magazine-article of 1795
suggested, the novel-reading mother might become 'the agent of corruption to her own offspring'.[67]

A number of women's novels dramatise this matrophobia. Reading
becomes a point of conflict between mothers and daughters in Lennox's
Life of Harriot Stuart and *Euphemia*, with mothers as the 'voice of convention, often discouraging learning'; even in *The Female Quixote* the romances which so damage Arabella's development are a legacy from her
dead mother. While in Charlotte Smith's conduct works mothers encourage their daughters' reading, in her novels, like *Desmond* (1792), *The
Old Manor House* (1793) and *Montalbert* (1795), they are more likely to
restrict their daughters' reading. In another extreme example, the *Lady's
Magazine* novel 'The Governess', Miss Hayward rescues the Miss Gas-
kins from a mother who is trying to preserve her own youth by refusing
to let her daughters grow up, and whose most effective weapon is to
refuse to allow them to read.[68]

A repeated pattern, then, is the figuring of literacy as a male realm to
which access is restricted by other women, especially the mother. The
daughter's 'relationship with her father is at the heart' of many contemporary texts, the source of the daughter's selfhood and social acceptance:[69] her relationship with her mother often seems more problematic,
emphasis often falling, as in Jane Austen's novels, on the 'absent
mother'.[70] Margaret Homans, indeed, suggests that 'the mother's absence is what makes possible and makes necessary the central projects of
our culture'.[71] In the Kristevan model, the child shares with the mother
the pre-Oedipal semiotic, and while a boy will easily move into the
symbolic order by identifying with the Word of the Father, for a girl this
transition is more difficult. If she accepts the law of the father, she
underwrites her own inferiority, but if she remains with the mother and
the semiotic, she identifies with 'countercultural' forces apparently incompatible with Enlightenment intellectuality and domestic ideology.[72]
In much nineteenth-century literature, the mother 'would repeal, not

encourage, her daughter's entry into the symbolic order';[73] for women writers, therefore, an identification with the law of the Father might have seemed the most profitable way to write themselves into culture.[74]

If Enlightenment women showed 'complicity' with the father and a tendency to reject or erase a mother equated with disturbing counter-cultural forces, Romantic women both resisted and desired identifica-tion with the mother. The Lacanian trope, in which the girl-child enters the symbolic order and arrives at language (and, in this case, literacy) only from the absence or death of the mother, is recurrent. In *Mrs Leicester's School*, the literacy of most of the girls seems contingent upon the disappearance of the mother. Almost all are separated from their mothers – by death (Elizabeth Villiers, Elinor Forester, Arabella Hardy), absence (Louisa Manners, Emily Barton), temperamental disaf-finity (Maria Howe), maternal neglect (Margaret Green), or more com-plex obstacles including uncertainty about who is the true mother (Ann Withers). Separation from the mother generates literacy for Elinor Forester in 'The Father's Wedding-Day', who accepts her widowed father's new family when her stepmother teaches her to read, and presumably for Ann Withers in 'The Changeling', educated in a family of a much higher class than her natal origins. In 'The Sailor Uncle', indeed, Elizabeth Villiers actually learns to read the 'alphabet from the letters on a tombstone that stood at the head of her mother's grave' (p. 276).

In the disquieting Lacanian landscape in which 'reading . . . begins with loss',[75] literacy depends on the erasure of the mother. The girl must leave her mother to enter a male-defined cultural order, as Elizabeth Villiers, who learns to read from her mother's tombstone, is educated in femininity by her father and uncle. To identify with the mother is to risk exclusion from language. Many novels by radical women of the 1790s, like Inchbald's *A Simple Story*, Hays' *The Victim of Prejudice*, Opie's *Adeline Mowbray* and Robinson's *The Natural Daughter*, foreground women's disturbed relations with mothers as these writers assess their actual and literary foremothers and their place within culture.

At the same time, the girl's identification with the absent mother might create a more optimistic, even subversive, resistance to the Word of the Father. In this counter-trope literacy figures as a feminised realm, with books and reading forming links with her lost mother which are crucial to the socialisation and maturing of the daughter. In Charlotte Smith's *Marchmont* (1796), Althea's mother dies shortly after her birth, and she is educated by an aunt, learning not only to be a competent reader of books but also 'the faculty . . . of reading the sentiments' of others (II, p. 177). After her aunt's death, Althea inherits her books, but is obliged to return to her unloving father and stepmother, where her room contains her mother's writing-desk, and 'a few books' in which 'she found her mother's name' (I, p. 128). In this lonely house, the link with the maternal figured by books and reading is crucial for Althea. Literacy in this novel embodies not the Law of the Father but the Word of the Mother, an impingement of the lost semiotic into culture which Althea can share with her man. Like a number of Smith heroes, Marchmont is feminised in the sense that he is domestic, sensitive and impoverished, and Althea's discovery of books signed with his name (I, pp. 306–7) recapitulates her forging of links with the lost maternal. In a novel where the father is so uncaring, Althea's best hope for happiness is not an Austenesque male mentor but a 'new man' whose masculinity rewrites the paternal by incorporating the emotional resonance of the lost maternal, and this is most powerfully figured in images of books, texts and reading. Literacy may, as in *Mrs Leicester's School*, point to a compliant, male-identified existence: but it may be less compliant than this model suggests, and in *Marchmont* it necessitates no less than the complete restructuring of the masculine on the model of the feminine.

But in the Age of Romanticism women writers tend to treat the lost maternal more ambivalently, even pessimistically. A vivid example is Mary Robinson's *The Natural Daughter* (1799), whose metaphors create troubling links between maternity and literacy. Martha, confined in a private madhouse because she is believed to be the mother of an illegitimate child, makes two discoveries. Reading a novel she herself had published, her 'first-born' (II, p. 129), now in its lucrative sixth edition although she was paid only £10 for it, frames her encounter with another inmate, her own mother, whom she believed dead. Literacy and motherhood become reciprocal metaphors, though in a much darker tone than in *Marchmont*. The identification of female writing and reading with economic oppression, imprisonment, insanity, illegitimacy and family breakdown creates a deeply pessimistic view of both literacy and maternity.

This view reaches a logical conclusion in Mary Shelley's *Matilda* (written 1819), a bleakly pessimistic rereading of *Marchmont*. Again the mother of the heroine dies shortly after her birth, and Matilda's literacy is conditional upon this loss and multiple recapitulations of it. Her mother's death, the departure of her nurse and the emotional withdrawal of her aunt leave her dependent on books, in which she finds heroines, Rosalind, Miranda, the Lady in *Comus* (p. 159),[76] who are conspicuously unmothered and who draw attention to her own exiled, disinherited state. Later, claimed by her absent father, Matilda returns to the house where she was born, and finds there tangible reminders of her mother: 'her work box, her writing table . . . and in her room a book lay open upon the table as she had left it' (p. 167). Her father even asks her to continue reading aloud from the copy of Dante that her mother had been reading to him. This effort to recapture a relationship with the lost maternal is, however, in this case disastrous. As she finds herself in the place of her mother, reading her mother's book, Matilda is seen by her father as too literally a repetition of the mother, and he falls incestuously in love with her. Reading no longer offers a pleasurable reestablishment of the nuclear family but a critical interrogation of it, and a source of guilt and teror, as the literature she knows suddenly includes sign after sign for incestuous affection.[77] After her father's death, paternity and even masculinity seem tainted to Matilda. Her Shelleyan friend Woodville, with whom she has a passionate platonic relationship, is firmly detached from the paternal and like Marchmont is instead identified with the maternal: he is unlike her father and 'in no degree reminded me of him' (p. 195), and in a quotation from Dante (who has already been associated with Matilda's mother) he is figured as a mother looking lovingly at a child (p. 198). Even the feminized Woodville cannot, however, rescue her from the trap which appears to be fabricated from maternity and literacy. Finally Matilda can find relief only in death, figured as a return to the semiotic in a union with the 'Universal Mother', Nature (p. 207). For Smith, Marchmont's recapitulations of the feminine render him an ideal partner for Althea: for Shelley even Woodville's association with the mother have insufficient power to transcend a malign masculinity figured as paternal incest, and, still more troublingly, the daughter's vulnerability to the seductive power of the patriarch.

THE PERILS OF READING: CHARLOTTE DACRE, THE BOOK AND THE FEMALE BODY

As Ina Ferris pointed out, early nineteenth-century writing about female reading persistently characterises it as an 'act of the body rather than the mind', often figured as eating (or, we might add, as sex). Women's reading thus becomes an important term in large-scale elite-class male paranoia about 'technology, the market, sexuality, the body . . . that which was defined as outside the literary sphere yet obscurely threatened to erupt from within',[78] as the Indians in *Euphemia* suggest a threat to culture both from outside and from within its weakest members. The materiality of the book might represent that of the female body, as in the examples given above where the open book is barely distinguishable from the openness of the female body to sexual activity.

One writer who specialises in images of books as weapons in a war whose battleground is domesticity, female sexuality and the female body is Charlotte Dacre. Dacre is better known by the pseudonym Rosa Matilda (whom Hannah More places in her bibliography of dangerous reading[79]): but 'Charlotte Dacre' was as much a false identity generated by her reading. Charlotte King (apparently the daughter of a famous Jewish money-lender and sister of Sophia King, author of the anti-Godwinian *Waldorf*) took the names Rosa Matilda from those assumed by the demon in *The Monk*, and Dacre from the heroine of Smith's *Marchmont*. She was herself her first great Gothic creation. In her work, reading is not an act of rational intellect but is associated with immorality and insanity. Helen Small sees Dacre's novels as 'obsessed' with female love-madness, but does not note that the missing link between transgressive sex and female insanity tends to be reading.[80]

Dacre's identification of reading with the unruly female body appears at its simplest in her first novel, *The Confessions of the Nun of St Omer* (1805). Cazire, alienated from her father by his cunning mistress, is placed in a convent where her loneliness can only be assuaged by books, especially novels: 'reading was my chief delight; dangerous, though charming power, capable alike to improve or destroy' (I, p. 62). In Dacre's world the second is much more probable. Whereas Radcliffe's heroines seek a legitimate temporary escape in reading, Dacre's illicitly seek a permanent alternative to real life, and ultimately lose a sure sense of the difference between the two. Cazire's reading draws her into a world of unhealthy sensuality, where '*Reason*' is 'blinded' by 'emotions', always a 'dangerous' scenario (I, p. 65). 'Passion', to use one of the key words of Dacre's fiction,[81] has a destructive power which operates through female reading. The novels Cazire reads are not the healthy opiates of Radcliffe's literary pharmacopia, but hard drugs, 'like the poisonous poppy', which 'under the fallacious mask of conveying *virtue*' are actually 'calculated to inflame the senses, and enervate the heart for *rational* pleasures' (I, p. 63).

As the illicit text figures the unruly female body, these novels exercise a 'dangerous fascination' over Cazire (I, p. 63): 'dangerous', indeed, becomes a key word in the context of female reading, with one chapter actually called 'Dangerous Reading' (I, p. 66). Cazire is 'seduced' by this, her 'mind was the wildest sea of anarchy and error' before the 'resistless power' of 'fiction and romance' (I, p. 67). Her favourite novels are 'most dangerous' because they depict love as 'happy only when *unfettered*' (I, p. 71). While apparently attacking novels like *The Wrongs of Woman* Dacre uses some Wollstonecraftian phrases, depicting Cazire's corruption by 'false sentiment' (I, p. 81). The consequences of her reading are predictable, the dark side of Radcliffe's elision of the roles of reader and heroine: Cazire grows 'weary of reading the actions of *others*' (I, p. 70) and seeks adventures herself. Although she is warned that 'real life and life depicted in romance, are widely different' (I, p. 221), she is unable to learn this basic and crucial lesson, and repeatedly throws away real happiness to pursue romantic delusions. In the climactic episode she is lured from her husband by Fribourg, 'The Fatal Seducer', whose most devastating weapon is a copy of 'Charlotte and Werter' (III, pp. 123, 116). After her seducer kills her husband and himself, Cazire is left, grief-stricken, to take monastic vows. She survives, but the only alternative to transgressive, book-generated sexuality is rejection of the world and the incarceration of the unruly female body.

It would be interesting to know how a contemporary woman read *The Confessions of the Nun of St Omer*. While Radcliffe uses the image of reading to reassure her readers, Dacre uses her novel to raise anxieties about novel-reading. Possibly her intention is to distinguish her allegedly moral text from such harmful fiction as *Werther*; possibly like her master Lewis she insists that moral 'responsibility lies with the reader', for what is dangerous is not how books are written but how they are read.[82] Nonetheless, one would suppose that the novel's 'fascination with the transgression it ostensibly condemns'[83] gave confusingly mixed messages to the female reader. P. B. Shelley, a keen reader of Dacre whose Gothic romance *Zastrozzi* was much influenced by her, produced his first published poems in an 1810 collection shared with his sister Elizabeth, who adopted the pseudonym Cazire. Perhaps she was more ambivalent about her entrance into literary culture than her brother could understand, registering her anxiety by choosing the name of this anti-heroine corrupted by literature. (Shelley used the pseudonym Victor, suggesting quite a different self-image.[84])

In *The Passions* (1811), books are even more blatantly weapons in the war over the female body. Countess Appollonia Zulmer is possessed by '*hatred*' of Count Weimar, who has rejected her for Julia Montalban (whose forename warns us that the novel will retell Rousseau). Pretending affection for Julia, Countess Zulmer sends her books, and although Julia at first returns them, suspecting her husband would disapprove, she gradually accepts and reads them. The most dangerous, Rousseau's *Julie* itself, unsettles Julia's mind, morals and marriage, making her vulnerable to seduction by Count Darlowitz. Julia's body and the text from which she is borrowed become indistinguishable, the power of reading dramatised in images of warfare and poison. Zulmer confesses that 'Books have been no small engines' of her skill in revenge – 'When I found my arguments fail . . . a volume of philosophy was the force I rallied, and it always proved a host in my favour' (II, p. 280) – and gloats in the 'subtle poison . . . extracted from . . . books', superior to all other venoms for they 'operate only on the physical system', while the 'deadly poison' of books 'affects not the body, but the mind' (I, p. 207).

It could be argued, borrowing the period's favourite distinction between 'good' and 'bad' books, that Radcliffe affirms female reading because her heroines read good books, while Dacre condemns it because her heroines read bad books, French and German novels and radical metaphysics, which in the light of the 'new conservatism' of the early nineteenth century seemed so dangerous.[85] But it is not as simple. Radcliffe offers no contrasting portraits of women who read bad books, so creating an affirmative verdict on reading which is strategic for her and her female readers, since it defends her literary activity and vindicates their reading pleasure. Dacre conversely has few full-length portraits of women who read good books. The brief, routine picture in *The Passions* of the virtuous Amelia Darlowitz, 'well versed in almost every species of useful and refined literature' (I, p. 97), hardly constitutes an exception. Nor does the slightly fuller picture in *The Libertine* (1807) of the apparent page-boy Eugene, actually the seduced Gabrielle de Montmorency, serving her seducer unknown to him: one of her duties is reading aloud, especially the Radcliffean diet of 'tender Tasso, or lovelorn Petrarch, or . . . romantic Ariosto' or history, although she worryingly also includes Voltaire and 'metaphysics' (I, p. 190). The libertine Angelo d'Albini recognises her when he sees her through a curtain, with her long hair let down, reading 'amatory verses' from a 'volume of Lorenzo de Medici' (I, pp. 242, 239). The reading of Amelia Darlowitz or Gabrielle de Montmorency is not associated with insanity or destructive passion, but it marks them as sexually vulnerable and, in the case of Gabrielle, as sexually transgressive: her adoption of transvestite disguise both figures and serves as an escape from sexual transgression, and the image of reading serves fundamentally ambiguous functions.

In *Zofloya, or the Moor* (1806), Victoria di Loredani's lover Berenza agonises over whether to marry her, since she has had such a poor education that he will have to 'new model the subject' (i, p. 200) to make her a fit wife, but it does not occur to him to do this by reading with her or offering her books (as, for example, Oswald successfully does in Roche's *The Nocturnal Visit*). In *Zofloya* the only attempt to educate through reading is that of the tyrannical Signora di Modena who tries to control Victoria by making her read 'religious books' (i, p. 141), but this strategy fails dismally, only increasing Victoria's resentment and desire to escape. Even *good* books have, it seems, only bad uses, in this case as the instrument of tyranny rather than virtue. Dacre may issue a 'challenge to the myths of Romantic self-hood', but her exclusion of women characters from any positive relationship to literacy worked in exactly the opposite direction to most women writers who were challenging those myths.[86]

Radcliffe's heroines form links with fathers (and, more rarely, mothers) through reading, links which enable their maturation into wives and mothers of perfected families. Radcliffe is clear that this, and the reading that facilitates it, are desirable. Dacre's heroines, though, come from dysfunctional and abusive families, so that the problem is not, as in Radcliffe, the need to remake links with parents, but a need to break those links and evade malign paternal – or, more often, maternal – power. If reading figures family, in a world of exploitative, neglectful and disintegrating families, reading takes on a sinister colouring. Daughters learn from parents either impracticably absolute prohibitions of pleasure, like Gabrielle in *The Libertine*, or selfish indulgence of the passions, like Cazire in *Confessions of the Nun of St Omer*. None of Dacre's heroines succeeds in establishing the Radcliffean reformed family: her families are unreformable, like the reading that figures them sites of transgressive and self-destructive passion rather than rational pleasure.

In Dacre's novels, then, women's reading is primarily associated with sexual transgression, tyranny and insanity, and hence they offer a much more uncomfortable experience than Radcliffe's for their female readers. Radcliffe's novels legitimise the activity in which readers are at that moment involved, while Dacre's implicitly attack her readers, their reading practices, and her own writing. Her attitude to her material seems 'troubled' and her use of conventions and images 'contradictory':

while her novels offer a 'warning against immorality', they are themselves 'more sensational and more explicitly sexual' than those of most
of her female contemporaries.[87] This might be intended to preempt
criticism by distinguishing her work from 'dangerous' fiction, but if so it
cannot be deemed to succeed. In my final chapter I shall examine this
curious phenomenon, the rise in the early nineteenth century of novels
embodying a specifically anti-novel discourse. Dacre may be seen to
belong to this movement and to express in exaggerated form the age's
anxieties about female literacy, with reading uncomfortably recapitula-
ting anxieties about the undisciplined female body.

PLEASURES AND PERILS OF READING: CONCLUSIONS

Reading, then, offers pleasures ranging from escape to domesticity,
community, and even resistance, but perils including family and marital
breakdown, incest, seduction and rape, and both can be especially
clearly seen in female Gothic. Radcliffe foregrounds the pleasures of
reading, especially its utility within a domestic discourse, and her imitators, like Regina Maria Roche, Eleanor Sleath and Eliza Parsons,
continued to make reading a significant element in the emotional lives of
their heroines. Dacre can be seen as a resisting, indeed a rebellious,
reader of Radcliffe, but like her she has something important and
coherent, though deeply pessimistic, to say about women's reading.
Although both use similar Gothic conventions, Dacre and Radcliffe
deal with female reading, and the female body for which it stands, in
very different ways.

CHAPTER 4

Pleasures and perils of reading: some case histories

The evidence for the reading-histories of real women in this period is both dauntingly rich and disappointingly meagre. Some left detailed records, but all are white, most from aristocratic, literary or professional families. Nonetheless, despite what seems a limitation, the readers studied in this chapter embody central contemporary themes. Laetitia Pilkington represents a late-Restoration identification of women's reading (and writing) with transgressive sexuality, which she simultaneously protests and uses to her own advantage; reading also serves her as a rhetorical means of claiming middle-class status as she struggled to survive as an impoverished divorced Irishwoman in London. Frances Burney's anxieties about self-assertion, authority, sexuality and a public role are typical of the new conservatism after 1750, and often focus around writing and reading. Elizabeth Carter demonstrates the problems faced by female intellectuals, and both she and Jane Austen demonstrate in different ways how tactics of vigorously resisting reading could be accommodated within apparently traditional modes of femininity. I cover the full chronological range of this study, from Pilkington who died in 1750 to Burney who survived until 1840: their different attitudes will therefore chart changing opinion as well as idiosyncratic differences or those conditioned by different social and family circumstances.

LAETITIA PILKINGTON (1712–50)

Laetitia Pilkington was born in 1712, and her treatment of reading strongly resembles that of women of the previous generation, like Aphra Behn whose transvestite adventuress Sylvia takes a 'little novel' to read in bed with her new lover, or Delarivier Manley who persistently identifies women's reading with seduction.[1] Like them, she equates women's reading with sexual desire; she thus accepts, but contrives to use for her own purposes, the association of reading and erotic pleasure which created so much embarrassment for respectable women of later generations like Burney.

The contradictions inherent in the scandalous autobiography have been demonstrated by recent critics.[2] Pilkington, Teresia Constantia Phillips, Lady Vane and others tried to vindicate themselves from scandal by publishing their own autobiographical accounts, and yet publication increased the scandal by making increasingly public the charges against them. Richardson complained such women contrived to 'perpetuate their infamy' by the very act of pleading their innocence.[3] Pilkington's *Memoirs* has two apparently incompatible aims. She vigorously defends her innocence and blames her husband for the breakdown of their marriage, but is also aware that her book will find a market only if she offers her readers titillating gossip, laudatory or scurrilous sketches of celebrities, and suggestively eroticised scenarios, which continually undercut her claims to feminine virtue. She must thus present herself as simultaneously innocent and experienced, a doubleness of focus which gives the memoirs their characteristic ironic flavour. Reading, with its potential to figure both virtue and seduction, is a peculiarly helpful metaphor, used constantly in the *Memoirs*.

Writing and reading are crucial elements in Pilkington's self-presentation, as she depicts her origins within a family whose systems of authority defined her reading practices as transgressive from the start. Her mother, although herself 'improv'd by reading' (p. 12), treated Laetitia with a 'Severity' (p. 13) which showed itself especially in an attempt to control her access to literacy, perhaps from jealousy of a daughter 'greatly indulg'd' (p. 12) by her father. The child Laetitia had a 'strong Disposition to Letters', but since her eyes were weakened by smallpox she 'was not permitted to look at a Book . . . neither was I allow'd to learn to read'. This prohibition only made her 'more earnest in the Pursuit of what I imagin'd must be so delightful', and although her mother punished her for it 'Twenty Times a Day', she taught herself to read. At the age of five, she was caught by her father reading Dryden: 'I dropt my Book, and burst into Tears.' However, instead of the expected punishment, her father gave her a shilling, and thereafter supplied her with 'the best, and politest Authors'. She was especially 'ravish'd' by poetry (p. 13), and became 'a perfect Devourer of Books', loving their 'sweet . . . and nourishing Food' (p. 173).

In this account of Pilkington's first literacy experience, reading is emphatically presented as transgression: it is the first of many occasions when she shows herself innocent of wrong-doing but punished, especially by powerful women, for transgressing arbitrary socially established boundaries. Literacy is equated with pleasure, even a specifically erotic pleasure – 'delightful', 'ravished' – and with money: like Moll Flanders learning to regard her sexuality as a marketable commodity, Pilkington finds literacy a site of profit as well as pleasure. Later, 'reading' not only comforts her when she is 'melancholy' (p. 168), but helps provide income in times of desperate need.

Pilkington uses images already noted, in which literacy is figured as a male realm to which she is welcomed by her father, while her mother tries to block access (a motif which recurs in her account of autodidact Constantia Crawley Grierson[4]). This forms a recurrent pattern in the *Memoirs*, by which Pilkington appeals to male readers by depicting herself as the innocent victim of autocratic, narrow-minded and hypocritical women. After her marriage fails she is insulted by women who are guiltier than she, cheated by landladies, neglected by ladies to whom she appeals for help, and a prey to procuresses.[5] Male readers are warned 'never to believe any thing that is said of me by a *Woman*' (p. 233). Indeed, Pilkington deliberately depicts herself as unlike other women and persecuted by them to such an extent that she 'never conversed with Women' (p. 189): even women writers, with the sole exceptions of the famously respectable Anne Dacier and Katherine Philips, are criticised for immorality and for gaining a bad reputation for women authors (pp. 227–8).

It suits Pilkington's purposes to present herself as a male-identified woman, repressed by actual and literary mothers, and dependent on male benevolence to survive. She addresses her readers constantly, generally envisaging the most skilled and sympathetic as male;[6] and since she has a special ability to 'read Men' they are also a text in which she has particular reading competence (p. 130). When she does address 'the *Female* Part of my Readers' (p. 9) specifically, it is not to offer reading pleasure, as she does to men, but to issue warnings (in this case, of the importance of '*Reputation*'), to attempt intimidation (p. 263), or to hope, though not expect, 'Compassion; tho' rarely met with from one Woman to another' (p. 290). Her treatments of women readers reflect deep unease. Although reading may, as in the case of Constantia Grierson, Lady Jane Grey (p. 217), or the daughter of the Duke of Richmond (pp. 159–60), figure virtue, it is more likely to demonstrate lust and hypocrisy: a 'lady of quality' who slanders her 'would have purchased my Book sooner than the Bible' (p. 227) if it had really been obscene.

Pilkington addresses male readers with a franker sense of fellowship and more expectation of fair treatment (e.g. pp. 233, 290), colluding in, but also ironising, their stereotypes of women. She presents herself simultaneously as vulnerable subject and powerful author. At one point, for instance, she invites the male 'Reader' who considers a 'Narrative' irrelevant to 'blot it out of his Book', ceding authority to reconfigure the text from female author to male reader: but even if the reader were to appropriate writerly power, he could not destroy the story, which would remain in her 'Manuscript' as a testimony to '*Truth*' (p. 285). Pilkington's text enacts a battle for meaning between male and female, writer and reader, over which she maintains an ambiguous authority.

One reason why reading seems transgressive in the *Memoirs* is that it can lead to still more transgressive behaviour: to sexual indulgence, and to writing, two acts which are persistently figured in terms of each other. As Pilkington tells us, 'from a Reader, I quickly became a Writer' (p. 13), and from this point writing and sexual activity become inseparable. The Duke of Wharton, in bed with his mistress, writes a letter using her 'Posteriors' as a 'Writing-Desk' (p. 171), and this scene serves as a humorous interlude generating an enjoyable frisson of shock: but the connection between writing and sex becomes more troubling in the case of a female subject. One of Pilkington's poems, working from the traditional metaphor of pen as penis, figures writing as an act of rape, but gender distinctions become confused, for the rapist is the female writer who assaults the 'Purity' of the paper, whose 'Innocence' is 'betray'd' by her, and whose 'Stains' (a word conventionally used of the loss of chastity) can never be washed away. The metapoem, and the poem with whose composition it deals, are specifically aimed at a male readership, written 'to please a Boy' (p. 45); their sexual suggestiveness aims to titillate this audience, and yet their images simultaneously deplore female (cultural and sexual) vulnerability and celebrate female power. The poem reflects the dual self-image that Pilkington creates in the memoir as both innocent and experienced, both victim and agent.

After separating from her husband, Pilkington survived through work directly dependent upon her literacy – selling prints, books and pamphlets, using her writing to gain the patronage of famous male writers like Richardson and Colley Cibber. She hired herself out as an amanuensis and letter-writer, a role combining the literary and erotic, since she specialised in 'Billet-Doux' (p. 137), even at one point functioning as 'Secretary for the Whores' (p. 278). The image of prostitution links reading and writing to sexuality. Her husband spread the story that she was a 'common Prostitute' (p. 161), a charge she refuted by writing narratives of heroic resistance to procuresses. And she resisted not only sexual but textual prostitution. Piratical publisher Edmund Curll tried to obtain 'valuable Manuscripts' (p. 193) from her, and to cash in on her notoriety by attributing to her works she never wrote, but she escaped his attempts to procure her works and reputation exactly as she evaded the procuresses.

Sometimes she cannot avoid prostituting the body of her writing, writing letters, poems and plays for others to claim as their own. But she has two self-defensive tactics against charges of literary harlotry. First, male writers are shown as equally guilty: male 'Bards will prostitute their wit' (p. 151), and her husband allows his work to be passed off as that of aspiring writer Worsdale just as she does (p. 101). And if men are (literary) prostitutes, literal female prostitutes are presented in a defiantly positive light: she works for them 'honestly' and they are 'liberal' in their pay (p. 278), a more positive relationship between writer and her public than she has elsewhere with women. Pilkington appropriates but re-evaluates the Restoration identification of female writing (and reading) with prostitution, of 'Punk and Poetess'.[7] She alternately resists and defiantly accepts the figuring of the female writer as whore, identifying female writing and reading with prostitution, but also mocking impotent male readers like Worsdale and literary (male) prostitutes such as Curll and her husband.

Pilkington's account of her disastrous marriage to her clergyman husband also gives centrality to reading and writing. At first shared literacy figures their harmonious union. Her early poems win his 'Applause' (p. 22), but when she demonstrates real ability he is jealous and 'very angry'. Men cannot endure literary wives, she writes bitterly, for literacy 'seems to set them too much upon a Level with their Lords and Masters', and her literary ability soon seems to him not the basis of domestic companionship but a threat to his superiority. He claims that she is 'mad', and in another traditional trope insists that 'a Needle became a Woman's Hand better than a Pen' (p. 50). His envy at her literary talent, not her unchastity, causes the breakdown of the marriage, and he punishes her most painfully through her literacy. When he deserts her, he prevents her access to the garden and the tea-chest, but what hurts most is his colonisation of her books: 'because I lov'd reading, Mr *Pilkington* took with him the Key of his Study, into which he had remov'd all my Books' (p. 82).

Eventually divorced for adultery with a Mr Adair, Pilkington protests her innocence. She was 'very indiscreet' in allowing Adair to be 'at an unseasonable Hour in my Bed-Chamber': but she was motivated by desire for reading, not for transgressive sex, 'the attractive Charms of a new Book, which the Gentleman would not lend me, but consented to stay till I read it through' (p. 88). Typically reading pleasure is contrasted with, but only by implication to be strongly identified with, adultery. The claim to innocence exists alongside a tongue-in-cheek challenge to the reader to reconsider the relation between textuality and sexuality, guilt and innocence. Pilkington simultaneously defends her innocence and markets her book by its naughty and knowing identification of reading with sexual pleasure.

Pilkington's style is highly allusive, for which she apologises,[8] while also defending her right to appropriate literary culture by invoking male precedent. She is not always accurate in her use and attribution of quotations,[9] though no worse than most contemporaries in informal modes. The range of her reading is not very wide, and is probably typical of the literate but not wealthy lower-middle-class woman of the mid century. She read much Shakespeare (favourite plays are *Othello, Macbeth, Henry IV, Julius Caesar, Hamlet* and *Measure for Measure*)[10] and poetry, especially Milton, Pope and Swift, with less Young, Dryden, Gay and Prior.[11] She records little fiction-reading (hardly any recent fiction except *Pamela*, whose image of embattled innocence is strategically useful to her self-presentation), and little history or travels, though she knew some religious and philosophical writing, and some periodical essays.[12] If eighteenth-century commentators feared the effect of reading on the imagination of a susceptible girl, Laetitia Pilkington might have served as a perfect negative role-model.

FRANCES BURNEY D'ARBLAY (1752–1840)

Frances Burney was a key figure in the history of novel-reading, the novelist who more than any other in the late eighteenth century legitimised the novel as an aesthetically and morally acceptable form. Her work is recommended in many conduct works, or specifically excluded from attacks on the novel.[13] Typically she was praised for both sound morality and educational realism: *La Belle Assemblée* for 1806, for instance, praises her for presenting a 'true picture of life' in 'reasonable' form (1, p. 531). The fictional heroine who reads Burney demonstrates virtue and sense, like Anne Elliot in *Persuasion*, Cecilia in Blower's *George*

Bateman, Lennox's *Euphemia*, Harriet Monson in 'The Rash Attempt: a Moral Tale', or the 'fair reader' Matilda Darnley in Eliza Taylor's didactic novel *Education: or, Elizabeth, Her Lover and Husband* (1817).[14] Readers who fail to respond to Burney are foolish and insensitive, like Mrs Wouldbe in Bennett's *The Beggar Girl and her Benefactors*, John Thorpe in *Northanger Abbey* who ridicules *Camilla*, or the Taddington sisters in *George Bateman* who misunderstand *Evelina*. In Hayley's *The Triumphs of Temper*, the idealised heroine Serena reads 'Sweet Evelina's fascinating power'[15] which 'exercise[s]' her 'virtues'. Burney was both a resource for women readers and an enabling precedent for novelists like Elizabeth Blower, Edgeworth, Austen, and Eliza Parsons, who found Burney's example caused 'trembling anxiety' about her own 'presumption', but was nonetheless inspiring.[16]

If Pilkington renegotiates the association of reading with transgressive pleasure and authority, Burney despite her love of reading and her high reputation as a writer associates women's reading squarely with anxiety and danger. The benevolent domestic dictatorship of her charismatic father Charles Burney put pressure on his children, and they reacted and rebelled in a range of ways, some as spectacular as theft and incest. Frances' reaction was to develop tactics of extreme reticence and self-effacement, and becoming a published writer exacerbated her dread of being thought bookish, pretentious, or simply different. Indeed, her fear of notice, often articulated in the context of reading and writing, is so emphatic as to appear a covert mode of resistance, an exaggeration which draws critical attention to, even works to subvert, the codes she seems so scrupulously to be keeping.

Books and reading are equivocally presented in Burney's fictional worlds, at least for women vehicles of anxiety as much as pleasure. Ostentatiously literate women made her uncomfortable, as is dramatised by Mrs Selwyn in *Evelina*, Mrs Berlinton in *Camilla*, and the bluestocking Lady Smatter in *The Witlings*, while some of her most lively and sympathetic heroines do not read. Joyce in *The Woman-Hater* is semi-literate, 'hate[s] reading' and cannot understand 'the use of Books', for she has 'words' of her own and so does not need 'to be poring over other people's'; Cleora in one of the manuscript sketches for *Camilla* cannot understand why 'one must always be reading' and is bored by 'reading Books'.[17] While Lady Smatter represents Burney's anxieties about being thought ostentatiously bookish, Joyce and Cleora offer utopian escape from the anxieties of literacy.

In the novels, women's reading is treated ambivalently. The heroine of her first novel, *Evelina* (1778), loves books – 'the young Lady *reads*', as Mrs Selwyn ironically announces to the fools who harrass her (p. 275) – and shared literacy sustains her growing attachment to Orville as they 'read' together, and he marks passages for her attention (p. 296). Books also provide useful self-protection – in an embarrassing interview with her guardian Villars Evelina 'pretended to employ [her]self in looking for a book', when Orville engineers her meeting with Macartney she 'pretended to be reading', and later she again 'took up a book' to avoid Orville's attentions (pp. 264, 320, 325). In an apparently last meeting with Orville, packing up her 'books' frames a scene of growing under-standing (p. 351).

Evelina is not only a reader but a 'book', which her foster-father 'read[s]', but which 'afflicts and perplexes' him (p. 263): and this is often the effect of reading in the novel. Evelina longs for letters from her guardian and friends, but they arrive too late to give her the advice she needs, are written in accordance with now-superseded informa-tion, or in an extreme case (p. 358) is even a forgery. Evelina is prepared to be compliant to textuality: indeed she longs for its author-ity to guide her, as she wishes for 'a book, of the laws and customs *à-la-mode*' (p. 83) to inform young people entering society. But she also fears textuality and the publication it threatens in a world where women should remain private and domestic. Sir Clement Wil-loughby's panegyric poem, like his forgery of Orville's letter, causes her 'the greatest confusion' (p. 334). Evelina's adventures in literacy em-body her creator's anxieties about her own entrance into the public world of print culture.

Although the protagonist of *Cecilia* (1782), wealthy, beautiful and independent, ought to be Burney's most powerful heroine, she is 'cul-turally silenced'[18] as much as Evelina, and this ambiguity is reflected in her relation to books. Cecilia loves reading, which provides an 'exhaust-less fund of entertainment', her 'richest, highest and noblest source of intellectual enjoyment'.[19] Burney satirises the 'patriarchal attitudes'[20] of Cecilia's snobbish guardian Delville, who thinks it ungenteel for a woman to read beyond 'The Spectator, Tatler, and Guardian' (p. 186), and we are clearly meant to sympathise with her love of books. And yet 'reading is intimately connected' with her 'loss of both fortune and status'.[21] Genuine authority, meaningful access to language and literacy, can hardly be held by women, however rich and independent, and Cecilia's buying of books causes her to fall dangerously into debt. Reading thus figures a dangerous assertiveness and concern for her own pleasure which prefigures her secret marriage and subsequent break-down.

In *Camilla* reading 'is a major theme', and many characters, from the pedantic Dr Orkborne to the careless Camilla, whose 'imagination . . . submitted to no control' (p. 63), are defined by reading practices and attitudes to books. It is clear that for women 'no reading matter is completely safe or instructive' (and nor is the avoidance of reading, which symbolises the thoughtlessness which leads the heroine into difficulties).[22] Eugenia is endangered because she has read classical epics but not novels which might have warned her against fortune-hunters (a reversal of the usual situation where the reading of novels generates the danger). Mrs Berlinton is also endangered, and inadvertently endangers the innocent Camilla, by her reading, which exaggerates her 'suscep-tible' and 'romantic' nature (p. 487), although the books specified (like Elizabeth Rowe's *Friendship in Death*, Akenside's *Pleasures of the Imagination*, and Collins' *Odes*) were generally thought legitimate for women readers: but even legitimate reading is dangerous in the terrifying textual world of *Camilla*.

The Wanderer is less profoundly anxious about female reading, since it polarises good and bad reading practices, at least allowing the possibility of the former. Elinor Joddrel's reading, by allusion largely from Rous-seau, Paine, Wollstonecraft, radical philosophy, and the dangerously imaginative Romantic poets,[23] constructs a transgressive Wollstonecraf-tian woman, who makes advances to the man she desires and when he refuses attempts suicide. Juliet's reading conversely demonstrates a moral, sensitive but self-sacrificing nature, and renders her worthy of Albert Harleigh. She reads Addison's *Guardian*, Boileau, Pope, Racine and Shakespeare, which 'proved alike her understanding and her feel-ing' (pp. 508, 116). While female-authored texts teach Elinor transgress-ive self-assertion, they give more competent readers a self-protective insight into their own situations, as Juliet consoles herself by reading her appalling employer Mrs Ireton as a satirical character from Jane Col-lier's *The Art of Ingeniously Tormenting* (p. 486).

Burney's life embodied the same ambiguities about literacy as her fiction. She came from a highly literate family, their house 'an *abyss* of literature'. To Charles Burney literacy represented the secure middle-class status he had fought so hard to achieve. Hester Thrale remarked on the pressure put on the young Burneys to conform, to 'write and read & be literary' in order 'not to disgrace' their father.[24] Dr Burney owned a famous library, estimated at 20,000 volumes in 1798 (though Frances claimed the only novel it contained was Fielding's *Amelia*[25]), and while a young unmarried woman she not only had access to this library but was also regarded as her father's '*Librarian*' (*ED* I, p. 212). Her brother Charles at his death also left a distinguished classical library which was bought for the nation.

Yet there was a dark side to reading, writing and the acquisition of books in the Burney household. Frances learned to read belatedly and slowly, characterising herself as the 'most backward' of her brilliant family, still unable to read at the age of eight, then springing from illiteracy to authorship in a single movement.[26] For young Frances, literacy was a link with her beloved mother, who died when she was ten: she later remembered, fondly and enviously, her mother reading with her elder sister Esther (*JAL* XI, p. 286). Her belated induction into literacy may indicate resistance to the pressure to conformity, or rivalry with her siblings for the attention of her mother. For Burney, as for Radcliffe's heroines, literacy constituted an important link with father and mother. Nonetheless, she persistently figured literacy as guilt and anxiety. Her earliest journals seek to legitimise '[r]eading & writing' by emphasising her ability to discipline her passion for her 'two *most* favourite pursuits': she never indulges in them in the morning, but sews 'like a good Girl', allowing herself the 'pleasure' of books only in the afternoon, when 'it does not take up the Time I ought to spend otherwise'.[27]

A good girl can, with negotiation and self-sacrifice, be a reader, but writing is more difficult, even in informal modes like the journal. Joyce Hemlow believes that the writing of the Burney children 'was by no means approved by their elders', and Frances at the age of fifteen burned her early writings, including plays and a novel detailing the tragic life of Evelina's mother, perhaps 'by command'.[28] Her early diaries certainly dramatise unease with female writing and male reading by telling a number of stories of young women made miserable when a male relative reads, or tries to read, their journals, most graphically an episode when a page of her own diary is lost and read by her father, causing her 'sad distress' and making her 'so frightened that I have not had the Heart to write since'. A female friend even urges her to give up journal writing, castigating it as a 'most dangerous employment' since it gives expression to 'things which ought *not* to be recorded' (Troide I, pp. 18–19, 20–1; cf. also p. 5). Even private writings risk being too public. For Burney writing raises anxieties about public versus private spaces and about the male reading of female texts, but reading is almost equally a source of gendered anxieties about pleasure and duty, self-assertion and self-sacrifice.

Anxieties about reading and writing recur throughout Burney's life. As a mother she thought it her duty to control the reading of her wayward son Alexander, curbing his consumption of the books of algebra and Romantic poetry which he particularly enjoyed. Her father's huge library became a liability when he had to move from his Chelsea apartments (*JAL* IV, p. 106). After the deaths of male relations their books assume a special emotional resonance, and in some cases become a site for family conflicts in which the guilt and suppressed anger inseparable from bereavement are played out.[29] But the most spectacular association of books with guilt and anxiety in the family history was a scandal in which her brother Charles was caught stealing and selling books from Cambridge University Library.[30] Frances thought him 'giddy' rather than criminal, overcome by 'a MAD RAGE for possessing a library' (*JAL* x, p. 795), but possibly Charles Jr's was an act of rebellion symptomatic of an Oedipal rivalry with his father and namesake whose bibliomania and need for middle-class respectability he parodies by exaggeration. This explains why the D'Arblays monitored their son's reading so scrupulously, with General d'Arblay on his deathbed urging his wife to limit Alexander's bookbuying to 'only such as belonged to his holy Profession, to Mathematics, & to general polite literature' (*JAL* x, pp. 897–8). Books, reading and writing were sites of pleasure and desire in the Burney and D'Arblay households, but they could manifest themselves in problematic, even transgressive forms. This was true of both sexes, but Frances seems to accept that women's writing and reading needed special control or excuse.

Even after childhood, Burney associated her reading with both pleasure and anxiety. She 'loved reading . . . I doat on nothing equally' (*ED* I, p. 47), and often chose to stay in the library when other female members of the party enjoyed more traditionally feminine activities (e.g. *DAL* I, p. 381): yet she dreaded a reputation for bookishness or pedantry. So well did she conceal her love of books that Dr Johnson remarked that he 'never see[s] her with a book in her hand', and when he asked what she was 'reading' she evaded the question (*DAL* I, pp. 82, 45). Burney haunted the Thrales' library at Streatham, hiding her book when a man appeared: she 'instantly put away [her] book', in this instance a translation of Cicero, when Mr Seward entered the library, or hid under her gloves his 'Life of Waller' when Johnson approached (*DAL* I, pp. 22, 82).

The same adjectives occur in her description of both incidents, her dread of being thought 'studious' and 'affected', repetition which emphasises the obsessively self-assertive quality of her self-concealment. She is happiest when she can conceal her reading or define it as negation, sometimes quite literally: she seems to enjoy a flirtatious joke by a male friend that she 'can't read', and only pretends to do so as 'make believe' (*DAL* I, p. 244).

She also displays revulsion at her stepmother's tactless joke about her having 'got Mr Charrier into a corner' in the library (*ED* II, pp. III, 119–20). Burney is angry at this definition of libraries as sites of assertive female desire, perhaps because she fears it might be true. A fear of a disturbingly uncontrollable element in reading pleasure is certainly suggested in an episode of 1784, when her reading group is reading two books, the last voyage of Captain Cook and the letters of Madame de Sévigné. She makes little progress with Cook because of her fascination with Sévigné, a 'siren' who 'seduces me from all other reading': she feels such an intense response to the letters that it is as if Sévigné 'were alive, and even now in my room, and permitting me to run into her arms' (*DAL* I, p. 572). This oddly sexualised image of female authority and the relationship between female reader and female writer reflects Burney's guilty sense of an intense, even potentially erotic, pleasure in reading.

The association of reading with both pleasure and danger is most obvious in Burney's early womanhood, but sometimes haunts her later life. This is revealed by small details in the 'Ilfracombe Journal' for 1817, which chronicles a terrifying episode in which, exploring alone in a sea-cave, she is trapped by the tide. As she is walking, she passes a 'lady . . . seated on a large flat stone, & composedly engaged with her Book', and 'this implication of security that all was safe' encourages her to explore. The episode is framed by her awareness of 'the lady who was reading in the neighbouring Recess' (*JAL* X, pp. 693–4). Female reading serves as a metaphor for ordinary everyday life which provides an effective backdrop for this crisis, but it also has a darker side. There is a buried sense that female reading conjures up danger to another female reader, and this female reader displays the author's anxieties about her audience, to whom she supplies pleasure but only at great cost to herself.

Solitary reading troubles Burney most: 'anything highly beautiful I have almost an aversion to reading alone' (*DAL* III, p. 6), and she emphasises reading as a vehicle for the pleasures of community. Perhaps she feels guilty about the selfishness of solitary pleasure, or fears the intensity of her own responses and needs the discipline of company to moderate them. When she is employed in the royal household the loss of reading community, 'one of the first gratifications of my life . . . reading with those who have an equal pleasure in it', is especially painful (*DAL* II, p. 568), and she makes a number of attempts to recreate it. It cannot be with the Queen and the royal princesses, although one of her professional tasks is reading aloud to them, because she is so bashful and self-conscious that the Queen often reads while Burney listens. (The Queen had strong if puritanical reading tastes, and was suspicious of novels, though she often gave Burney gifts of approved books.[31]) Her attempt to revive reading community with Col. Digby (called 'Mr Fairly' in the printed diaries) was no more successful. Their relationship is defined in the printed diaries almost wholly in terms of shared books and reading, though anxiety and the need for concealment remain prominent. She fears being thought 'sentimental' or 'pedantic', so they hide their book when anyone appears (*DAL* III, pp. 8, 7). Indeed, he seems even more nervous than she, possibly implying that he is in fact guilty of using reading as a cover for sexual desire. On one occasion he takes the copy of Pope she is reading, opens it at 'Eloisa to Abelard', and remarks that ''tis but too beautiful, and that is its greatest fault' (*DAL* III, pp. 135). He especially dreads the accusation that they are 'two blue stockings' (*DAL* III, p. 7): reading seems to him, paradoxically, both sexualising and emasculating.[32] Burney's uncertainty about his intentions, her loneliness, and her anxiety about sexuality, are displaced into anxieties about reading.

That reading was a vehicle for problematic desire and pleasure is indicated by the repeated recurrence of the theme, especially in her journals for 1788 and 1789. She tends, indeed, to code her relationship to literature in terms of negation and absence: her first novel was submitted anonymously to the bookseller, with her siblings concealing her involvement and negotiating on her behalf with the publisher, and her earliest journal is dedicated to its female reader 'Nobody' (Troide I, p. 2). Throughout her life she emphasises how few books she herself has read or owns, telling Queen Charlotte that her 'free access' to her father's library has made it 'unnecessary' and 'impractical' for her to buy 'books of my own' (*DAL* II, p. 258). The dutiful daughter accepts her father's choice of books and his ownership of the books she reads: a room of her own, even a book of her own, are not necessities but dangerous temptations to independence and self-assertion.

Indeed, one of her favourite rhetorical ploys is to present herself as not having read some book that everyone else has read, defending herself from charges of inappropriate, unfeminine literary professionalism by defining herself in terms of lack of reading. In 1771 she reads Pope, 'I blush to say for the first time' (*ED* I, p. 138), she has not read Miss Aikin's poems (*ED* I, p. 289), or Rousseau's *Nouvelle Eloise* (*ED* I, p. 290), or *Candide* (*DAL* I, p. 153),[33] or Wraxall's *Memoirs* (*DAL* I, p. 163), or *Les liaisons dangereuses* (*DAL* I, p. 503), or enough Rousseau or Voltaire to discuss them with the King, or any of the comedies he names (*DAL* II, pp. 46–7), or Madame de Genlis' latest work (*DAL* II, p. 48), or the *Sorrows of Werther* (which when she does read she abandons 'from distaste at its evident tendency') (*DAL* II, pp. 49, 412), or the poems of Churchill (*DAL* II, p. 442), Akenside (*DAL* II, p. 568), or Goldsmith (*DAL* III, p. 245), or Falconer's *The Shipwreck* (*DAL* II, p. 569), or Gessner's *The Death of Abel* (*DAL* II, p. 472), or Captain Bligh's memoirs (*DAL* III, p. 256), or Dermoustier's *Les femmes* (*JAL* III, p. 308), or Bürger's 'Lenore' (*JAL* IV, p. 40), or Elizabeth Montagu's *Letters* (*JAL* VII, p. 209), or the latest 'Work of Mme Neckar' (*JAL* XI, p. 162). Indeed she 'astonished' Mr Fairly by her revelation of 'the number of authors I have never yet read' (*DAL* II, p. 568).

Sometimes the claim not to have read particular books is intended to distance herself from morally suspect works, *La Nouvelle Eloise* or *Werther* or *Les liaisons dangereuses*. Otherwise her emphasis on the narrowness of her reading guards her against accusations of pedantry or professionalism. It is an important element in her self-presentation to show herself as no different from other gentlewomen, bound by the same rules and not exempted by professionalism or other special pleading. Mr J-, recommending *Les liaisons dangereuses* in 1782, tells her, presumably as a compliment, 'you, we all know, may look into any work without being hurt by it'. However, she resents rather than is flattered by the assumption that she is different from other women readers, and responds forbiddingly that she 'never looks into any books that could hurt me' (*DAL* I, p. 503). Indeed, so central a part of her self-definition is this rhetoric of non-reading that sometimes it is more important than telling the simple truth: her claim not to have read Bligh's memoirs, for instance, contradicts what she said a few pages before (*DAL* III, p. 246).

However as she grew older Burney came to see liberating ways to use for her own purposes the association of reading with pleasure, assertion and sexual desire. Reading and writing, books and libraries, paper and pens, played key roles in her courtship by Alexandre d'Arblay. He hides love-letters in her books, they exchanged literary gifts of a pen and an escritoire, and he gave her 'long daily lessons in reading' (*JAL* II, pp. 107,

116, 163, 19). Their 'acquaintance began, in intimacy, by reading . . . together', and they are 'united' by shared literary tastes (*JAL* IV, p. 77). In particular, Burney cleverly overcomes family opposition to their match by insisting that d'Arblay was not an outsider but a spiritual member of the Burney reading community. She encouraged her father to lend and give him books (*JAL* III, pp. 5, 16, 36), and repeatedly emphasises that d'Arblay is 'passionately fond of literature', unable to 'stir without a Book in his Hand or his pocket' (*JAL* II, pp. 19, 181). After they married, the emotional centre of their home, paid for from the proceeds of her novel and called Camilla Cottage, is 'the Book Room' (*JAL* IV, p. 62), which they later reconstruct in their Paris lodgings (*JAL* VI, p. 600), and which figures their union.

Hester Thrale thought Burney 'a very desultory reader' (*DAL* I, p. 153). In some respects she is a textbook case, reading all those genres generally recommended to women, conduct and devotional works, history, letters and memoirs, travels, periodical essays. She had a good knowledge of the classic eighteenth-century *belles lettres* – Shakespeare, Swift, Pope, Johnson, *Don Quixote*, the *Spectator* and *Tatler*, the most famous plays. She knew Italian and 'had always loved Reading French' (*JAL* VI, p. 720). As a young woman she wrote that 'I doat on poetry' (*ED* I, p. 213), and she read Pope, Milton, Thomson and Young as well as Whitehead, Samuel Rogers, Anna Letitia Barbauld, Elizabeth Carter and others, probably including the *Lyrical Ballads*.[34] In later life she lost the taste for poetry, though individual poems, like Barbauld's 'Life', retained special meaning for her, but she showed little interest in recent poetry, though she read some Southey (*JAL* IX, p. 450) and was familiar with some Byron poems, probably because of her son's passion for them (*JAL* XI, p. xxiv).

One might have expected Burney, a published novelist, to show more interest than she does in fiction. She shared her family's distrust of novels, and tends to evade the term for her own writing, calling *Camilla* '*sketches of Characters & morals, put in action*, not a Romance' (*JAL* III, p. 117), and *The Wanderer* 'a Work', not 'a Love-tale' (*JAL* VII, p. 104). In youth her 'taste in reading [was] moral and sentimental',[35] a favourite book being Sterne's *Sentimental Journey*, which she had read three times by 1769. She also knew, and was stylistically influenced by, *Tristram Shandy*. (Later she absorbed the dislike of Sterne shown in Elizabeth Montagu's circle.[36]) She knew *Gulliver's Travels* and *Robinson Crusoe*, reread *Don Quixote*, was '*surprised into Tears*' by *The Vicar of Wakefield* although she did not much like it (Troide I, p. 12), and enjoyed *Clarissa* and recommended it to her son. She read some new novels, though not often with approval: she disliked the politics of *Caleb Williams* (*JAL* III, p. 245), was not impressed by Samuel James Arnold's *The Creole*, Lady Morgan's *The Missionary*, Edgeworth's *Patronage*, which she thought 'dull & heavy', or Hannah More's *Coelebs*, which she found 'monotonously without interest of ANY kind', despite her approval of its politics (*JAL* IX, pp. 451–2, X, p. 537). She did however enjoy Charlotte Smith, reading *Celestine* in 1791, by which time she knew, and preferred, *Emmeline* and *Ethelinde* (*JAL* I, p. 26). Fictionality generally disturbed her: she complains that *The Vicar of Wakefield* lacks 'genuine' truth to appeal to her (Troide I, p. 13), and is ambivalent about the Gothic fictionality of Ann Radcliffe (*JAL* III, p. 337). As a novelist with strong reservations about story-telling, Burney's position is a deeply problematic one.

Reading continued to have strong emotional force for Burney, enlivening 'solitary intervals' (*JAL* III, p. 337), but increasingly life confronts her with sorrows that reading cannot salve. She is unable to read during the crisis caused by the madness of George III, or when she learns of the execution of Louis XVI, or when Alex is ill (*DAL* III, p. 85; *JAL* I, p. 8; IV, p. 258). In her last years, she records less reading, in the 1820s lamenting that she has 'totally lost her pleasure in reading . . . I have no longer that resource!' (*JAL* XI, p. 414). She still reads some of Scott's fiction, and corresponds with Benjamin Disraeli about *Contarini Fleming* (*JAL* XI, p. 162; XII, p. 753), but her lack of interest in fiction, indeed in new literature of any kind, prevents some intriguing observations: this predecessor of Jane Austen lived long enough to read *Pickwick Papers*. The last years of her correspondence show little reference to recent books, but much harking back to the favourite reading of her youth, with many references to Pope, *The Rehearsal*, and Shakespeare, especially *Hamlet*, where she poignantly figures herself as the 'Mobbled Queen' Hecuba, widowed and deprived of her children (*JAL* XII, pp. 970, 785–6, 813; XI, pp. 171, 455, 463; XII, p. 723).

ELIZABETH CARTER (1717–1806)

Elizabeth Carter represents a minority but influential model of female authorship at the opposite extreme from Pilkington's scandal chronicle. 'Moral Carter' was a heroine of educationalists, praised in the *Lady's Magazine*, and admired by Richardson, Johnson and Hannah More, who lauded her as an example of both 'profound and various learning' and 'Christian humility'. Indeed it has been argued that she 'established a new image of female "authority"' which was enabling to women writers in modes other than the novel.[37] At the centre of her reputation was the ability to balance learning with domestic virtues – in Johnson's terms to 'make a pudding as well as translate Epictetus' – though Carolyn D. Williams has demonstrated that 'the demands of learning and domestic duty set up tensions which she resolved only partially, and with enormous effort', which is not concealed by her playful appropriation of the metaphor of the pudding in her own writings about writing.[38]

Carter is most famous as a member of the group that has gone down in history as the 'Bluestockings', though to use this term causes more problems than it resolves, for they can hardly be seen as a coherent school with shared projects and a shared programme, or even common attitudes to female reading, as can be seen in Carter's letters to fellow Bluestockings Catherine Talbot, Elizabeth Montagu and Elizabeth Vesey. While Carter presents herself as an advocate of moral and informative reading and an enemy of the indecent, irreligious and politically radical, she creates interestingly different views of herself as reader for her different female correspondents.

Her letters to Catherine Talbot show girlish playfulness, little moralising, and even an amused pleasure in mildly shocking her younger, more timid friend. She claims, for instance, a 'charity to all kinds of books' which allows her to read sympathetically even the scandalous memoirs of Teresia Constantia Phillips (*Series Of Letters* I, p. 307). To Elizabeth Vesey, Carter presents a sterner and more didactic persona, chiding her for unwise reading, warning her against Voltaire and the fashionable but to Carter's mind spurious benevolence of *A Sentimental Journey*, and castigating her for reading the 'licentious profligate' work of Abbé Raynal: ''tis dangerous amusement to a mind like yours, indeed to any mind' (*Series of Letters* II, pp. 166–7; 96–7; 272–3; 394). Carter seems to think that Vesey, the 'Sylph', witty, imaginative, possibly 'irresponsible',[39] needed firm guidance, and so adopts a repressive tone very different from her letters to Talbot. Her correspondence with Elizabeth Montagu also shows anxiety about the dangers of unsuitable reading, and though she does not criticise the reading of Montagu, a married woman and her social superior, she stresses her censorship of her own reading, not only avoiding irreligion and 'indecency', but also requiring more than moral correctness to make her read. She rejects even 'good' books if she finds them tedious or long-winded, finding unreadable Hooker's 'extremely good' *Laws of Ecclesiastical Polity* and the 'very profound learning' of 'Dr Shuckford's Connection' (*Letters . . . to Mrs Montagu* I, p. 49; II, pp. 226, 237).

Carter's most unusual quality as a reader was her expertise in the classical languages: she read widely in Greek including Thucydides and Xenophon, translated Epictetus, and had a good knowledge of Latin literature, with Livy, Cicero and Tacitus being at different times her 'favourite'.[40] However, she was not a slavish admirer of a classical culture of whose masculine bias she was acutely aware. She often writes iconoclastically, regarding Terence, the *Odyssey*, Pindar, Plutarch, Quintilian, Aristotle, Longinus and Lucan as overrated.[41] Indeed, she playfully describes herself as an 'arrant . . . Goth' in aesthetics, defending a female-friendly medieval culture against the 'usurped authority' of the classics.[42] (She was also a resisting reader of some classic English texts, like Pope, whom she 'creatively misread', correcting his deism and misogyny in her own poems.[43]) This alignment positions her not with a male-dominated high culture but with a feminised popular culture, including the Gothic novel (which, as we shall see, she did not despise). It was important to Carter, as to Burney, to emphasise what she shared with other women rather than what separated them.

In the intellectual circles around Carter there was lively debate about how a female reader should deal with questionable texts. In 1760, Mary Delany and Mrs Clayton 'had a furious argument about reading books of a bad tendency', Delany arguing for 'preserving a purity of mind' by not reading, Mrs Clayton for 'trusting to her *own strength* and *reason*'.[44] Carter sided with Delany, Elizabeth Montagu with Clayton. Carter's nephew and editor Montagu Pennington certainly presents her as scrupulously avoiding questionable reading (e.g. *Series of Letters* II, pp. 146, 273). In a letter to Elizabeth Vesey she attacks *A Sentimental Journey*, which 'I neither have read nor probably ever shall; for indeed there is something shocking in whatever I have heard of the author, or of his writings' (*Series of Letters* II, p. 166). Nor will she read Voltaire, Rousseau, or other French sceptics: 'I should as soon think of playing with a toad or a viper, as of reading such blasphemy and impiety' (*Series of Letters* II, pp. 272–3). She began *Candide* but 'threw it aside, and nothing, I believe, will tempt me ever to look into it again' (*Letters . . . to Mrs Montagu* I, p. 49).

The Bluestockings generally disliked Sterne, Rousseau and Voltaire but Carter's self-censorship is extreme. Elizabeth Montagu's circle read Voltaire with interest: although Montagu shared Carter's 'detestation' of *Candide* she read his work 'thoughtfully', and her sister Sarah Scott in a letter makes a playful allusion to the loss of one buttock by Cunégonde's maid.[45] Carter 'thought it tempting Providence to read books of scepticism or infidelity', and 'always refused to read' them,[46] while the more socially confident Montagu believed even bad books might have good uses: the sceptical writing of 'that foul fiend my Lord Bolingbroke' led her back to devout writers Locke and Clarke; and she argued that even Rousseau's *Confessions* had educational uses: 'had I expected such stuff I should not have meddled with the book, but as it gives the strangest specimens of the human kind that ever I was shown I am glad I was not prevented reading it'. But even Montagu's arguments that Carter, 'a pure Virgin',[47] will be able to read his work safely cannot persuade her, since she thinks Rousseau 'the most dangerous writer I ever read', his work 'of so bad a tendency that, after a few trials, I have determined never to look into any thing he should publish' (*Letters . . . to Mrs Montagu* II, p. 268; III, p. 179).

While Carter avoided sceptical and indecent books increasingly as she grew older, she was throughout her life unusually liberal in her views on fiction and ready to admit its recreational and even its moral functions. In 1773 she affectionately described her sister, 'who is sitting at my elbow reading all the novels she can get in the world' (*Letters . . . to Mrs Montagu* I, p. 235), and she seems to value novel-reading partly as a link between herself and other female readers. She shared an enthusiasm for Richardson with other women in her circle, but she also, perhaps surprisingly, admired Fielding, enjoying *Joseph Andrews* and defending Tom Jones as 'no doubt an imperfect, but not a detestable character, with all that honesty, good nature, and generosity of temper'. She accused of 'wrongheadedness and perplexity of understanding' those who believe the novel 'immoral' and 'dangerous'; she even believed Fielding's work superior to the beloved Richardson in its 'natural representation of what passes in the world' (*Series of Letters* I, pp. 16, 207).

Carter and Talbot read fiction and corresponded about it, including *Roderick Random*, the novels of Eliza Haywood, French romances, and Charlotte Lennox's *Henrietta*, in which Talbot finds a number of objectionable qualities including 'irreligion' and the 'pride and sauciness' of the heroine. Their 'favourite' among woman novelists was Sarah Fielding, many of whose works they read and discussed (*Series of Letters* I, pp. 166, 320, 58, 350, 427, 373, 41, 335, 369, 415).

Carter read and enjoyed fiction until the end of her life. Pennington reveals her enthusiasm for a number of novelists 'of considerable genius, as well as strict morals', who provided 'a very pleasing relaxation from her severer studies' (*Letters . . . to Mrs Montagu* I, p. 69). According to him, she disliked realist fiction, though she made an exception for Burney's, which she read 'with increasing approbation more than once': her favourite was *Evelina* (*Memoirs*, p. 299). She also enjoyed Jane West (who dedicated *A Tale of the Times* to her) and Ann Radcliffe, who impressed her, according to Pennington, by 'the good tendency of all her works, the virtues of her principal characters . . . and her accurate, as well as vivid, delineation of the beauties of nature' (*Memoirs*, p. 300). She thought *A Sicilian Romance* 'elegant' and praised its 'good' moral (*Letters . . . to Mrs Montagu* III, p. 323).

Hannah More, who condemned novel-reading, was outraged by Pennington's editing of Carter's letters, complaining that he depicted her as 'a woman of the world', so that 'Every novel-reading Miss will now visit the circulating library with a warrant from Mrs Carter'.[48] Pennington tried to avoid the stereotype of the humourless learned lady, and used her recreational reading to humanise Carter, and yet a modern reader may feel that he tries too hard to stress her moral correctness. He emphasises, for instance, that she 'highly disapproved' the novels of Charlotte Smith, believing their morality 'very defective', if not 'positively bad' (*Memoirs*, p. 299). Carter's letters however show enthusiasm at least for *Emmeline*, and deep sympathy for Smith's domestic situation: she tries hard to be fair even to the 'democratical' *Desmond*, suggesting its critics are 'perhaps prejudiced against it', while she has found the included poems 'very beautiful' (*Letters . . . to Mrs Montagu* III, pp. 295, 333).

The women of Carter's circle were especially interested in reading female writers, Carter having 'an extreme partiality', even a 'decided bias' for 'writers of her own sex', reading their works 'with a mind prepared to be pleased'. She 'felt a kind of triumph' when she discovered the author of the admired *Plays on the Passions* was a woman, Joanna Baillie (*Memoirs*, pp. 303–4, 301), and read 'a system of false philosophy' by Madame de Chatelet 'for no other reason than because it was wrote by a lady' (*Series of Letters* I, p. 144). She also 'worked on behalf of other women writers', despite her limited means subscribing to books by women poets, including Sarah Dixon (1740), Jane Brereton (1744), Mary Jones (1750), Mary Masters (1755) and Anna Williams (1766); her tastes were reasonably robust, too, for she did not share Catherine Talbot's dislike of the Swiftian pastiche in Jones' *Miscellanies in Prose and Verse*.[49] In his discussion of her love for women's writing, Pennington continues to insist on her unimpeachable conservative and moral tastes: his Carter 'detested the principles displayed in Mrs Woolstonecroft's (sic) wild theory concerning the "Rights of Women"', and only approved of women writers whose 'principles were good' and 'personal characters' feminine and 'amiable' (*Memoirs*, p. 304). But Carter's sympathies were wider than it suits her nephew to admit: despite her conservative principles she is sympathetic to women of different views, like Charlotte Smith or Helen Maria Williams, whose books she finds 'too democratical', but still praises as 'exprest with decency and moderation' and 'very prettily written' (*Letters . . . to Mrs Montagu* III, p. 333).

Yet while Carter admires and promotes female talent, she sets high standards of behaviour. In 1775 she admired Catherine Macaulay despite her radical views, having a 'higher opinion of her talents' than Montagu. However as Macaulay's popularity grows, as her friend Dr Wilson set up a statue of her in his church, and as Carter hears about the celebrations for her forth-sixth birthday, she criticises the highly public model of authorship represented by Macaulay, castigating her for lacking 'sober common sense' and 'principles'. As Pennington remarks, this 'language . . . is rather warmer than Mrs Carter generally made use of, except in cases of flagrant vice' (*Letters . . . to Mrs Montagu* II, p. 309; III, pp. 40–1, 98): she is clearly disturbed about a highly visible woman writer transgressing boundaries of modesty and, perhaps, endangering what legitimation had been won by women.

Carter and Talbot read many women letter-writers and autobiographers, and their tastes were wide and unprudish, including the scandalous autobiographies of Phillips, Lady Vane and Laetitia Pilkington as well as the lives of extraordinary women like Mary Wortley Montagu.[50] They were searching not only for female contemporaries but also for their own legitimation through a moral female tradition counter to that of the scandal writers which would vindicate and validate their own literary ambitions. Thus they read and admired the work of Elizabeth Rowe, and questioned each other excitedly about the almost forgotten Katherine Philips, the 'matchless Orinda', impressed that her work is mentioned with 'the highest respect, admiration and reverence by the writers of that time'. Having heard that the work of another virtuous woman writer, Catherine Trotter Cockburn, was to be published, they displayed great interest in this literary foremother, and when the 1751 edition of her work appeared, they were struck by her 'most remarkable clear understanding and an excellent heart' (*Series of Letters* I, pp. 207, 305; 490–2; 219, 242, 279).

JANE AUSTEN (1775–1815)

Although Austen's place in the 'great tradition' of English fiction is more secure than any of her female contemporaries, in her own time she was less influential than Burney, Edgeworth or More, although she was praised by female readers including Anne Grant, Lady Byron, Mary Russell Mitford, Susan Ferrier and Maria Edgeworth. Edgeworth, for instance, used allusions to Austen characters in satirical sketches of acquaintances, and her copy of *Persuasion* survives, with marginal notes approving Anne Elliott's account of the constricting effect of domesticity on the construction of the female subject.[51]

Although Austen was 'no bluestocking', playfully defining herself as 'the most unlearned and uninformed female who ever dared to be an authoress',[52] her letters and the dense allusiveness of her fiction suggest a wide range of 'miscellaneous' reading and a full internalisation of some favourite texts. Her brother thought 'Her reading was very extensive in history and belles lettres', including Shakespeare, Milton, Chaucer, Richardson, Thomson and Locke.[53] As we have seen, she had no high opinion of conduct books, sceptical that 'written material . . . has much power to convert or rectify the individual': her fiction mocks 'the unfeeling pomposity and self-interest of homiletic discourse' which produced Mr Collins and Mary Bennet and the inevitable failure of moral publications to construct the moral reader (Mary Crawford in *Mansfield Park* is an approving reader of Blair's sermons).[54] She read sermons and other religious books, her favourite sermons being 'professedly *practical*', without too much 'Regeneration and Conversion', especially Sherlock's (*Letters*, pp. 252, 467, 406). She also read histories, memoirs and lives, periodical essays, travel books and plays, and was 'well-read in the poetry of her contemporaries'.[55] References to Pope and Johnson are frequent in her letters (*Letters* e.g. pp. 323, 362, 363, 368), and significant allusions to both have been identified in her fiction.[56]

Like many contemporary women, she retained a strong interest in writers of a previous generation and generally resisted male Romanticism, though she read Southey, Byron's *The Corsair*, and Scott, and seems to use Coleridge's newly published 'Kubla Khan' in *Persuasion*. In her fiction, love of Romantic poetry is associated with self-indulgence or false morality: *Persuasion* in particular interrogates male Romanticism in the person of Capt. Benwick, transposing it into a female dialect distinguished by acute but disciplined feelings and self-concealment. Austen's style of 'female Romanticism' depends on resistance to the language of male Romanticism.[57]

She loved Cowper, whom her earliest biographers singled out as a 'favourite'. However, while More's *Coelebs* identifies him with sound religious and moral views, Austen enjoys him but because she identifies him with sensibility rather than sense tends to adopt a self-defensive mockery. She laughs at a relative who 'has more of Cowper than of Johnson in him, fonder of Tame Hares & Blank Verse than of human existence at Charing Cross', and Fanny Price's susceptibility to Cowper dramatises a sensitivity which is not quite immune to humorous undercutting: more seriously, Marianne Dashwood's exaggerated response to Cowper represents the dangers of an uncritical indulgence in emotion.[58] Austen is only a little less mocking toward another favourite poet, the realist Crabbe, whose hold on her imagination she resisted by 'smother[ing him] . . . in jokes', including the long-running family joke that she planned to marry him.[59] If Cowper's presence in Fanny Price's tiny library emphasises her sensibility, Crabbe's stresses her sense (*MP*, ch. 16): and she is a literary daughter of Crabbe in more senses than one, her name being borrowed from a heroine of *The Parish Register*.

Austen was 'a compulsive reader of novels',[60] she and her family 'great Novel-readers and not ashamed of being so' (*Letters*, p. 38). While Burney tried to ensure her respectability by labelling her writing not novels but works or moral tales, Austen directly protested her culture's hypocrisy about novel-reading, attributing it to 'pride, ignorance or fashion'.[61] She consistently satirises those – generally men – who ostentatiously reject fiction, like John Thorpe or Mr Collins, who protests that he 'never read novels', and 'started back' on finding a circulating library book in the Bennet house (*Pride and Prejudice*, p. 113), and she laughs at the mindset that accuses novel-reading of causing a tendency to spout 'unmeaning Gibberish'.[62] Austen read especially novels by women, including Mary Brunton, Frances and Sarah Harriet Burney, Maria Edgeworth, Charlotte Lennox, Lady Morgan, Ann Radcliffe, Regina Maria Roche, Charlotte Smith, Jane West, Laetitia-Matilda Hawkins and Hannah More. She also, apparently, read the fiction of the *Lady's Magazine*, deriving names, Willoughby, Brandon, Knightley, from it but correcting its 'monological' discourse.[63]

She valued verisimilitude in fiction, but still read Radcliffe and Brunton with pleasure, even while laughing at inexperienced readers who take Gothic literally, and at the lack of 'Nature or Probability' in Brunton's *Self-control* (*Letters*, p. 344). She enjoyed comic didactic novels, with Lennox's *The Female Quixote* and Barrett's *The Heroine* being especially admired (*Letters*, pp. 123, 377), both satires on female misreading which shaped her fullest treatment of the subject in *Northanger Abbey*. Her favourite novels included those of Burney, whom she thought 'the very best of English novelists', and of Richardson, especially *Sir Charles*

Grandison. She makes frequent allusion to both, borrowing names from them, employing them to describe characters and situations to her correspondents and allowing fictional characters the same intertextuality, and using them to shape her own fiction. She loved but resisted Richardson, 'tests' him by 'pushing him to absurd extremes' and 'invert[ing] his priorities', while never rejecting his morality or densely verisimilar techniques.[64]

She knew *Evelina* (as did Anne Elliott), and her treatment of Darcy in the early part of *Pride and Prejudice* alludes to, perhaps 'caricature[s]', its hero Orville: Darcy's behaviour at the Meryton ball, when he is heard to criticise Elizabeth Bennet, invokes Orville's response to his first meeting with Evelina, though Austen treats the male mentor/female pupil topos more ironically than Burney. Austen also read *Cecilia*, which was 'an important source', giving her the title for *Pride and Prejudice*: Darcy's first proposal may allude to Mortimer Delville's explanation of why he cannot marry Cecilia. She was also a subscriber to *Camilla*, which remained a favourite, influencing plots from as early as *Sense and Sensibility*. That Catherine Morland has not read *Camilla* tells against her as much as her excessively literal reading of Gothic (though the fact that she finds *Grandison* 'very entertaining' proves she is reformable).[65]

For Austen Burney's fiction figures not only the aesthetic but the moral authority of fiction. In *Sanditon*, Charlotte is tempted to overspend on trivia at the circulating library cum trinket shop: but 'She took up a Book; it happened to be a vol: of *Camilla*', and thinking of the financial embarrassments suffered by Burney's heroine strengthens her resolve to be more careful with her own money (*MW*, p. 390). In this instance Austen demonstrates the moral usefulness of fiction in the education of the woman reader, and Charlotte's reading is sharply contrasted with the irresponsible reading practices of Denham.

Austen read and enjoyed not only the realist-didactic fiction she tends to praise but also Gothic and sentimental fiction, though she protects herself with humour from their hold on her imagination. Mrs Sykes' Minerva Press novel *Margiana, or Widdrington Tower* (1808) gains tongue-in-cheek applause for 'two or three sets of victims already immured under a very fine villain', and she reports reading the novels of Lady Morgan in cold weather, and wishing that the 'warmth of [the] Language' could literally 'affect the Body', as anti-novel moralists argued (*Letters*, pp. 248, 251). Here, as in *Northanger Abbey* where she defines novel-writers and readers as 'an injured body', Austen shows her awareness of the cultural politics that presented women's reading as a physical, and therefore dangerous, act, and resists it through humour.[66]

While Austen mocks Gothic and sentimental novels, she still read, enjoyed and remembered them: the name Charles Bingley is, for instance, borrowed from Roche's *The Children of the Abbey*, and she tendered an 'ambiguous tribute' to Radcliffe. A youthful enthusiasm for Charlotte Smith's novels, especially *Emmeline*, is clear from her juvenilia, where Smith's Delamere is comically intruded as a model of heroic masculinity into 'The History of England', and from other works.[67] In 'Catharine, or the Bower', a prototype for *Northanger Abbey*, the heroine is a 'great reader' who dislikes her aunt's choice of moral works but is a devotee of 'Mrs Smith's Novels'. Her sensible new acquaintance Camilla Stanley, whose name conflates Burney and More heroines, shows her incompatibility with her romantic friend by her inability sufficiently to prize Smith (*MW*, pp. 198, 232, 199).

Austen disliked 'indelicacies' in fiction: she is 'disgusted' by Genlis' *Alphonsine*, and after twenty pages returns the book to the library and takes out an old favourite, *The Female Quixote* instead (*Letters*, p. 173). But her weapon against indelicacy is not outraged virtue or moralising but mockery. She shows discomfort about the morality of Goethe, for instance, only by making Laura, the outrageous anti-heroine of 'Love and Freindship', criticise a 'Sensible, well-informed, and Agreeable' young man simply because 'he had never read the Sorrows of Werter' (*MW*, p. 93). Although Austen believes in the difference between good and bad books, she does not advocate a *Coeleb*esque patriarchal control over female reading. Catherine Morland must learn to read correctly, not accept her father's or husband-to-be's injunctions not to read novels; and in 'Catharine, or the Bower', Austen laughs at Mrs Percival's doomed attempts to limit her niece's reading to 'Blair's Sermons, and Coelebs in Search of a Wife' (*MW*, p. 232). In any case, the heroine's reading practices are generally superior to those found elsewhere in the patriarchal family, as with Fanny Price or Anne Elliott, rendering patriarchal control ironically misplaced.

Reading is important in Austen's fiction as allusion, as symbol, as verisimilar detail, and as means of characterisation. It has ramifications both political and moral, functioning as a vehicle for discussing 'the problem of mediating self and society within a professional middle-class culture'.[68] She constantly makes reading practices revealing of character. Emma devises improving reading-lists but is never seen reading anything more challenging than a riddle or the letters in a word-game (although she obviously does read, and her reading feeds her fantasy life, as she reads Jane Fairfax's situation through allusions to *Romeo and Juliet* and *A Midsummer Night's Dream*[69]). Austen's ideal female character is literate – Lady Middleton in *Sense and Sensibility* is mocked for assuming that because the Dashwood sisters were 'fond of reading' they must be unfemininely 'satirical' (p. 246) – but not too bookish, for reading might represent 'a withdrawal from a woman's proper social concerns': Mrs Musgrove in *Persuasion* is obliquely criticised because she is unable to take care of Louisa after her accident but instead gets 'books from the library and changed them . . . often'.[70]

Books and reading, and their misuse, are, then, crucial motifs. Female misreading may become a central issue, especially in the early work, like *Northanger Abbey* and *Sense and Sensibility*, but in her later novels Austen unusually focuses on male misreading rather than female, for the mis-shaping of male authority has potentially serious consequences in the family and society. Male misreading and its relation to a failure of male authority is especially prominent in *Persuasion*, whose men are guilty of misreading not only books but women. The novel even begins with an act of faulty male reading, as Sir Walter Elliott is shown with the only book he ever reads for his own amusement, the Baronetage. This reading dramatises his snobbishness and superficiality, as does the way he generates allusions to Chesterfield's *Letters*: indeed the novel has been seen as a 'satire' on the aristocratic and misogynist ideology promulgated by Chesterfield.[71]

Men in *Persuasion* are the 'only people . . . who have satisying relations to books' because they can read themselves and 'their own place in national history' in the Baronetage or navy lists. The novel works, though, to unsettle their confidence in the authority of a male-authored, male-centred textuality, not only presenting 'an indictment of a masculine literary tradition'[72] but also suggesting substitutes for that tradition or new ways of reading it. Men are able to enjoy an untroubled relation to textuality because 'the pen has been in their hands', but the novel not only enacts a feminised control of fiction but also praises other women writers like Burney (p. 234): for Anne Elliot, there is a 'bond between emotional maturation and reading', which implies the superiority of female over male reading practices. The novel uses male-authored intertexts to unsettle rather than confirm masculine authority. The *Rape of the Lock* is quoted, for instance, to apply to Sir Walter the narcissism of Belinda:[73] the result is to undercut not only the male character but also the authority of the male author, who is by implication accused of misogynist bias. Moreover, *Persuasion* reverses the male mentor–female pupil relationship of a novel like *Evelina* around the issue of male misreading. The 'dejected, thinking, feeling, reading Captain Benwick' (p. 135) feeds his grief with Romantic poetry, especially Scott and Byron, while the rational Anne recommends 'a larger allowance of prose', and in particular moralists, letters and memoirs (ch. 11). Male Romanticism is self-indulgent, as the male satire of the eighteenth century is biased, and both male author and male reader are implicated. The novel may end 'with quotations from Shakespeare and Richardson' which reassert male literary authority, but this is done in a wittily equivocal way since these quotations praise female constancy, and the evocation of the debate between the transvestite Viola and Orsino in *Twelfth Night* complicates gender distinctions. Jocelyn Harris sees Austen's relations to male literary authority as that of a dutiful daughter, abrogating a Bloomian anxiety of influence and displaying a confidence in her 'affiliative relation to a loved literary past':[74] but *Persuasion* at least suggests that her intertextual practices are more rebellious than this recognises.

Austen's fullest portrait of a male misreader is Sir Edward Denham in the unfinished *Sanditon*. Like Benwick a devotee of Romantic poetry, Denham is a flawed 'Man of Feeling' (*MW*, p. 396), enthusiastic in his praise of Burns, Wordsworth, Campbell and Scott (though the latter is criticised for 'want of Passion'). Denham values 'illimitable Ardour', and regards as prudish 'Pseudo-philosophy' Charlotte's moral reservations about male Romanticism. For him 'high toned Genius' absolves a man from the need to keep conventional moral rules, the 'grovellings of a common mind' (*MW*, pp. 397, 398): he anticipates, in fact, the arguments of Moore's life of Byron.[75] Like Austen's most criticised misreaders, he despises novels, liking only those which vindicate a sensibility too acute to be controlled: he thus misreads *Clarissa*, identifying with Lovelace and deriving 'only false Principles from Lessons of Morality, & incentives to Vice from the History of it's Overthrow' (*MW*, pp. 404–5).

While it is still sometimes claimed that Austen is essentially '[u]npolitical', most recent commentators have seen her as very much involved in the 'War of Ideas' of the 1790s and its reactionary aftermath, though they have disagreed fundamentally over whether her political allegiances are strongly conservative (Marilyn Butler), radical especially in an espousal of Wollstonecraftian feminism (Margaret Kirkham), or superficially compliant to conservative tradition while covertly expressing a subversive anger (Gilbert and Gubar).[76] Austen is certainly indirect and evasive in her engagement with political issues, though 'in the

Revolutionary aftermath . . . this could be another way of being political'.[77] Uncertainty on these vital issues is unlikely to be resolved without new evidence, and the most hopeful source of this is an ever closer and more nuanced understanding of Austen's intertextual practices: 'Imitation is . . . not repetition, but the completion of an act of interpretation',[78] and to understand how Austen reads predecessors and contemporaries will be to understand a good deal about her opinions and achievement.

Austen is a resisting reader first and foremost, reading against the grain and interrogating concepts of literary authority. Particularly, though not exclusively, in her juvenilia, the most obvious form of resisting reading is parody, a favourite parodic form being miniaturisation, as in her tiny 'History of England' which parodies Goldsmith's four-volume work, or her dramatic abridgement of *Sir Charles Grandison*, where the 'essence of the joke is the reduction of a mammoth novel to a miniature play'. Parodies are 'acknowledgements of respect, as well as acts of criticism', and the play of *Sir Charles Grandison* is both 'a tribute' to and 'a skit' of a favourite novel.[79]

Her 'History of England', written when she was sixteen, is a funny but serious interrogation of the dominance of history in women's education, the lack of objectivity of male historians, the fact that history may be no more than a 'convenient fiction', and history's exclusion of women. It not only recklessly and hilariously reveals ignorance and prejudice (like a marginal note in her copy of Goldsmith's *History* it reveals a shameless partisanship for the Stuarts), it also more seriously enacts 'a series of refusals', of assumptions about the 'rationality of history and historians' and of the 'transparency of historical narrative' for instance, and protests about history's entry to high culture while the (feminised) narratives of fiction are excluded.[80]

In her mature fiction her intertextual strategies become more complex and subtle. It is demonstrable from her borrowings that she knew the key novels of the conservative reaction, More's *Coelebs*, Jane West's *A Gossip's Story*, Elizabeth Hamilton's *Memoirs of Modern Philosophers*, Opie's *Adeline Mowbray*. The episode in *Pride and Prejudice* where Miss Bingley criticises Elizabeth Bennet for walking to visit her sick sister and arriving with muddy petticoats, alludes to an incident in *Memoirs of Modern Philosophers* centred on Bridgetina Botherim. In both cases, the issue is 'the unseemliness of female "energy"', a much-debated word in the controversy around Godwin's *Political Justice*; but Bridgetina Botherim is clearly convicted of transgressive self-assertion, while Elizabeth's energetic enactment of sisterly affection is sympathetically presented. Later in the same novel, when Lady Catherine de Bourgh 'attempts to discredit' Elizabeth by asking her age, Austen 'reconfigure[s]' an episode in *Adeline Mowbray*, where Dr Norberry, 'the novel's moral guide', reveals the immaturity of Adeline's revolutionary politics by asking her age.[81] Again, the moral authority of the conservative text is challenged, its insistence on the rightness of the status quo interrogated.

Austen's reading of these conservative texts goes to correct what she must have seen as their artistic faults, the palpable design of political novels and their tendency to mechanistic planning and melodramatic excess. Her reading of *A Gossip's Story* in *Sense and Sensibility*[82] edits out West's melodramatic exaggeration, translates her political and social monsters into believable human beings, and avoids tragedy. But Austen's revision might mark political as well as aesthetic priorities. If in conservative fiction sensibility figures commitment to a self-assertive and even revolutionary agenda, Austen's more sympathetic treatment of Marianne – whose sensibility is 'never really scorned, or even fully dismissed', unlike West's similarly named character[83] – may mark her as a resistant reader of the texts of reactionary conservatism.

Austen's reading of More's *Coelebs in Search of a Wife* also demonstrates resistance to the texts of conservatism. As her letters show, Austen disliked the idea of this novel from the start, and her revision of 'Catharine, or the Bower' adds it as a comic example of Mrs Percival's futile attempt to control her niece's reading. *Mansfield Park* and *Emma* may also offer resisting readings of *Coelebs*. In *Emma*, More's conviction that female subordination and silence will 'pay off in the end' is subverted and reversed.[84] It has been argued that 'Hannah More is at the centre of *Mansfield Park*', a novel functioning as a 'serious challenge' to *Coelebs*, correcting its 'internal contradictions', More's 'failure to take into account' the complexity of real relationships, and the ideology of female silence which is central to her characterisation of the heroine. Mary Waldron lists Austen's probable allusions to More, and argues that Austen challenges Fanny's 'silence, the approved female virtue' as at best 'impotent' to effect moral change. The evidence suggests that *Mansfield Park* is not intractably committed to conservative ideology but is a novel which 'tests the parameters of conservative mythology', even a 'bitter parody of conservative fiction'.[85]

While resisting, critical, even parodic readings of conservative novels can be discerned even in Austen's mature work, it is difficult to claim more because as yet critics have failed convincingly to identify a balancing radical intertextuality. While Edgeworth's *Belinda* and Burney's *The Wanderer* include explicit critical pictures of the female reader of Mary Wollstonecraft, Austen does not, and indeed seems to make no direct references to Wollstonecraft, Robinson or Hays (although her sister-in-law owned a set of Hays' *Female Biography*), or to use their novels to shape her own as she does West's or More's. Critics who have claimed Austen as 'a committed disciple of Wollstonecraft's teaching' who frequently quotes the *Vindication* have yet to prove their case.[86] It is not clear whether one should conclude from this aporia that Austen takes it as self-evident that radical texts require no serious rebuttal, or that her failure to attack them suggests a covert sympathy with their aims. At present, without further evidence for Austen's reading of the radicals, we can only note her critical revisions of the aesthetics and politics of reaction. To date, Claudia Johnson's Austen, neither a doctrinaire radical nor a dyed-in-the-wool reactionary, but a sometimes ambivalent 'progressive' aiming to 'defend and enlarge a liberal middle ground' by 'interrogating the political mythology of reaction',[87] is the most convincing in the light of her intertextual practices and her treatments of reading and literary authority.

CONCLUSIONS

These case histories reveal the importance in women's lives of reading, how reading permits critical engagement with issues of authority, and the variety of forms that the coexistence of reading pleasure and anxiety could take. Laetitia Pilkington figures reading as sexual pleasure, which proves to be morally disturbing but potentially empowering. Frances Burney resists this association, and finds alternatives which include an exaggerated rhetoric of denial and absence. Elizabeth Carter both claims a place within a male-centred culture and criticises that culture, identifying herself both with a classical gynephobic and a modern gynocentric literature. Finally Jane Austen, although an admirer of Burney's fiction, shows none of Burney's anxiety about reading and confidently assumes its relations with both pleasure and power, using it as a vehicle to claim and to challenge cultural authority.

CHAPTER 5

Where and how should women read?

It was not enough to read the right books: they had to be read in the right manner, the right company and the right places. In this chapter I deal with two revealing side-issues. First I examine libraries as gendered spaces and library-use as a gendered practice, for libraries offer a clear example of the consequences of perceived gender-differences in literacy and culture. The private library tended to be seen as a masculine space, even a symbol of male power and rationality, while the commercial library (the 'circulating library' which the literature so often denounces) was perceived, apparently in defiance of historical reality, as a female-dominated space representing both second-rate literature and transgressive sexuality. Libraries became a contested space.

Secondly I explore the different significances for women of reading silently and reading aloud. Roger Chartier finds this distinction one of the 'fundamental oppositions' of our culture, with the movement from reading aloud to reading silently a 'macroscopic' historical change. '[S]olitary' and 'silent' reading was potentially rebellious or self-indulgent, while reading aloud formed the 'bond and expression of social ties'[1] and was especially appropriate for women within domestic ideology.

THE REALM OF THE FATHER: PRIVATE LIBRARIES, GENDER AND POWER

By the mid eighteenth century the private library had become a 'major feature of the rebuilding projects of noble families'. Darcy feels it a duty to future generations to maintain the fine library at Pemberley, and Sir Charles Grandison also has a remarkable library. The trend also began to spread downwards to the middle classes,[2] a visible sign of class and economic as of gender privilege. Stories in the *Lady's Magazine*, a publication most read by lower-middle-class women, repeatedly offer utopian images of lower-class girls who visit country houses and are allowed to participate in an elite-class lifestyle whose most appealing feature is ready access to books: sometimes they are able through their literacy to prove their right to join the library-owning classes by marrying the son of the house.[3]

Despite the growing importance of the private library, its history is hard to write: even in the clearest case, a man like Samuel Pepys who bequeathed his library to his Cambridge college, Magdalen, where it remains as a unit, we know he owned books which did not become part of the library (like the obscene *L'escholle des filles* which he bought and read, but destroyed out of guilt[4]). Following the fortunes of women's libraries is still more problematic since few women had independent libraries of their own, though they might have access to those of fathers, husbands, or sons. Where this is so it is usually impossible to be confident which books reflect her taste rather than his. A few wealthy women who were widowed or separated did have their own libraries, and the literary tastes of Mary Wortley Montagu, Hester Thrale or Elizabeth Vesey can be gauged from surviving evidence about their libraries.[5] It was expected that a young middle-class woman would accumulate books of her own, as the instructions offered by writers like Addison and Vicesimus Knox demonstrate, but what is intended is a library in the sense of a number of books rather than a private space where they can be enjoyed. Austen, and probably other women writers, had 'no separate study to retire to',[6] for a room of one's own offered independence and withdrawal from domestic society that was incompatible with women's role. Mary Wortley Montagu believed even in the highest classes it was unusual for a woman to own her own library, naming Lady Isabella Finch as the 'only Lady at Court' who did.[7]

Private libraries, indeed, often specifically figure patriarchal power. In Mary Shelley's *Falkner*, Falkner visits Oswi Raby to persuade him to acknowledge Elizabeth, the angelic granddaughter he rejects because of her father's unfortunate marriage, and meets him in a 'library of vast proportions . . . very imposing, but very sombre'. It is the only scene where Raby appears, and his library defines the desiccated patriarch, 'shrivelled . . . by . . . the narrowness of his mind' (p. 140). Books, it will be noted, do not feature in the description of the space designed for their enjoyment, a space which reflects Raby's anachronistic and snobbish values. The scene confirms Elizabeth as the true child not of Raby but of Falkner who has adopted her and educated her. The private library is here identified only with outmoded forms of authority (also figured by Raby's Anglo-Saxon forename and Roman Catholicism).

The genteel library services patriarchy by protecting men from women. In Elizabeth Blower's *Maria*, Dr Edgeware 'withdrew to his library' to escape his ill-tempered sister (I, p. 81), and Mr Bennet's library in *Pride and Prejudice* provides an escape from a female-dominated domestic world. In particular the genteel library symbolises the superiority of male rationality over female passion and the unruly female body: in Roche's *The Nocturnal Visit* (1800) Greville is 'reading' when his friend Netley tells him that Miss Barclay loves him: but he is warned of her 'Treachery' in a letter, and hiding in her 'reading-closet' discovers she only wants to marry him because she is already pregnant by Netley (pp. 42–6). In Edgeworth's *The Absentee* (1812) Lord Colambre, 'sitting in one of the recesses' of the library, hears Lady Isabella, unaware of his presence, revealing that her 'soft, gentle, amiable' appearance hides an 'evil spirit': he is thus enabled to curb his growing love for her.[8]

However, in novels by women, the male authority and rationality figured by the library is likely to have a marked dark side, which becomes explicit in Gothic fiction. In Eliza Parsons' *The Mysterious Warning* (1796) Baron S- keeps in the library the keys of the cell in which he has imprisoned his wife, and in the same author's *The Castle of Wolfenbach* (1793), as in Catherine Cuthbertson's *The Romance of the Pyrenees*, the library contains the entrance to a secret passage, which plays a significant role in the victimisation of the heroines.[9] In Gothic fiction such images powerfully express women's anxieties about male domination of culture and what might really lie behind the surface of a male-identified rationality.

In Gothic fiction the ruined library recurs as a potent symbol for the bankruptcy of male authority and literary culture. In Shelley's *The Last Man* (1826), the hero journeys to Rome, where in an abandoned library he finds manuscripts 'scattered about': the inability of an author to find readers becomes the most poignant manifestation of the end of humanity. In Sophia Troughton's 'Sketches from Nature' (1808–9), a ruined Gothic library containing a 'few books, in old English'[10] symbolises Walsingham's broken marriage-vows. The ruined library is a particularly significant image for the bankruptcy of male-dominated culture in Charlotte Smith's novels. Althea in *Marchmont*, Monimia in *The Old Manor House*, and the heroine of *Emmeline* all find themselves in semi-ruinous libraries. The last, for instance, educates and entertains herself in a library 'in the most deserted part' of the castle, which serves as an evocative woman's-eye symbol for androcentric literary culture, 'injured by time . . . almost effaced by mould': here she reads Spenser,

Milton, the *Spectator*, Shakespeare, 'an odd volume or two' of Pope, and 'some tracts of devotion' (pp. 7–8).

Even in non-Gothic writing, libraries are associated with male privilege and female confinement and deprivation. Susan Sibbald's father has 'Romances' and 'novels' in 'his library', which his daughters long to read, but he forbids access, and the girls must get books from the circulating library: Emma Courtney's father keeps the cases in his library 'locked' so as to control his daughter's access. (Keeping library cases locked was the practice in reality as well as fiction, a sign of the expensiveness of books and the prestige access to them conferred. Lady Louisa Stuart, for instance, laments the 'grievous misfortune' of 'breaking the key to the library, and as every press has been carefully locked fast, we must bid farewell to the books'. Tensions 'between the encouragement and fear of reading' are everywhere apparent in representations of the private library, nowhere more obviously than when gender is an issue.[11])

The private library figures male power, especially patriarchal authority over the sex-lives of women and younger men. In Edgeworth's *Helen* the General questions Helen in the library over indiscreet letters of which he believes she is the author (p. 288). Interviews between fathers and sons or prospective sons-in-law about marriage routinely take place in libraries. In Roche's *The Nocturnal Visit*, Mr Frankland takes Egbert Oswald into his library to ask his intentions toward Jacintha Greville, and Oswald takes Mr Greville 'to his library' to ask for his daughter's hand (I, pp. 25, 155). The power figured by such libraries is often, however, presented critically. In Eliza Fenwick's *Secresy*, Valmont cruelly manipulates his foster-children Sibella and Montgomery in the library, introducing them there and later forbidding any relationship but a fraternal one.[12] Such motifs readily became part of the symbolic vocabulary of magazine fiction. In 'The History of Augustus Pembroke and Miss Woodley' Charles Campley's father threatens in the library to disinherit him if he will not marry according to his dictates; in 'The Inconsistent Father' Mr Webster, who 'spent much of his time in the library' studying philosophy, acts in a tragically unphilosophical way by forcing his daughter to marry a man she dislikes; and in 'Virtuous Love Rewarded' Adolphus' father castigates him in the 'library' for being unwilling to marry his choice, preferring Clementina whom he has seen 'busily employed in reading'.[13]

The private library also serves as a site for eroticism, using the identification of textuality and sexuality I have outlined. However it is notable that relationships in which private libraries, symbols of male power and rationality, are prominent, tend to be painful for the woman. In Caroline Lamb's *Glenarvon* (1816), the dangerous attraction between Calantha and the Byronic anti-hero first becomes explicit in the library: 'he leant over her; she held a book in her hand; he read a few lines . . . Calantha looked up; he fixed his eyes on hers . . .' (II, p. 153). In Hays' *Emma Courtney* the library is the central locus of the heroine's troubled relationship with Augustus Harley (e.g. p. 80): in a crucial episode they spend the night together in the library during a storm, which externalises the 'cruel conflict' in Emma's mind (p. 161).

In Amelia Opie's *Madeline* (1822), the difficult relationship between the heroine and her lover is played out over books and his library. She is 'a woman of intellectual superiority', educated by gentry friends in London although she is only a Scots cottager's daughter. She loves reading, especially poetry, and when she returns home a major difficulty is how to obtain books. The Laird of Glencarron, the local landowner, offers her the 'key of his library' and 'unlimited power' over his books, and is resentful when she is offered books by other men.[14] Her parents readily discern the coded meaning of the library key, and fear he means to seduce her. Instead he persuades her to a secret marriage, and although the conclusion is ultimately happy, the power imbalance represented by his library allows him to conceal the marriage and inflict protracted ill-treatment on her, while she suffers agonies of doubt and guilt before their problems are resolved.

A similar scenario occurs in less sinister register in Roche's *The Children of the Abbey*. Amanda is staying in a cottage with her old nurse, for 'Peculiar circumstances had driven her from the shelter of a parent's arms', and she has 'lost all her books' (I, pp. 8, 64). Her nurse manages to procure her access to the library at Tudor Hall, and Lord Mortimer meets her in the library and encourages her to use it. By reading his books she discovers that Mortimer is the son of her father's friend, and by falling in love with her over the books Mortimer repeats the circumstances of her parents' courtship and so demonstrates the legitimacy of his love (I, pp. 97, 34). The economic anxieties faced by women in Roche's novels are often expressed through the desire for books and the difficulty of obtaining them, and books repeatedly give Amanda a coded language for revealing or concealing emotion.[15] While in *Madeline* the male power figured by the library causes the heroine so much pain that the happy ending hardly atones, in Roche's more utopian vision the inequalities which the library figures at the beginning of the novel are largely removed by the end. Amanda regains the status and money she is entitled to as the granddaughter of an earl, and Mortimer loses his money so that his 'title' becomes an 'empty one' (IV, p. 253). Perhaps Amanda will help to choose the books in their new, more equal relationship.

Books, reading and libraries are vital elements in a war of the sexes for power and love in Elizabeth Inchbald's *A Simple Story* (1791).[16] In the first generation, men use books and libraries as emotional barriers: Sandford reads at meals and in uncongenial company (pp. 225, 263), and at moments of tension Dorriforth 'take[s] up a pamphlet and affect[s] to read' (pp. 26–7). Miss Milner, intelligent, playful, and willful, uses books, as she uses masquerade costume, to assert her control over her identity and to further her power-struggle with her foster-father and later husband Dorriforth. At an auction she buys 'a lot of books on chemistry, and some Latin authors', although she 'can't read a word' and cares only 'how elegantly they are bound' (p. 125): for her, books are part of a dream of conspicuous consumption and female participation in male cultural authority. Her concern for appearance rather than truth predicts the breakdown of her marriage. In the lives of Dorriforth and his daughter books and libraries are revised to symbolise a female emotion now seen as positive, and to allow the men to express not conceal emotion. This is possible because, by correcting her mother's reading crimes, Matilda regains Dorriforth's affection. She can develop a relationship with the father who refuses to see her only by borrowing books from his library (p. 203), and when he decides he has treated her too harshly, the first manifestation is his supervising her choice of books. In his library Dorriforth questions Rushbrook about his love for Matilda (pp. 236, 292), and Rushbrook, having confessed his love for Matilda, is sent to the library to await his fate. Dorriforth intends to dismiss him, but when he sees Matilda, 'who was arranging her music books' (p. 293), weep, she too is sent to the library, now revised as a place of emotional frankness rather than concealment. Matilda's relationships with both father and lover can now be reinforced. In this novel Inchbald both uses and interrogates the identification of the private library with patriarchal power.

If private libraries figure male authority, it can be seen why women's ownership might give rise to anxiety. Bridgetina Botherim's library in Hamilton's *Memoirs of Modern Philosophers* expresses her lack of intelligence, for without going there to 'study for the discourse of the evening' (I, p. 184) she is unable to 'say three sentences upon any given subject' (II,

p. 56). In Lennox's *The Life of Harriot Stuart* (1751), the heroine, alone and without resources in England, meets Lady Cecilia, 'a lady of great distinction about court, remarkable for the brilliancy of her wit, and her taste for the Belles-Lettres' (I, pp, 233–4), who promises her support. Harriot is 'prodigiously struck' by her 'library . . . The number of books of which it was composed, gave me a very advantageous idea of a lady, who could be at such an expense to furnish herself with intellectual entertainments' (I, p. 238). This library, though, like Miss Milner's choice of books, indicates false 'appearances' (II, p. 16) rather than true intellect. The library-owning lady offers no help, and quickly turns against the genuinely accomplished Harriot, affecting to believe, when Harriot is almost raped, that she was the aggressor, and displaying a 'tempest of rage' when she tries to vindicate herself (II, p. 53). It is obvious why Mary Wortley Montagu resented this portrait of her friend Lady Isabella Finch, for library ownership figures hypocrisy, selfishness and transgressive sexuality (Lady Cecilia has a taste for young lower-class men, and accuses Harriot of sexual misdemeanours to conceal her own greater guilt). If these were the subtextual meanings of female library-owning, it is clear why women tended to avoid the word 'library', often preferring more modest terms like 'closet', 'reading closet', or 'Book-room'.[17]

In dysfunctional families like the Bennets', Valmont's or Dorriforth's, the library aggressively figures male power, and many women writers mock this power through misuses of the private library, often veiling their attacks as criticism of illiterate aristocrats or ostentatious parvenus. Many aristocrats, like Sir William in *A Tale of the Times*, have 'lofty and extensive' libraries where 'the multitude of busts, models, and statues left no space for books' (I, p. 68). Hawkins' *The Countess and Gertrude* repeatedly contrasts the impecunious heroine's longing for books with misuses of books and libraries: noblemen buy books by the 'twelve-inch rule', or even display 'wooden editions' only for interior decoration (III, p. 284; I, pp. 129–31). In Burney's *Cecilia* Mr Harrel and his wife, in 'his library' (p. 73) planning to build an expensive private theatre, are too caught up in an unrealistic dream of conspicuous consumption to pay their debts, and in Bennett's *The Beggar Girl and her Benefactors* the Wouldbes reveal their failure to understand polite culture by having 'a large well-chosen library . . . converted into a theatre' (IV, pp. 158–9).

However, in the course of the period the genteel library ceased to be seen primarily as symbolic of male power and became instead an image of domesticity, a 'family space'. *A Simple Story* could be seen as dramatising and negotiating a historical shift from the private library as the preserve of the male to the private library as a shared domestic space where power and pleasure can be more evenly distributed. Maria Edgeworth especially depicts the genteel library as a democratised space where families and friends meet to talk or share reading. Visiting the family of economist David Ricardo, Edgeworth instantly notices the 'family party – books open on the table', and is pleased to find an 'excellent library and . . . books in every sitting room', which she decodes as evidence of the family's 'affection and openness and hospitality': the walls of the private library with its embodiment of male authority have dissolved, and the domestic space itself has become coterminous with, and undistinguishable from, the library. Edgeworth contrasts the literate and domestic Ricardos with the superficially elegant Carrington family, whose lack of shared literacy provokes her to punish them with literary allusions, especially to *Mansfield Park, Emma* and *Persuasion*. Such imagery is also vital in Edgeworth's fiction. The Percy library in *Patronage* is a place the family 'all loved so much' (p. 66), and in *Helen* the heroine meets her mentor Lady Davenant 'in the library', which is equipped with books which give 'an idea of the range and variety of the [female] reader's mind' (p. 18).[18]

In some utopian examples, a library figures revised and democratised heterosexual relations, or even resistance to compulsory heterosexuality. In Frances Brooke's *History of Emily Montague* the heroine after marriage will retain a room of her own, a 'closet of books' into which even her husband 'will never intrude', for we all need 'some place which . . . is peculiarly our own' where 'we can retire even from those most dear to us' (p. 262). In utopian novels like Scott's *Millenium Hall* and Lady Mary Hamilton's *Munster Village* books and libraries are central, indeed an 'emblem' of their revisionist female-friendly societies.[19] Many accounts of visits to the Ladies of Llangollen make special mention of their 'charming' library, which becomes symbolic of their freedom from the constraints of fathers or husbands and the joys of female friendship. Shared reading was a vital element in the relationship of Eleanor Butler and Sarah Ponsonby ('they were always reading'): in three months in 1789 they read eighty-two volumes, in English, French and Italian.[20] The heroine of the *Lady's Magazine*'s 'Matilda: or, the female Recluse', probably in allusion to the Ladies, sets up a similar utopian home. Having discovered that the man who courts her cares only for her money, she retires from the world to a house in a romantic spot. Heavy emphasis falls on the library, where 'she intended to spend the greatest part of her time' and which is 'well stocked with an excellent collection of the best authors' as well as china, flowers, and busts of great contemporaries, 'an equal number of both sexes'. Here she lives 'perfectly contented' with 'one constant, one unalterable friend . . . They live in one house – they know but one purse – they possess but one heart' (10, 1779, p. 203).

NEGOTIATING THE PUBLIC–PRIVATE DIVIDE: ALTERNATIVES TO THE PRIVATE LIBRARY

Eighteenth-century Britain experienced a 'library revolution',[21] with the rise not only of private aristocratic and genteel libraries but also of library societies, reading clubs, civic libraries, early public libraries and commercial libraries. Subscription libraries, in which a number of 'proprietors' pooled resources and took joint decisions about purchases, book clubs, and civic and parochial libraries offered a compromise space between the private library and the dangerous public space of the circulating library, which was attractive to women readers. Charlotte and Harriet Grove were, for instance, members of the Book Society of Yeovil, of which Harriet was president in 1823, and also of the Salisbury Reading Society, borrowing Stukeley's *Avebury* in 1822.[22]

The Bristol Library Association was founded in 1773 (its registers of borrowings survive and are an important resource) and the London Library Society in 1785, and Liverpool, Leeds and Birmingham also had early subscription libraries. One aim of such libraries was to counteract the allegedly malign influence of the circulating library while still allowing for recreational reading: in the stock of the Leeds Library Society 35 per cent of the total stock was imaginative literature, with 64 per cent devoted to biography, history, commerce, law and politics, geography and the sciences. Cathedral libraries sometimes allowed borrowing by outsiders, by 1804 at least one dissenting temple kept a 'Circulating library' of respectable books to counter the threat of novels, from 1737 Shrewsbury School library allowed outsiders to borrow books, an extraordinary library for working-class readers was founded at Innerpeffray in 1680 and survived throughout the period, and in smaller communities informal schemes of lending and borrowing were often implemented.[23]

The evidence suggests that women used all these semi-private, pseudo-genteel libraries or borrowing networks, although they generally constituted a small proportion of all readers. In 1782 only four of a membership of 137 of the Bristol Library Society were women, and by 1796 this had risen only to five, although membership had increased to 198. In 1798 Birmingham Library had thirty-two women readers out of 459, and in 1760 Liverpool had six female readers out of 140, though by the end of the century they boasted a membership of 950 including 'many ladies', one of whom, Miss Twentyman, had been a member for seventy-eight years![24] Women also borrowed from cathedral, school and parochial libraries: the parochial library at Witham, Essex, had a 'unique proportion of women readers', thirty-three out of fifty-seven borrowers being women.[25]

The ambiguously pseudo-private space of such libraries provided opportunities for women that were not only cultural. Anne Lister, for instance, regularly visited the library at Halifax: it was a vital resource, meeting enough of her literary needs for her to refuse to subscribe to another 'book society' in 1821. (It was still not perfect, and she complains about insensitive refurbishment in 1818, and of its failure to stock Byron's poems.) The library was not only, however, a cultural but an erotic resource: it was one of the few quasi-public places where respectable women could go alone, and lesbian Lister often used it as a meeting-place with the women she was in love with, Elizabeth Brown or M- .[26]

Women joined book clubs and reading circles, informal or more formally constituted. Eugenia de Acton, born in 1749, records that in her youth 'reading assemblies were much in vogue amongst young people of both sexes', in which books 'of various descriptions' were read aloud, and each member was requested to 'give some opinion of what had been read'.[27] Women joined male-dominated clubs – at Kibworth, Leicestershire, from 1774, at Clavering, Essex, from 1790, at Thaxted from 1805, to give a few examples – or formed women-only reading groups (for example at Penzance in 1770 and at Taunton in 1790).[28] A *Lady's Magazine* article of 1791 praises the newly formed Stockton library association and recommends the establishment of such associations elsewhere, since they gave women access to 'rational entertainment' to replace the 'love tales and romantic nonsense, called Novels' which form the 'nonsensical trash of the circulating library' (22, 1791, pp. 645–6). As we shall see, circulating libraries' associations with nonsense, novels, a public space and transgressive sexuality made them problematic for respectable female users, while book clubs, reading groups and library associations by simulating private life gave vital opportunities for non-transgressive access to books.

Finally, if their home was too remote from any library, if the book they wanted had a discouragingly long waiting list (as Wollstonecraft's *Vindication* or More's *Coelebs* had when Anne Grant tried to borrow them, or the memoirs of actress George Anne Bellamy when Betsy Sheridan wanted them in 1785),[29] if they were intimidated by being one of few females to use a library, or if they could not afford the cost of borrowing, women might borrow books more informally. John Griffiths, clergyman in Carmarthenshire, kept a catalogue of 'Books lended' from his private library from 1763 to 1796, which includes a number of women borrowers: a translation of Aristotle, for instance, was loaned first to Sarah Evans, then to Miss Mary Lewis, then to Mrs Lloyd. Kaufman argues that this private lending library was 'probably unique', but its uniqueness lies in the survival of its documentation rather than the enterprise itself, and John Brewer has discovered a number of other generous private lenders and grateful borrowers, either of whom could be female.[30] A friend of Elizabeth Hamilton's capitalised on the popularity of *The Cottagers of Glenburnie* by 'lending her copy at so much a head', and the *Lady's Magazine* assumes that even women of the servant class will be able to read it by borrowing copies from purchasers (a system of informal patronage that was, as we shall see, vital for labouring-class women writers).[31]

FEMALE SPACE: THE CIRCULATING LIBRARY

It was the commercial or 'circulating' library, however, that had most impact on the English novel. A customer paid a yearly, half-yearly or quarterly subscription (the Minerva charged a guinea a year in 1798, rising to two guineas by 1814), or for less affluent patrons, a weekly or even overnight fee (perhaps 2d a day or a shilling a week to borrow a single volume): such fees could be met occasionally even by non-affluent readers such as servants.[32] Circulating libraries flourished in fashionable watering places (in Bath possibly as early as 1724, certainly in Bristol by 1728), in the growing industrial centres (in Birmingham by 1729), in prosperous county towns (in Salisbury by the 1730s) and in London (there are references to the renting of books as early as the Restoration period, and a number of circulating libraries by the 1740s).[33] They rapidly spread to the remotest parts, until not only all sizeable towns but even 'every intelligent village' had a library by the turn of the century.[34] In 1808, Hester Thrale Piozzi remarks on recent changes in the distribution of literacy, including the innovation of 'a Circulating Library at

Holyhead'.[35] By 1800, Paul Kaufman records 112 libraries in London and 268 in the provinces, only Hertfordshire and Rutland failing to provide evidence of libraries.[36]

Circulating libraries were vital in the democratisation and regionalisation of literature, playing a crucial 'popularizing role', since most readers, especially of fiction, 'were not library-owners, but library-goers'.[37] Books were so expensive that hardly anyone beyond the very wealthiest could afford ephemeral reading like novels: 'who buy novels?', Charlotte Smith asks bitterly.[38] The price of novels rose steeply in the 1790s, when *Camilla* would have cost £1 5s and *The Mysteries of Udolpho* £1 4s (for the same price one could buy eight to ten pairs of women's shoes).[39]

Circulating libraries, then, were vital in allowing access to literature to less affluent readers, but were also the subject of vigorous hostile propaganda. Library proprietors sought to preempt this by a number of tactics. Library premises were 'designed to suggest privacy and even domesticity', and advertising through trade cards and catalogue engravings offered 'romanticised pictures' of elegant respectability, including even a subtle 'emphasis on checks to untutored and irresponsible reading'. Despite such attempts, however, the evidence suggests even in the managers of such libraries a 'tension between promotion and guardedness, between commercialization and exclusivity':[40] the public–private space of the circulating library was also viewed ambivalently by library users and even writers who depended on sales to libraries for their livelihood.

In reality, many respectable families and individuals were ready to risk the circulating library's ambiguous space. The Austens, Anne Grant and her family and friends, Anna Larpent, the Grove sisters and countless other respectable but not affluent readers depended upon its resources. Even the respectable middle-class dissenting family of Anne Milnes Lumb were occasional borrowers: her accounts books for 1775 and 1777 record some predictable literary purchases (ten shillings for a copy of Watts' sermons, thirteen shillings for a family prayer book), but also budget for one shilling and twopence for borrowing the seven volumes of *Sir Charles Grandison*.[41]

However, except for the self-promotion of library proprietors, '[o]pen vindication of circulating libraries was very uncommon'. Prevailing stereotypes saw them as culturally and morally inferior, marketing 'illiterate authors for illiterate readers': they were imaged as an 'evergreen tree of diabolical knowledge', 'filthy streams of spiritual and moral pollution', 'the gin-shop of [female] minds', a 'great evil', simultaneously conveying 'food and poison' to the young reader'.[42] Often the circulating library was run by a bookseller or stationer, but it could also, as in Austen's *Sanditon*, be only a sideline in a shop which predominantly traded as a haberdasher's, milliner's, or jeweller's, giving opportunities to hostile critics to identify book-lending with sordid commercialism rather than culture. While proprietors argued their exclusiveness and respectability, critics emphasised transgression of class and gender boundaries.

Proprietors' advertisements tried to counter stereotypes of circulating libraries as haunts of unbridled sexuality: Theophilus Shrimpton's library at Bath even provided separate reading rooms for men and women.[43] Nonetheless the stereotypes persisted, and the hostile propaganda denigrated circulating libraries by representing them as places dominated by women, from the 'young ladies at the counter'[44] to female customers whose ignorance and folly are satirised. Circulating libraries certainly offered women employment, important in an age when job-opportunities for women were elsewhere in decline.[45] Ann Yearsley's library in Bristol Hot Wells from 1795 is only the most famous of many run by female proprietors (including at least six others in Bristol alone between 1770 and 1800[46]). Fictional and non-fictional accounts of circulating libraries are dominated by the presence of women, like Robert Bisset's account of the Margate library in *Douglas*, or the Edinburgh library in *Noctes Ambrosianae* where a lady with thick ankles borrows 'the Secrets o' Sensibility, in four volumes'.[47] A *Lady's Monthly Museum* poem of 1799, 'A Circulating Library at a Public Watering-Place', has numerically more male customers, but is framed by its female clients, beginning with 'Misses' and ending with 'Beauties' and 'Old Women' (3, p. 162).

Satire on circulating libraries virtually always depicts library use as a practice where gender is a dominant factor. In Courtney Melmoth's *Family Secrets* (1797) the 48th chapter, 'The Secrets of a Circulating Library', satirises Mr Page's female clients, even though the library's success depends on young female 'consumers' who devour sentimental fiction ('Delicate Distresses', 'Excessive Sensibility', 'Seduction', etc.) and 'can run over a novel of three, four or five volumes faster than book-men can put them into boards'. Women figure a range of transgressive reading practices: one complains she has been sent history, philosophy and science when she reads only the 'last plays and novels', while another complains that she has been given novels when she 'stud[ies] only metaphysics'. Page's library is a feminised space, its books strictly gendered: bad books, novels and sceptical metaphysics, are read by women, while Page keeps good literature, Gibbon, Robertson, Bacon and Newton, for himself.[48]

Not only circulating libraries but also their books become feminised spaces in unpleasant ways, as popular books are ruined by 'powder and pomatum between the leaves', or are returned 'soil'd and dog-ear'd' by a sluttish female borrower, reeking of 'spirits, and . . . snuff'.[49] The book, the library and the female body become disturbingly identified, an identification further exaggerated by the constant assumption that women borrow from circulating libraries only the most pernicious kind of novels, texts which themselves were constantly identified with the female body and sexuality.

If women learned false sensibility and transgressive sexuality from novels, these dangers were doubly acute if the books came from circulating libraries. In Bage's *Barham Downs* (1784) and William Combe's *The Devil upon Two Sticks in England* (1791) 'lady novel reader[s]' are corrupted by 'circulating library' novels (Combe, II, pp. 170–4; cf. Bage, pp. 275–6), in Edgeworth's 'Mademoiselle Panache', Lady Augusta reveals her lack of 'delicacy – of decency' by getting the second volume of 'one of the very worst books in the French language' from 'the circulating library at Cheltenham' (pp. 396–7), and in Kett's *Emily*, Caroline Sparks enjoys the 'delusive and pernicious . . . reading' of novels from the circulating library (*Werther* is specifically named), and urges Emily to give up her charitable works and aspire to the more 'genteel' modes of 'sensibility' she can acquire from the library (II, pp. 91, 90, 92–3). Conservative, liberal and radical writers use the same images to convey the same messages about the dangers of female literacy. In all these cases, reading circulating library fiction directly causes seduction and/or elopement with an unsuitable man: access to the circulating library is tantamount to sexual and class transgression. Moreover, circulating libraries became associated with a morally questionable conspicuous consumption itself focused on women. A print of 1782 shows an opulently dressed woman about to enter a circulating library, and Charlotte Smith symbolises the selfishness of the rich by the sending of a richly dressed footman 'to pass on a message of his lady to the Circulating Library over the way'. (Smith also shows children learning the opposite lesson by reading, in a domestic library, 'Thomson, on the subject of the thoughtlessness of the affluent'.)[50]

The most familiar criticism of the circulating library for its effect on female readers is Sir Anthony Absolute's in Sheridan's *The Rivals* (1775), which equates women's reading with 'the black art', the circulating library being its most 'diabolical' manifestation (I, ii, p. 39). Sir Anthony's exaggeratedly reactionary views are, of course, mocked, but Lydia Languish, who borrows sentimental fiction and absorbs unrealistically romantic views, demonstrates their essential correctness. Lydia first appears 'sitting on a sopha with a [circulating library] book in her hand', multiply demonstrating bad reading practices in her pose and her choice of reading. Her maidservant has failed to track down the sentimental novels she has ordered – *The Reward of Constancy, The Fatal Connexion* and *Mistakes of the Heart* (I, ii, p. 32) – but has managed to get some Smollett, *A Sentimental Journey, The Man of Feeling, Tears of Sensibility,* Elizabeth Griffith's *The Delicate Distress* and *The Innocent Adultery*.[51] As her aunt Mrs Malaprop confuses words, Lydia confuses sense and sentiment, fantasy and reality, licit and illicit texts: access to the circulating library leads to at worst sexual transgression, at best false sensibility and unrealistic aspirations.

Sheridan could afford to deride the circulating libraries, but women writers were dependent on them both as a source of otherwise unobtainable reading and as a reliable market for their writing. Some novelists therefore attempted to rehabilitate the institution by creating virtuous heroines who are also library users, like the Bennet girls in *Pride and Prejudice,* Jacintha Greville in Roche's *The Nocturnal Visit,* or the *Lady's Magazine* heroine Harriet Vernon.[52] When Laura Montreville in Brunton's *Self-control* visits Edinburgh, she notes its 'ancient castle' and 'splendid scenery', but is most struck by 'its public libraries' (p. 47). Previously she had dreamed of cheering her father with 'new books' for his library (p. 29), but when this proves impossible she is still able to buy him 'the cheap luxury of some books from a circulating library' (p. 55). This shift from a private genteel library to dependence on a circulating library poignantly marks the decline of the family's fortune.

Women depended on circulating libraries both as writers and readers – Charlotte Smith remarks that libraries are the 'principal' buyers of novels, and Elizabeth Griffith records that of a print run of a thousand copies of a novel, circulating libraries took four hundred[53] – but they nonetheless view circulating libraries with marked ambivalence. Smith noted the novelist's dependence on the library trade, allowed virtuous heroines like Emmeline and Ethelinde to be users, and argued that any young woman endangered by novels would be 'foolish . . . though she had never heard of a circulating library': but she also criticised the libraries and their users in her didactic work for children.[54] Mary

Robinson's *Walsingham* (1797) depicts the circulating library in North Parade, Bristol, as a space malignly dominated by women. *Walsingham* is much influenced by *Family Secrets*, which is specifically cited; Courtney Melmoth actually appears as a character, a 'liberal observer' and 'the author of many excellent and beautiful productions', who rebukes the Duchess of Riversford and her daughters for their rudeness (III, pp. 236, 234). These women who 'torment' (III, p. 231) Walsingham demonstrate their folly by transgressive reading practices. The Duchess mocks women novelists (III, pp. 229–30), dislikes Melmoth's novels only because their titles embody 'Truth' and 'Liberal Opinions' (III, p. 235), hates exemplary heroes, preferring 'a Werter, or a St. Preux, nay, even a Lovelace, or a Tom Jones' (III, p. 229), and reads novels only in search of scandal (III, p. 236): Lady Arabella is semi-literate, knowing of the poems of Spenser only because the story of Una is 'painted on [her] fan' (III, p. 242).

While in *Walsingham* Robinson accepts the male-identified view that the circulating library is a female-dominated space and this is a bad thing, her later novel *The Natural Daughter* (1799) shows circulating libraries as female-friendly spaces in more positive ways. Early in the novel Martha leaves money at the circulating library to help a mysterious lady in desperate circumstances: she is later revealed as Mrs Sedgeley, whose friendship proves a vital resource to Martha. In this novel, indeed, literacy figures bonds of female friendship and kinship and Martha's heroic commitment to these bonds despite repeated betrayal. This episode is later recapitulated when, at a circulating library where she is trying to sell a novel of her own, Martha hears a maidservant ask for a book, 'something about Virtue Rewarded' (II, p. 41), for her impoverished and dying mistress. By a letter in the novel the servant returns, Martha recognises this lady as her own sister Julia, and sends her money. The circulating library might exploit the labours of women writers, but still allows a space for women to offer help to each other. In this subversive novel, such a space is not available in the home, for domesticity is stiflingly oppressive. Martha is falsely believed to unfaithful and is cast off by her husband because she dares support the abandoned child Frances (who is finally, ironically, revealed as the illegitimate daughter of her own husband). Even her mother and sister reject her. The patriarchal home does not allow supportive relations between women, even between sisters or mother and daughter, and Martha must find other spaces to express her support for her unworthy mother and sister, her foster-daughter and her female friends. She finds such opportunities only in unrespectable spaces, the theatre, the asylum[55] and the circulating library.

Similar ambivalences can be found in the *Lady's Magazine*'s 'The Rash Attempt: a Moral Tale', which again depicts the library as a female-friendly space. George Dalton falls in love with Harriot Monson when he sees her in the bookseller's, where she is lodging, immediately discerning her virtue from her borrowing of Burney's *Evelina*. A notorious rake also comes to lodge at the shop, and to forestall George's jealousy Harriot moves out, but her letter goes astray and he assumes the rake is to blame for her disappearance. In a melodramatic conclusion George is killed in a duel with the rake and Harriot, dressed as a man, is badly wounded. Harriot is safe morally and physically within the world of the library, protected from dangerous male sexuality by twin guardian angels, the bookseller and Frances Burney. When she leaves this haven, the results are a failure of communication, gender transgression, and the loss of her lover and her 'peace of mind' (17, 1787, p. 598).

Circulating libraries, then, constituted a vigorously contested space. Proprietors' propaganda tried to imply that the library was a respectably quasi-domestic space, while conservative critics attacked it as a public arena transgressively dominated by women, even as women novelists, themselves increasingly dependent on the library market, expressed ambivalence about a market economy or fought to establish other images. While Smith imaged circulating library use as conspicuous consumption, she also, like Brunton and Austen, demonstrated its importance in extending culture to the non-affluent, and Robinson in *The Natural Daughter* went so far as to imply that what was good about the libraries was exactly what made them different from the patriarchal home.

What dominates the literature, in the twentieth century as in the eighteenth, is the stereotype of the circulating library as a place 'mainly . . . patronised by women' renting out novels: but neither half of this seems to be literally true. Paul Kaufman's research indicates that, in one of few circulating libraries where information remains, James Marshall's in Bath from 1793 to 1800, women constituted only between 22 and 35 per cent of the clientele: this was higher than in most surviving lists of other types of libraries, but still significantly less than half.[56] Most of the great male figures of the turn of the century used circulating libraries – Macaulay, Southey, Chatterton, Scott, Leigh Hunt, Coleridge, Shelley, Burns, Cowper, Keats, Wordsworth.[57] Moreover, circulating libraries did not stock only, or even mainly, novels. Some certainly specialised in fiction: *The Use of Circulating Libraries Considered* (1797) recommends that 80 per cent of the stock should be fiction, and some libraries had an even higher proportion (90 per cent at libraries in Newton Abbot and Darlington, over 95 per cent at one in Whitehaven), but this was unusual. Some kept very small stocks of fiction (only 5 per cent in Allen's library, Hereford, and about the same for a library in Leicester): the three libraries in Bath whose catalogues survive show proportions of fiction of 45, 10 and 8 per cent.[58] Despite the usefulness to hostile propagandists of an image of libraries dominated by women reading pulp fiction, this was not historically true.

WHERE NOT TO READ

Reading acts were judged not only on the book chosen and its source but on where it was read and even the physical posture of the reader: 'if you read in inappropriate places, then it was likely that your reading material was worthless',[59] and this was believed particularly in the case of women and girls. They were accused of reading novels in bed, for instance, so that reading becomes at best a slothful activity, risking dangers from seduction to conflagration from an injudiciously placed candle ('the insurance offices against Fire are not much pleased with this Mode').[60] Women read novels in coaches, while putting on makeup, at meals, in hospital, even in church: one reader has a special 'cover . . . ornamented with religious emblems' behind which she hides volumes 'from the circulating library'.[61]

In particular, women were accused of reading, or listening to reading, while having their hair done.[62] *Clarissa* is read aloud while a lady's hair is curled, and Anna Larpent read novels while having her hair done. Hester Thrale compared herself to Swift's Vanessa who 'held Montaigne and read / While Mrs Susan comb'd her Head', and read the *Spectator* to her daughters while her 'Maid . . . was dressing [her] Hair'.[63] This may simply indicate how busy women's lives were and how time-consuming eighteenth-century hairstyles, but the image tended to be used to figure women's reading as trivial and to characterise some of the period's most transgressive female readers. The deist Mrs– in Lennox's *Henrietta* reads stoic Epictetus 'while her maid is combing her hair', and then very unstoically rages at her maid for hurting her (II, p. 112): her reading represents not only irreligion but also hypocrisy and bad temper. Lady Isabella Rackrent reads *Werther* while having her hair done, indicating her withdrawal from family duties into a world of self-indulgent sentiment and superficial appearances.[64] In Robinson's *Walsingham* the trivial Lady Arabella never reads except in sound-bytes of six minutes, while her maid is putting her hair 'in *papillots*' (III, p. 246).

Even physical posture while reading mattered. Ina Ferris has demonstrated how women's reading became associated with 'sofas and softness' as opposed to the 'legitimate, upright reading' of men. When women 'spread themselves on the sofa' their 'supine, erotic' reading becomes a form of sensuality rather than intellectuality. Moreover, women who read in this way trespass on the body language of the male: Sarah Green warns young women never to 'lounge, or loll', for such 'masculine deportment' is as inappropriate in a woman as other male behaviour, like loud laughter, humming, or talking too much.[65]

Working- as well as leisure-class women were castigated for reading in inappropriate times, places and postures. The female shopkeeper 'at the counter' was blamed for keeping a novel at hand, maids for reading novels in the kitchen, the 'scullion-wench' for working inefficiently 'with a dishclout in one hand and a novel in the other, sobbing o'er the sorrows of a *Julia* or a *Jemima*'.[66] Hannah More complains that seamstresses 'of the lowest class' spend 'half their night' listening to one of their number reading a novel aloud, so that 'the labour of one girl is lost, and the minds of the rest are corrupted'. (More is shocked by novel-reading but not, apparently, by the economic necessities which drove young women to spend the whole night in physically hard low-paid work.) Charles Lamb also associates seamstresses, milliners and mantua-makers with novel-reading, though he writes more sympathetically of their need for the 'Lethean' escapism provided by circulating-library books.[67]

READING SILENTLY AND READING ALOUD

A woman who hid books among her linen for private pleasure, or who read when she should be working, obviously performed a transgressive act, but all solitary recreational reading by women tended to be associated with idleness and selfishness. Central to J. Paul Hunter's prehistory of the novel is the idea of the genre's 'addictive engagement with solitariness' and its construction of a 'lonely . . . anti-social' reader.[68] While the spectre of the anti-social novel-reader of either sex certainly haunts eighteenth- and early nineteenth-century writing, Hunter's analysis misses a key cultural fact of the period, the importance of reading aloud: 'Reading may be a social as well as a solitary occupation.

Thus one person may entertain many others in a domestic party.' When a girl leaves domestic company to read novels ('these delusive books'), she indulges in 'selfish pleasure' instead of performing domestic duties.[69] Instead she should read to friends or family, or listen to her father, husband or brother reading, especially if she can sew at the same time. Frances Burney at Windsor missed the pleasures of social reading, and Betsy Sheridan, whose father barred family readings of poetry, longed to read Cowper but was unhappy about reading as a 'solitary pleasure', which she felt was like 'sitting down to a feast alone'.[70]

Scenes of social reading reinforce or create family ties, for they can also function as vehicles of a legitimised eroticism: in Brunton's *Self-control* Montague de Courcy courts Laura by bringing her books, 'and would spend hours in reading aloud, an accomplishment in which he excelled' (p. 100). In didactic novels characters are often judged by their willingness to read to entertain others. De Courcy reads to his mother and sisters (p. 76); in *George Bateman* the hero reads 'Hume's History of England' to his adoptive mother and sister as they sit 'at their needle-works' (I, p. 41); in Lennox's *Euphemia* Maria Harley reads Plutarch's *Lives* to her sick uncle, and Clara Bellenden 'books of devotion' to her widowed mother (I, p. 10; IV, p. 79); Amanda in *The Children of the Abbey* reads the Bible to her dying father (II, p. 332); Charles Lennox in Ferrier's *Marriage* reads to his aged mother (p. 346); Hawkins' Gertrude reads to her patroness for such long periods as to cause ill-health, and to the Countess's sick husband when he is deserted by his relations, and lists the ability 'to read aloud for hours together' among her qualifications for employment (I, p. 311, III, pp. 292, 249); and in Brunton's *Discipline* Emma Percy's moral reawakening is marked by a shift from a carelessly unfulfilled plan to read to Miss Mortimer to the actual accomplishment of this 'reading' (pp. 114, 204). Such reading practices do not seem to be gendered, but are acceptable in both sexes. To clinch the point that such reading is virtuous, the chosen reading is, if specified, carefully legitimate, its devotional or historical subject-matter being emphasised.

Only the selfish and foolish refuse to participate in social reading. In *Memoirs of Modern Philosophers*, Bridgetina Botherim is so intent on her own reading pleasure that she will 'never read aloud to any one' (II, p. 76). Thus in the novel's value-scheme she is contrasted with Henry Sidney, who generously reads to the injured Julia (II, p. 72), with Julia Delmond, who reads to entertain her father (I, p. 46), and with the 'active and judicious' Harriet Orwell, who 'performed every domestic task, and having completely regulated family economy for the day, was quietly seated with her aunt and sisters, listening to Hume's History of England, as it was read to them by a little orphan girl she had herself instructed' (I, pp. 107–8).

Contemporary fiction, journals and letters are full of domestic scenes where communal reading reveals the unity of the family group. A girl was educated to read aloud, often to her mother in the first instance (as was Frances Thynne Seymour) and to listen to reading, often by her father (as was Mary Delany).[71] It was important for a girl to be able to read aloud. In Thomas Day's male-centred educational novel *Sandford and Merton* (1783), virtually the only female character is the idealised girl Miss Simmons, who has no individual qualities except to be 'famous for reading well'.[72] If a young woman read aloud, it was usually to her family or female companions: Mary Hamilton read the *Iliad* aloud to Mary Delany, translating from the Greek as she went along, Frances Boscawen read Mason's *Life of Gray* while her female companion sewed, and Lady Melmoth in Blower's *Maria* reads Hayley's *Marcella* to female friends. Occasional complaints, sometimes disguised, are, nonetheless, heard about the pressure on women to spend time reading aloud from books they have little interest in themselves. Charlotte Smith attacks Milton for making his daughters read him classical texts without educating them to understand 'what they read', thus transforming an expression of domestic ties to an 'irksome task' imposed by patriarchal authority.[73] Such a comment attacks not just the misuse of sociable reading, but, by implication, the centrality of the system itself in women's cultural lives.

There was no impropriety in a wife reading to her husband, especially if he were tired or ill, or occupied in manual work: landscape gardener Humphrey Repton's wife read to him while he drew, and Thomas Turner's wife read *Clarissa* to him as he was writing.[74] But generally the stereotype approvingly depicted the husband reading, while the womenfolk listen (and often sew). Thomas Moore regularly read to his wife for two hours after dinner, at one point 'going through Miss Edgeworth's works', Dr Delany read his wife an eclectic range of books from Eusebius' *Life of Constantine the Great* to *Peregrine Pickle*, and Shelley read aloud constantly to the women in his life.[75] In Mary Shelley's *Lodore*, Villiers reads *Troilus and Cressida* while his wife nets a purse, and its 'profound philosophy, and intense passion' cements their relationship despite their financial troubles (pp. 233–4). The harmony of reading husband and sewing, listening wife is central to many didactic novels promulgating domestic ideology including More's *Coelebs*: but so seductive was it that it appealled even to radical women who were otherwise critical of the patriarchal home. In *Original Stories from Real Life* (1788), Wollstonecraft creates the ideal domestic woman Mrs Trueman, whose 'bookcase, full of well-chosen books' reveals her virtue, and whose husband, 'a man of taste and learning, reads to her, while she makes clothes for her children' (p. 386). Later, in 1793 in a letter to Gilbert Imlay she tried to figure the two as a similar family and so reconstruct him as a domestic gentleman and draw him into her picture of domestic happiness even without marriage with the poignant memory of him reading to her 'whilst I mend my stockings'.[76]

The husband reading to the wife, the virtuous suitor reading to his intended, the mother reading to daughters, constituted central images in domestic novels. Reading aloud by women, however, can suggest anxieties even about these most legitimate kinds of reading. While in her happy second marriage Mary Delany and her husband shared reading, in her unhappy first marriage she used reading aloud as a narcotic and was relieved when her husband had 'fallen asleep with my reading'.[77] Moreover, a woman reading aloud might generate a less legitimate eroticism, however innocent she is. Elizabeth Blower's *Maria* attracts the unwanted attentions of the married Mr Aubrey when he hears her reading a poem aloud (1, p. 15). In a *Lady's Magazine* story, 'The Rape of the Marriage Contract', the heroine attracts an elderly gentleman who hears her reading, although the 'book had more charms, in her eye, than the good man'. He proposes for her and her mother insists she accept, but the heroine frees herself by adopting male disguise and, pretending to be a highwayman, stealing the marriage contract (3, 1772, p. 412). This tale unusually offers unconditional sympathy to its Amazonian heroine and to the idea of reading for personal pleasure.

Much of most women's reading time was probably occupied not in reading but in listening to reading, and these two experiences are different. For most people in a print culture the visual stimulus will create a deeper and more memorable impression than simply hearing something read. Silent reading establishes 'a freer, more secret, and totally private intercourse with the written word'[78] which might be desired but is frequently thought dangerous for women. As Alberto Manguel writes, reading aloud 'both enrich[es] and diminish[es] the act of reading'. To offset the pleasures of sociability of reading aloud are the pleasures of silent reading, which allows both a more 'personal' relationship with the text and 'more rapid reading'.[79] Even Hannah More, great exponent of the domestic scene of shared reading, realises that to hear reading is in some respects inadequate: when asked her opinion of Scott's poetry, she replied that '[h]aving only *heard* it, and not yet read it myself, I do not feel competent to speak decidedly as to its merits'.[80] Reading aloud establishes a 'hierarchy',[81] often a gendered hierarchy. The man who reads aloud will gain a more intimate, more authoritative relationship with the book than his female listener, and his power might go even further, since he is likely to choose the text and the time it is read. In 1753 Catherine Talbot stayed with the Berkeley family and participated enthusiastically in readings of *Sir Charles Grandison*. One evening the women were all longing to have the book read, but were too delicate to ask their usual male reader directly, 'and he punishes them by saying nothing and condemning them to an evening of ennui and fretting'.[82]

Even the cosy image of the man reading aloud while the woman sewed did not escape unchallenged: and, paradoxically, one of its acutest critics was its most articulate exponent, Hannah More. To some extent this scenario always offers a compromise, with women allowed partial access to literacy without neglecting their proper business, and imaginative escape being moderated by domestic labour. More simultaneously recommends this compromise and hints at its inadequacies. Lucilla Stanley in *Coelebs* is praised because she submissively 'laid down her work' to concentrate better when one of the men is reading. While the women 'pursue their little employments', they will miss the 'sublimity' of the male-authored texts of elite culture, Addison's *Cato*, *Hamlet*, *King Lear*, *Macbeth*, *Henry VI* and Southey's *Life of Nelson*. This passage is typically complex and contradictory, and Lucilla has to steer a difficult way between neglecting domestic tasks and neglecting the great works of patriarchal culture. However, the passage might offer less repressive messages. It serves, for instance, to legitimise women's reading without the alibi of needlework. Perhaps it even presents a covert portrait of women in rebellion against patriarchal culture, as one is shown more concerned with a broken needle than with the death of Nelson (XI, pp. 323–4).

One final way in which sociable reading could offer not conformist but subversive possibilities is its potential for a democratisation of reading. When women read aloud among themselves, or when husband and wife read to each other, this reading could be shared by female servants. The maidservant in Thomas Turner's family often listens to sociable reading; Hester Thrale's maid hears her read the *Spectator* to her daughters, and is confident enough about her own status as a family member to laugh at its dated manners; the hairdressing maid who hears *Clarissa* read and weeps is rewarded for a display of the sensibility she shares with her superiors.[83] Such lower-class women gained unwonted access through the process of reading aloud to elite culture. My next chapter will examine in more detail the intersection of class and gender at the site of reading.

CHAPTER 6

Preparing for equality: class, gender, reading

Things are getting worse and worse in France. A lady of quality,
the other day in Paris, rung her bell, and desired the footman to
send up her maid Jeannotte. In vain she rung and rung: the man
told her, Jeannotte refused to come, or be any longer under any
body. At last Jeannotte walked into the room with a pamphlet open
in her hand, and sat down. The lady astonished, asked her what she
meant. 'I'm reading', said Jeannotte, without taking her eyes off the
book. The lady insisted on an explanation of this impertinence.
The maid replied with great sang froid, 'Madame, we are all going
to become equals, and I am preparing for equality'.[1]

In this letter to her sister in 1790, Hannah More deplored the disorder in
France after the fall of the Bastille. The More sisters were pioneers in the
movement to educate the poor: yet here a servant's reading provides a
readily decipherable symbol of anarchy, still sharper because the servant is a woman. More's anecdote extends its theme of the class
specificity of good reading from the rebellious servant to possible
readers of the letter. Although I have translated the maidservant's
words, More gives them in French. Her, and her sister's, knowledge of
that language demonstrates genteel education and status, and no lower-
class person who saw the letter could emulate the maid's transgressive
reading act because the account of it is coded in a form only accessible to
the genteel reader.

Hostile accounts of the French Revolution, like More's description of
the throne 'overturned by fisherwomen!' or Elizabeth Montagu's account of the 'Wives of Shopkeepers' in Paris gloating over the severed
head of an executed enemy and the women in a mob at Nimes cutting
two aristocrats to pieces,[2] often focused on its lower-class female members. The collocation of female gender, low class and reading recurs in
writing about the revolution in Europe. In 1803, Mary Berry noted the

spread of revolutionary ideology to Switzerland: 'The women consider *liberty and equality* as an equal right for everyone to read *novels from morning till night, which they do*, from the lowest *servante* to the first *citoyenne*.' Social levelling finds its most appalling expression in undisciplined female reading.[3]

As Roger Chartier has shown, contemporary discourses of reading focus on 'three fundamental figures of nineteenth-century mythology – the child, the woman, and the people', all of whom represent 'new classes of print consumers',[4] wooed by writers seeking to extend literary markets but feared by the guardians of a traditional culture in which reading and writing figure power. One could add to Chartier's trinity a fourth mythic figure, the ethnic Other, who is also significant in discourses of reading. This chapter deals with the double impact of class and gender on the conceptualisation of reading, but race and nationality also impinged on the gendering of literacy, with reading taking a key role in developing discourses of ethnic and national identity, as of gender. Ethnic or religious difference reinforced stereotypes of female misreading: even in radical Charlotte Smith's fiction a Jewish woman obsessed 'with the heroes of novels' embodies bad reading practices, contrasted with the Christian heroine's reading of religious books, poetry and periodical literature. Similar stereotypes confronting women faced Anglophone readers of African and Afro-American origin. As too much reading might cause insanity in women, it was sometimes argued that the 'African head is not adapted by nature to . . . profound contemplations', and an African who read might go 'mad . . . from too much learning'.[5] Reading was a crucial medium through which Black writers argued their intellectual equality, and illustrations of Black personalities frequently code them as civilised by depicting them with books or in libraries. For such readers, the acquisition of literacy was 'as much a political act as an educational one'.[6]

Olaudah Equiano, an Ibo kidnapped as a child in Eastern Nigeria in 1756, frequently quotes the classic texts of English poetry, including Pope's Homer and *Paradise Lost*, to stake a claim to civilisation.[7] Ignatius Sancho, born aboard a slaving ship in 1729, was brought to England as a baby and given 'books', which were his 'chief pleasure', by his patron the Duke of Montagu. Sancho frequently alludes to English literature and planned a 'useful, elegant, little library' similar to that recommended for women – travels, history, sermons, periodical literature, Milton, Young's *Night Thoughts*, Thomson's *Seasons*.[8] Phillis Wheatley, a Fulani born in Senegal and sold into slavery in Boston in 1761, had a double burden of colonisation as woman and slave, and she demonstrates her intellectual equality by stressing that, although 'brought an uncultivated Barbarian from *Africa*', the 'land of errors', she has gained knowledge of the master-texts of English civilisation, the Bible, the 'best of Books', sermons, Homer, Virgil and Ovid, Pope, and poets like Young, Akenside and Milton.[9]

For early Black Anglophone writers, literacy was the key element proving their potential for intellectual equality. Mary Prince was taught to 'read in the Bible' by Moravian ladies, and shared reading forms links between her and her white benefactors; Rebecca Jackson was given the 'gift of power' to read mystically by God, thus avoiding her literate brother's attempts to colonise her language.[10] Equiano, first encountering white men and print culture, 'had a great curiosity to talk to the books as I thought they did . . . I have often taken up a book and talked to it and then put my ears to it . . . in hopes it would answer me: and I have been very much concerned when I found it remained silent' (p. 40). James Albert Ukawsaw Gronniosaw was astonished to discover a book could 'talk' to a reader, and 'greatly disappointed' that it 'would not speak' to him, which he attributed directly to the fact that he 'was black'. The 'trope of the Talking Book' became a way to 'measure the humanity of authors struggling to define an African voice in Western letters'.[11] For them, reading constituted a revolutionary act, but, they are keen to imply, spiritually and culturally, not politically. Mary Prince and Phillis Wheatley read the Bible and learned their own inferiority; Sancho finds that books 'mended my heart – they improved my veneration of the Deity – and increased my love to my neighbours'.[12]

PREPARING FOR (CLASS) EQUALITY

One of the most important cultural events of the period was the extension of literacy to the labouring classes and the spread of reading habits in the lowest social groups. This can be attributed to broad changes in thinking about class and society; to changes in education, especially the rise of books for young readers which created habits of literacy; to changes in methods of book production and marketing (the demise of perpetual copyright in 1774 allowed the rise of cheap reprints, and remainders and other cheap forms of book-buying became significant); and to new ways of making books accessible to the non-affluent (like libraries and book clubs). The 'distribution of printed matter in society' remained 'unequal',[13] but less so than in previous centuries.

While radicals like Mary Wollstonecraft saw the ability to read as crucial in allowing lower-class women a stake in culture, and cultural liberals like Johnson sympathetically depicted lower-class female readers, and argued that 'the publick' was the ultimate arbiter of literary worth, conservatives especially after 1789 show 'fear of the influence of mass literacy', in terms of how it would change both society and literature.[14] In 1787 Humphrey Repton believed that 'some degree of ignorance' was necessary to make the poor accept their subordination; Mary Berry thought revolution the inevitable result of teaching 'the lower order of people' to read; Thomas Moore, using the language of counter-revolutionary politics, 'letting the mob in to vote', argued that the spread of literacy would necessarily erode literary standards; and Coleridge, who apparently coined the term 'Reading Public', thought it a 'luxuriant misgrowth' of elite writerly activity. This anxiety about mass literacy includes gender anxieties. Christopher North's *Noctes Ambrosianae* personifies the '*reading* Public' as 'an old woman', in defiance of the fact that one of the *Noctes* regulars, the 'Shepherd' James Hogg, was a product of the very extension of literacy to the labouring classes that he condemns.[15]

The radical right drew on Mandeville's 'Essay on Charity and Charity Schools' (1723), arguing that society would not benefit from increased lower-class literacy, for reading 'keeps the Poor from Working'. It is not 'the want of Reading and Writing' that causes crime; quite the contrary, for education only produces cleverer criminals. Educating poor children should specifically be avoided, since it 'looks like a Reward for being Vicious and Unactive'.[16] Hester Thrale's marginalia in her copy express unqualified approval and praise Mandeville's prescience in predicting a major social problem of the turn of the century.[17] In the light of this contest over mass literacy, Hannah More's project of village schools and cheap mass-market literature can be seen to aim at social control more than enlightenment, and was a conscious attempt to prevent the disruption of class and gender hierarchies she saw in revolutionary Europe.

In this period class was more vital than gender as a determinant of reading practices. Little is known about labouring-class women's reading, and although entrenched stereotypes persisted, these often have little to do with historical reality. Region as well as class was important. Urban workers were more likely to need to read, and to be able to find reading material, than rural labourers. In some regions, like New England and Scotland, commentators believed literacy was particularly widespread and 'democratized': even in 'the humblest conditions of the Scottish peasants every one can read'.[18] In Hamilton's *Memoirs of Modern Philosophers* Henry Sidney is impressed that in the Scottish 'peasantry . . . all can read' (I, p. 222), and William Weller Pepys believed the example of Scotland 'supersedes all argument' about the advantages of More's project to educate the poor. Susan Sibbald knew Scottish shepherd Wully Carruthers who was a fellow-subscriber to the circulating library at Melrose, but while she borrowed Ann Radcliffe, he read 'Ancient and Modern History', though he did sometimes read 'a novel or nonsense buke', like *Sir Charles Grandison*. He had also read Alan Ramsay's *The Gentle Shepherd*, and contrasted it ironically with the life of a real shepherd.[19]

Class-distinctions in this period are impossible to recapture in all their complexity. The Duchess of Gloucester sent one of her ladies to ask an orange-woman 'if she ever sold ballads?' The tradeswoman is indignant: 'No indeed . . . I don't do anything so mean, I don't even sell apples': popular textuality ranks for this working woman as the lowest form of commodity. The aristocratic ladies are entertained by this display of class pride in a worker, 'as they did not know there were so many ranks and gradations in life'.[20] But it was precisely on such gradations that the self-respect of many depended, and which conditioned – enabled or constrained – their reading practices.

Class-distinctions were vital but to some degree fluid, and reading opportunities could change abruptly. A woman could rise by marriage or fall by being orphaned or widowed. Charlotte Smith, despite an elite-class education, became too poor to buy books and found it 'misery *past compute* . . . to hear of books, & hunger & thirst after them without being able to get them': Philippa Hayes, an impoverished middle-class widow who became housekeeper to George Lucy at Charlcote Park near Stratford-on-Avon, was a 'bookworm', and some record of her reading survives.[21] The family of Ellen Weeton (later Stock, 1776–?) of Upholland in Lancashire, who also left some record of her reading, included most ranks except the very highest. Her paternal grandfather was a tenant farmer on an estate which had once belonged to his ancestors: her mother was a butcher's daughter who had been a lady's maid, but her family, the Rawlinsons, also included wealthy upwardly mobile merchants whose career provides a poignant counterpoint to her downward trajectory.[22]

Class and money were likely to determine reading experience: kitchen-maid, poet and keen reader Mary Leapor probably earned £3 10s a year, which put her far below the £50 per annum which James Raven believes was the minimum which would permit regular book-buying.[23] Reading figures the middle-class identity which belongs by right to a number of mysterious foundlings (like Ella Worthy in a *Lady's Magazine* serial), or reveals the low origins of some aspirers to middle-class status (like nabob's daughter Miss Silvertop in Thomson's *The Denial*).[24]

At the same time, books 'crossed social boundaries and drew readers from very different social and economic levels'.[25] Very popular books, from *The Rights of Man* to More's Cheap Repository Tracts, from *Paradise Lost* to *Clarissa*, crossed the whole range of literate society. Sharing books, and this is most visible among women, offered democratising opportunities, opening up professional-class culture to those below (or above). Maidservants listened to family reading; Philippa Hayes and Mary Leapor 'certainly' had access to employers' libraries; Ann Hayman, in 1797 appointed sub-governess to Princess Charlotte, was loaned books, including Roche's *The Children of the Abbey*, by the Princess of Wales.[26] Princess Charlotte wrote of reading as 'a great passion'; in a poignant attempt to construct bourgeois domestic intimacy in the dysfunctional household of the divorced Prince Regent, she discussed and exchanged books with her friend Margaret Mercer Elphinstone, including memoirs and recent history, Byron's poems, and novels, including Gothic fiction and works by Anne Plumptre and Jane Austen. (The perceptive Charlotte especially enjoyed *Sense and Sensibility* because she discerned in herself 'the same imprudence' as Marianne's.[27])

Though popular books crossed class divides, different classes might read the same text differently. Mary Shelley's life of her father offers 'antithetical', class-specific readings of *Caleb Williams*, suggesting that readers of the 'lower classes' supported Caleb, for they 'saw their cause espoused, & their oppressors forcibly & eloquently delineated': readers 'of higher rank' instead 'felt the nobleness, sensibility and errors of Falkland with deepest sympathy'.[28] For Shelley, reading is a political act conditioned by, among other things, class-identification.

Class-distinctions and their relations to literacy functioned differently for men and women. Ellen Weeton's family history demonstrates the gendered nature of social mobility, and the effect on female reading of the trap of downward mobility. Weeton's father, a sailor, was killed in action, leaving his wife impoverished, with an aged mother, two children and an orphaned niece to support. With few alternatives before her, she started a school, in which her daughter also worked. Life was a struggle to survive and preserve the appearance of middle-class status and middle-class contacts. Ellen felt patronised by her more affluent equals, but that she had nothing in common with her working-class inferiors. The two women worked hard and endured privation to support Thomas Weeton Jr. through his education as a lawyer, but he thought this no more than his due, 'for we were but *female* relatives, and had only done our duty' (I, p. 23). When he qualified and married advantageously he was unwilling to offer a home to his sister, for his wife and her relations despised one who had exercised the '*degrading* profession of schoolmistress' (I, p. 79).

Weeton's life demonstrates that 'unless a father can provide independent fortunes for his daughters, they must either be made mop squeezers or mantua makers, whereas sons can easily make their way in the world' (I, pp. 6–7). Poor women could only rise through marriage. Weeton met one real-life Pamela, Mrs Pedder of Dove's Nest near Ambleside, who had been her wealthy future husband's dairy-maid. Such a meteoric rise was exceptional, and there was a high price to pay – her husband's insulting behaviour, 'the sorrow that person must undergo who marries above herself' (I, p. 239). For Weeton, intelligent, fond of books, with a talent for writing and dreams of becoming an author, there was no escape from poverty and dependence, in a world where, as Wollstonecraft bitterly observed, there were no professions for women:[29]

I often feel as if I were not in my proper sphere, as if I possessed talents that only want awakening . . . I could have been something greater, something better than I am . . . why are not females permitted to study physic, divinity, astronomy, &c, &c . . . chemistry, botany, logic, mathematics, &c. To be sure the mere study is not prohibited, but the practice is in great measure. Who would employ a female physician? who would listen to a female divine, except to ridicule? (I, pp. 196–7)

In such circumstances it is unsurprising that Weeton clung doggedly to her literacy and the habit of reading as crucial signs of middle-class status when all others were lost: reading was 'the greatest comfort of my life, and its greatest blessing' (I, pp. 195–6). As a child, a 'Story Book' her father gave her became an 'inseparable companion', and when he commissioned her portrait she insisted on being painted with the book. When her father died, she 'saved, and gave to my mother all the half pence I received', a real sacrifice, because 'such was my excessive fondness for books, that I used to spend all my money that way', and when she passed bookshops unable to buy their 'tempting' wares, her 'heart . . . ached' (p. 9). Later, when she could, she visited bookshops and circulating libraries wherever she happened to be (I, p. 212; II, p. 376).

For Weeton books were not only objects of desire perpetually kept from her by poverty: they were also proof of middle-class status distinguishing her from uncultured parvenus around her, like her employer Mr Armitage, who objects in a 'cavilling manner' to spending money on books for her pupils (II, p. 75), or ex-dairymaid Mrs Pedder, who 'cannot bear books, nor even to *hear* one read' (I, p. 315). Weeton's reading becomes important in communication with friends, but also a point of conflict: when she visits her brother and his wife, they complain that she spends all her time reading, though she insists that she read very little ('only . . . Gil Blas, now and then a newspaper, two or three of Lady M. W. Montagu's letters, and a *few* pages in a magazine'), and only because her hosts rose so late (I, pp. 111, 105). Since her literacy is important as a sign of status, she repeatedly presents herself not as a reader of low-status texts like novels but of travels, education works, memoirs and letters, including Boswell's *Tour of the Hebrides*, the Travels of Mungo Park, and Mme de Genlis' work (II, pp. 33, 77). She approves some novels, like Hamilton's *The Cottagers of Glenburnie* (II, p. 78), but generally finds them a 'dangerous, fascinating kind of amusement' which 'destroy all relish for useful, instructive studies' (I, p. 275).

If literacy was difficult for impoverished middle-class women, it was still harder in the classes below. Labouring-class literacy, especially among women, tended to be relatively low, though rising in the later period thanks to Hannah More and others. Dr Johnson's view that literature 'now pervades society through all its ranks' may be only 'complacence',[30] but there is substantial anecdotal evidence suggesting a trend in that direction. Carl Philip Moritz met a tailor's widow whose husband fell in love with her because of the 'good style' in which she read Milton: Moritz thinks this typical of 'the common people' of England, whose literacy 'brings them nearer to the higher' classes than in Germany, because of the accessibilty of 'cheap . . . editions'.[31] Johnson's *Idler* is full of literate working women, like Betty Broom and Molly Quick. However the increase in labouring-class female readers was accompanied by a growth of anxiety about them. Broom's employers think it 'criminal or dangerous to know how to read', and she gains an unjust reputation for 'sauciness' simply because she is literate.[32]

At best, lower-class female reading may be presented in oddly ambivalent ways, as in Charles Lamb's *Rosamund Gray* (1798). The cottager household of Rosamund and her grandmother has a tiny library of a Bible, a prayer book, *The Complete Angler*, the first part of *Pilgrim's Progress*, and Wither's *Emblems* (pp. 9, 51, 11). While she confines herself to such old-fashioned reading, Rosamund is safe, though the episode in which she disobeys her grandmother and almost falls into 'a deep chalk-pit' marks her as vulnerable to the 'sexual failing' of Eve (p. 22). This 'fall' (p. 23) symbolises a sexual awakening, itself caused by reading: as she reads Mackenzie's *Julia de Roubigné* with Allan Clare they recognise their mutual attraction and are 'changed' (pp. 37, 40); later her reading of Burns at Margate (presumably from a circulating library) also adumbrates sexual danger. Although Rosamund and her reading remain innocent (*Julia de Roubigné* was often cited as a moral novel[33]), her implication in the sin of Eve, embodied in a shift from traditional to genteel reading, makes her vulnerable to rape by Matravis and resulting death. While elsewhere Lamb writes sympathetically of the reading of lower-class girls, *Rosamund Gray* is more ambivalent. Its nostalgia for old books and 'the purity and simplicity of childhood', its desire to escape 'the stains of manhood' (p. 113) or mature womanhood, lead it to find sexuality, and the modern adult reading which figures it, a source of anxiety, especially in lower-class women.

The problem for lower-class readers was acquiring not only the ability to read but also, as James Raven argues, books to read. Since books were so expensive, even a very small number were out of the question for the poorest readers. William Cobbett, on his way to find a job, spent all his money, 3d, on Swift's *Tale of a Tub* and passed the rest of the day reading it; Thomas Holcroft, a stable-boy in the 1760s, learned to read from the Bible but could find nothing else to read but ballads pasted on walls; Bristol milk-seller Ann Yearsley learned about classical mythology from 'little ordinary prints that hung in a shop-window', and when she had nothing else read the 'verse' on tombstones in Clifton churchyard.[34]

Literacy rates were probably lower for women than men in the labouring classes. The mother of labouring-class John Clare, born in 1793, 'knew not a single letter', while his father could 'read a little in the Bible', and this pattern may have been typical.[35] There is little evidence on how lower-class women actually read: the early nineteenth-century vogue for lives of self-made men, from which much evidence for reading can be drawn, is quite gender-specific.[36] However, in Clare's class the identification of culture with print culture was not as strong as for the elite classes, and he depicts women hearing stories and ballads read aloud, and as the special guardians of traditional oral narratives of 'Giants, Hobgoblins and Fairies'.[37] Moreover, labouring women could profit from the cultural reformations of Romanticism: Ann Yearsley argues that 'the touch of Ecstacy' which inspires poetry 'strikes/ Most pow'rful on . . . untaught Minds'.[38] While for an Augustan writer the lack of a classical education was a crippling handicap, like playing whist 'not only *without* but *against* the Ace of Trumps', for a Romantic poet to be untaught was a positive advantage, a rhetorical claim of which many women poets took full advantage.[39]

FARMERS AND SERVANTS

Treatments of lower-class female reading tend to focus on two groups – farmers and agricultural labourers, and domestic servants. Farmers were central in ensuring that 'capital is . . . constantly circulating', especially in the years of revolution and war: hard-line conservatives were therefore shocked that they should read when they could be working, finding such behaviour by women especially culpable. Mrs Orgueil in Sarah Fielding's *Adventures of David Simple* criticises David for teaching farmer's daughter Betty Dunster to read, fearing that 'instead of minding her Dairy' she would waste time 'poring over a romance' (p. 328), and a review of 1772 echoes this, arguing that when a 'farmer's daughter sits down to read a novel, she certainly misspends her time', because she could be engaged in 'real service to her family'. While conservatives deplored such changes, bookseller James Lackington paints an idyllic world where even 'the poorer sort of farmers' kept '*Tom Jones, Roderick Random*, and other entertaining books, stuck up on their bacon-racks', and their children happily read fiction, and read it in a gendered way, the sons enjoying *Peregrine Pickle* and the daughters *Pamela*.[40] What for Lackington was a utopia of literacy, though, was a nightmare for conservatives like More.

Ivy Pinchbeck demonstrated that in this period the wives and daughters of wealthy farmers ceased to be involved in production and 'joined the ranks of the leisured classes', and More's 'The Two Wealthy Farmers; or, the History of Mr Bragwell' offers a moralistic reading of this shift. The farmer's daughters read circulating library novels, and so waste time and fail to learn the virtues appropriate to their 'station . . . humility, economy, meekness, contentment, self-denial and industry', becoming 'discontented', and aping elite-class '*elegance . . . sentimental feeling . . . sensibility*'.[41] As a result Polly marries a strolling player she mistakes for a gentleman, and Betsey a dissipated gentleman who kills himself when the money is spent, leaving her to die in childbirth. Stereotypes persisted of lower-class women as ravenous readers of fiction and little else, and this was especially believed of servants. In contemporary satire female servants devour novels, 'the *Pupil of Pleasure*, or else *Man of Feeling*', and later commentators tend to take this self-interested rhetoric at face value: Ian Watt, for instance, assumed that 'Servant girls . . . constituted a fairly important part of the reading public' of fiction.[42]

Jan Fergus, though, has produced evidence that 'servants' devotion to novels' has been exaggerated.[43] Her researches, using the records of a Midlands firm of booksellers, suggests that novels constituted rather a small element of servants' reading, with guides (including cookery books and self-improvement manuals) and conduct books, followed by religious works, constituting by far the largest categories, especially for women. Servants 'did not order or buy any English novels' in these records: Richardson is 'the only novelist shown . . . to have attracted servants', but it is two male servants who borrow *Clarissa*. Women prefer book-keeping manuals, *The Complete Servant Maid*, or religious books (though a few read fiction, including *Robinson Crusoe*, Eliza Haywood's *The Invisible Spy*, and Maria Susannah Cooper's *The Exemplary Mother*). While in conservative stereotypes servant women were corrupted by novels, this small sample suggests that their reading actually 'reflects that of the middling ranks', demonstrating aspirations to self-improvement.[44]

Upper servants needed to read: a manual of 1773 finds the ability to 'read well aloud' essential in a lady's maid, and servants clearly read even lower down the household hierarchy. The Scottish cook in the Sibbald household read *Paradise Lost*, and in 1778 Hester Thrale won a bet about servant literacy with Dr Johnson by demonstrating that of her eighteen servants, four women and Mr Thrale's valet had read *Don Quixote*.[45] Servants might have the advantage over other labourers both in time to read and access to books. Molly Quick in the *Idler* acquires 'learning' as maid to a lady who has 'many books' and allows her 'much time to read', and Ellen Weeton's mother, having 'a great desire to improve her mind and manners . . . read much' as a lady's maid in Lancashire.[46]

Conservative commentators accused ladies who allowed their maids to 'read . . . novels' of neglect and even irreligion: but others argued that concern for servant literacy was part of an employer's duty. Utopian patriarch Sir Charles Grandison kept 'a Servants Library, in three classes', '*divinity* and *morality*', '*housewifery*' and 'innocent amusement' including history, travels and true adventures (though not, apparently, novels): there is a separate 'Library of Gardening' (vii, p. 286). Fictional successors of Grandison, like Mrs Villars in Cooper's *The Exemplary Mother* (1769), also allow servants to borrow books (i, pp. 13–14). Mrs Taylor's *Practical Hints to Young Females on the Duties of a Wife, a Mother, and a Mistress to a Family* (1818) suggests that in 'every kitchen there should be a library' of books adapted to the comprehension of 'kitchen readers' (p. 41). This democratising of reading clearly happened in real life, though probably only on a small scale.[47]

Accounts of servant literacy show anxiety, and not only about servants reading novels. The breakdown of the Middleton marriage in 1796 demonstrates the 'high level of literacy' of the family servants who could all read and write, except 'the dairymaid and the wetnurse', and who kept notes and wrote letters about their employers which were used in the divorce proceedings. Servant literacy could thus lead to anxiety about the real privacy of the private sphere.[48] It might also be equated with laziness and incompetence. The *Gentleman's Magazine* account of servant-poet Mary Leapor imagines her writing 'while the jack was standing still, and the meat scorching', and a number of her poems deal with accusations that she neglects work to read, charges which caused equal anxiety to other working-class women poets, like dairy-women Ann Yearsley and Janet Little.[49] So entrenched were these images that when Lovelace arranges a fire to flush Clarissa out of her lodgings, he blames it on a servant-girl reading romances late at night (p. 723). A key theme among women servant poets, indeed, is self-defence from charges of inappropriate reading and writing: Christian Milne defends her 'foible' of loving novels, which does not prevent her reading the Bible, 'Travel . . . and history', and Elizabeth Hands satirised attacks on her poems simply because of her servant status.[50]

READING AND LABOURING-CLASS WOMEN POETS

The vogue of 'uncultivated genius', which aided the success of poets like Clare and Burns, extended to women, and labouring poets like Mary Collier (1690?–c. 1762) and Ann Yearsley (1752–1806), and servant poets like Mary Leapor (1722–46), Janet Little (1759–1813), and Elizabeth Hands (fl. 1789), became culturally significant, the most self-aware of them producing poems which explicitly or implicitly 'distinguish a gendered class identity'. Such women rarely, unlike Clare, wrote their own stories, so it is difficult to discover how they learned to read, what they read and how they obtained access to it. Mary Collier, child of 'poor, but honest' parents, was taught to read by them, and Ann Yearsley learned to read from her mother and to write from her brother.[51]

Probably most literate working-class women had read little apart but the Bible, which was 'crucially formative' for them. Elizabeth Hands' *The Death of Amnon* (1789) took a Biblical theme, though she satirises the view that anything beyond religious reading is 'out of [the] sphere' of women servants, and mocks elite-class readers for their ignorance of the Bible, which must be borrowed from the housekeeper.[52] The next most significant authors were probably Shakespeare, Milton and Pope. Some servant poets, like Phillis Wheatley, managed some acquaintance with classical authors, presumably in translation: Ann Yearsley's favourite book was a translation of Virgil's *Georgics*, Mary Leapor may have learned a little Latin and certainly knew Greek and Latin poetry in translation, and Mary Collier asserts that despite her 'low' birth and life of 'labour', she had none the less 'seen, and read' stories 'of the Pagan Gods'. Yearsley knew some poems of Milton, Pope and Young, Janet Little could allude to 'Swift, Thomson, Addison an' Young' and to Dr Johnson's *Lives of the Poets*, and Collier had read some history, Fox's *Book of Martyrs*, Josephus, and some *Spectators*.[53]

Some women acquired books. Working-class York poet Charlotte Richardson (1775–?1850) had a 'library [which] consisted of a Bible, a Common-prayer Book, the Whole Duty of Man, the Pilgrim's Progress, and one or two other books of like description', and had also managed to read 'Gray's poems, Goldsmith's poems, and the Death of Abel . . . the Vicar of Wakefield, and one volume of [Frances Brooke's] Lady Julia Mandeville'; Mary Leapor owned 'sixteen or seventeen single volumes', including 'Part of Mr. *Pope's* Works, *Dryden's* Fables', and some plays. Equally important, women like Leapor, Hands and Little, might have access to libraries of employers or could borrow books from friends: even Yearsley's impoverished mother managed to borrow books for her daughter from '*her betters*'.[54]

Lack of time was as constraining as lack of reading material. The parents of Mary Leapor, at first proud of her poetic talents, tried to prohibit her writing and reading when they feared it impeded 'more profitable Employment' as a servant.[55] The double burden of work outside and within the home chronicled in Mary Collier's *The Woman's Labour* (1739) made reading and writing especially difficult for labouring-class women. Ann Yearsley felt obliged to present herself as compliant to domestic ideology as well as class hierarchies, and explains over and over that her reading did not prevent her work either within or outside the home, for she 'never allowed herself to look into a book till her work was done and her children asleep'.[56]

Although labouring-class women could read the same books as their 'betters', they could not do so in the same quantities. Yearsley admired Milton, Young and Pope, but had only read *Paradise Lost*, *Night Thoughts*, and 'Eloisa to Abelard', and had never heard of 'Dryden, Spenser, Thomson and Prior'.[57] Of course we have only the word of Hannah More for this, and her rhetoric depends on presenting the poet's lack of education as a guarantee of 'genuine' genius. This is a major problem in studying working writers, and the patrons of Mary Leapor also 'minimize her reading',[58] although of all contemporary labouring-class women poets she shows the widest reading. The very image of the natural genius, initially enabling, might later prove inhibiting in ghettoising the labouring woman poet and separating her from broader literary culture.

Yearsley's first, More-influenced, collection, *Poems, on Several Occasions* (1785) colludes with this image, presenting herself in a cascade of negatives as 'Unaided, unassisted' (p. 6), 'guideless . . ./ Uncouth, uncivilized . . . / Unpolished' (p. 10). She displays limited knowledge of literature, though alluding to Milton (p. 63), Beattie's *Minstrel* (p. 101) and *The Castle of Otranto* (p. 87ff), of which she offers early images-of-women criticism. In this collection writing (and perhaps reading: see 'Clifton Hill') is connected with the poet's search to 'find a home' and 'a long lost mother' (p. 6): Yearsley associates her reading with the 'proud maternal care' of the mother who died before her daughter acquired patronage.[59] Possibly Yearsley hoped to rediscover that lost mother in her patron Hannah More, the 'Stella' of her poems. But already there are tensions. Stella is invoked to 'assist' and 'aid' (pp. 5, 10), but instead 'soars' out of sight, and cannot be claimed even as a 'Friend' because friendship 'cou'd dare exist/ But in equality' (p. 85). Reading and writing for Yearsley may have promised a preparation for equality, allowing her to reject class and gender stereotypes of the 'passive' woman capable only of 'low submission' (p. 91). But if so, she found More uncooperative.

More's patronage of Yearsley came to a bitter end, Yearsley complaining that More had insisted on controlling the profits from her work (and, equally a source of conflict, that she had kept from her a gift of books sent by an aristocratic patroness), More accusing Yearsley of pride and vanity. Yearsley, bright, acerbic and difficult, refused to be compliant to More's conservative vision: indeed, as herself only recently fallen from the property-owning classes,[60] she was reluctant to regard More as her superior. After the break with More, Yearsley used her profits to become proprietor of a circulating library at Bristol Hot-wells, in deliberate defiance of the reading ideologies of the acutely anti-circulating library More. Yearsley's second collection, *Poems on Various Subjects* (1787), published after the break-up, is visibly less keen to emphasise a lack of reading experience, and although she continues to identify herself with 'Nature' (pp. 4, 67, 94), she also quotes *The Tempest* (p. 73), alludes to Chatterton (p. 145ff), Pope (p. 139), *Werther* (pp. 109–10) and, probably, Thomson, Frances Greville and Voltaire,[61] and uses many classical references (e.g. pp. 94–9).

Mary Leapor's experiences of reading, writing and female patronage were markedly different. She loved reading, was 'committed to educating herself', and had read classics in translation, Shakespeare, works of Locke, Chaucer, Gay, periodical literature, and plays, including Otway, Rowe and Congreve. She also knew the work of Swift and Pope well and was influenced by them: her patroness hailed her as the 'successor of Pope'.[62] Leapor may have gone to school – her probable teacher, Richard Cooper, a bookbinder, probably loaned her books – and had good networks of acquaintance through which books could be borrowed. Her employer, Susanna Jennens of Weston Hall in Northamptonshire, probably allowed the kitchen-maid poet to use her library – its contents have been reconstructed by Richard Greene, and offer clues to what Leapor may have read – and may have been more supportive, for there was a 'group of women poets associated with Weston Hall'.[63] Another patron was the 'well-read' clergyman's daughter Bridget Freemantle who loaned books including the *Odyssey*. Her account of Leapor is remarkable for its 'self-effacement and absence of class prejudice'[64] and its reversal of class-expectations: the higher-class woman 'Fear[s] . . . being troublesome' to her lower-class friend, the servant issues 'Invitations' and is so 'obliging' that Freemantle fears she would be 'ungrateful' if she did not accept.[65]

Because of this sympathetic support from a class above her own, Leapor was able to write poems which do not erase the issue of class and are, indeed, unusually 'class-conscious', but in a form which is playful rather than explicitly reformist. Her masterpiece *Crumble-Hall* offers a radical rereading of the country-house poem which 'seeks to demystify the values of the gentry'[66] by marginalising the landowners and laying bare things usually concealed, life below stairs and the laborious construction of the apparently natural landscape. In its class criticism textuality takes a significant place, with the monopolisation of books by upper-class men a crucial symptom of the exclusion of women and the lower classes from the cultural project: Biron, who sleeps surrounded by the 'dusty Volumes' she would love to read, may be William Henry Chauncy of Edgcote House, Leapor's last and least happy employment.[67]

Perhaps because of the success of her experience of patronage, Leapor's view of class is critical but unembittered, and her poems emphasise gender inequalities, what she shared with Susanna Jennens and Bridget Freemantle, rather than the inequalities of class that divided them. In the second volume of *Poems upon Several Occasions* (1751), 'Man the Monarch' satirises the male sex as 'envious' of women's abilities and 'Greedy of Power' (p. 10), 'Complaining Daphne' warns the young woman of the predations of man (p. 77), and 'An Essay on Woman', another radical revision of Pope, concludes that 'Unhappy Woman's but a Slave at large' (p. 67).

Though both see class and gender as related mechanisms, Leapor's social critique concentrates on gender, Yearsley's on class. Yearsley's novel *The Royal Captives* (1795) implicitly supports the early stages of the French Revolution, presenting the poor as victims of the *ancien régime*'s 'audacious tyranny' (I, p. 105), while in particular 'Oppression hangs on women' (II, p. 103). In this novel, reading is certainly a preparation for equality. Henry, unknown to himself Louis XIV's unacknowledged elder twin, is brought up by peasants. Later when he is taken away to be educated for his true class, his foster-mother tries to console him by insisting that 'Without reading good books . . . [he] can never know the world' (I, p. 93), and that such 'good books' are not available in the peasant household. However, although men's reading is explicitly a preparation for equality, it is dubious that equality can be available to women, whose reading, especially in the labouring classes, seems positively dangerous. The shepherd's daughter Anna (note the autobiographical resonances) is an enthusiastic reader, though we are assured, as in Yearsley's autobiographical writing, that she does not neglect her work but only 'reads when she should take her natural rest' (I, p. 185). Anna, though, is seduced by the upper-class Antonio, and dies in childbirth. For a labouring woman reading, however scrupulously disciplined, is almost inevitably equivalent to transgression. Anna, who begins as a figure of autobiographical self-vindication, ends as an embodiment of Yearsley's anxieties about class and gender transgressions, especially focusing on literacy.

Both Leapor and Yearsley read and critically rewrote their male elite-class predecessors, using their forms of georgic, Gothic, satire, horatian epistle and country-house poem to very different effect. But while Leapor's reading prepared for some degree of social equality with her patron and her circle, Yearsley's reading – and this is what worried Hannah More – might have formed a preparation for political equality and a qualified support for revolutionary change.

CLASS, GENDER, READING: HANNAH MORE

As I have shown, a vigorous contest ensued over mass literacy, and whether its effect would be the erosion of standards or the effective maintenance of social control. Even the most committed to the project were aware of its dangers, the most conservative of its advantages. Hester Thrale, whom I have quoted as fellow-traveller of Mandeville, also saw the possibilities of using increased access to print culture as a form of social control, relating how Mrs Townsend, angry at her coachman for getting drunk, read him the story of Alexander the Great's murder of Clytus: as a result, 'the Coachman shed Tears' and had 'never . . . been drunk since'.[68]

Lower-class reading as a mechanism of social control was central to the work of Hannah More. Strongly opposed to novel-reading and the circulating library, and anxious about the reading of milliners, servants, farmers and manual labourers, she channelled these anxieties into a movement not to prevent but to direct the literacy of such new readers, which has been described as 'the effective colonisation of an entire class'.[69] Much of her work targets specific social groups and their reading situations, from *Hints towards Forming the Character of a Young Princess* designed for Princess Charlotte (who disliked it, since it made 'the hours so long'[70]), through *Thoughts on the Importance of the Manners of the Great to General Society* and *Stories for the Middle Ranks* to the Cheap Repository Tracts aimed at the lowest class of readers. More sought to involve all levels of society in her project for a moral and religious revolution designed to prevent political revolution.

On labouring-class education More considered herself a moderate, attacking extremists of both sides. Farmer Hoskins in 'The Sunday School' argues the Mandevillian case that lower-class reading 'always does more harm than good' by making labourers 'think themselves too good to work'.[71] This is not what is intended by More or her fictional persona Mrs Jones: 'to teach good principles to the lower classes, is the most likely way to save the country. Now, in order to do this, we must teach them to read.' It would still be dangerous then to 'turn them adrift to find books for themselves', but More intends constant surveillance, providing the poor with '*safe* books'. Mrs Jones always has 'a few little good books in her pocket to give away', and More herself records distributing annually 'nearly 200 Bibles, Common Prayer Books, and Testaments'.[72] Female authority, More's and Mrs Jones', could operate most legitimately on lower-class people, especially women (as Mrs Jones so triumphantly demonstrated, and More, at least in the case of Yearsley, so signally failed to).

More did more than distribute Bibles. Knowing 'the school of Paine had been labouring to undermine' religion and 'good government' by distributing 'in cottages, and in highways . . . into mines and coal pits' cheap editions of 'alluring . . . novels' with an implicit revolutionary agenda, she decided to 'fight them with their own weapons', producing the *Cheap Repository Tracts* as 'antidote' to their 'fatal poison'. She is uneasy about using fiction even as the tool of a greater good, aware that some 'strict people' will think 'invention should have been entirely excluded'; but she accepts the received wisdom that the lower orders love fiction, and uses this for her own purposes – 'alas! I know with whom I have to deal'.[73]

More disagrees that social stability can only be ensured by keeping workers illiterate: but by the 1820s, when the immediate danger of revolution had passed, she began to fear that her movement had gone much further than she had intended. In correspondence with William Wilberforce in 1823 she objected to any broadening of the curriculum of education for the poor. Some reformers aimed to teach 'ancient history, and even the sciences', which a labourer could learn only by neglecting his employment. Some argued that 'there is *nothing* that the poor ought not to be taught', but this is a manifest 'absurdity', which she fears will precipitate exactly the social unrest her own reforms were designed to preempt.[74] More's, and Mrs Jones', programme was much more modest. The poor were to be taught 'only to enable them to read the Bible'. For '*labourer's* children' reading was sufficient, and she did not 'approve of teaching charity children to write', which she believed incompatible with 'hard and laborious employments'.[75] Their immediate superiors, the children of 'common farmers', might also learn writing, arithmetic and other knowledge 'necessary for persons of this class'. Exceptions might be made for children of 'superior capacities', but such cases would be few.[76]

As a woman, More's special mission was to labouring-class women: indeed, it has been plausibly proposed that, by arguing that the family was the 'originary site of historic endeavour' and devising a range of 'woman-directed discourses', More's 'counter-revolutionary feminism' offered women more opportunities to 'enlarge [their] sphere of activity and influence' than revolutionary feminists like Wollstonecraft.[77] There was often a 'female club' attached to More's Sunday Schools: members subscribed 6d a month, and a girl who maintained a virtuous reputation would receive a 'bride's portion' on marriage. These female clubs were popular, in one instance having a roll three times the size of the male list. The 'Weekly School' for girls taught 'sewing, knitting and spinning' as well as elementary reading, and aimed to *'make good wives for working men'* by teaching 'industry and good management'.[78] Like the ladies of Millenium Hall, More entered public life through acts of charity modelled on the family, and used her own unconventional position and role to argue for entirely traditional female roles.

For More, literacy is an issue which is both class- and gender-specific. Her stories of labouring-class reading often focus on female readers and show high levels of ambivalence. On the one hand, they can be positive: the daughter of Jack Anvil in *Village Politics* comes home from the charity-school with a 'story-book' containing a 'fable about the Belly and the Limbs' (p. 9), which had been used as a conservative allegory of the organic unity of society from the time of Shakespeare's *Coriolanus*.[79] The agenda of the charity-school is explicitly political as well as religious, and the key vehicle for these messages is female reading. Another positive story of female reading centres on Hester Wilmot, a labouring-class girl who learns to read and is educated out of rebelliousness, and whose story legitimises and publicises More's project. She goes on to convert her parents and win the school prize of 'a handsome Bible' before going on to become a teacher herself.[80]

However, despite her youthful love of literature and despite positive models of the female reader, when dealing with low-class characters More tends to figure competent reading acts as male, incompetent as female, as the reading maidservant who opens this chapter might indicate. In correspondence about the education of poor girls, she rejoices over the high recruitment for female clubs, but even in this passage the ideal reader is a boy who 'called for passages of scripture frequently'. Many stories turn on acts of misreading by sub-genteel females, like 'The Two Wealthy Farmers', where Farmer Bragwell's daughters read novels and are, with tragic consequences, familiarised with 'ADULTERY, GAMING, DUELS AND SELF-MURDER'. Fortunately Polly is reclaimable, and by reading Doddridge's *Rise and Progress of Religion in the Soul* she is able to refashion herself, although this text at first seems 'ill suited to a taste formed by novels and plays'.[81]

Moreover, when More mocks misguidedly ambitious schemes to educate the poor, her examples of misreaders are almost always female: the 'poor little girl' who says she is learning 'the whole circle of the sciences' from one 'very small book'; the 'little girl, a servant's child' who does not know the catechism but is learning '*Syntax*'; another girl who is subjected to an over-ambitious education programme which she cannot even articulate grammatically – 'I learns geography, and the harts and senses'; another girl who recites a poem 'extremely well' but lacks the most basic knowledge of the Bible.[82] Even More, a female reader and writer centrally concerned with issues of female literacy, tends to accept the rhetorical device that figures misreading as feminine.

CHAPTER 7

A dangerous recreation: women and novel-reading

The argument about women's reading centred on the novel, with novel-reading one of the most contested areas in cultural debate. The *Lady's Magazine*, for example, ran a series of articles on novel-reading, representing virtually all imaginable ideological positions. Novels were subject to large-scale 'obloquy and censure', but this did not convince either the reading public or less repressive critics who defended them on grounds both aesthetic and moral.[1] In reviews of novels, unlike other genres, 'questions of audience came into explicit focus', with novel-reading attributed to 'the young, the ignorant and the idle', and especially the female.[2] A 'stable' – and 'negative' – association was drawn between women and fiction, and in reviews novel-readers were 'commonly . . . figured as female' rather than the implied reader, the 'gentleman or the scholar' of traditionally sanctioned genres.[3]

The anti-novel literature is voluminous and repetitive: the same stereotypes, like the vulnerability of the novel-reading girl to seduction, and even the same words, like 'poison' and 'soften', recur compulsively. This certainly suggests, as E. J. Clery maintains, that arguments about the novel were really about larger issues, 'unregulated social and economic forces, and the erosion of established hierarchies of value and authority', displaced on to a more manageable canvas, and that relocating these arguments on to the novel disguised a culture-specific issue as one allegedly of timeless universality, female sexuality.[4] Nonetheless, I shall proceed on the assumption that these arguments may have been about more than the novel, but were also about the novel.

The loudest voices in the controversy over novels came from the conservative opposition. The heroines of the didactic novelists of the turn of the century did not themselves read novels: West's Maria Williams, More's Lucilla Stanley or Sandham's Ellen Stanley prefer books 'on a serious subject', which tell 'truth, which novels never do'.[5] This extends even to Gothic writers: in Eleanor Sleath's *The Orphan of the*

Rhine, Laurette's mother 'prohibited' her daughter's reading of 'fictitious tales of distress' because they 'might have a dangerous tendency' (p. 147): ironically, Laurette would not have been allowed to read the novel whose heroine she is.

Most accounts of novels are, it is true, more nuanced. As Ina Ferris points out, commentators repeatedly contrast dangerous 'ordinary novels' with an exceptional few which are instructive as well as entertaining, like those of Burney.[6] Other women novelists achieved comparable status: Mary Brunton's work, for instance, is recommended as the opposite of received stereotypes, for reading it will keep the female reader 'safe from seduction'. The *Lady's Magazine* carefully discriminates between common novels – 'the powerful engine with which the seducer atacks the female heart' – and the exceptional few which can be recommended: this latter category includes Burney's *Evelina*, Mackenzie's *The Man of Feeling*, Scott's *Millenium Hall*, Brooke's *Julia Mandeville*, Lennox's *The Female Quixote*, Inchbald's *A Simple Story*, and the novels of Richardson.[7]

Even the term 'novel' became problematic, so that respectable writers resisted applying it to their work. Burney experimented with less provocative formulations, even though in the preface to *The Wanderer* she protests at anti-novel 'prejudice', and in the preface to *Evelina* praises novel-writers including Fielding, Richardson, Smollett and Johnson.[8] Amelia Opie in 1801 published *The Father and Daughter* as a 'SIMPLE, MORAL TALE', not a 'NOVEL', although she alludes approvingly to Inchbald's *Nature and Art* and *Clarissa*; in the same year Maria Edgeworth described *Belinda* as 'a Moral Tale – the author not wishing to acknowledge a Novel', although this preface praises novels including those of Burney and Inchbald. Novelists and their readers, by creating oppositions between good novels and ordinary novels which are receptacles of 'folly, error, and vice',[9] seek both to defend their preferred novels and express ambivalence about the form.

Toward the end of the period, cultural paranoia about the novel abated somewhat, particularly after the publication of *Waverley* in 1814, a crucial watershed, after which women writers' domination of the novel lessened and the reputation of some previously well-regarded women novelists declined, but the legitimacy of (at least certain) novels for women readers increased.[10] In 1815 Anne Grant thought 'a bad novel is the worst of bad things', but that 'a good one confers a material benefit on society', and rejoiced that novels were showing 'a gradual amendment of taste and morals'; Eliza Fenwick also believed the 'high tone of the present race of Novels is a blessing to the rising Generation', citing Scott and Fenimore Cooper as evidence.[11] This last quotation implies the true nature of the change, for the improving reputation of novels was intimately connected with the rise of a new cadre of male novelists after a period of virtual female hegemony, with Scott 'the man who finally redeemed the novel as literary discourse', a redemption which depended on the ejection of the female.[12]

In this chapter I examine four novels which foreground women's reading of fiction – Charlotte Lennox's *The Female Quixote* (1752), which, perhaps, satirises the reading of French romance, Eaton Stannard Barrett's *The Heroine* (1813), which criticises the reading of practically all imaginative fiction, Jane Austen's *Northanger Abbey* (1818), which makes comic mileage out of the misreading of Radcliffean Gothic, and Sarah Green's *Scotch Novel Reading* (1824), which guys the vogue for Scott's novels. What is actually going on in each, though, is more important than this, for what is under scrutiny is women's stake in culture.

The heroine misled by novel-reading is a common plot-motif especially in the early nineteenth century, and it is unsurprising that treatments by women novelists are often 'paradoxical', ambivalent and conflicted. There *were* novels that warned of the dangers of male reading: Aubrey in Polidori's *The Vampyre* (1819) and Scott's Edward Waverley are misled by romance-reading until they become 'masculine version[s] of Catherine Morland'.[13] But the woman misreader is central in the fullest and most popular accounts, raising the vital issue of women's place, as readers and writers, within the newly professionalised world of literature.

NOVEL AND ROMANCE

Before continuing, the nomenclature of fiction needs some elucidation. Many commentators, especially early in the period, vigorously distinguished between the romance and its 'younger Sister' the novel. Novels 'are meant to represent beings like ourselves, and the probable incidents of human life', whereas romance 'describes what never happened nor is likely to happen'.[14] The language and structure of the two were different, with the 'lofty and elevated' language of romance contrasted with the novel's language of everyday reality, and the 'detached and independent adventures' of romance with the 'Unity of design' of the novel.[15] Such distinctions, however, are only useful up to a point, and tend to collapse later in the period under the weight of the Gothic novel, sometimes seen as a hybrid of novel and romance: Godwin in 1797 uses the two terms as if they were absolutely synonymous.[16] Nonetheless, the distinction remained useful for making moral and aesthetic points.

Although fiction was generally seen as a feminised field, when novel and romance were specifically compared, the realism of the novel tended to be gendered as masculine, the fantasy of romance as feminine. When in the early nineteenth century a canon of the novel began to be formulated, it centred on the (allegedly) realist male writers, Richardson, Fielding, Smollett and Sterne.[17] Since, as we have seen, three of these writers raised moral reservations in some female readers, it is clear that the act of canon-formation participated in the cultural movement to counteract female hegemony over the novel and reconfigure it as a form more amenable to male control.

The comparison between novel and romance may work to the advantage of either. To a male-identified faction, realism was obviously superior to fantasy, the 'dangerous tendency' of fiction tamed only by its subservience to the real. Johnson's Imperia becomes umarriageable by learning false expectations from 'the perusal of romances'; Lennox prescribes the realism of *Clarissa* as a cure for her female quixote; and Maria Edgeworth in 'Angelina; or, L'Amie Inconnue' prescribes *The Female Quixote* for a similar disease.[18] To such writers, it is self-evident that romances encourage foolish idealism and unjustified paranoia, and that a male-identified realism is needed to counteract a female taste for fantasy.

There was equally, however, a vocal faction who found the realism of novels their most troubling characteristic, arguing that romance was harmless precisely because its blatant fictionality would not mislead the female reader. A romance-reader might not be a female quixote but a paragon of virtue and sensitivity, her chosen reading figuring her 'sublimity of soul' and – at least in the case of one *Lady's Magazine* story – making her a worthy bride for a hero who wanders about 'with a book in his hand'.[19] If the unreality of the romance could figure sublimity of soul, the realism of the novel might serve as the vehicle for corruption or deception, for the more realistically '*human passions*' are depicted, the more the effect is to 'cloud the reason' and lead readers into 'dangerous errors'.[20]

Moreover, the fantasy of romance might be more amenable than the realism of the novel for the encoding of morality, or so commentators including James Fordyce argued. Defenders of romances praised their 'good morals', their overwhelmingly affirmative images of women, and their provision of positive role-models, men who are 'good, generous, full of virtue', and women who display 'Virginal and Conjugal Chastity'.[21] The 'extravagances and absurdities of Romances' are obvious, but the 'good effects they have produced' also require acknowledgement: they 'speak to all the noblest feelings of the human heart', teach women the importance of 'virtue' and men 'respect' for women.[22] If these are false expectations, such commentators might argue, so much the worse for society.

As Ros Ballaster has suggested, 'what was at stake' in the argument over romance was quite simply 'female power'.[23] Clara Reeve's *The Progress of Romance* (1785) builds this battle of the sexes over literary authority into its dialogic form, as Hortensius debates the value of fiction with Sophronia and Euphrasia, and generally gets the worst of the argument. The dialogue allows Reeve to represent the contradictions about fiction endemic in her culture, and the ambivalences experienced by a woman novelist of the mid century. Hortensius is the spokesman for a traditional elite male-centred culture, his ideal literature classical epic poems: while he would not 'prohibit reading *all* works of fiction' he would destroy most, especially since he believes women 'read more of these books' than men, and as the weaker sex are more likely to be 'hurt by them' (II, pp. 80–1). Euphrasia denies that fiction is read mostly by women (II, p. 81), and she and Sophronia defend fiction and fiction-writers even while acknowledging their faults. Euphrasia, indeed, goes so far as to recognise the 'fine and amiable qualities' of the then-notorious Aphra Behn, despite her 'improper' fiction (I, pp. 118, 117).

The argument which Hortensius finds most troubling, and which ultimately proves decisive, is that the central plank of elite masculine culture, classical epic poems, are actually 'on an equality with . . . Romance' (I, p. 2), only considered superior because of cultural 'prejudices': both are forms founded 'in real History', though the 'superstructure was pure fiction' (I, p. 17). In some respects, indeed, epic is 'of worse tendency' than romance, because it contains so much that is indecent and unchristian (II, p. 81). Reeve dissolves the distinctions between high-status masculine forms, history and epic, and low-status female forms, novels and romance. Hortensius is 'astonished – admonished – and convinced!' (II, p. 82). This is, however, only one strand in a polyvalent argument: despite its defence of romance, Reeve's treatise concludes with bibliographies for children and young women which contain virtually no fiction (except Richardson) but which depend heavily on conduct-books and history.

LENNOX AND *THE FEMALE QUIXOTE*

Lennox's *The Female Quixote* is unusual, for in 1752 a full-length account of female misreading is rare, though briefer accounts are common. Lennox's fiction in general is interested in women's reading, especially romance-reading: Harriot Stuart is 'deeply read in romances', though her mother considers these books 'horrid', and Clara Bellenden in *Euphemia* is a great romance-reader, and although her mother is critical, the heroine defends romances for their 'excellent lessons of morality'.[24] In these novels, although romance-reading is a point of conflict between mothers and daughters (perhaps because, as we shall see, they encode potentially oppositional models of femininity), Lennox is apparently not herself critical, and romance-reading seems at best a resource for women, at worst a harmless waste of time.

Why then does romance-reading become so serious a moral issue in *The Female Quixote*, and why does Lennox concentrate on the apparently anachronistic issue of the reading of French romances? Clara Reeve certainly thought this weakened the novel, that its 'satire . . . lost its aim' because in the 1750s the taste was 'extinct' and French romance 'exploded'.[25] *Euphemia* though suggests that even by 1790 the taste was not quite extinct. But a more important answer lies in Lennox's 'not . . . unequivocal' treatment of her subject.[26] Possibly by 'scapegoating romance . . . Lennox protected novels', implicitly defending her own practice. Kate Levin has argued that Lennox's early work, especially 'The Art of Coquetry' in *Poems on Several Occasions* (1747) and *The Life of Harriot Stuart*, were read as affirming passion rather than morality, and were thus 'characterised as morally problematic', and that the repudiation of romance in *The Female Quixote* attempted 'to dramatize and advertize her own literary reform'. Levin's argument is persuasive up to a point,[27] but it does not disprove the ambivalence which most modern readers have discerned in the novel: indeed, it explains its personal as well as cultural origins.

The heroine of *The Female Quixote*, Arabella, motherless and brought up in isolation by her father, models herself on the heroines of French romances, which she believes are historically true. Her cousin Glanville wants to marry her, but she resists, even after her father's death, insisting on the lengthy and exaggeratedly deferential courtship of romance. Her literal reading of romance leads to absurd errors, as she mistakes prostitutes for fellow heroines, believes a servant is a disguised wooer, almost falls victim to an opportunistic suitor who can manipulate the

language of romance for his own purposes, and is constantly in unnecessary terror of rape, until, in a climactic act, she imitates Clelia by
throwing herself into the Thames to escape some innocent passers-by.
Dangerously ill as a result, she is finally persuaded of her folly by a wise
clergyman, based on and perhaps written by Dr Johnson, enabling her
and Glanville to marry. The satire on romance-reading reaches its
natural conclusion in the cure of the deluded heroine.

The previous paragraph gives an accurate but loaded summary of the
plot, for the novel is more complex and ambiguous. 'Arabella's invest-
ment in romance is related to her preoccupation with power',[28] but it
needs to be noted why power is so important to her. Her father was a
nobleman and politician of 'extensive Authority' until, embittered by
the 'Malice of his Enemies', he retires to a 'very remote Province' (p. 5),
where he establishes an 'Epitome of *Arcadia*' (p. 6). Arabella's pathology
is not endogenous but learned from her situation: her romantic disposition reflects her father's values, but while a taste for Arcadian romance
in landscape gardening is, apparently, reasonable in the father a similar
taste in reading seems unreasonable in the daughter. He chooses retirement while she lives by necessity in a 'Confinement' (p. 9) whose
extreme nature needs to be noted: the 'only Diversion she was allowed,
or ever experienced' is to be 'sometimes' permitted to ride (p. 19). Her
little world is dominated by male authority: Glanville thinks it entirely
reasonable that he should have the right to command her servants (p.
31), or come into her apartment whenever he wants (p. 34). It is hardly a
delusion born of romance-reading to envisage herself as a 'Prisoner' of
'the tyrannical Exertion of parental Authority' (p. 35), prevented from
expressing her 'Will' (p. 43), and to dream of power.

What Arabella finds in romances and not in the real world are
powerful women obeyed by their suitors, and a feminocentric love-ritual
allowing women to exercise 'Authority' and 'Power' (p. 320). She must
apparently learn to put aside these desires, but while the surface of the
novel seems decorously compliant to patriarchal imperatives, this is
constantly undercut in a range of startling and disturbing ways. Images
of gender-reversal, for instance, of 'feminine' men (p. 279) and 'masculine' (p. 71) women, of Amazons and transvestites, recur repeatedly, and
challenge the traditional gender-ideologies and hierarchies that the
novel seems to maintain. Arabella's romances were originally the property of her mother, who also 'used them to soften a Solitude which she
found very disagreeable' (p. 7): mother and daughter, both without
power to change their world, choose to escape it. While in *The Life of*

Harriot Stuart and *Euphemia* romances were a point of tension between rebellious heroines and more traditionally socialised mothers, here they constitute a 'female inheritance' between dissatisfied mother and dissatisfied daughter.[29]

Lennox's novel used to be read unproblematically as a satire on romance-reading, but recent critics have convincingly reinterpreted it rather as a covert critique of the position of women in the real world, 'a secret cache of resistance to . . . the plot of the patriarchy', allowing access to the resisting 'feminist reader', even a 'satire on women's education'.[30] In particular it presents an intense but covert struggle between male and female over language and texts, over women's writing and reading and the control of 'modes of narration'.[31] Male power seeks to control female texts: Arabella's father's 'absolute Commands' compel her to write summoning Glanville (p. 46), he threatens to confiscate and burn her books (p. 55), and even the servant William 'resolved to supress [the] Letter' from Lucy to Arabella's suitor until he questions her about it (p. 17). Conversely, Arabella tries to share texts with Glanville, but he is daunted by their length and 'acted extremely wrong' in not trying to understand her by sharing her reading (p. 52). Women seek to share texts, men to monopolise or deny them.

'[L]anguage itself' becomes the 'site of conflict' between men and women in the novel.[32] Indeed, 'language' is a key word (e.g. pp. 10, 22, 32, 53, 374, etc.) whose repetition draws attention to competing linguistic modes, a feminocentric 'Language of Romance' (p. 329) destabilising the 'man made language' of everyday reality by allowing 'the possibility of an alternative "reality"'. The ambiguity of certain words whose meanings shift between contexts in romance and reality generates much of the action.[33] In reality, for instance, the word 'servant' denotes an employee, while in romance dialect it means a declared suitor (e.g. p. 100). Another complex word is 'adventure', which Arabella uses in its romance sense, dramatic episodes demonstrating female power and sensibility: she therefore wishes to hear the 'Adventures' of Miss Groves (p. 69), of Miss Glanville (p. 89), of the 'Fair Unknown' (p. 343), and of the Countess (p. 327). Unfortunately, as the Countess finally persuades her, this word had by 1752 developed 'licentious' overtones, so should not be used of 'those few and natural incidents' in the lives of respectable women (p. 327). Probably the word seemed so unfortunate because of its widespread use about the scandalous female autobiographies popular in the 1750s: Laetitia Pilkington admitted having been a 'Lady of Adventure', and in a poem by Richard Graves she is attacked for making herself the 'heroine of her own romance'.[34] This is a role unavailable to respectable women, who do not, by definition, have adventures, or think of themselves as heroines: to be respected as a romance heroine and to be respectable as an eighteenth-century woman are not the same, or even compatible. The seductions of romance could not be more poignantly or sympathetically explained.

Another word with competing gendered meanings is 'history'. Arabella uses it in a romance sense to mean a feminocentric story of feelings (e.g. pp. 61, 110). Good women, though, have no histories as they have no adventures, for their lives should be 'a History of nothing' (p. 305). However, Arabella's dispute with Mr Selvin reveals the hidden agenda in the argument over history. His history is a record of the deeds of men, while hers seeks to acknowledge women as the hidden agents for historical change: she attributes Pisistratus' struggle for the crown, for instance, to 'violent Affection . . . for the beautiful *Cleorante*' (p. 266). Selvin, who 'read[s] no Authors, but the Antients' (p. 267) lives in a fantasy world as much as Arabella, but is less skilled in its lore and language, and this *reductio ad absurdum* of male history is as much satirised as her romance-reading. Arabella is not so much 'trapped within a child's view of history' by romance-reading as endowed with a subversive covert language for problematising history's 'exclusion' of women.[35]

The ending has a poignant ambivalence. Lennox's original intention may have been for Arabella's cure to be effected by a woman, the Countess, who is also 'deep read in Romances' but has not been deluded by them, for she has access to what is unavailable to Arabella, 'an early Acquaintance with the World' (p. 323). Possibly the instrument of the cure was to be *Clarissa* (p. 377).[36] However, in the completed text the Countess vanishes back into her own world of domestic duties because of 'her Mother's indisposition' (p. 330): if a good woman's history is necessarily a blank, a good woman cannot fulfil even a virtuous extra-domestic role. The novel's action must be extended, and the cure finally effected by the clergyman Dr–. Terror of incest and rape, Arabella is told, is only paranoid delusion, the result of women's 'wild imaginations' (p. 371), not male power. This view, summed up by Doody as 'non-sense',[37] seeks to reconcile Arabella to proper female powerlessness. Her delusions of female power cannot be cured by another woman but only by her, and the female author's, submission to the cultural authority of the male, of Dr– and his real-life prototypes, Young, Richardson and Johnson (p. 253). The novel's central 'problem of defining female identity' can only be accomplished through the male, the positive term against which female absence stands.[38]

However, while the surface of Lennox's text is compliant to male cultural authority, rebellious impulses lurk below. When Lennox allows Arabella to appropriate masculine texts – Temple Stanyan's *Grecian History*, for instance, and in all probability other unidentified intertexts[39] – the effect is not only to acknowledge male cultural superiority but more subversively to erase the differences between male history and female romance. Arabella provides, as Levin argues, Lennox's self-justification, but she also represents 'the novelist's own hidden danger', the 'powerful, subversive forces' present in all writing.[40] Because these subversive forces are so strong, in order to be a good daughter of Richardson and Johnson Lennox must show the triumph of male realism and the failure of female cultural authority – of the feminocentric romance entirely, and even to some extent of Charlotte Lennox herself, whose voice is silenced when Arabella's is. And yet part of Lennox does not want to be a good daughter, and there is an 'underlying pathos', even 'bitterness', that renders the 'highly equivocal' ending 'more problematic and ironic than intended'.[41] Romance alone gives Arabella a story and a language in which it can be told: her cure means her disappearance into a private world which has no story and into which by definition we cannot follow her. So 'complete' is the identification between women and romance that 'a woman cannot take herself out of romance without disappearing altogether', and when Arabella 'loses her voice', so does Lennox. Cure for Arabella means capitulation to 'the ordinary',[42] acceptance of a world where 'Topicks of Conversation among young Ladies' do not include heroic virtue but only 'their Winnings and Losings at *Brag*, the Prices of Silks, the newest Fashions, the best Hair-Cutter, the Scandal at the last Assembly, &c' (p. 361). Lennox cannot help stressing what is lost as much as what is gained by the shedding of romantic illusion.

The ambivalence of Lennox's conclusion becomes clear by comparing it with an American imitator, Tabitha Gilman Tenney's *Female Quixotism* (1801). While Arabella retains the love of Glanville even at her most ridiculous, Dorcasina Sheldon loses her chance to marry the sensible Lysander by her 'whimsical and romantic' belief, learned from novels, that 'violent emotion' is the vital ground for marriage (p. 13).[43] Afterwards she has no suitors except manipulative fortune-hunters who despise her, and she ends the novel middle-aged, unattractive and alone, lamenting the 'serious evils' of perverted judgement and 'visionary expectations' caused by novel-reading (p. 325). Dorcasina cannot be forgiven for preferring fantasy to reality: Arabella's preference for a fantasy which 'give[s] women voice'[44] over a reality where they have neither adventures nor history, is altogether explicable.

BARRETT, THE HEROINE

Eaton Stannard Barrett's conservative satire also educates its protagonist Cherubina to accept that she cannot be the heroine of her own life, and that the fiction she has enjoyed simply lies to her about the world and women's place in it. *The Heroine* (1813), published the year before *Waverley*, participates in the same cultural project, the reappropriation of the novel by male writers to express a reinvigorated masculine literary authority. Barrett's 'unquestioning faith in patriarchy' leads him to attempt to exorcise the 'socially disruptive potential of women authors and readers'. Indeed, the novel envisages 'female authority and female imagination' as so terrifying that they must be 'defin[ed] as illusory'. Barrett associates novel-reading and writing with a range of 'to him subversive values, practices and writing',[45] including female desire, women's writing, Frenchness, revolution and class transgression. For him, bad writing, fantasy and femininity are identified, and realism and masculinity go naturally together, although he allows the honorary immasculation of a few rationalist women like Burney, Hannah More (III, p. 283), and Maria Edgeworth, whose fictional characters are 'too comic, moral and natural' to be heroines in Cherubina's sense (I, p. viii).

The Heroine begins by contextualising itself within a world of solid male cultural and political authority: it is dedicated to Canning and compares itself with Sterne dedicating to Pitt, and even the prefatory epistle, 'The Heroine to the Reader', defines the voice of its female protagonist through authoritative male intertexts, Pope, Cervantes, Milton and Sterne (I, pp. vii–viii, xii). The novel ends by similarly replacing the central female first-person voice with the 'authoritative "voice" of the hero',[46] and replacing her female-authored reading by safe male authors like Johnson. A novel about female disorderliness figured as misreading, *The Heroine* is framed by contrasting, allegedly superior, male-authored and male-authorised texts and reading practices.

Cherubina sins against her literal father and her literary forefathers as a result of bad reading: the Gothic novel teaches her a dangerously inflated idea of the feminine, especially the maternal. Rebelling against the benevolent patriarchy of the real world, she denies her name and lineage, leaves her father's house, and has him imprisoned in an asylum (a regendering of an anti-patriarchal motif of radical women's fiction like Wollstonecraft's *Wrongs of Woman* and Robinson's *The Natural Daughter*). Cherubina's allies in her battle against male authority are the promiscuous governess who 'instigated me against my father' (III, p. 244), and women novelists, who by implication share, by the very act of writing, the heroine's rebellion against ordered gender relations. Barrett burlesques 'successful novels by women',[47] especially Radcliffean Gothic and the novel of sentiment. *The Mysteries of Udolpho* is Cherubina's favourite, appearing twenty times in the notes to burlesqued passages, and there are also allusions to *A Sicilian Romance* (II, p. 135), *The Romance of the Forest* (III, p. 19) and *The Italian* (III, pp. 142, 156). Roche, especially *The Children of the Abbey*, and Lady Morgan are also favourite targets.[48]

Cherubina's crimes against male authority revolve around the powerful but ambiguous figure of the mother. In the late eighteenth and early nineteenth centuries, as Jessamyn Jackson has pointed out, a 'reconceptualisation . . . of motherhood' fed into a reassessment of the role of the woman author.[49] Like virtually all Gothic heroines, Cherubina is motherless, but the presence of the absent mother generates some disturbing episodes. While Smith or Radcliffe or, more ambiguously, Lennox, link the heroine's reading to a potentially subversive quest for the lost mother, Barrett parodies this to reinforce a traditional male authority. Cherubina's aristocratic birth, dependent on a lost mother who is, in a spoof of *A Sicilian Romance*, rediscovered alive, is simply a delusion: this 'mother', indeed, is actually a man in disguise. The dream of discovering the lost mother, the lost female language of the semiotic, is simply a foolish illusion fuelled by a desire to trespass on the prerogative of the male, as the transvestite imagery symbolises.

Like *Northanger Abbey*, *The Heroine* mocks the improbability of Gothic and its mysterious fragmentary manuscripts (III, p. 149), ghosts (III, pp. 182–93), castles, missing mothers and fortuitously rearranged identities. Barrett is especially concerned that Cherubina's misreading of the nature of the real leads her to violate gendered behaviour codes. Both the broad comedy of *The Heroine* and its didactic purpose exploit the chasm between proper female behaviour and that endorsed in novels. Cherubina commits a catalogue of solecisms and crimes, from leaving her father's house alone and rampaging around the country in masquerade costume to theft (I, p. 104), accepting kisses from strange men (I, pp. 155–6), and blowing up a house with gunpowder (I, p. 66)! Each time she can, like Lennox's Arabella, justify her behaviour from the examples of fictional heroines. The heroine, female novelists seem to believe, is exempted from normal moral, and gender, codes, and 'need not so much consider whether [her] conduct be prudent or indiscreet, as whether it be graceful . . . The grand criterion is, "how will it read?" ' (I, p. 56). Moreover, the textualised heroine will be a sexualised heroine. Although Cherubina escapes actual contamination, novels expose her to attempts at seduction.

The Heroine becomes increasingly surreal in its humour as Cherubina's hold on reality grows more tenuous. In a climactic episode at the castle of Baron Hildebrand, she encounters some of the 'heroes and heroines' (III, p. 163) of her favourite novels, but the realities of time have ravaged them: Sir Charles Grandison is now 'an emaciated old oddity', Harriet Byron 'bursting with fat and laughter' (III, p. 175), Burney's Mortimer Delville a 'plain . . . hard-featured fellow' and Cecilia a 'fashionable grandmother', and Lord Mortimer and Amanda from *The Children of the Abbey* respectively 'fallen into flesh' and 'with a face like scorched parchment' (III, p. 176). Even realist fiction is not real, Grandison warns her. Happy endings are 'All irony': 'Why do their biographers always conclude the book just at their wedding? Simply because all beyond it, is unhappiness and hatred' (III, p. 177). Evelina and Orville quarrel, Pamela has eloped with Rasselas and Rosa, Bennett's beggar girl, with Sterne's Corporal Trim (III, pp. 178–9). Barrett undercuts even the cultural authority of realistic fiction and of the women writers like Burney whom he elsewhere praises.

The masquerade is meant to persuade Cherubina she might as well marry a man she does not love, since happy endings do not really exist, but it backfires, and she is overwhelmed with 'rage, horror, and desperation' (III, p. 199) to discover she has been tricked through her love of fiction. She is rescued by Robert Stuart and, following *The Female Quixote*, becomes seriously ill. The loss of illusion is necessary but dangerous. A clergyman persuades her of the 'plain and simple truths' of religion (III, p. 229), and she acknowledges her own guilt: her love of novels has given her 'a distaste for sober occupations, perverted my judgement, and even threatened my reason' (III, pp. 230–1).

As medication, Robert Stuart prescribes *Don Quixote*. The novel began by invoking male cultural authority, and ends with a male speaker recommending a male writer. A male-identified rationality is privileged over feminised fantasy. Stuart believes some fiction can 'be read without injury' (III, p. 232), as long as it draws 'man as he is, imperfect'. Women writers can contribute to this discourse: Barrett praises Burney's *Cecilia*, Edgeworth's *Fashionable Tales*, More's *Coelebs* and even Lady Morgan's *O'Donnel*, as 'both instructive and entertaining', and even Radcliffean Gothic with its 'appeal to the imagination alone', is 'captivating, and seldom detrimental'. Praise for a gynocentric literary tradition is now safe within the reinforced masculine authority of the novel, but is nonetheless instantly withdrawn, for fiction for and by women still seems dangerous, so 'seductive' that 'people can become too fond of it', so that it 'act[s] upon the mind, like inebriating stimulants' (III, p. 233).

Moreover, if novels have damaging effects on immature individuals, they have analogous effects on societies. In cultures without firm moral values, like *ancien régime* and revolutionary France, novels develop a 'pernicious sentimentality' which contributes to the collapse of society. The key example is Rousseau's *Julie*, attacked not only for preaching a socially disruptive sensibility, but for reproducing its mechanisms through the reading practices it necessitates. 'What St Preux is to Heloise, the book is to the reader' (III, p. 234): the novel not only depicts seduction, it is seducing; and, perhaps even more dangerous, feminising, for if the book is male the reader, of either sex, must be positioned as female. Novels have political as well as moral significance in Barrett's conservative vision, 'at once a test and a source of national virtue' (III, p. 236). The echoes of Pope reinforce the privileging of a male, English literature over a feminising, French culture.[50]

Barrett's novel ends with Cherry 'no longer a heroine' (III, p. 242), married to Robert Stuart and receding into a domestic life of 'practical morality' and 'social duties' (III, p. 237). The stability of the state depends on that of private life, which itself relies on women relinquishing the desire to be the heroines of their own stories and accepting their place within domestic ideology; and this is figured especially in their subordination as writers and readers. Novel-reading is a feminised, feminising, female-empowering act in this novel, and consequently must be strictly disciplined. The uncontrolled female reader is identified not only with class, gender and sexual transgression, she also transgresses against 'national virtue' and is implicated in the politics of revolution.

JANE AUSTEN, *NORTHANGER ABBEY*

Until recently criticism took at face value the surface messages of this group of novels, reading *The Female Quixote* unproblematically as a

parody of French romance, and *Northanger Abbey* as a text which 'satir-
ized the Gothic novel' and showed Austen's 'congenital distaste for the
absurdities of contemporary literature'.[51] More recently critics have
focused on their disjunctions and ambiguities. In *Northanger Abbey* these
are closer to the surface than in *The Female Quixote*, for Austen's novel
not only laughs at its heroine's uncritical addiction to Gothic fiction, it
also revises Barrett's attack on women writers by using the female
quixote plot as a smokescreen behind which to launch a vigorous
defence of the novel in general, and women writers in particular.

Although for some critics the centrality of the Gothic criticism has
obscured this point, *Northanger Abbey* is fundamentally concerned with
reading, and writing, as a woman: reading and writing not only
Gothic (and other) novels, but also periodicals (pp. 58–9), poetry (p.
39), epitaphs (p. 193), newspapers (p. 199–200), history (p. 123), moral
fables (p. 38) and essays (p. 238), letters, journals (pp. 48–9), even
laundry lists (p. 177). More than any other Austen lovers, Catherine
Morland and Henry Tilney's relationship grows through discussions of
gender, language and textuality: even their first encounter in the Assembly Rooms centres round a discussion of the gendering of private
textual modes like letters and journals. Like Arabella, Catherine misuses language, leading Miss Tilney to believe she is predicting revolutionary disorder in London when she is only discussing the forthcom-
ing publication of a new Gothic novel, and having no term of
approbation more specific than 'nice' (pp. 126, 122). She learns from
Henry 'a series of lessons in semantics'[52] which facilitate her maturation.

But Henry Tilney is not Glanville or Robert Stuart, authoritative
voices of androcentric culture in *The Female Quixote* and *The Heroine*. In
some respects, indeed, he critiques rather than maintains male authority, claiming that far from reading 'better books', men 'read nearly as
many [novels] as women' (pp. 122–3), and even assuming an oddly
androgynous quality, as when he claims to be an authority on muslin
(pp. 49–50), so allowing Austen to challenge the assumptions about male
cultural authority encoded in Glanville or Stuart. The Tilneys allow
Catherine to see a literary world much less male-dominated than
Barrett's: even the elite masculine form of history is adjudged equal to
fiction, both depending on 'invention' and 'imagination' (p. 123). The
end of the novel effects a dazzling reversal of gendered textualities:
Henry's love for Catherine is shown arising from his gratitude for her
attraction to him, a direct gender reversal of Gregory's conduct-book

pontificating that women's love is reactive rather than proactive, arising in 'gratitude' to the man who favours her (p. 240).[53]

In chapter 5 Austen, unusually, speaks in the first person:

I will not adopt that ungenerous and impolitic custom so common with novel writers, of degrading by their contemptuous censure the very performances, to the number of which they are themselves adding. . . . 'I am no novel reader . . .' – Such is the common cant . . . 'Oh! it is only a novel!' . . . 'It is only Cecilia, or Camilla, or Belinda': or, in short, only some work in which the greatest powers of the mind are displayed, in which the most thorough knowledge of human nature, the happiest delineation of its varieties, the liveliest effusions of wit and humour are conveyed to the world in the best chosen language. (pp. 57–8)

Burney and Edgeworth are praised as the equals, or superiors, of the patriarchs of the past. Addison and Steele's *Spectator*, once recommended to young women and even now read proudly by them, shows only 'improbable circumstances, unnatural characters', outdated topics and 'coarse' language (p. 59). Alert to repressive associations of the novel with the female body, Austen renegotiates this by presenting female novelists as victims of prejudice, an 'injured body' (p. 58).

This passage not only vindicates the novel and novel-reading, it also reverses the strategy with male intertexts of *The Heroine*, using them not to embody a legitimate but to attack a spurious cultural authority. Male copyists, 'the nine-hundredth abridger of the History of England', or the 'man who collects and publishes in a volume some dozen lines of Milton, Pope and Prior' are 'eulogized', while the innovative women novelists are slighted (p. 58). Austen reverses Barrett's privileging of male literature, questioning the priority of androcentric modes like history or the periodical essay, and attacks the classic male texts as coarse, outmoded or immoral: the foolish John Thorpe 'never read novels' except the morally questionable *Tom Jones* and *The Monk* (p. 69). *Northanger Abbey*'s attack on Radcliffe, if such it is, is vigorously underpinned by a defence of women novel-writers and readers.

The novel certainly laughs at Catherine Morland's appetite for 'horrid' literature (p. 61). But as a very young woman learning to understand herself and her world, Catherine's need for fiction is touchingly rather than satirically depicted: 'while I have Udolpho to read, I feel as if nobody could make me miserable' (p. 62). Something as important as happiness depends on a range of trivial things, and the love of Radcliffe is no worse than a love of hyacinths, for 'it is well to have as many holds upon happiness as possible' (p. 179).

Catherine's dependence on regular fixes of Radcliffe has, however, two serious consequences. It fosters an unfortunate intimacy with Isabella Thorpe. The attractions of a female reading community are sympathetically depicted, but Catherine would profit more from reading with her sensible mother, whose favourite book is *Sir Charles Grandison* (p. 62), or with Eleanor Tilney, who is 'fond of history' (p. 123). It also teaches her to read real life in the light of Radcliffe, expecting Northanger Abbey to shelter spectres, dark secrets and mysterious manuscripts, and General Tilney to be 'a Montoni' (p. 190) who has murdered or imprisoned his wife. Catherine must learn that 'Charming as were all Mrs Radcliffe's works . . . it was not in them perhaps that human nature, at least in the midland counties of England, was to be looked for' (p. 202). Armed with this momentous discovery, she is 'awakened' to reality (p. 201), educated to put aside unrealistic expectations, to accept that even Henry might have 'some slight imperfection' (p. 202), and to grow up.

So far the novel sounds like *The Female Quixote* or a less misogynistic *The Heroine*: but this is not the last word. Austen 'is . . . criticizing female gothic in order to reinvest it with authority', and she does so by emphasising the 'political subtext' of Gothic.[54] Radcliffe may describe the patriarch's oppression of women in an excessively melodramatic vocabulary of images, but this does not discredit her basic insights. Northanger Abbey may not harbour an imprisoned wife, but a dark secret is 'concealed' there (p. 189), the selfish reality beneath General Tilney's courtly façade. He may not be Montoni, but his terrorising of his wife and daughter, and his ejection of Catherine from his house when he discovers she is not a wealthy heiress, present a critique of patriarchy in an only slightly lower key: the 'anxieties of common life' may not be so very dissimilar from the 'alarms of romance' (p. 203) after all. Indeed this last episode, General Tilney precipitately sending Catherine away on a Sunday without a servant, struck at least one contemporary reader as altogether too Gothic, 'quite outrageously . . . out of nature'.[55] Unlike Arabella, who must learn that her fears of rape are only self-dramatisation, or Cherubina, taught that Gothic has given a false idea of her own importance, Catherine's final lesson is not only the unreality of romance but also its reality. Her reading of Gothic has been educational as well as escapist, having taught her not to judge naively by appearances, to assume that General Tilney is 'perfectly agreeable and good-natured' simply because he has good manners and is 'tall and handsome' (p.

139). As far as he is concerned, her 'anxiety had foundation in fact, her fears in probability' (p. 225).

Austen's parody of Gothic in *Northanger Abbey* shows, as Linda Hutcheon argues, 'a tension between her desire to exorcize the naive clichés of sentimental 'women's' fiction and her inability or unwillingness to do so'.[56] Indeed, I would go further and argue that the apparent attack on Gothic serves in reality as a covert defence of woman's reading and writing: the final result is not to discredit but to recredit female Gothic.

SARAH GREEN, *SCOTCH NOVEL READING*

If Barrett's *The Heroine* represents a backlash against female literary authority, which *Northanger Abbey* sought to stem but which was confirmed by the success of the *Waverley* novels, Sarah Green's *Scotch Novel Reading* (1824) turns the joke against Scott himself. Although formally following the pattern established in *The Female Quixote* and *The Heroine*, in which female misreading is castigated and cured by male authority, Green rebukes not only female misreading but also the male appropriation of literary authority that makes that misreading not only possible but necessary.

Very little is known about Sarah Green: she gets only eight lines in the *Dictionary of British and American Women Writers*, and even her sex has been doubted.[57] She presents herself as female and as a Londoner (the title-page of *Scotch Novel Reading* refers to her as a 'Cockney'). By 1824 she had published a conduct book for young women, which bans virtually all novels,[58] but also a number of novels, including *Romance Readers and Romance Writers* (1810), a routine depiction of the female quixote whose unwise reading of novels leads to seduction and lifelong unhappiness. The easy targets – French fiction, Gothic, heroic romance – are again set up, and the usual justifications of fiction, like the morality of Richardson and Burney, are again rehearsed, but little that is new is added to the motif.

Scotch Novel Reading shows a more assured presentation of the argument, and a more challenging approach to issues of gender and fiction-reading. While Barrett's satire is directed against women readers and writers, in *Scotch Novel Reading* Green's kinder humour is aimed not only at an exuberant heroine who prefers fiction to reality, but also, as the subtitle tells us, at 'Modern Quackery' of all sorts: quack doctors, patent medicines, sham evangelists and bad actors (I, pp. 20–2) offer analogies for literary quackery, challenging Barrett's view of the political and aesthetic superiority of male cultural hegemony. Although the novel revolves around the heroine Alice Fennel's uncritical reading of his work, Scott is given due credit: his poems are praised, and his novels credited with being without 'a single impropriety' (III, p. 6), and for 'chasteness . . . elegance and morality', which makes them eminently suitable for a female reader, who if forbidden Scott will 'read worse' books (I, p. 58). The fashion for Scott is as much criticised as the work itself. In the decades from 1814, *Waverley* and its successors were 'in everybody's hands,'[59] and the heroine's book-loving father, who represents sense and moderation, rapidly gets bored with the 'one beaten track' (I, p. 23) prescribed by fashion.

Nonetheless, even Scott is not exonerated from charges of literary quackery. He is accused of carelessly 'rapid' composition (II, p. 87), prolixity (II, p. 115), the excessive 'quantity' and cost of the novels (I, p. 235; II, p. 185), their 'improbabilities' and lack of 'variety' (II, p. 186; I, p. 48), and a dangerous blurring of the line between historical fact and fiction (II, pp. 186–7, 196). Like *Northanger Abbey*, *Scotch Novel Reading* allows its attack on fashionable reading to defend female writers and challenge an increasingly male-dominated culture. While Barrett attacks female writers as well as readers, Green like Austen defends herself by praising foremothers and female contemporaries, and only the neo-puritan Mr Hartfield condemns them, foolishly preferring 'the dryest prose writer, and vilest poetaster of his own sex' to the 'most sprightly or witty' of women writers (I, pp. 89–90). As a result, Green punishes him by envisaging him as the hero of a novel by a woman, engaged in 'Coelebs-like search' for a wife, which his misogyny renders comically futile (I, p. 91).

While Barrett attributes the follies of his heroine to excessive exposure to women writers, Green's heroine has read too little by women because of her obsession with Scottish authors, not only Scott but also Hogg (I, p. 10), Ramsay, Burns (I, p. 44) and Galt (II, p. 109). Part of the problem with Scottish writers, indeed, seems to Green to be not only that they encourage national transgression, leading Alice to undervalue her English culture, but also that they form a monstrous regiment of men, with little interest in the cultural needs of women readers.

Alice, like Arabella, is an idealised heroine, 'truly feminine and lovely . . . intelligent, full of sweetness . . . chastity and pureness of heart' (I, p. 16). Her only fault is a fondness for 'Scotch stories' (I, p. 9) so extreme that her conversation is virtually confined to 'quotations' from them, and she adopts a fantastic version of 'highland' dress and dialect which makes her lover Robert Butler think she has an 'impediment in her speech' (I, pp. 47, 51). She has however misread Scott, having only 'skimmed . . . over' his novels, reading only the 'romantic parts' (I, p. 4; II, p. 87). Still, she never neglects 'those household concerns, which every female ought to be well acquainted with': indeed her true nature is 'very domestic' (III, p. 128). Green is careful to maintain our sympathy for Alice and not to identify female reading (and writing) as such with folly and transgression.

Misreading, indeed, runs in the Fennel family. Alice's sister Elizabeth suffered from a severe case of '*Byronomania*' (I, p. 43) in youth but was 'cured' (I, p. 1) by marriage and motherhood. Now, like Miss Tilney in *Northanger Abbey* or the Countess in *The Female Quixote*, she represents an ideal model of female reading. This model, striking by its absence in *The Heroine*, is multiplied in *Scotch Novel Reading*, embodied not only in Elizabeth Fennel but also in minor characters like the good old maid Hannah Meredith, whose library contains Scott's poems but not his novels (I, p. 184). Elizabeth Fennel now reads not only *Domestic Cookery* which 'every lady ought to know', but also the work of 'the best and most approved writers of fiction', though she is not 'a slave to novel-reading' and reads other 'ingenious works' (II, p. 103). Green is more relaxed than Barrett or Lennox about female misreading: a freak of girlhood, it will not interfere with the proper socialisation of the heroine, but will naturally 'wear off in time' (III, p. 6). Alice's cure takes three volumes, and Robert Butler is only one element in this: she was already 'weary of Scotch novel reading' (III, p. 68) before his intervention. Alice's 'dawn of reformation' begins much earlier when she meets some real Scots-women and finds them 'very different from the heroines of her favourite novel-writer', being especially shocked that Lady Macbane can 'neither read nor write' (I, pp. 173, 175).

While Cherubina and Arabella are brought up in male-dominated households, Alice although like them motherless grows up in a more female-friendly atmosphere: her father, while accepting a proto-Victor-ian ideology of separate spheres, 'firmly believed women to be endowed with capacity equal to that of a man' (I, pp. 24–5), and supports female employment by having only women servants (I, p. 31). He guards Alice from 'improper and hurtful publications', especially the 'trash' of a century ago which 'disgraced both the publishers and authors', but allows her to read freely 'every amusing and celebrated work of fiction' (I, pp. 34–5). Indeed, attempts to curtail female reading unnecessarily are castigated throughout the novel: Mr Hartfield's 'philippic' against the 'dangerous indecency' of Byron's work shows more 'indelicacy' than the poems he is criticising: 'the ears of chastity are . . . wounded by the outrageous . . . purity of the over-nice' as often as by actual obscenity (I, pp. 102–3).

While in *The Female Quixote* and *The Heroine* wrong-headed females are cured by right-minded men, the balance in *Scotch Novel Reading* is different. Alice is not only less seriously deluded than Arabella or Cherubina, the men in her life are less self-evidently superior. Her 'romantic disposition' may like Arabella's be an inheritance from her mother, but her father also has a 'strong portion of the romantic in his own temperament, however he might laugh at . . . many a "romance writer and romance reader"' (I, pp. 32–3), so her tastes are legitimised by paternal example. Moreover, while Glanville and Robert Stuart are identified with rationality and reality, Robert Butler errs equally but oppositely to Alice. He has a 'rooted aversion to all fictitious tales', however 'good' or 'instructive', considering even the best only 'abominable lies' (I, p. 118),which is a reaction against his own father's 'excess of mistaken sensibility' (I, p. 41). Even a short 'novel or romance, though with plenty of margin, and in very large print, always so disgusted him . . . that he could never have patience to read it through . . . he may safely say he never read one novel through in his whole life'. This is not positive male rationality, but 'excess' as 'faulty' as Alice's over-enthusiasm (I, pp. 74, 79).

Alice's cure is completed when Butler disguises himself as Duncan Macgregor, a caricature of Scott's Rob Roy whom her father pretends to compel her to marry. She is shocked by this compulsion and by the unromantic appearance of this spoof highlander, a 'coarse savage' with only one arm, one eye and a crippled foot and with 'red mustachios', who wears the 'extremely indelicate' kilt which horrifyingly reveals 'bare knees'. She learns at last the difference between fiction and reality: 'Oh, how charming descriptions read in books of warlike Gallic chiefs! See them in reality, and they scarce appear a degree above barbarians' (III, pp. 76, 77, 75).

So far this accords with the traditional pattern of the taming of a misreading heroine: but a number of factors undercut this pattern. In particular, it is less that Butler cures Alice than that they cure each other. As she has to learn not to take romance too literally, he has to learn the pleasures of fiction and fantasy, as he does by assuming the Macgregor disguise. She both loses her obsession for things Scottish – indeed, she comes to 'hate every thing that is Scotch' (III, p. 85) – and learns to respect and then love Macgregor, despite his unprepossessing appearance. He helps to moderate her 'romantic folly' by teaching her 'geography . . . and the scientific part of music' (III, pp. 120, 91). As with Catherine Morland, the real lesson is not to stop reading romance, but to stop judging by appearances, and romance may facilitate rather than impede this lesson. Finally Alice discovers that Butler and Macgregor are the same, and the novel ends happily. Her spirit is not broken, unlike Cherubina and Arabella she is not brought to the brink of death, and unlike them she need not give up her 'favourite author': in fact she ends the novel singing a song of Scott's (III, p. 243–4).

Moreover, while Glanville and Robert Stuart represent coherent images of patriarchal authority, Robert Butler is paradoxical and self-divided. While his rejection of romance appears a reaction to his father's excessive sensibility, it is also a self-protective façade, for he has been guilty of a 'romantic' (I, p. 120) folly surpassing any of Alice's – he has fallen in love with a woman in a picture. Exactly as the Macgregor disguise allows Alice to discover she has always loved Butler, it allows him to find that he has always loved her, for in a clumsy turn of plot it is revealed that the lady in the picture is actually Alice herself. Butler first fell in love with the lady in the picture when he saved her from a fire 'which [owed] its origin to novel reading', since it was caused by a maidservant carelessly reading by candlelight a tale of the supernatural (III, p. 215). Female reading may be dangerously inflammatory, but it also works ultimately to the benefit of the heroine and her lover.

While Barrett's repressive fable shows a rebellious female reader tamed by male rationality, Green's liberal tale allows equality between male and female readers. Excessively 'romantic' behaviour is not gender-specific, being shared by Alice's father, her father-in-law and her lover (I, pp. 33, 41, 120). Alice, a 'romantic female Prometheus' (II, p. 140), constructs an imaginary hero, exactly as Butler like 'Pygmalion' has developed a 'romantic passion' for a picture (I, p. 120). Where Barrett and Lennox seek to curb female authority, Green delights in it, praising women writers and queens, like Elizabeth I, 'to whom the English nation owes almost every thing' (III, pp. 27–8). Even when reading is figured as cultural or national transgression or conflagration, Green allows high levels of gender equality and legitimises the activity of her readers by demonstrating that its final results are positive.

CONCLUSIONS

In all the novels investigated in this chapter, women's writing as well as reading become significant issues in a battle of the sexes for cultural authority. This is simplest in *The Heroine*, where Barrett mocks and attacks female writers, their work, and their readers, revealing the desire to be the heroine of one's own story as politically and morally dangerous. In *The Female Quixote* and other female-authored texts the desire to have a history is more sympathetically understood and ambivalently presented. Austen centres her novel on issues of gender, language and textuality, defending female novelists and dramatising the superficial falsehood but also the underlying truth of Radcliffean Gothic. In *Scotch Novel Reading* Sarah Green playfully turns the attack on the author of the Waverley novels, by creating a simultaneously mocking and utopian vision of men and women sharing reading and writing in an idealised, stable, domestic, English community. Female novel-reading may have seemed to some timid or misogynist commentators a 'dangerous recreation',[60] but it also gave women writers a series of potent images to deal with their anxieties about, or even to fight for their rights to, literary authority.

Conclusion

Books and reading were vital to women in the late eighteenth and early nineteenth century, offering job-opportunities to women in a catastrophically shrinking jobs-market, and occupying time for middle-class women increasingly defined as a leisured rather than productive group. Study of their reading not only allows a glimpse of an apparently minor issue: in some important respects it takes us to the heart of a series of cultures, and their characteristic anxieties, evasions and contradictions, those things they thought too obvious to articulate, and those things they could not articulate at all.

Texts of all kinds draw constant attention to the figure of the woman reader: fictional female characters are defined through their reading; novels employ extraordinary intertextual strategies in which the female characters in the book we are reading discuss the books they are reading. Our activity as readers is kept constantly before us, directing our own reading strategies, creating a rich self-consciousness. Women's reading is depicted, though, in highly contradictory ways. The good girl reads books with 'pleasure'[1] yet pleasure is deeply problematic; reading may be seductive or protect from seduction; it is a means of emotional maturation or perpetual juvenility; informative reading constructs a virtuous subjectivity or encourages vanity and folly; reading fosters or compromises good domestic relations.

What is finally, to me, the most surprising thing is not the age's anxieties about the woman reader, its elision of sexuality and textuality, the difficult tightrope act required of the woman reader, the repetitiveness of discourses especially of fiction-reading with their constant use of words like 'dangerous', 'seductive', 'poison' and 'soften', or even their deeply self-contradictory nature. What surprises me most is simply the ubiquity of the woman reader in discourses of all kinds – of gender and sexuality, education, economics, class, 'race', social stability and revolution, science, history and so on. The woman reader is a key icon for this period, noticeable both for her occasional omnipresence and for the occasional invisibility which draws attention to her absence. Students reading Mary Shelley's *Frankenstein*, for instance, sometimes find it a problematically male-identified text, struck by the fact that all three of its major voices, Walton, Frankenstein and his creature, are male. Yet the novel also depends on women readers within the text, like Safie, whose reading enables the creature's entrance to culture. In contrast male reading practices, like the ambitious and individualistic reading of Frankenstein or Walton, are deeply flawed. In fact the text exists because of an absent and invisible female reader, Margaret Walton, to whom the whole is addressed, and whose domestic virtues imply a different and superior kind of reading and of social organisation from Walton's or Frankenstein's. The woman reader is the novel's touchstone for moral and social value, and its very reason for existing. In *Frankenstein*, as in contemporary culture, the woman reader is a central, enabling figure for the whole cultural project.

Notes

PREFACE

1 Edward Copeland, *Women Writing about Money: Women's Fiction in England, 1790–1820* (Cambridge, 1995), p. 3.

INTRODUCTION

1 Samuel Johnson, *The Idler and The Adventurer*, ed. W. J. Bate, John M. Bullitt and L. F. Powell (New Haven and London, 1963), II, p. 411.

2 *Lady's Magazine* 29 (1798), p. 364; see below, p. 176; Mary Wollstonecraft, *The Wrongs of Woman; or, Maria* (orig. 1798) in Gary Kelly, ed., *Mary and the Wrongs of Woman*, (1980), p. 155; Ann Yearsley, *The Royal Captives* (1795), e.g. I, pp. 93, 184–5.

3 Kate Flint, *The Woman Reader, 1837–1914* (Oxford, 1993), p. 22.

4 J. Paul Hunter, *Before Novels: the Cultural Contexts of 18th-Century English Fiction* (New York, 1990), p. 84; Alan Richardson, *Literature, Education, and Romanticism: Reading as Social Practice 1780–1832* (Cambridge, 1994), p. 44.

5 Judy Simons, *Diaries and Journals of Literary Women from Fanny Burney to Virginia Woolf* (1990), p. 3; Mary Wollstonecraft, *Thoughts on the Education of Daughters* (orig. 1787) in Janet Todd and Marilyn Butler, eds., *The Works of Mary Wollstonecraft* IV (1989), pp. 20, 19; Helena Whitbread, ed., *I Know My Own Heart: the Diaries of Anne Lister 1791–1840* (1988), pp. 265–6; Sarah Fielding, *The Governess, or Little Female Academy* (orig. 1749; rcpr. Oxford, 1968), p. vii; David Alexander, *Richard Newton and English Caricature in the 1790s* (Manchester, 1998), plates 39a, 39b; p. 130.

6 E. J. Clery, *The Rise of Supernatural Fiction 1762–1800* (Cambridge, 1995), pp. 81–2; Cecilia Lucy Brightwell, *Memorials of the Life of Amelia Opie* (2nd edn, Norwich, 1854; New York, 1975), p. 118; Nancy Armstrong, *Desire and Domestic Fiction: a Political History* (Oxford, 1987), p. 203.

7 Armstrong, *Desire*, p. 3; Leonore Davidoff and Catherine Hall, *Family Fortunes: Men and Women of the English Middle Class 1780–1850* (orig. 1987; 1992), esp. pp. 149–92; Caroline Gonda, *Reading Daughters' Fictions 1709–1834: Novels and Society from Manley to Edgeworth* (Cambridge, 1996), p. 27.

8 Maggie Kilgour, *The Rise of the Gothic Novel* (1995), pp. 8, 80; Markman Ellis,

The Politics of Sensibility: Race, Gender and Commerce in the Sentimental Novel (Cambridge, 1996), pp. 41, 16; Toni Bowers, *The Politics of Motherhood: British Writing and Culture 1680–1760* (Cambridge, 1996), p. 226.

9 J. P. Grant, ed., *Memoirs and Correspondence of Mrs Grant of Laggan* (1844), II, pp. 235–6.

10 *Lady's Magazine* 12 (1781), p. 472; Edgeworth, *Belinda* (orig. 1801), ed. Eiléan Ni Chuilleanain (1993), p. 3; Anon., *Fatal Obedience; or, the History of Mr Freeland* (1780), I, p. 72.

11 *Letters for Literary Ladies*, ed. Claire Connolly (1993), pp. 27, 11, 33, 21, 39, 48, 37.

12 Earl of Bessborough, ed., *Georgiana: Extracts from the Correspondence of Georgiana, Duchess of Devonshire* (1955), p. 57; Cecil Aspinall-Oglander, *Admiral's Wife: Being the Life and Letters of the Hon. Mrs Edward Boscawen from 1719 to 1761* (1940), pp. 54, 77, 79, 125; Cecil Aspinall-Oglander, *Admiral's Widow: Being the Life and Letters of the Hon. Mrs Edward Boscawen from 1761 to 1805* (1942), pp. 186, 193.

13 [Richard and Elizabeth Griffith], *A Series of Genuine Letters between Henry and Frances*, 2 vols. (1757), I, p. 182; William Roberts, *Memoirs of the Life and Correspondence of Mrs Hannah More* (1834), III, p. 362.

14 Isaac D'Israeli, *Curiosities of Literature* (1865), I, pp. 85–6.

15 Betty Bennett and Charles Robinson, *The Mary Shelley Reader* (1990), p. vii; Mary Shelley, *Frankenstein* (orig. 1818), ed. Marilyn Butler (Oxford, 1994), pp. 95, 103.

16 Isaac Watts, *The Improvement of the Mind* (1782), II, p. 139; Robert Halsband, ed., *The Complete Letters of Lady Mary Wortley Montagu* (Oxford, 1956–7), II, p. 449.

17 Ina Ferris, *The Achievement of Literary Authority: Gender, History and the Waverley Novels* (Ithaca, 1991), pp. 37, 40; John Gregory, *A Father's Legacy to his Daughters* (orig. 1774; new edn, 1814), p. 56; *Lady's Magazine* 10 (1779), p. 89; cf. Eliza Parsons, *The Errors of Education* (1791), I, p. 226; Laetitia-Matilda Hawkins, *Rosanne; or, a Father's Labour Lost* (1814), III, p. 43.

18 William Godwin, cit. Kilgour, *Rise of the Gothic Novel*, p. 8.

19 Frances Pagett Hett, ed. *The Memoirs of Susan Sibbald (1783–1812)* (1926), p. 176; Hawkins, *Rosanne*, I, p. 316, II, p. 74; Hawkins, *The Countess and Gertrude; or, Modes of Discipline* (1811), I, pp. 262, 364 (I am grateful to David Thame for drawing my attention to this novel); Mary Hays, *Memoirs of Emma Courtney* (orig. 1796; repr. 1987), pp. 13, 20–1; *Memoirs of Laetitia Pilkington* (orig. 1748–54), ed. A. C. Elias Jr (Athens, Georgia, 1997), p. 13; Alicia Lefanu, *Memoirs of the Life and Writings of Mrs Frances Sheridan* (1824), p. 4; Sarah Fielding, *The Adventures of David Simple* (orig. 1744–53), ed. Malcolm Kelsall (Oxford, 1987), pp. 101–2, 108; Ernest de Selincourt, ed., *The Letters of William and Dorothy Wordsworth*, vol. I, *The Early Years 1787–1805* (2nd edn, Oxford, 1967), pp. 6, 8.

20 Edgeworth, *Moral Tales* in *Tales and Novels by Maria Edgeworth*, 12 vols. (1870), I, pp. 388–9, 393; Lee Monroe Ellison, '*Gaudentio di Lucca*: a forgotten utopia', *PMLA* 50 (1935), p. 508; Lady Llanover, ed., *The Autobiography and Correspondence of Mary Granville, Mrs Delany* (1861), II, p. 523; modern opinion

attributes *Gaudentio* to Simon Berington (Ellison, '*Gaudentio*', pp. 494–509); Edgeworth, *Moral Tales*, p. 396.

21 For Gibbon and Boswell, see below, pp. 16, 31–2; David Hume, 'Of Essay Writing', *Essays Moral, Political and Literary* (1963), p. 572; D'Israeli, *Curiosities* I, p. 71, II, p. 446; D'Israeli, *A Dissertation on Anecdotes* (1793), p. 28.

22 D'Israeli, *Curiosities*, II, p. 502; *Lady's Magazine* 26 (1795), p. 452.

23 Lady Theresa Lewis, *Extracts from the Journals and Correspondence of Miss Berry* (1865), I, pp. 11, 7–8; III, p. 332.

24 *Lady's Magazine* 26 (1795), p. 137; William Ray, *Literary Meaning: from Phenomenology to Deconstruction* (Oxford, 1984), p. 11; *Lady's Magazine* 12 (1781), pp. 409–11.

25 Jacques Derrida, *Positions*, trans. Alan Bass (Chicago, 1981), p. 63.

26 *The Use of Circulating Libraries Considered* (orig. 1797) in Devendra P. Varma, ed., *The Evergreen Tree of Diabolical Knowledge* (Washington, DC, 1972), p. 203.

27 *Memoirs of Laetitia Pilkington*, pp. 304–5; Teresia Constantia Phillips, *An Apology for the Conduct of Mrs Teresia Constantia Phillips* (1748–9), III, pp. 90–1; M. J. Levy, ed., *Perdita: the Memoirs of Mary Robinson* (1994), p. 54.

28 John Brewer, 'Reconstructing the reader: prescriptions, texts and strategies in Anna Larpent's reading' in James Raven, Helen Small and Naomi Tadmor, eds., *The Practice and Representation of Reading in England* (Cambridge, 1996), p. 230.

29 Roche, *The Children of the Abbey* (1796) I, pp. 22–3.

30 *Lady's Magazine* 11 (1780), p. 265; Hamilton, *The Cottagers of Glenburnie* (2nd edn, Edinburgh, 1808), pp. 19–20; Hannah More's *Coelebs in Search of a Wife* (orig. 1808: vols. XI and XII of *The Works of Hannah More*, 1818), XI, pp. 116–19.

31 *Lady's Magazine* III (1772), p. 349; 7 (1776), p. 43.

32 Ann H. Jones, *Ideas and Innovations: Best Sellers of Jane Austen's Age* (New York, 1986), p. 27.

33 See below, pp. 72, 74–5, 78–82, 110–12; note 30 above.

34 *Marriage* (orig. 1818; repr. 1986).

35 Flint, *Woman Reader*; Roger Chartier, esp. *Frenchness in the History of the Book: from the History of Publishing to the History of Reading* (Worcester, Mass., 1988); James Raven, *Judging New Wealth: Popular Publishing and Responses to Commerce in England, 1750–1800* (Oxford, 1992); Ferris, *Achievement of Literary Authority*.

36 Sara Mills, *Feminist Stylistics* (1995), p. 3.

37 Luce Irigaray, 'Les marchandises entre elles' in Elaine Marks and Isabelle de Courtivron, eds., *New French Feminisms* (Brighton, 1981), p. 200; cf. Julia Kristeva, 'La femme, ce n'est jamais ça' in Marks and de Courtivron, p. 137.

38 Catherine Macaulay, *Letters on Education* (1790; Oxford, 1994), p. 202.

39 Michel Foucault, *The History of Sexuality: an Introduction*, trans. Robert Hadley (New York, 1980), p. 103; Roy Porter and Lesley Hall, *The Facts of Life: the Creation of Sexual Knowledge in Britain, 1650–1950* (New Haven, 1995), p. 4.

40 Randolph Trumbach, 'Modern prostitution and gender in *Fanny Hill*: libertine and domesticated fantasy' in G. S. Rousseau and Roy Porter, eds., *Sexual Underworlds of the Enlightenment* (Chapel Hill, NC, 1988), pp. 72–3.

41 Jane Spencer, *The Rise of the Woman Novelist: from Aphra Behn to Jane Austen* (Oxford, 1986); Gonda, *Reading Daughters' Fictions*, p. 35; Raven, *Judging New Wealth*, p. 55.

42 Ann B. Shteir, *Cultivating Women, Cultivating Science: Flora's Daughters and Botany in England 1760–1860* (Baltimore, 1996), p. 17; Marjorie Garber, *Vested Interests: Cross-Dressing and Cultural Anxiety* (1992), p. 16.

43 Randolph Trumbach, 'London's sodomites: homosexual behaviour and western culture in the 18th century', *Journal of Social History* 11 (1977), pp. 1–33 and 'London's Sapphists: from three sexes to four genders in the making of modern culture' in Julia Epstein and Kristina Straub, eds., *Body Guards: the Cultural Politics of Gender Ambiguity* (1991), pp. 112–41; Rictor Norton, *Mother Clap's Molly House: the Gay Subculture in England 1700–1830* (1992).

44 Mary Anne Radcliffe, *The Female Advocate* (orig. 1799; Oxford, 1994), pp. 17–76; *La Belle Assemblée* 4 (1808), pp. 217–19.

45 Porter and Hall, *The Facts of Life*, pp. 65–90.

46 Elizabeth Freund, *The Return of the Reader: Reader-response Criticism* (1987), p. 7; Judith Fetterley, *The Resisting Reader: a Feminist Approach to American Fiction* (Bloomington, 1978); Ross Chambers, *Room for Maneuver: Reading (the) Oppositonal (in) Narrative* (Chicago, 1991); Garrett Stewart, *Dear Reader: the Conscripted Audience in Nineteenth-Century British Fiction* (Baltimore, 1996).

47 Eleanor Ty, *Unsex'd Revolutionaries: Five Women Novelists of the 1790s* (Toronto, 1993), p. 63.

48 Lucien Dällenbach, *The Mirror in the Text*, trans. Jeremy Whitely with Emma Hughes (Cambridge, 1989), p. 1.

49 Jan Fergus, 'Women readers of fiction and the marketplace in the midlands, 1746–1800', cit. Clery, *Rise of Supernatural Fiction*, p. 190; 'Provincial servants' reading in the late 18th century' in Raven, Small and Tadmor, eds., *Practice and Representation*, pp. 202–25.

50 Jonathan Barry, 'Literacy and literature in popular culture: reading and writing in historical perspective' in Tim Harris, ed., *Popular Culture in England, c. 1500–1850* (Basingstoke, 1995), p. 86.

51 Amy Cruse, *The Englishman and his Books in the Early Nineteenth Century* (1930), p. 9; Margaret Anne Doody, 'Jane Austen's reading' in J. David Grey, ed., *The Jane Austen Handbook* (1986), p. 347; Roy Porter, *English Society in the Eighteenth Century* (Harmondsworth, 1982), p. 183; Raven, *Judging New Wealth*, pp. 23–4.

52 Porter, *English Society*, p. 183; Barry, 'Literacy and literature', p. 82; Raven, *Judging New Wealth*, pp. 56–7; Richardson, *Literature, Education and Romanticism*, p. 46.

53 Hunter, *Before Novels*, pp. 62–3; Porter, *English Society*, p. 183.

54 Linda Colley, *Britons: Forging the Nation 1707–1837* (orig. 1992; 1994), p. 226.

55 Raven, *Judging New Wealth*, pp. 35–6.

56 Griffith, *A Series of Genuine Letters between Henry and Frances*, 6 vols. (1786), v, p. 15.

57 Raven, *Judging New Wealth*, pp. 35–6; Cheryl Turner, *Living by the Pen: Women Writers in the Eighteenth Century* (1992), pp. 96, 115.

58 Raven, *Judging New Wealth*, pp. 57–8.
59 Mary Brunton, *Emmeline, with some other Pieces* (orig. 1819; repr. 1992), p. xv; Hett, *Memoirs of Susan Sibbald*, p. 27.
60 Raven, *Judging New Wealth*, p. 53; Ellis, *Politics of Sensibility*, pp. 200, 37, 39; Hunter, *Before Novels*, p. 65; Richardson, *Literature, Education and Romanticism*, p. 45; Roberts, *Memoirs of Mrs Hannah More* III, p. 61; Richardson, *Literature, Education and Romanticism*, p. 45.
61 A. G. L'Estrange, ed., *The Life of Mary Russell Mitford . . . Related in a Selection from her Letters to her Friends* (1870), p. 30; C. G. Luard, ed., *The Journal of Clarissa Trant 1800–1832* (1925), pp. 237–8; Brewer, 'Reconstructing the reader', p. 229.
62 Henry Fielding, *Tom Jones* (orig. 1749), ed. R. P. C. Mutter (Harmondsworth, 1966), p. 532; Hawkins, *Countess and Gertrude* II, p. 174; Hays, *Memoirs of Emma Courtney*, p. 17.
63 See below, p. 135.
64 Whitbread, *I Know My Own Heart*, pp. 131, 151; Helena Whitbread, ed., *No Priest but Love: the Journals of Anne Lister from 1824–1826* (Otley, 1992), pp. 26, 32, 33; Emma Donoghue, *Passions between Women: British Lesbian Culture 1668–1801* (1993), p. 214; *I Know My Own Heart*, pp. 42, 203; *No Priest but Love*, p. 54.
65 Mrs Edwin Gray, *Papers and Diaries of a York Family, 1764–1839* (1927), pp. 24, 258.
66 Sir John Hawkins, *The Life of Samuel Johnson* (orig. 1787), ed. Bertram H. Davis (1961), p. 113.
67 *Lady's Magazine* 8, (1777), p. 538; Edgeworth, *Letters for Literary Ladies*, p. 16; Lewis, *Journals and Correspondence of Miss Berry* I, p. 7.
68 Ellis, *Politics of Sensibility*, p. 24; Thomas Broadhurst, *Advice to Young Ladies on the Improvement of the Mind and Conduct in Life* (Bath, 1810), pp. 4–6.
69 Jacques DuBosq, *The Accomplish'd Woman* (1753), p. 4 (cit. Armstrong, *Desire*, p. 102); Brunton, *Emmeline*, p. xcvii.
70 Jane Austen, *Pride and Prejudice* (orig. 1813; repr. Harmondsworth, 1972), p. 37; Helen Maria Williams, *Julia* (orig. 1790; 1995), II, p. 43; Elizabeth Inchbald, *Nature and Art* (1796), I, p. 180; Hawkins, *Countess and Gertrude* I, p. 15.
71 Ellis, *Politics of Sensibility*, p. 219; Williams, *Julia* II, pp. 202–3; for *Coelebs*, see below, p. 89; Eliza Taylor, *Education; or, Elizabeth, Her Lover and Husband* (1817), I, pp. 115–20.
72 Margaret Anne Doody, *Frances Burney: the Life in the Works* (Cambridge, 1988), p. 244.
73 Eaton Stannard Barrett, *Woman, a Poem* (1810), p. 61.
74 See esp. Copeland, *Women Writing about Money*.
75 Anne K. Mellor, *Romanticism and Gender* (1993), p. 7.
76 [Richard and Elizabeth Griffith], *Series of Genuine Letters* (1757), I, p. 65; *Lady's Magazine* 4 (1773), p. 81; J. H. Adeane, ed., *The Girlhood of Maria Josepha Holroyd* (1896), p. 201.

77 Flint, *Woman Reader*, p. 42; see below, pp. 36–41.
78 Barry, 'Literacy and literature', pp. 84, 76.
79 Joan Didion, 'Why I write' in Janet Sternberg, ed., *The Writer on her Work* (New York, 1981), p. 17; Catherine Sharrock, 'De-ciphering women and de-scribing authority: the writings of Mary Astell', in Isobel Grundy and Susan Wiseman, eds., *Women, Writing, History 1640–1740* (1992), p. 109.
80 John B. McKee, *Literary Irony and the Literary Audience: Studies in the Victimization of the Reader in Augustan Fiction* (Amsterdam, 1974).
81 Wolfgang Iser, *The Implied Reader: Patterns of Communication in Prose Fiction from Bunyan to Beckett* (Baltimore, 1974), p. xii; Stewart, *Dear Reader*, p. 91; Jon P. Klancher, *The Making of English Reading Audiences, 1790–1832* (Madison, 1987), p. 22; Kilgour, *Rise of the Gothic Novel*, p. 81.
82 Mary Wollstonecraft, 'Hints' in Ashley Tauchert, ed., *A Vindication of the Rights of Woman* (1995), p. 230.
83 Roberts, *Memoirs of Mrs Hannah More* iii, p. 74.
84 R. W. Chapman, ed., *Jane Austen. Minor Works* (Oxford, 1958), pp. 404–5; *Lady's Magazine* 22 (1791), p. 571.
85 Christina Colvin, *Maria Edgeworth: Letters from England 1813–1844* (Oxford, 1971), p. 23.
86 Doody, *Frances Burney*, p. 272.
87 Harold Bloom, *The Anxiety of Influence: a Theory of Poetry* (1973), p. 5.
88 Ioan Williams, *Novel and Romance 1700–1800: a Documentary Record* (1970), pp. 208–9.
89 Ibid., pp. 240–1.
90 J. H. Adeane, ed., *The Early Married Life of Maria Josepha Lady Stanley* (1899), p. 255.
91 Edgeworth, *Letters for Literary Ladies*, pp. 2–3.
92 Austen, *Northanger Abbey* (orig. 1818; Harmondsworth, 1972), p. 121.
93 Peacock, *Nightmare Abbey* (orig. 1818; Harmondsworth, 1986), p. 60.
94 See below, pp. 30, 118.
95 Edwin J. Marrs Jr, *The Letters of Charles and Mary Lamb* (Ithaca, 1976), ii, pp. 278–9.
96 Elizabeth Bergen Brophy, *Women's Lives and the 18th-century English Novel* (Tampa, 1991), p. 40.
97 David Bleich, 'Gender interests in reading and language', cit. Patrocinio P. Schweickart and Elizabeth A. Flynn, eds., *Gender and Reading: Essays on Readers, Texts and Contexts* (Baltimore, 1986), p. xxv.
98 See below, pp. 69–71.
99 Joseph Wittreich, *Feminist Milton* (Ithaca, 1987), p. 55.
100 Roger Sales, 'Pierce Egan and the representation of London' in Philip W. Martin and Robin Jarvis, eds., *Reviewing Romanticism* (1992), p. 154.
101 Brophy, *Women's Lives*, p. 30; T. C. Duncan Eaves and Ben D. Kimpel, *Samuel Richardson: a Biography* (Oxford, 1971), pp. 346, 360.
102 Edgeworth, 'The Good French Governess', *Moral Tales for Young People* (orig. 1801; n.d.), p. 193; Malcolm Elwin, *Lord Byron's Wife* (1962), pp. 363–4.

103 Edgeworth, *Ormond* (orig. 1817; Gloucester, 1990), p. 82.
104 B. G. MacCarthy, *The Female Pen: Women Writers and Novels 1621–1818* (orig. 1944), ed. Janet Todd (Cork, 1994), pp. 362–7; Austen, *Northanger Abbey*, pp. 69, 58; Colvin, *Maria Edgeworth: Letters from England*, p. 525.
105 Flint, *Woman Reader*, p. viii.

1 PYMALIONESSES AND THE PENCIL UNDER THE PETTICOAT: RICHARDSON, JOHNSON AND BYRON

1 Sandra Gilbert and Susan Gubar, *The Madwoman in the Attic: the Woman Writer and the Nineteenth-Century Literary Imagination* (New Haven, 1979).
2 See, e.g., Cheryl Turner, *Living by the Pen*, esp. p. 35; James Raven, *British Fiction 1750–1770: a Chronological Check-list of Prose Fiction* (1987), p. 18.
3 Roger Lonsdale, *Eighteenth-Century Women Poets; an Oxford Anthology* (Oxford, 1989), p. 220; see below, pp. 36–7.
4 John Gibson Lockhart, *The Life of Sir Walter Scott* (Edinburgh, 1902–3), VI, p. 376.
5 Lestrange, *Life of Mary Russell Mitford* I, p. 300.
6 Katharine C. Balderston, ed., *Thraliana: the Diary of Mrs Hester Lynch Thrale (later Mrs Piozzi) 1726–1809* (Oxford, 1942), p. 547; Thomas Middleton Raysor, ed., *Samuel Taylor Coleridge: Shakespeare Criticism* (1960), II, p. 35.
7 *Humphrey Clinker*, ed. Lewis M. Knapp, revd. Paul-Gabriel Boucé (Oxford, 1984), pp. 128, 92.
8 Fielding, *Joseph Andrews and Shamela*, ed. Douglas Brooks-Davies (Oxford, 1980), p. 344.
9 Ibid., p. 344; *Tom Jones*, pp. 471–2, 532, 531, 265; and see below, pp. 61–2.
10 Charlotte Lennox, *Henrietta* (1758), I, p. 36; Macaulay, *Letters on Education*, p. 145.
11 Eugenia de Acton, *Essays on the Art of Being Happy* (1803), II, pp. 41–2; John Carroll, ed., *Selected Letters of Samuel Richardson* (Oxford, 1964), p. 128; Roberts, *Memoirs of Mrs Hannah More* I, p. 169; *The Vicar of Wakefield*, ed. Arthur Friedman (Oxford, 1981), p. 37.
12 See below, p. 140; West, *A Tale of the Times* (1799), I, p. 164; *Lady's Magazine* 34 (1803), p. 77; *Lady's Monthly Museum* 2 (1799), p. 145; Brunton, *Emmeline*, p. lxxii.
13 *George Bateman* II, p. 198; *Maria* I, p. 193; *George Bateman* II, p. 22.
14 Hawkins, *Countess and Gertrude* III, p. 30; *Ormond*, pp. 71–3; *Northanger Abbey*, p. 69.
15 Ferrier, *The Inheritance* (orig. 1824; Bampton, 1984), pp. 392–3; Brunton, *Self-Control* (orig. 1810/11; repr. 1986), p. 64.
16 Tom Keymer, *Richardson's Clarissa and the Eighteenth-Century Reader* (Cambridge, 1992), p. xiii.
17 James Fordyce, *Sermons to Young Women* (orig. 1765; 3rd edn, 1766), I, pp. 147–8; Burton R. Pollin, ed., *Godwin's Italian Letters; or, the History of the Count de St Julien* (Lincoln, Neb., 1965), p. xii.

18 Wollstonecraft, *Vindication of the Rights of Woman*, p. 82; Macaulay, *Letters*, p. 145; Lady Louisa Stuart in 1802 (Mrs Godfrey Clark, ed., *Gleanings from an Old Portfolio*, Edinburgh, vol. III, 1898, p. 95); Macaulay, *Letters*, p. 145; Anne Grant, *Letters from the Mountains: Being the Real Correspondence of a Lady between the Years 1773 and 1807* (4th edn, 1809), II, p. 45; Desmond Hawkins, ed., *The Grove Diaries: the Rise and Fall of an English Family 1809–1925* (Wimborne, 1995), p. 144.

19 Lawrence Sterne, *The Life and Opinions of Tristram Shandy* (orig. 1759–67), ed. George Saintsbury (1967), pp. 458–9.

20 Keymer, *Richardson's Clarissa*, p. xvii.

21 For *Clarissa*, see below, pp. 61–2; Bowers, *Politics of Motherhood*, pp. 168–9; *Sir Charles Grandison*, e.g. I, p. 180; II, pp. 315 (Bible), 56 (*Paradise Lost*), 231, 348 (Swift), 348 (Dryden), 298 (Young), 229 (*Clarissa*); VII, p. 398.

22 Carroll, *Selected Letters*, p. 158; Eaves and Kimpel, *Samuel Richardson*, pp. 585–6.

23 Carroll, *Selected Letters*, p. 296; Keymer, *Richardson's Clarissa*, pp. xviii, 82.

24 Carroll, *Selected Letters*, p. 184; William M. Sale Jr, *Samuel Richardson: Master Printer* (Cornell Studies in English 37, Ithaca, 1950), pp. 106–14; Elspeth Knights, 'A "licensuous" daughter: Mehetabel Wesley 1697–1750', *Women's Writing* 4 (1997), p. 16; *Clarissa* (orig. 1747–8), ed. Angus Ross (Harmondsworth, 1985), pp. 231–4; Carroll, *Selected Letters*, p. 268.

25 Duncombe, *The Feminiad: A Poem* (1754), lines 15–16; Keymer, *Richardson's Clarissa*, p. 97.

26 Keymer, *Richardson's Clarissa*, p. 248.

27 Carroll, *Selected Letters*, pp. 164, 182.

28 Montagu Pennington, *A Series of Letters between Mrs Elizabeth Carter and Miss Catherine Talbot, from the Year 1740 to 1770* (1808), I, p. 291.

29 Carroll, *Selected Letters*, pp. 182–3, 312; and cf. p. 244.

30 Ibid., p. 306; Keymer, *Richardson's Clarissa*, p. 76.

31 Carroll, *Selected Letters*, pp. 321, 316.

32 Keymer, *Richardson's Clarissa*, p. 198; Carroll, *Selected Letters*, pp. 315, 73; Keymer, review in *Eighteenth-Century Fiction* 6 (1994), p. 195.

33 Carroll, *Selected Letters*, p. 270.

34 Ibid., pp. 117, 103.

35 Eaves and Kimpel, *Samuel Richardson*, pp. 220–3; Keymer, *Richardson's Clarissa*, pp. 214–18.

36 Keymer, *Richardson's Clarissa*, pp. 217, 219.

37 Carroll, *Selected Letters*, pp. 84, 117.

38 Eaves and Kimpel, *Samuel Richardson*, pp. 286, 222, 224.

39 Katherine Sobba Green, *The Courtship Novel 1740–1820: a Feminised Genre* (Lexington, 1991), p. 46; Grant, *Letters from the Mountains* II, p. 46.

40 *Lady's Magazine* 11 (1780), p. 275; 12 (1781), p. 84.

41 Roberts, *Memoirs of Mrs Hannah More* II, p. 101; Reginald Blunt, ed., *Mrs Montagu, 'Queen of the Blues'. Her Letters and Friendships from 1762 to 1800* (1923), I, p. 150; Grant, *Letters from the Mountains* II, p. 46.

42 Halsband, *Complete Letters of Mary Wortley Montagu* III, p. 9.

43 Johnson, letter to Thomas Cadell, 1779, cit. Robert DeMaria Jr, *The Life of Samuel Johnson* (Oxford, 1993), p. 1.

44 Hawkins, *Life of Samuel Johnson*, pp. 62, 130.

45 James Boswell, *Life of Johnson*, ed. Pat Rogers (Oxford, 1980), p. 52; Hester Thrale Piozzi, *Anecdotes of Samuel Johnson* (Gloucester, 1984), pp. 7–8.

46 James G. Basker, 'Radical affinities: Mary Wollstonecraft and Samuel Johnson' (in Alvaro Ribeiro and James G. Basker, eds., *Tradition in Transition: Women Writers, Marginal Texts, and the Eighteenth-Century Canon* (Oxford, 1996), pp. 46–7; Boswell, *Life*, p.36; *Thraliana*, p. 178; see also Eithne Henson, *'The Fictions of Romantick Chivalry': Samuel Johnson and Romance* (Ganbury, NJ, 1992).

47 Thrale, *Anecdotes*, p. 67.

48 Boswell, *Life*, p. 50; Thrale, *Anecdotes*, p. 7.

49 DeMaria, *Life of Samuel Johnson*, p. 3.

50 Johnson, *Adventurer*, p. 412; *Boswell's London Journal 1762–1763*, ed. Frederick A. Pottle (Edinburgh, 1991), p. 302; *Adventurer*, p. 490.

51 *Rambler* 12, 28 April 1750, ed. W. J. Bate and Albrecht B. Strauss, Yale Johnson edition (New Haven and London, 1969), III, pp. 64–7; *Idler* 26 and 29, pp. 80–3 and 90–2; *Rambler* 51, pp. 276–8.

52 James G. Basker, 'Dancing dogs, women preachers and the myth of Johnson's misogyny', *Age of Johnson* 3, (1990), p. 65; Sylvia Harcstark Myers, *The Bluestocking Circle: Women, Friendship, and the Life of the Mind in Eighteenth-Century England* (Oxford, 1990), p. 158; Isobel Grundy, 'Samuel Johnson as patron of women', *Age of Johnson* 1 (1987), pp. 59–77; see below, pp. 204–5.

53 Boswell, *Life*, p. 979; Hawkins, *Life*, p. 162.

54 Basker, 'Dancing dogs', p. 63; DeMaria, *Life of Samuel Johnson*, p. 34.

55 *Rambler*, pp. 78–9.

56 Hawkins, *Life*, p. 166; Boswell, *Life*, p. 696.

57 George Birkbeck Hill, *Johnsonian Miscellanies* (orig. 1897; repr. 1966), II, p. 11.

58 *Adventurer*, p. 458.

59 *The History of Rasselas, Prince of Abyssinia* (orig. 1759; repr. 1994), pp. 23–4; *Idler*, p. 312; *Adventurer*, pp. 345–8.

60 See above, pp. 5–6; *Helen*, pp. 62–3; Claudia Johnson, *Jane Austen: Women, Politics, and the Novel* (Chicago, 1988), pp. 78–9; Basker, 'Radical affinities', pp. 46, 48, 54; West, *A Tale of the Times* II, p. 181.

61 See Marlon Ross, *The Contours of Masculine Desire: Romanticism and the Rise of Women's Poetry* (Oxford, 1989); Alan Richardson, 'Romanticism and the colonization of the feminine' in Anne K. Mellor, ed., *Romanticism and Feminism* (Bloomington, 1988, pp. 13–25); Mellor, *Romanticism and Gender*.

62 Anne K. Mellor, 'Why women didn't like Romanticism: the views of Jane Austen and Mary Shelley' in Gene W. Ruoff, ed., *The Romantics and Us: Essays on Literature and Culture* (New Brunswick, 1990), p. 278; J. P. Grant, *Memoir and Correspondence of Mrs Grant* II, p. 60; Mellor, 'Why women didn't like Romanticism', p. 278.

63 Mellor, *Romanticism and Gender*, p. 1; see Nicola J. Watson, 'Trans-figuring Byronic identity' in Mary A. Favret and Nicola J. Watson, *At the Limits of Romanticism: Essays in Cultural, Feminist, and Materialist Criticism* (Bloomington, 1994), pp. 185–206.

64 They were Agnes Maria Bennett, Regina Maria Roche, Eliza Parsons, Mary Meeke, Mrs Howell, Isabella Kelly, Elizabeth Bonhote, Anna Maria Mackenzie, Agnes Musgrave and Mary Charlton (Dorothy Blakey, *The Minerva Press, 1790–1820*, Oxford, 1935, p. 53).

65 Ross, *Contours of Masculine Desire*, p. 16.

66 Henry F. Chorley, *Memorials of Mrs Hemans* (1836), II, pp. 112, 117; I, p. 174; II, pp. 117–20.

67 Q. D. Leavis, *Fiction and the Reading Public* (orig. 1932; repr. Harmondsworth (1979)), p. 184; Davidoff and Hall, *Family Fortunes*, pp. 159–60, 27, 159.

68 Ferrier, *The Inheritance*, pp. 221, 391.

69 Grant, *Memoir and Correspondence* II, pp. 37, 17; Chorley, *Memorials of Mrs Hemans* II, pp. 21–3.

70 Jane Blumberg, *Mary Shelley's Early Novels* (Basingstoke, 1993), pp. 71–3, 206–15; Leslie A. Marchand, *Byron: a Portrait* (1971; repr. 1993), pp. 193, 245, 250; Bradford Keyes Mudge, *Sara Coleridge, A Victorian Daughter: Her Life and Essays* (New Haven, 1989), pp. 14, 3. For Shelley as editor, see Mary Favret, 'Mary Shelley's sympathy and irony: the editor and her corpus' and Susan J. Wolfson, 'Editorial privilege: Mary Shelley and Percy Shelley's audiences', both in Audrey A. Fish, Anne K. Mellor and Esther Schor, eds., *The Other Mary Shelley: Beyond Frankenstein* (New York and Oxford, 1993), pp. 17–36, 39–72; Blumberg, *Mary Shelley's Early Novels*, as above, and Jerome McGann, *Lord Byron: the Complete Poetical Works* (Oxford, 1986), V, p. xxii.

71 *Wordsworth's Literary Criticism*, ed. Nowell C. Smith, revised by Howard Mills (Bristol, 1980), p. 23.

72 Germaine Greer, *Slipshod Sibyls: Recognition, Rejection and the Woman Poet* (1995), pp. 248–51; Chorley, *Memorials of Mrs Hemans* I, p. 167; II, pp. 141, 143.

73 Nicola J. Watson, *Revolution and the Form of the British Novel, 1790–1825* (Oxford, 1994), p. 126; Scott, *Waverley* (orig. 1814), ed. Andrew Hook (Harmondsworth, 1972), pp. 33–4, 10.

74 Homans, 'Keats reading women, women reading Keats', *Studies in Romanticism* 29 (1990), pp. 347, 361–2, 363.

75 R. C. Dallas, quoted in *His Very Self and Voice: Collected Conversations of Lord Byron*, ed. Ernest J. Lovell Jr (New York, 1954), p. 49.

76 Leslie A. Marchand, *Byron's Letters and Journals* (1973–81), III, p. 109 (further references appear parenthetically in the text); *Lady Blessington's Conversations of Lord Byron*, ed. Ernest J. Lovell Jr. (Princeton, NJ, 1969), p. 196; Marchand, *Letters and Journals* VII, p. 98; VIII, p. 15; Franklin, *Byron's Heroines*, p. 101.

77 *Medwin's Conversations with Lord Byron*, ed. Ernest J. Lovell Jr (Princeton, NJ, 1966), p. 206.

78 *Beppo* in *Byron: Poetical Works*, ed. Frederick Page, revised by John Jump (Oxford 1970), p. 632.

79 E.g. Marchand, *Letters and Journals* VI, pp. 91, 95; VII, p. 115; IX, p. 68; XI, p. 171.
80 *Medwin's Conversations*, p. 178.
81 Ross, *Contours of Masculine Desire*, p. 28.
82 Sonia Hofkosh, 'The writer's ravishment: women and the romantic author – the example of Byron' in Mellor, *Romanticism and Feminism*, p. 93; *Byron: Poetical Works*, pp. 180, 128, 252.
83 Horace, *Satires* 1.4.62; cf. Ovid, *Amores*, 3.7.65; Marchand, *Letters and Journals* VI, p. 207.
84 Henry Blyth, *Caro: the Fatal Passion* (1972), pp. 112, 155; *Medwin's Conversations*, p. 44; Marchand, *Letters and Journals* II, p. 559, note 1.
85 Marchand, *Letters and Journals* VII, p. 161; Blessington, *Conversations*, p. 91.
86 *The Blues: a Literary Eclogue* in *Poetical Works*, p. 151.
87 *His Very Self and Voice*, p. 91.
88 Elwin, *Lord Byron's Wife*, p. 110.
89 Marchand, *Letters and Journals* III, p. 238; cf. VI, p. 29.
90 Ibid. VII, p. 232; V, p. 168; VI, p. 232.

2 WHAT SHOULD GIRLS AND WOMEN READ?

1 Lefanu, *Life and Writings of Mrs Frances Sheridan*, p. 196: but contrast *Rambler* 4, p. 21.
2 Lefanu, *Life and Writings*, p. 197.
3 Ibid., p. 4; William LeFanu, ed., *Betsy Sheridan's Journal: Letters from Sheridan's Sister* (Oxford, 1986), p. 88.
4 Hawkins, *Rosanne* I, p. 46; Rozsika Parker, *The Subversive Stitch: Embroidery and the Making of the Feminine* (1984), p. 1.
5 *Lady's Magazine* 3 (1772), p. 239; Maria and Richard Lovell Edgeworth, *Practical Education* (1798), I, pp. 332–3.
6 Gregory, *Legacy*, p. 59; Fordyce, *Sermons* I, pp. 271, 273.
7 *Lady's Magazine* 31 (1800), pp. 283–4; Adeane, *Girlhood*, pp. 328, 347, 124; *Early Married Life*, pp. 65, 278, 285; *Girlhood*, pp. 268, 332.
8 Charlotte Lennox, *The Lady's Museum* 2 (1760–1), p. 776; *Lady's Magazine* 7 (1776), p. 123.
9 Hawkins, *Rosanne* II, p. 15; *Twin Sisters*, p. 80; More, *Coelebs* XII, pp. 45, 79; Hawkins, *Countess and Gertrude* I, pp. 226, 254; *Marriage*, p. 195; *Lady's Magazine* 4 (1773), p. 84.
10 Anley, *Miriam* (6th edn, 1839), p. 362; Green, *Mental Improvement*, p. 92; Gregory, *Legacy*, p. 16.
11 Wollstonecraft, *Thoughts on the Education of Daughters*, p. 21; Macaulay, *Letters on Education*, p. 138.
12 *Lady's Magazine* 4 (1810), p. 454; Hamilton, *Memoirs* I, p. 148; Lewis, *Journals and Correspondence of Miss Berry* I, pp. 7–8; Frances Burney, *Diaries and Letters of Madame D'Arblay*, ed. Charlotte Barrett (orig. 1842–6; 1893), 4 vols. (hereafter abrev. *DAL*), I, p. 275; Hunter, *Before Novels*, p. 241; *Tales of Fashionable Life* in

Tales and Novels by Maria Edgeworth (1870), v, pp. 326, 333; Hawkins, *Countess and Gertrude* III, p. 41.

13 See below, pp. 107–8; Gregory, *Legacy*, p. 17; *Belinda*, pp. 254–5; *Lady's Magazine* 13 (1782), p. 28; Vicesimus Knox, *Essays, Moral and Literary* (orig. 1778) in *Works* (1824), II, p. 248; *The World* 19 (9 May, 1753) cit. in Ioan Williams, *Novel and Romance*, p. 209.

14 Frances Burney, *The Journals and Letters of Fanny Burney (Madame D'Arblay)*, ed. Joyne Hemlow *et al.* (Oxford, 1972–84), 12 vols. (hereafter abbrev. *JAL*), v, pp. 102–3.

15 Lewis, *The Monk* (orig. 1796), ed. Louis Peck (New York, 1952), p. 258.

16 Lady Sarah Pennington, *An Unfortunate Mother's Advice to her Absent Daughters* (1761), pp. 18–19, 24; Burney, *DAL* I, p. 560; *Lady's Magazine* 22 (1791), p. 420; More, *Coelebs* XI, p. 386; *Strictures on the Modern System of Female Education* (1799), I, p. 234; *Twin Sisters*, p. 80.

17 Doody, 'Jane Austen's reading', p. 349; Elwin, *Lord Byron's Wife*, p. 262; Augustus J. C. Hare, *The Life and Letters of Maria Edgeworth* (1894), II, p. 92.

18 Armstrong, *Desire*, pp. 292, 100–1.

19 Green, *Mental Improvement*, p. 100; Joyce Hemlow, 'Fanny Burney and the courtesy books', *PMLA* 45 (1950), pp. 734–6; Reeve, *The Progress of Romance* (Colchester, 1785), II, pp. 103–4; Wollstonecraft, *Vindication*, pp. 105–9; *Female Reader*, pp. 70–2, 75–6, 120, 324, 325.

20 Green, *Courtship Novel*, p. 20; Armstrong, *Desire*, pp. 60, 258; More, *Strictures* I, p. 6; Nancy Armstrong, 'The rise of the domestic woman' in Armstrong and Leonard Tennenhouse, eds., *The Ideology of Conduct: Essays in Literature and the History of Sexuality* (1987), p. 98.

21 Vivien Jones, ed., *The Young Lady's Pocket Library, or Parental Monitor* (Bristol, 1995), pp. vi–vii.

22 Hemlow, 'Burney and the courtesy books', p. 739; John Bennett, *Letters to a Young Lady* (1792), II, p. 101; Wollstonecraft, *Thoughts on the Education of Daughters*, p. 14; Gregory, *Legacy*, pp. 33, 40, 63.

23 Armstrong, *Desire*, p. 109; Jones, *Young Lady's Pocket Library*, p. vii.

24 Wollstonecraft, *Vindication*, p. 109; 'natural' is a key-word in Gregory's *Legacy*, e.g. pp. 7, 11, 12, 14, 61, 81.

25 *The Woman-Hater* in Peter Sabor, ed., *The Complete Plays of Frances Burney* (1995), vol. I, II.iv.44; Hemlow, 'Burney and the courtesy books', pp. 737, 735; Austen, *Pride and Prejudice*, p. 113; R. W. Chapman, *Jane Austen's Letters to her Sister Cassandra and Others* (2nd edn, 1952), pp. 141–2; Barbara Horwitz, 'Lady Susan: the wicked mother in Jane Austen's work' in J. David Grey, ed., *Jane Austen's Beginnings* (Ann Arbor, 1989), p. 184; *Northanger Abbey*, p. 125 (cf. Gregory, *Legacy*, p. 36).

26 Ferrier, *Destiny* (orig. 1831; repr. 1929), pp. 568, 591–2.

27 Anna Seward, *The Letters of Anna Seward* (Edinburgh, 1811), IV, p. 350; *Lady's Magazine* 41 (1810), pp. 456–7; Seward, *Letters* IV , p. 350; ref. to Thomas Gisborne, *An Enquiry into the Duties of the Female Sex* (1797); Hawkins, *Countess and Gertrude* III, p. 46; Wollstonecraft, *Vindication*, pp. 109, 25, 105, 106, 108,

105, 109.

28 Gonda, *Reading Daughters' Fictions*, p. 180; *Betsy Sheridan's Journal*, p. 40; Claudia Thomas, ' "Th'instructive moral, and important thought": Elizabeth Carter reads Pope, Johnson and Epictetus', *Age of Johnson* 4 (1991), p. 139; Miss Benger, *Memoirs of the Late Mrs Elizabeth Hamilton* (1818), I, pp. 45, 49–50.

29 *The Repository or Treasury of Politics and Literature for 1770*, ii, 290; More, *Strictures* I, pp. 175–95; *Hints Towards Forming the Character of a Young Princess* (orig. 1805) in *Works* IV (London, 1834), pp. 264–6; Green, *Mental Improvement*, pp. 93, 99; Pennington, *Unfortunate Mother's Advice* (8th edn, 1817), p. 43, recommends 'Rollin's Ancient History', 'Hooke's Roman History', 'Hume's History of England' and 'Robertson's History of Scotland', etc.; More, *Coelebs* XI, p. 381; *Lady's Magazine* 5 (1774), p. 692; West, *Advantages of Education* I, p. 170; Bridget Hill, *The Republican Virago: the Life and Times of Catherine Macaulay, Historian* (Oxford, 1992), p. 25.

30 Gregory, *Legacy*, p. 59; *Lady's Magazine* 3 (1772), pp. 68, 9, 53, 103, 151, 207.

31 Joan Wallach Scott, *Gender and the Politics of History* (New York, 1988), pp. 9, 7, 18; Kathryn Sutherland, 'Hannah More's counter-revolutionary feminism' (in Kelvin Everest, ed., *Revolution in Writing: British Literary Responses to the French Revolution* (Milton Keynes, 1991), p. 27; *Lady's Magazine* 3 (1772), p. 68; More, *Strictures*, p. xii; *The Polite Lady* (1760), p. 139; Grant, *Letters from the Mountains* III, p. 65; Henry Kett, *Emily: a Moral Tale* (1809), II, pp. 28–9; Hester Chapone, *Letters on the Improvement of the Mind, addressed to a Young Lady* in *Works* (Dublin, 1775), p. 120; [Elizabeth Montagu], Dialogue XXVIII from *Dialogues of the Dead* (1760; Williams, *Novel and Romance*, p. 225).

32 *Northanger Abbey*, p. 123; *The Milesian Chief* (1812), I, p. 90; *The Errors of Education* (1791), II, pp. 68, 170–3; *The Cottagers of Glenburnie*, p. 75; *Helen* (orig. 1834; repr. 1987), pp. 94–5; *Mansfield Park*, (ed. Tony Tanner (Harmondsworth, 1966), p. 57; Smith, *Rambles Farther* I, p. 21; Hawkins, *Countess and Gertrude* III, pp. 34, 36; Shelley, *Falkner* (orig. 1837; repr. 1996), pp. 39–40; Edgeworth, *The Parent's Assistant*, p. 11.

33 Kett, *Emily* II, pp. 30, 31, 38, 39; Fordyce, *Sermons* I, p. 274; West, *Advantages of Education* I, pp. 43, 54; Ralph M. Wardle, ed., *Collected Letters of Mary Wollstonecraft* (Ithaca, 1979), p. 126.

34 Kett, *Emily*, II, p. 40; Green, *Mental Improvement*, p. 58.

35 *Lady's Magazine* 4 (1773), p. 402; Kett, *Emily* II, p. 38; More, *Hints*, p. 267; Knox, *Essays* I, p. 82, II, p. 247; Stella Tillyard, *Aristocrats: Caroline, Emily, Louisa and Sarah Lennox, 1740–1832* (1995), pp. 16, 39; *Lady's Magazine* 3 (1772), p. 196.

36 Joyce Hemlow, *The History of Fanny Burney* (Oxford, 1958), p. 20; Burney's reading included Plutarch's Lives (1768, *The Early Diaries of Frances Burney, 1768–1778*, ed. Annie Raine Ellis, 1889, 2 vols., hereafter abbrev. *ED* I, p. 21), Guthrie's *General History of England*, which was one of her 'favourite books' (1793, *JAL* III, p. 2), Anquetil's History of Greece, Voltaire's life of Charles XII of Sweden, and a life of Catherine the Great (1804–5, *JAL* VI, pp. 771–2,

780). Sarah Harriet Burney read a history of the Crusades, Robertson's history of Charles V, Plutarch's Lives, Wilkinson's *Manners and Customs of the Ancient Egyptians* (p. 150), and memoirs including those of Crabbe and Mrs Siddons (Edith J. Morley, 'Sarah Harriet Burney, 1770–1844', *Modern Philology* 39, 1941, pp. 132–58); *ED* I, pp. 8, 13; Seward, *Letters* II, p. 314.

37 *Lady's Magazine* 18 (1787), p. 425.

38 West, *Letters to a Young Lady* (1806), I, p. 21; More, *Coelebs* XII, p. 10; *Strictures*, p. 28; Smith, *Desmond* (1792), I, pp. iii–iv.

39 Sheila Rowbotham, *Hidden from History: 300 Years of Women's Oppression and the Fight against it* (1973).

40 Doody, 'Jane Austen's reading', p. 350; Edgeworth, preface to *Castle Rackrent* (orig. 1800; Oxford, 1980), pp. 1–3.

41 Pennington, *Series of Letters between Elizabeth Carter and Talbot* I, p. 147; Hays, *Emma Courtney*, p. 24; Seward, *Letters* I, p. 250; Hamilton, *Letters on the Elementary Principles of Education* (orig. 1801; 5th edn, 1810), II, p. 202; *Translation of the Letters of a Hindoo Rajah* (1796), I, p. 14; Edgeworth, *Early Lessons* (orig. 1801; 6th edn, 1829), III, p. xx; *Practical Education* I, p. 352; Hamilton, *Letters on . . . Education* II, p. 202.

42 Pennington, *Series of Letters* I, pp. 56–7; Jane Rendall, 'Writing History for British Women: Elizabeth Hamilton and the *Memoirs of Agrippina*' in Clarissa Campbell Orr, ed., *Wollstonecraft's Daughters: Womanhood in England and France 1780–1920* (Manchester, 1996), p. 82; Lars E. Troide *et al.*, ed., *The Early Journals and Letters of Fanny Burney* (Oxford, 1986–; hereafter abbrev. Troide), I, p. 25; Edgeworth, *Castle Rackrent*, p. 11; *Lady's Magazine* 9 (1778), p. 452; Joanna Baillie, *A Series of Plays: in which it is attempted to delineate the stronger passions of the Mind . . .* (orig. 1798; repr. Oxford, 1990), p. 18; Rendall, 'Writing History', p. 82; Wollstonecraft, *Vindication*, p. 168; Baillie, p. 18.

43 Edgeworth, 'The Good French Governess' (*Moral Tales*), p. 236, referring to Hume's 'Of the Study of History' in *David Hume, Philosophical Historian*, ed. David Fate Norton and Richard H. Popkin (Indianapolis, 1965); J. M. S. Tompkins, *The Popular Novel in England, 1770–1800* (orig. 1932; repr. 1962), p. 223.

44 Hunter, *Before Novels*, p. 341; Mary Campbell, *Lady Morgan: the Life and Times of Sydney Owenson* (1988), pp. 222, 183–5; *Lady's Magazine* 12 (1781), p. 13; Hamilton, *Letters of a Hindoo Rajah* II, p. 18.

45 Philip Edwards, *The Story of the Voyage: Sea-Narratives in Eighteenth-Century England* (Cambridge, 1994), pp. 1, 3; Kett, *Emily* I, p. 86; Austen, *Mansfield Park*, p. 177; Hawkins, *Countess and Gertrude* I, p. 261–3.

46 More, *Hints*, p. 267; Knox, *Essays* I, p. 82; Green, *Mental Improvement*, p. 91; Boswell, *Life of Johnson*, p. 44; Edwards, *Story of the Voyage*, p. 1; John Hawkesworth, *The Adventurer* 4, 18 Nov. 1752 (Williams, *Novel and Romance*, p. 192).

47 Billie Melman, *Women's Orients: English Women and the Middle East, 1718–1918* (orig. 1992; repr. 1995), p. 1; Fordyce, *Sermons* I, p. 275; Sara Mills, *Discourses*

of Difference: an Analysis of Women's Travel Writing and Colonialism (1991), p. 58; Melman, *Women's Orients*, p. 4; Kay Schaffer, *Women and the Bush: Forces of Desire in the Australian Cultural Tradition* (Cambridge, 1989), p. 82.

48 More, *Hints*, p. 267; Edwards, *Story of the Voyage*, p. 86; Carole Fabricant, 'The literature of domestic tourism and the public consumption of private property' in Felicity Nussbaum and Laura Brown, eds., *The New 18th Century: Theory, Politics, English Literature* (1987), p. 257.

49 Melman, *Women's Orients*, p. 301; Halsband, *Letters* I, p. 328; Melman, p. 1; Reginald Blunt, ed., *Mrs Montagu, 'Queen of the Blues': Her Letters and Friendships from 1762–1800* (1923), I, pp. 45, 279; Seward, *Letters* I, pp. 83, 330.

50 Wollstonecraft, 'Hints', *Vindication*, p. 225; Blunt, *Mrs Montagu* I, p. 279.

51 Blunt, *Mrs Montagu* II, pp. 31, 251.

52 *Mansfield Park*, p. 177; Doody, 'Jane Austen's reading', p. 352; Joseph Lew, ' "That abominable traffic": *Mansfield Park* and the dynamics of slavery' in Beth Fowkes Tobin, ed., *History, Gender, and Eighteenth-Century Literature* (Athens, Georgia, 1994), p. 293; Hunter, *Before Novels*, p. 351.

53 Wollstonecraft, 'Hints', *Vindication*, p. 225; *Lady's Magazine* 5 (1774), p. 403; Chapone, *Letters*, p. 120; Kett, *Emily* II, p. 46; Mudge, *Sara Coleridge* p. 245.

54 Roberts, *Memoirs* II, p. 386; More, *Coelebs* XII, pp. 244, 246, 245, 243, 31.

55 Margaret and Susannah Minifie, *The Histories of Lady Frances S- and Lady Caroline S-* (Dublin, 1763), pp. 26, 33, 93, 117, 148; 20–1, 133–44.

56 Burney, *Camilla* (orig. 1796), ed. Edward A. Bloom and Lillian D. Bloom (Oxford, 1986), p. 487; Samuel Jackson Pratt, *Shenstone-Green; or, the New Paradise Lost* (1779), I, p. 22; Frances Brooke, *The History of Emily Montague* (orig. 1769; repr. 1961, Aylesbury and Slough), p. 300; Roche, *Clermont: a Tale* (orig. 1798; repr. 1968), p. 5.

57 *Lady's Magazine* 38 (1807), p. 581; Pennington, *Unfortunate Mother's Advice*, 1761 edn, p. 25; 1817 edn, p. 43.

58 Smith, *Conversations, Introducing Poetry* (orig. 1804; repr. 1863), p. 233; see also pp. 13, 18, 131, 159, 240; *Rural Walks* (1795), I, pp. 93–4, 138–40, II, p. 71; *Rambles Farther* (1796), I, p. 114, II, pp. 148–9; More, *Coelebs* XII, p. 288; Maturin, *Women: or Pour et Contre* (1818), I, pp. 200–1; Kett, *Emily* II, pp. 236–7; *Romance of the Forest*, ed. Chloe Chard (Oxford, 1986), p. 261; *Sir Charles Grandison* III, p. 122; *Falkner*, p. 223; *Destiny*, p. 415; James Thomson, *The Denial: or, the Happy Retreat* (1790), I, p. 24.

59 *The Mysteries of Udolpho* (orig. 1794; repr., Oxford 1980), pp. 1, 15, 17, 54, 56, 140, 213; Smith, *Rural Walks* I, pp. 18, 26, 86, 125, II, p. 31, etc.; *Rambles Farther* I, p. 80; Hawkins, *Countess and Gertrude* III, pp. 37, 170; West, *Tale of the Times* I, pp. 27, 136; *Lady's Magazine* 12 (1781), p. 693; Burney, *Camilla*, p. 201; Ferrier, *Marriage*, pp. 38, 487.

60 *Marriage*, p. 487; *Falkner*, p. 148.

61 Donna Landry, *The Muses of Resistance: Labouring-Class Women's Poetry in Britain, 1739–96* (Cambridge, 1990), pp. 45–6.

62 Pope, 'Epistle to Dr Arbuthnot' (1734), line 128; Paula R. Backscheider and Hope D. Cotton, eds., *The Excursion: Frances Brooke* (Lexington, 1997), p. 16;

Donald C. Mell, *Pope, Swift, and Women Writers* (Newark, 1996), p. 18; Landry, *Muses of Resistance*, p. 110.

63 *The Excursion*, e.g. pp. 16, 28, 35, 129, 152; Ann Messenger, 'Arabella Fermor, 1714 and 1769: Alexander Pope and Frances Moore Brooke', ch. 6 of *His and Hers: Essays in Restoration and 18th-Century Literature* (Lexington, 1986); *Emily Montague*, pp. 218, 237; in *Belinda* Lady Delacour quotes *The Rape of the Lock* (pp. 29, 68), 'Epistle to a Lady' (pp. 129, 160) and 'On the Art of Sinking in Poetry' (p. 450).

64 *Lady's Magazine* 11 (1780), p. 659; Benjamin Silliman, *Letters of Shahcoolen* (Boston, 1820; repr. Gainesville, 1962), p. 55.

65 Green, *Mental Improvement*, p. 116; Smith, *Desmond* II, p. 170.

66 Burney, *Evelina* (1778), ed. Edward A. Bloom with Lillian D. Bloom (Oxford, 1982), p. 78; Edgeworth, *Harrington* in *Harrington and Ormond, Tales* (2nd edn, 1817), I, pp. 144–55; *Hortensia* I, pp. 68, 162–70.

67 *Lady's Magazine* 22 (1791), p. 520; de Acton, *Essays* II, p. 38; West, *Letters* I, p. 202; Green, *Mental Improvement*, p. 117.

68 Gregory, *Legacy*, p. 66; *Thoughts on the Education of Daughters*, pp. 46–7; *Lady's Magazine* 22 (1791), p. 520.

69 Landry, *Muses of Resistance*, p. 85; Llanover, *Autobiography and Correspondence of Mrs Delany*, e.g. I, pp. 123, 188, 251; III, pp. 28, 65; Susan Staves, 'Fatal marriages? Restoration plays embedded in eighteenth-century novels' in Douglas Lane Patey and Timothy Keegan, eds., *Augustan Studies: Essays in Honor of Irvin Ehrenpreis* (Newark, NJ, 1985), pp. 95, 97, 99; Richardson, *Pamela* (repr. 1974), II, pp. 253–4; *Sir Charles Grandison* II, p. 273, III, p. 8, IV, p. 264; II, p. 348, VI, pp. 251, 201, VII, p. 436; Fielding, *Tom Jones*, p. 706; *Amelia* (orig. 1751), ed. A. R. Humphries (1974), II, p. 194.

70 Staves, 'Fatal marriages', p. 97.

71 *Recruiting Officer* I.i.293, I.ii.59.

72 Keir, *Interesting Memoirs* (1785), II, p. 147; *George Bateman* II, p. 56; *Romance of the Forest*, pp. 261, 284; *Marriage*, p. 65; Williams, *Julia* II, p. 44.

73 Michael Dobson, *The Making of the National Poet: Shakespeare, Adaptation and Authorship, 1660–1769* (Oxford, 1992), p. 7; Austen, *Mansfield Park*, p. 335; Williams, *Julia* I, p. 17; Lewis Theobald, *Shakespeare Restored* (1726) in Ann Thompson and Sasha Roberts, *Women Reading Shakespeare, 1660–1900* (Manchester, 1997), p. 1; ibid., pp. 1, 58, 47, 30.

74 Thompson and Roberts, *Women Reading Shakespeare*, p. 23; Edgeworth, *Patronage*, p. 378, and 'Emilie de Coulanges' in *Tales and Novels* VI, p. 353; Maturin, *Women* III, p. 43.

75 *Interesting Memoirs* I, p. 165; *Twelfth Night* II.iv.106–22; *Sir Charles Grandison* III, pp. 153, 157; Brooke, *Emily Montague*, p. 160; Roche, *Clermont*, p. 24; *Hartley House, Calcutta* (1789; repr. 1989), p. 110.

76 Acton, *Essays* II, p. 39; More, *Hints*, pp. 285–9.

77 Robert Altick, *The English Common Reader* (Chicago, 1957), pp. 112–13; Kett, *Emily* I, p. 313; Altick, *English Common Reader*, pp. 112–13.

78 Thompson and Roberts, *Women Reading Shakespeare*, p. 1; Wardle, *Collected*

Letters of Mary Wollstonecraft, pp. 30, 33, 38, 39, 42, 44, 49; Susan J. Wolfson, 'Explaining to her sisters: Mary Lamb's *Tales from Shakespeare*' in Marianne Novy, ed., *Women's Re-visions of Shakespeare* (Urbana and Chicago, 1990), p. 18; Virginia Sapiro, *A Vindication of Political Virtue: the Political Theory of Mary Wollstonecraft* (Chicago, 1992), p. 220.

79 Roberts, *Memoirs of the Life and Correspondence of Hannah More* I, p. 234.

80 Shteir, *Cultivating Women*, p. 2; Londa Schiebinger, *The Mind Has No Sex? Women in the Origins of Modern Science* (Cambridge, Mass., 1989), p. 233; Davidoff and Hall, *Family Fortunes*, p. 27.

81 Shteir, *Cultivating Women*, p. 5; Edgeworth, *Letters for Literary Ladies*, p. 20; *Harry and Lucy Concluded* (1825), I, pp. 272, 114; xiv, 7, II, p. 121, III, p. 27; I, pp. 2–3; I, pp. 4, 14, 23–4, III, pp. 27, 223.

82 G. S. Rousseau, 'Science books and their readers in the 18th Century' in Isobel Rivers, ed., *Books and their Readers in 18th-Century England* (Leicester, 1982), p. 227; Ann B. Shteir, 'Botanical dialogues: Maria Jacson and women's popular science writing in England', *Eighteenth-Century Studies* 23 (1989–90), p. 301.

83 E.g. Maria Jacson's *Botanical Dialogues* (1797) and *Sketches of the Physiology of Vegetable Life* (1811), Priscilla Wakefield's *Domestic Recreation; or, Dialogues Illustrative of Natural and Scientific Subjects* (1805), and Jane Marcet's 'conversations' on chemistry (1806), 'political economy' (1817), 'natural philosophy' (1819) and 'vegetable physiology' (1829); Shteir, 'Botanical dialogues', p. 301.

84 For science reading, see Patricia Phillips, *The Scientific Lady: a Social History of Woman's Scientific Interests 1520–1918* (1990), e.g. pp. 90–104; *Lady's Magazine* 26 (1795), p. 435; Llanover, *Autobiography and Correspondence of Mrs Delany*, 2nd series, I, p. 474; orig. series, I, pp. 259–60; Halsband *Complete Letters* I, p. 180; Paula R. Feldman and Diana Scott-Kilvert, *The Journals of Mary Shelley 1814–1844* (Oxford, 1987), I, p. 68; Haywood, *The Invisible Spy* (1755), III, pp. 266–7.

85 *Lady's Magazine* I (1770), pp. 466–9; *La Belle Assemblée* I (1806), pp. 41, 42, 105, 541.

86 Phillips, *The Scientific Lady*, pp. 96–7; Shteir, *Cultivating Women*, p. 28; West, *Letters* I, p. 362.

87 William Rowley, *A Treatise on Female . . . Diseases* (1780), cit. Rousseau, 'Science books and their readers', p. 248.

88 *Lady's Magazine* 4 (1773), pp. 400–2; Emily J. Climenson, *Elizabeth Montagu, the Queen of the Blue-Stockings: Her Correspondence from 1720 to 1761* (1906), II, p. 198; *Lady's Magazine* II (1780), pp. 265, 310; Chapone, *Letters*, p. 119.

89 *Letters for Literary Ladies*, p. 21.

90 Llanover, *Autobiography and Correspondence of Mrs Delany* I, pp. 259–60; Montagu Pennington, *Memoirs of the Life of Mrs Elizabeth Carter . . .* (1807), p. 11; see above, p. 65; *Thraliana*, p. 383; Roberts *Memoirs of the Life and Correspondence of Hannah More* I, p. 16; Kett, *Emily* I, ch. 15; Mary Hays, *Emma Courtney*, p. 71 and *The Victim of Prejudice* (orig. 1799), ed. Eleanor Ty (Ontario, 1994), p. 6;

Radcliffe, *Romance of the Forest*, p. 275; Hawkins, *Countess and Gertrude* I, p. 340, II, p. 203; Austen, *Mansfield Park*, p. 139.

91 Davidoff and Hall, *Family Fortunes*, p. 453.

92 Letter from Peter Collinson to Linnaeus, cit. Rousseau, 'Science books and their readers', p. 225; Edgeworth, *Letters for Literary Ladies*, p. 21; Shteir, *Cultivating Women*, p. 19; Burney, *JAL* XII, pp. 628–9.

93 Schiebinger, *The Mind Has No Sex?*, p. 241; Shteir, *Cultivating Women*, p. 147.

94 Shteir, *Cultivating Women*, p. 2; Schiebinger, *The Mind Has No Sex?*, p. 241; *Coelebs* XII, p. 287; *Hortensia* II, pp. 64–7; West, *Advantages of Education* I, pp. 77–8; Rosamund in Edgeworth's 'The Rabbit' (*Early Lessons* II), Susan in 'Simple Susan' (*The Parent's Assistant*); Shteir, *Cultivating Women*, p. 3.

95 West, *Advantages of Education* I, pp. 77–8; Ruth Hayden, *Mrs Delany, Her Life and Her Flowers* (1980); Judith Pascoe, 'Female botanists and the poetry of Charlotte Smith' in Carol Shiner Wilson and Joel Haefner, eds., *Re-visioning Romanticism: British Women 1776–1837* (Philadelphia, 1994).

96 Shteir, *Cultivating Women*, p. 56; Smith, *Rural Walks* II, p. 128; Shteir, *Cultivating Women*, p. 117.

97 Alan Bewell, '"Jacobin plants": botany as social theory in the 1790s', *Wordsworth Circle* 20 (1989), p. 137; Shteir, *Cultivating Women*, pp. 21, 242, 35, 15, 16.

98 Shteir, *Cultivating Women*, pp. 13, 16, 17, 4, 23; Hawkins, *Countess and Gertrude* III, p. 8–9; Londa Schiebinger, *Nature's Body: Sexual Politics and the Making of Modern Science* (1994), p. 30.

99 Richard Polwhele, *The Unsex'd Females; a Poem* (1798), p. 8.

100 Eaton Stannard Barrett, *The Heroine; or, Adventures of Cherubina* (orig. 1813; 3rd edn, 1815) II, p. 158; Seward, *Letters* VI, p. 83; Hawkins, *Countess and Gertrude* III, p. 9; Edgeworth, *Letters for Literary Ladies*, pp. 20–1; and see Pascoe, 'Female botanists', pp. 199–201.

101 John Berkenhout, *A Volume of Letters from Dr Berkenhout to His Son at the University* (Cambridge, 1790), p. 307; Wollstonecraft, *Vindication*, p. 139; Milton, *Paradise Lost* III, lines 47–8; Polwhele, *Unsex'd Females*, pp. 8–9, 7, 6.

102 Hawkins, *Countess and Gertrude* II, pp. 130, 132; Penelope Wilson, 'Classical poetry and the 18th-century reader' in Rivers, *Books and their Readers*, p. 72; *Letters of the Earl of Chesterfield to his Son*, ed. Charles Strachey (1901), I, p. 230; *Coelebs* XII, p. 231; Sarah Scott, *Millenium Hall* (orig. 1762), ed. Gary Kelly (Toronto, 1995), p. 225; Minifies, *Histories of Lady Frances S-*, p. 169; see above, p. 49; *Lady's Magazine* 10 (1779, p. 512; 3 (1772), p. 9.

103 Shteir, *Cultivating Women*, p. 56; Mudge, *Sara Coleridge*, p. 26; Shelley, *Lodore* (orig. 1835; repr. 1996), p. 214.

104 Halsband, *Complete Letters* III, p. 22; More, *Coelebs* XII, p. 234; Burney, *DAL* III, p. 133.

105 *ED* I, p. 63; *DAL* I, pp. 132, 43, 149.

106 Frances Sheridan, *Memoirs of Miss Sidney Biddulph* (repr. 1987), p. 73.

107 Edgeworth, *Practical Education* II, pp. 387–8, 550; More, *Coelebs* XII, p. 232; Knox, *Works* I, p. 432; *Coelebs* XII, p. 235; Knox, *Works* II, pp. 109–10.

108 Chapone, *Letters*, p. 122; Blunt, *Mrs Montagu* II, p. 184.

109 *Grandison* II, p. 431, IV, p. 294; see below, p. 106; Green, *Mental Improvement*, p. 108; J. C. Austen-Leigh, *Memoir of Jane Austen* (orig. 1870), ed. R. W. Chapman (Oxford, 1926), p. 88; *Thaddeus of Warsaw* II, p. 165.

110 Chapone, *Letters*, p. 117; Carol Barash, *English Women's Poetry, 1649–1714: Politics, Community, and Linguistic Authority* (Oxford, 1996), p. 34; Mary Seidman Trouille, *Sexual Politics of the Enlightenment: Women Writers Read Rousseau* (Albany, 1997), p. 238.

111 More, *Strictures* I, p. 93.

112 Carolyn D. Williams, 'Poetry, pudding, and Epictetus: the consistency of Elizabeth Carter' in Ribeiro and Basker, *Tradition in Transition*, p. 20; Blakey, *Minerva Press*, p. 38; Schiebinger, *Nature's Body*, p. 168.

113 More, *Strictures* I, p. 43; *Coelebs* XI, p. 33; *Mansfield Park*, pp. 161–3, 175; Seward, *Letters* VI, p. 144; Ferrier, *Marriage*, pp. 115, 237; Edgeworth, *Patronage*, p. 58, *Leonora*, p. 9; Maturin, *The Wild Irish Boy* (1808), I, pp. 261–2, III, pp. 300, 303.

114 Lady Louisa Stuart, Wilfred Partington, *The Private Letter-Books of Sir Walter Scott* (1930), p. 273; Adeane, *Girlhood*, pp. 332, 302, *Early Married Life*, p. 191; Florence May Anna Hilbish, *Charlotte Smith, Poet and Novelist (1749–1806)* (Philadelphia, 1941), e.g. pp. 297, 310, 318; Whitbread, *I Know My Own Heart*, p. 283; Burney, *Evelina*, p. 7; William Hayley, *The Triumphs of Temper: A Poem, in Six Cantos* (1781), IV, 330, 372; Hawkins, *Countess and Gertrude* I, p. 329, II, p. 30.

115 More, *Strictures* I, pp. 44–5; Grant, *Letters from the Mountains* II, p. 141; Trant, *Journal*, p. 62; Mary Hays, *Letters and Essays, Moral and Miscellaneous* (1793) repr. in Folger Collective on Early Women Critics, *Women Critics 1660–1820* (Bloomington and Indianapolis 1995), p. 298; Edgeworth, *Leonora*, pp. 31, 179; Edgeworth, *Castle Rackrent*, pp. 65–6; *Marriage* p. 475; Smith, *Emmeline: or the Orphan of the Castle* (orig. 1788; repr. 1987), p. 184.

116 Nicola J. Watson, *Revolution and the Form of the English Novel 1790–1825* (Oxford, 1994), p. 27; Trouille, *Sexual Politics*, pp. 57, 163, 3, 1.

117 William Ray, 'Reading women: cultural authority, gender, and the novel: the case of Rousseau', *Eighteenth-Century Studies* 27, no. 3 (1994), pp. 423, 429, 430.

118 Sydney Owenson Morgan, *St Clair; or, the Heiress of Desmond* (1803), p. 178; Wardle, *Collected Letters of Mary Wollstonecraft*, p. 145; Hays, *Letters and Essays*, p. 299; for Rousseau in Wollstonecraft's work, see Sapiro, *Vindication of Political Virtue*, esp. pp. 167–72, 292–7, and Trouille, *Sexual Politics*, pp. 221–36; Watson, *Revolution and the Form of the English Novel*, p. 46; Trouille, *Sexual Politics*, p. 227; Wollstonecraft, *Wrongs of Woman*, p. 49.

119 Watson, *Revolution and the Form of the English Novel*, p. 51; Trouille, *Sexual Politics*, p. 55.

120 Sydney Owenson Morgan, *Lady Morgan's Memoirs: Autobiography, Diaries and Correspondence* (1862), I, p. 134.

121 Brigid Brophy, ed., *The Wild Irish Girl* (1986).

122 Watson, *Revolution and the Form of the English Novel*, pp. 114–15.

123 More, *Strictures* I, pp. 178–9; Johnson, *Jane Austen: Women, Politics, and the Novel*, p. 11; *Boswell's London Journal*, p. 278.

124 Benger, *Memoirs of . . . Hamilton* I, p. 211; Knox, *Works* I, p. 429; Roberts, *Memoirs* III, p. 56; Dacre, *The Passions* (1811), II, pp. 229–30.

125 Tobias Smollett, *The Adventures of Roderick Random*, ed. Paul-Gabriel Boucé (1979), pp. 117–18, 132.

126 Burney, *DAL* I, p. 273.

127 More, *Strictures* I, pp. 30–1; West, *Letters* I, pp. 16, 20–1, 359–65; Benger, *Memoirs of . . . Hamilton* I, pp. 132–3.

128 'Mr Fantom; or, the History of the New Fashioned Philosopher and his Man William' in *Stories for the Middle Ranks*, *Works* (1818), vol. IV).

129 Silliman, *Letters of Shahcoolen*, pp. 39, 44, 48, 61.

130 *The Vagabond* I, p. 177; Silliman, *Letters of Shahcoolen*, pp. 31, 23; Pam Hirsch, 'Mary Wollstonecraft: a problematic legacy' in Orr, ed., *Wollstonecraft's Daughters*, p. 43.

131 Regina M. Janes, 'On the reception of Mary Wollstonecraft's *A Vindication of the Rights of Woman*', *Journal of the History of Ideas* 39 (1978), pp. 293–302; *Lady's Magazine* 18 (1787), pp. 227–30, 369–70; 26 (1795), p. 453; 29 (1798), p. 261; 36 (1805), pp. 82, 79, 81.

132 Hamilton, *Letters on . . . Education* I, pp. 142, 184.

133 Grant, *Letters from the Mountains* II, pp. 268, 272–3, 270, 273; *Much Ado about Nothing* II.iii.64–5.

134 *Adeline Mowbray* (orig. 1804; repr. 1986).

135 Johnson, *Jane Austen: Women, Politics, and the Novel*, p. 12.

136 Brewer, 'Reconstructing the reader', p. 232; Whitbread, *I Know My Own Heart*, p. 146; Bennett, *Letters to a Young Lady* II, p. 38; Markman Ellis, *Politics*, p. 164; Chesterfield, *The World* 25 (1753), I, pp. 215–22; Mackenzie, *The Man of Feeling* (orig. 1771; repr. Oxford, 1970), p. 58; Blunt, *Mrs Montagu* I, p. 15.

137 Clery, *Rise of Supernatural Fiction*, p. 7; Sidney Smith, *Edinburgh Review* 15 (1810), p. 312; Fordyce, *Sermons* I, p.149; *Lady's Magazine* 22 (1791), p. 74; Fordyce, *Sermons* I, pp. 148–55; Gregory, *Legacy*, pp. 22, 47; Gisborne, 'On the Employment of Time by the Female Sex', *Lady's Magazine*, 34 (1803), pp. 418–19; Pennington, *Unfortunate Mother's Advice*, p. 39; Green, *Mental Improvement*, pp. 101–2; Chapone, *Letters* p. 127; More, *Strictures* I, pp. 185–7; West, *Letters to a Young Lady*, e.g. II, pp. 442–54; Hamilton, *Letters on . . . Education* II, p. 214; de Acton, *Essays on the Art* II, p. 40.

138 Roberts, *Memoirs* III, pp. 145, 168; Gisborne, 'On the Employment of Time', p. 419; Hugh Murray, *The Morality of Fiction* (Edinburgh, 1805), cit. W. F. Galloway Jr, 'The conservative attitude toward fiction, 1779–1830', *PMLA* 55, (1940), p. 1045; Hamilton, *Translation of the Letters of a Hindoo Rajah* II, p. 38; Reeve, *Progress of Romance* II, p. 78; Mackenzie, *Man of Feeling*, p. 55.

139 Knox, *Works* I, p. 430; Goldsmith, *The Citizen of the World* (1760) in *Collected Works of Oliver Goldsmith*, ed. Arthur Friedman (Oxford, 1966), II, p. 123;

Honoria, *The Female Mentor; or, Select Conversations* (1798), pp. 71–2; West, *Advantages of Education* I, p. 3; Eliza Parsons, *The Errors of Education*, II, p. 171; Hawkins, *Countess and Gertrude* II, p. 174.

140 Edgeworth, *Practical Education* I, p. 334; Eleanor Sleath, *The Orphan of the Rhine* (1798; repr. 1968), p. 147.

141 Pope, 'An Epistle to a Lady' (orig. 1735), line 3; *Eclectic Review* 8, June 1812, p. 606, cit. John Tinnon Taylor, *Early Opposition to the English Novel: the Popular Reaction from 1760 to 1830* (New York, 1943), p. 69; D'Israeli, *Curiosities of Literature* II, p. 60.

142 Wollstonecraft, *Vindication*, pp. 306, 152, 306; More, *Hints towards Forming the Character of a Young Princess* (orig. 1806) in *Works* (1834), IV, p. 29; *Moriana* in *Works* (1837) VI, p. 373; *Strictures* I, p. 171.

143 *Lady's Magazine* 12 (1781), p. 123; *Lady's Monthly Museum* I (1798), p. 258; 3 (1799), p. 375; Anna Letitia Barbauld, 'On the Origin and Progress of Novel-Writing', cit. Taylor, *Early Opposition*, p. 112; Charles Jenner, *The Placid Man* (1770), I, p. 125.

144 Austen, *Northanger Abbey*, p. 58; Brunton, *Emmeline*, p. lxxii; Brooke, *The Excursion*, p. 1; *La Belle Assemblée* I (1806), p. 531.

145 Lamb, *Glenarvon* (2nd edn, 1816), p. 138; Darwin, *A Plan for the Conduct of Female Education* (Derby, 1797), p. 34.

146 Mary Anne Schofield, *Masking and Unmasking the Female Mind* (Newark, 1990), p. 150; *The Old Manor House* (orig. 1793; repr. Oxford, 1989), p. 293; *Ethelinde or, the Recluse of the Lake* (1789), II, p. 166; *Emmeline*, pp. 245, 78; *The Young Philosopher* (1798), I, p. 110; *Conversations, Introducing Poetry* (1804), I, p. 106; *Rural Walks* II, p. 6.

147 *Old Manor House*, pp. 26–7, 42; *Ethelinde* II, p. 124; *The Young Philosopher* I, p. 73; *Montalbert* (1796), I, p. 59; Diana Bowstead, 'Charlotte Smith's *Desmond*: the epistolary novel as ideological argument' in Mary Anne Schofield and Cecilia Macheski, eds., *Fetter'd or Free? British Women Novelists 1670–1815* (Athens, Ohio, 1986), p. 237.

148 *Rural Walks* II, pp. 141, 7–10; *Letters of a Solitary Wanderer* (1800), I, p. 25; *Rural Walks* II, pp. 122–3.

149 *Emmeline*, p. 78; *Desmond* II, p. 173; *Letters of a Solitary Wanderer* I, pp. vi–vii.

150 *Ethelinde* II, p. 166; *The Romance of Real Life* (1787) is a translation of French law cases.

151 Knox, *Works* I, p. 82, II, p. 247.

152 Morgan, *St Clair*, p. 183; Seward, *Letters* VI, pp. 142.

3 THE PLEASURES AND PERILS OF READING

1 Grant, *Memoirs and Correspondence* II, p. 235; I, p. 225; Halsband, *Complete Letters* III, p. 144; Grant, *Letters from the Mountains* III, p. 126.

2 A. F. Wedd, *The Love-Letters of Mary Hays (1779–1780)* (1925), p. 28.

3 Adeane, *Early Married Life*, p. 252.

4 M. J. Levy, *Perdita: the Memoirs of Mary Robinson*, pp. 38, 54.

5 Sutherland, 'More's counter-revolutionary feminism', pp. 38, 52.

6 Gregory, *Legacy*, p. 33.

7 *Tears of Sensibility* is a novel by John Murdoch (1773); Rosa Matilda was the pseudonym of Charlotte Dacre; I have not found *Too Civil by Half*, though perhaps More is thinking of *Too Friendly by Half*, a play performed at Covent Garden in 1807; Goethe's *The Sorrows of Young Werther* was translated in 1779; *The Stranger* was a play by Kotzebue, adapted by Sheridan (1798); *The Orphans of Snowdon* is a novel by Elizabeth Gunning (1797), *The History of Jemmy and Jenny Jessamy* a novel by Eliza Haywood (1753); *Perfidy Punished* is the subtitle of *Emily Herbert* (1786), a novel, perhaps by Elizabeth Inchbald; *The Fortunate Footman* is the subtitle of a chapbook ballad, *The Resolute Lady* (Glasgow, 1805: though novel-titles including 'fortunate' had a mid-eighteenth-century vogue, and More may be thinking of one); I have not traced *Sympathy of Souls* or *The Illustrious Chambermaid* (though there was a vogue for novels about servants, generated by *Pamela*). Perhaps these are meant to be generic rather than snipes at specific books.

8 Sutherland, 'More's counter-revolutionary feminism', p. 37.

9 Joan Rees, *Shelley's Jane Williams* (1985), p. 67; Halsband, *Complete Letters* III, p. 207; Llanover, *Autobiography and Correspondence of Mary Delany* III, p. 214; Grant, *Memoirs* II, p. 58; Robert Gittings and Jo Manton, *Claire Clairmont and the Shelleys* (1992), p. 185.

10 Grant, *Memoirs*, e.g. I, pp. 87, 198–90; Wollstonecraft, *Wrongs of Woman*, p. 81; Robinson, *The Natural Daughter* (1799), II, p. 129; Janet Schaw, *Journal of a Lady of Quality . . . in the Years 1774–1776*, ed. Evangeline Walker Andrews and Charles McLean Andrews (2nd edn, New Haven, 1934), p. 256; Richardson, *Pamela* I, p. 95; Smith, *Emmeline*, p. 184.

11 Walter Marion Crittenden, *The Life and Writings of Mrs Sarah Scott – Novelist (1723–1795)* (Philadelphia, 1932), p. 62; James L. Clifford, *Hester Lynch Piozzi (Mrs Thrale)* (2nd edn, Oxford, 1968), pp. 113, 422; Ralph M. Wardle, *Godwin and Mary: Letters of William Godwin and Mary Wollstonecraft* (1987), pp. 119–20.

12 Feldman and Scott-Kilvert, *Journals of Mary Shelley* I, p. 135; Gittings and Manton, *Claire Clairmont*, p. 223; Louise Schultz Boas, *Harriet Shelley: Five Long Years* (Oxford, 1962), pp. 60–1; Wollstonecraft, *Female Reader*, p. 274.

13 *Lady's Magazine* 35 (1804), pp. 698–9.

14 Parodied in, e.g., Eaton Stannard Barrett's *The Heroine* I, p. 183.

15 Staves, 'Fatal marriages', p. 98.

16 Stewart, *Dear Reader*, p. 127; Edgeworth, *Belinda*, pp. 162–3; Maturin, *The Milesian Chief* IV, p. 157; *Women* I, p. 263, III, p. 208; *Thraliana*, pp. 560–1.

17 Kilgour, *Rise of the Gothic Novel*, p. 82.

18 Betty A. Schellenberg, *The Conversational Circle: Re-reading the English Novel, 1740–1775* (Lexington, 1996), p. 2.

19 *Lady's Magazine* 10 (1779), p. 399; 7 (1776), p. 543; Crittenden, *Life and Writings of Sarah Scott*, p. 63; *Lady's Magazine* 4 (1773), p. 47.

20 *Lady's Magazine* 10 (1779), pp. 544–5; 9 (1778), pp. 20–3; cf. *Spectator* 37, 12

April 1711.

21 Tompkins, *Popular Novel*, p. 120.

22 See below, pp. 159–60.

23 Watson, *Revolution and the Form of the British Novel*, p. 54; Janet Todd, *Women's Friendship in Literature* (New York, 1980).

24 Boas, *Harriet Shelley*, p. 45; Desmond Hawkins, *Shelley's First Love: the Love Story of Percy Bysshe Shelley and Harriet Grove* (1992), pp. 128, 139.

25 Feldman and Scott-Kilvert, *Journals of Mary Shelley*; M. K. and D. M. Stocking, *The Journals of Claire Clairmont* (Cambridge, Mass., 1968).

26 Mary and Percy Bysshe Shelley, *History of a Six Weeks Tour* (orig. 1817; repr. Oxford, 1992), pp. 54, 62.

27 *Shelley and his Circle 1773–1822*, ed. Kenneth Neill Cameron (Cambridge, Mass., 1961), II, pp. 522, 568, 592, 575, 595, 580.

28 Boas, *Harriet Shelley*, p. 227.

29 Ibid., pp. 34, 36; Sydney Owenson Morgan, *The Missionary: an Indian Tale* (2nd edn, 1811), I, p. 35.

30 Boas, *Harriet Shelley*, p. 164.

31 Kilgour, *Rise of the Gothic Novel*, p. 6; Susan Wolstoneholme, *Gothic (Re)Visions: Writing Women as Readers* (Albany, 1993), p. xi.

32 Hett, *Memoirs of Susan Sibbald*, p. 176.

33 *Thraliana*, p. 886; Edward Mangin, *Piozziana; or Recollections of the Late Mrs Piozzi* (1833), pp. 75, 78; Pennington, *Memoirs of the Life of Mrs Elizabeth Carter*, p. 300; Christine Colvin, ed., *Maria Edgeworth in France and Switzerland* (Oxford, 1979), p. 5; Hare, *Life and Letters of Maria Edgeworth* I, p. 25; Wollstonecraft, *Letters*, p. 385; Seward, *Letters* III, p. 389; Burney, *JAL* III, p. 337.

34 *Lady's Magazine* 33 (1802), p. 314; Marilyn Butler, 'The woman at the window: Ann Radcliffe in the novels of Mary Wollstonecraft and Jane Austen' in Janet Todd, ed., *Gender and Literary Voice* (New York and London, 1980), pp. 128–48.

35 David H. Richter, 'Reception of the Gothic novel in the 1790s' in Robert W. Uphaus, ed., *The Idea of the Novel in the 18th Century* (East Lansing, 1988), p. 121.

36 Kilgour, *Rise of the Gothic Novel*, pp. 6–7, 150, 172, 169.

37 Radcliffe, *The Mysteries of Udolpho*, pp. 49–50. References to Radcliffe in the text are as previously cited; *A Sicilian Romance* to the first edition; and *The Italian*, ed. Frederick Gerber (Oxford, 1981); Kilgour, *Rise of the Gothic Novel*, p. 244.

38 See introductions and notes to the editions cited above for the range of Radcliffe's allusions.

39 Weak or wicked men in Radcliffe often have phallic 'mountain' names, like the Marquis de Montalt and La Motte in *The Romance of the Forest*.

40 Radcliffe's followers appropriate this topos: cf. Roche's *The Nocturnal Visit*, where Jacintha reads in an 'inner parlour which opened into the garden' (I, p. 243), and *The Children of the Abbey*, where Amanda takes books to read 'at

the root of some old moss-covered tree' (I, p. 71); Eleanor Sleath's *The Orphan of the Rhine* (orig. 1798; repr. 1968), p. 154, where Laurette keeps her books in a room which 'opened upon a lawn'. Radcliffe perfects but does not invent this pattern: cf. *Lady's Magazine* 4 (1773), p. 304; 7 (1776), pp. 141, 12 (1781), p. 692, etc.

41 *Udolpho*, p. 319; her followers even more often emphasise the desperate nature of the heroine's situation by showing the failure of the escapist powers of literature – e.g., Roche, *The Nocturnal Visit* I, p. 132, IV, pp. 38, 71, 290; *Clermont*, pp. 179, 332–3.

42 Burney, *JAL* III, p. 337; Wollstonecraft, *Letters*, p. 385.

43 Cf. Roche's *The Nocturnal Visit*, where Jacintha finds in a secret room a book belonging to her mysteriously absent mother (IV, p. 12); 'De Courville Castle: a Romance, by a young Lady', *Lady's Magazine* 26 (1795), pp. 324–5, where the hero, visiting his uncle's castle, finds it deserted and discovers a book, 'stained with blood', bearing his mother's name.

44 Wolstoneholme, *Gothic (re)Visions*, p. 30.

45 Elizabeth Kowaleski-Wallace, *Their Father's Daughters: Hannah More, Maria Edgeworth and Patriarchal Complicity* (New York, 1991), p. ix.

46 Jacqueline Pearson, 'Women reading, reading women' in Helen Wilcox, ed., *Women and Literature in Britain 1500–1700* (Cambridge, 1996), pp. 86–8; Whitbread, *I Know My Own Heart*, p. 90; Joseph Mason Cox, *Practical Observations on Insanity* (1804), pp. 64, 67, cit. Helen Small, *Love's Madness: Medicine, the Novel, and Female Insanity, 1800–1865* (Oxford, 1996), pp. 45, 47.

47 Stocking, *Journals of Claire Clairmont*, pp. 101, 102, 104, 111; Burney, *ED* I, p. 243.

48 See above, p. 34; Morley, 'Sarah Harriet Burney', p. 148.

49 Partington, *Private Letter-Books*, p. 273.

50 *Lady's Magazine* 35 (1804), p. 222; Roberts, *Memoirs* III, p. 423; Swift, *Gulliver's Travels* in Philip Pinkus, ed., *Jonathan Swift: A Selection of his Works* (Toronto, 1965), p. 49; Hawkins, *Rosanne* II, p. 95.

51 'Mackery End, in Hertfordshire' (orig. 1823), ed. Jonathan Bate (Oxford, 1987), pp. 87, 86.

52 Charles and Mary Lamb, *Mrs Leicester's School; or, the History of Several Young Ladies, Related by Themselves* (orig. 1808) in E. V. Lucas, ed., *The Works of Charles and Mary Lamb* (1903) III.

53 See Jane Aaron, ' "On Needlework": protest and contradiction in Mary Lamb's essay', *Prose Studies* (1987), pp. 159–77.

54 See chapter 5 below.

55 *Lady's Magazine* 11 (1780), p. 16; see Pearson, ' "Books, my greatest joy": constructing the female reader in *The Lady's Magazine*', *Women's Writing* 3 (1996), esp. p. 13; *Lady's Monthly Museum* 1 (1799), pp. 131, 133.

56 Kate Levin, ' "The Cure of Arabella's Mind": Charlotte Lennox and the disciplining of the female reader', *Women's Writing* 2 (1995), p. 282.

57 Gonda, *Reading Daughters' Fictions*, p. 255.

58 Ellis, *Politics of Sensibility*, p. 188.

59 Sarah Scott, *The History of Cornelia* (orig. 1750; repr. Bristol, 1992), p. 89; Sheridan, *Sidney Biddulph*, p. 371; Lennox, *Henrietta* I, p. 149; Roche, *Nocturnal Visit* I, p. 244.

60 Fordyce, *Sermons* I, p. 148; *Monthly Mirror* 4, Nov. 1797, pp. 277–9; Edward Barry, *Essays* (Reading, 1806), pp. 56–7; *Edinburgh Review* 8 (1806), p. 207; Adam Sibbitt, *Thoughts on the Frequency of Divorces in Modern times* (1800), p. 10; *The Evils of Adultery and Prostitution* (1792), p. 54.

61 Delarivier Manley, *The New Atalantis*, ed. Ros Ballaster (1992), pp. 35–9.

62 Varma, *Evergreen Tree*, p. 15; James White, preface to *The Adventures of King Richard Coeur-de-Lion* (1791); Courtney Melmoth, *Family Secrets* (1797), I, pp. 338–9; Leigh Hunt, *The Maidservant* (1816), cit. Raymond Irwin, *The English Library: Sources and History* (1966), p. 255.

63 John Cleland, *Memoirs of a Woman of Pleasure* (orig. 1748–9; ed. Peter Sabor, Oxford, 1986), p. 71.

64 Lawrence Stone, *Broken Lives: Separation and Divorce in England 1660–1857* (Oxford, 1993, pp. 35, 301).

65 See above, pp. 4–5.

66 Kowaleski-Wallace, *Their Father's Daughters*, p. ix.

67 Fénélon, *Treatise on the Education of Daughters* (orig. 1687 but this edition 1805), cit. Vivien Jones, *Women in the Eighteenth Century: Constructions of Femininity* (1990), p. 103; *The Sylph* 5, 6 Oct. 1795, pp. 35–8.

68 Brophy, *Women's Lives and the Eighteenth-Century English Novel*, p. 57; *Lady's Magazine* 10 (1779), pp. 580, 579.

69 Caroline Franklin, *Byron's Heroines* (Oxford, 1992), p. 166.

70 Susan Peck MacDonald, 'Jane Austen and the tradition of the absent mother' in Cathy N. Davidson and E. M. Broner, eds., *The Lost Tradition: Mothers and Daughters in Literature* (New York, 1980), pp. 58–69.

71 Margaret Homans, *Bearing the Word: Language and Female Experience in Nineteenth-Century Women's Writing* (Chicago, 1986), p. 2.

72 Jean Wyatt, *Reconstructing Desire: the Role of the Unconscious in Women's Reading and Writing* (Chapel Hill, NC, 1990), p. 5.

73 Homans, *Bearing the Word*, p. 136.

74 Kowaleski-Wallace, *Their Fathers' Daughters*.

75 Homans, *Bearing the Word*, p. 75.

76 Janet Todd, ed., *Wollstonecraft's Maria and Shelley's Matilda* (Harmondsworth, 1993).

77 E.g. *Oedipus* (p. 153), Fletcher's *The Captain* and Alfieri's *Myrrha* (p. 165).

78 Ferris, *Achievement of Literary Authority*, pp. 36–7.

79 See above, p. 90.

80 For what is currently known about Dacre's life, see Kim Ian Michasiw, introduction to *Zofloya, or the Moor* (1997), pp. x–xiv, and Appendix p. 269; Small, *Love's Madness*, p. 82.

81 E.g. *Confessions* I, p. 65; II, p. 42; *Zofloya* I, pp. 23, 27, 126, 127, 212, 223; II, p. 81; III, p. 235; *The Passions* I, pp. 31, 43, 61, 193; *Libertine* II, p. 72, 104; etc.

82 Kilgour, *Rise of the Gothic Novel*, p. 168.

83 Gary Kelly, 'Women novelists and the French revolution debate: novelizing the revolution/revolutionizing the novel', *Eighteenth-Century Fiction* 6 (1994), p. 385.

84 [P. B. and Elizabeth Shelley], *Original Poetry by Victor and Cazire* (1810).

85 Small, *Love's Madness*, p. 81.

86 Michasiw, introduction, p. xxv.

87 Small, *Love's Madness*, pp. 85, 89; Ann H. Jones, *Ideas and Innovations*, p. 227.

4 PLEASURES AND PERILS OF READING: SOME CASE HISTORIES

1 Aphra Behn, *Love Letters between a Nobleman and his Sister* (orig. 1687; repr. 1987), p. 413; Manley, *New Atalantis*, e.g. pp. 35–7, 83, 224–5, etc.

2 Felicity Nussbaum, 'Heteroclites: the gender of character in the scandalous memoirs' in Nussbaum and Brown, eds., *The New 18th Century*, pp. 144–67; Clare Brant, 'Speaking of women: scandal and law in the mid-eighteenth century' in Brant and Diane Purkiss, eds., *Women, Texts and Histories 1575–1760* (1992), pp. 242–70.

3 Carroll, *Selected Letters of Samuel Richardson*, p. 173.

4 *Memoirs*, pp. 17–18.

5 Ibid., e.g. pp. 179–80, 227, 233, 266–7, 296–7, etc.

6 Ibid., e.g. pp. 117, 131, 139, 141–2, 179–80, 209, 298; etc.

7 Robert Gould, *Works* (1709), II, p. 16.

8 *Memoirs*, e.g. pp. 88, 252.

9 She thinks, e.g., that the description of the music of the spheres from Act v of *Merchant of Venice* is by Milton (p. 290).

10 *Othello* pp. 9, 48, 67, 86, 161, 201; *Macbeth* pp. 14, 55, 76, 117, 232; *Henry IV* pp. 17, 80, 109, 174, 177, 302; *Julius Caesar* pp. 39, 157, 174, 209, 235, 309; *Hamlet* pp. 49, 52, 106, 172, 325; *Measure for Measure* pp. 51, 86, 104, 263, 318. She also knows *Henry VIII* (p. 85), *Henry V* (pp. 145, 315), *Midsummer Night's Dream* (p. 298), *As You Like It* (pp. 56–7, 185, 198, 205), *Merchant of Venice* (p. 197), *Winter's Tale* (p. 212), *Tempest* (pp. 253, 292), *Timon of Athens* (pp. 110, 301), *Merry Wives of Windsor* (p. 131), *King Lear* (p. 314), and *Richard III* (pp. 176, 303).

11 Milton, e.g. pp. 30, 33, 94, 158, 198, 235, 266; Pope, e.g. pp. 13, 23, 34, 55, 87–8, 188, 199, 233, 289; Swift, e.g. pp. 16, 17, 38–9, 75, 92, 174, 279, 326; Young, e.g. pp. 159, 181, 233, 304, 312; Dryden, e.g. pp. 16, 65, 84, 142, 156, 175, 181, 340; Gay, e.g. pp. 82, 130, 146, 168, 303; Prior, e.g. pp. 51, 85, 232, 264. She has also read Ramsay (p. 87), Waller (p. 35), Katherine Philips (pp. 227–8), Cowley (p. 272), Mary Barber (pp. 18, 283), Savage (p. 306), and Horace in translation (pp. 49–50).

12 In fiction, she only refers to the *Arabian Nights* (p. 166), *Don Quixote* (p. 267) and *Pamela* (p. 209); she has read Addison (pp. 33–4) and Steele (pp. 180, 182, 205); she knows plays by Ambrose Philips (p. 308), Rowe (pp. 104, 187, 194, 245, 321), Congreve (pp. 220, 300, 310), Buckingham (p. 248), and Farquhar (pp. 276, 279, 302). Among historians she refers only to Xenophon (p. 304); her references to religious works include Hutcheson's *Essay on the Passions* (p.

304–5) and Wollaston's *Religion of Nature Delineated* (p. 305).

13 E.g. Green, *Mental Improvement*, p. 101; Barrett, *The Heroine* II, p. 283.

14 *Persuasion*, p. 234; *George Bateman* II, p. 11–12; *Euphemia* II, pp. 107–8; *Lady's Magazine* 17 (1787), p. 596; *Education* I, p. 116.

15 Bennett, *The Beggar Girl and her Benefactors* (1799), IV, p. 144; *Northanger Abbey*, pp. 58, 69; *George Bateman* II, pp. 9–12; Hayley, *Triumphs of Temper*, canto I, lines 68–9.

16 Colvin, *Maria Edgeworth: Letters from England*, p. 169; Hare, *Life and Letters* I, pp. 142, 212, 225; Colvin, *Letters form England*, p. 525; *Harrington* I, p. 118. There are references to *Evelina* in Butler, *Life*, p. 106; to *Cecilia* in Colvin, *Letters from England*, pp. 45, 277 and Colvin, *Maria Edgeworth in France and Switzerland*, p. 108; and to *Camilla* in Colvin, *Letters from England*, pp. 169, 360 and *Patronage* p. 201; Eliza Parsons, preface to *The History of Miss Meredith* (1790), I, p. v.

17 *Woman-Hater* II.iv.96, 89–91; Doody, *Frances Burney*, pp. 244–5.

18 Joanne Cutting-Gray, *Woman as 'Nobody' and the Novels of Fanny Burney* (Gainesville, 1992), p. 33.

19 *Cecilia* (orig. 1782: repr. 1986), p. 27.

20 Judy Simons, *Fanny Burney* (1987), p. 72.

21 Catherine Gallagher, *Nobody's Story: the Vanishing Acts of Women Writers in the Marketplace 1670–1820* (Oxford, 1994), p. 244.

22 Doody, *Frances Burney*, pp. 244, 245; *Camilla* (orig. 1796), ed. Edward A. Bloom and Lillian D. Bloom (1972).

23 *The Wanderer* (orig. 1814), ed. Margaret Anne Doody, Robert L. Mack and Peter Sabor (Oxford, 1991), pp. 152, 168, 175, 177, etc.

24 *ED* II, p. 311; *Thraliana*, p. 399.

25 Burney, dedication to *The Wanderer*, p. 9.

26 Burney, *Memoirs of Dr Burney* (1832), II, p. 123.

27 Troide, I, pp. 14–15.

28 Joyce Hemlow, *The History of Fanny Burney* (Oxford, 1958), pp. 20, 1.

29 E.g. *JAL* VII, pp. 292, 326–7, 333–4; XII, pp. 919, 930.

30 Ralph S. Walker, 'Charles Burney's theft of books at Cambridge', *Transactions of the Cambridge Bibiliographical Society* 3 (1959–63), pp. 313–26.

31 E.g. *DAL* II, pp. 47, 178, 300.

32 Myers, *Bluestocking Circle* (pp. 9–11) points out that the term referred originally to a male member of the circle, then became gender-neutral and finally female. In the 1780s it could still refer to either sex, though its use as gender-neutral would be somewhat anachronistic by 1788.

33 As a married woman she was more relaxed about her reading – she quotes from *Candide* in 1794 (*JAL* III, p. 46).

34 Pope *ED* I, pp. 138, 140, *JAL* VIII, p. 506; Milton *JAL* VIII, pp. 375, 410, 526, X, pp. 788, 850; Thomson, *Camilla* pp. 100–1; Young *DAL* III, p. 164, *JAL* IX, p. 279; Whitehead *ED* I, p. 181; Rogers *JAL* I, p. 203; Barbauld *JAL* IV, p. 188; Carter *JAL* IV, p. 272; *Lyrical Ballads*, Doody, *Frances Burney*, p. 329.

35 Troide I, p. xxiii.

36 Doody, *Frances Burney*, p. 36; Blunt, *Mrs Montagu* I, p. 78.

37 Hannah More, epilogue to *The Search after Happiness: a Pastoral Drama* (orig. 1773) in Lonsdale, *Eighteenth-Century Women Poets*, p. 325; *Lady's Magazine* 3 (1772), p. 220; 4 (1773), pp. 47, 402, 531; 7 (1776), pp. 89, 300–1; 9 (1778), p. 22 etc.; see above, pp. 26, 30–1; More, *Coelebs*, p. 207; see also Jane West, *Letters to a Young Lady* III, p. 355, *The Infidel Father* III, p. 297 and *Advantages of Education* II, p. 236; Thomas, 'Th'instructive moral, and important thought', p. 142.

38 Williams, 'Poetry, pudding, and Epictetus', pp. 6, 3–9, 22.

39 R. Brimley Johnson, *Bluestocking Letters* (1926), p. 12.

40 Montagu Pennington ed., *Letters from Mrs Elizabeth Carter to Mrs Montagu* I, pp. 12, 201, 256; II, pp. 291 etc.; I, pp. 14, 262; II, p. 179.

41 Montagu Pennington, ed., *Series of Letters between Elizabeth Carter and Catherine Talbot* I, pp. 56–7, 80, 110, 240; II, p. 31; *Letters . . . to Mrs Montagu* I, p. 242; II, pp. 22, 273, 337.

42 *Letters . . . to Mrs Montagu* II, pp. 332, 311.

43 Thomas, 'Th'instructive moral, and important thought', p. 152.

44 Llanover, *Autobiography and Correspondence of Mrs Delany* III, p. 593.

45 Climenson, *Elizabeth Montagu* II, p. 163; Dr Doran, *A Lady of the Last Century* (1873), pp. 151, 243.

46 *Letters . . . to Mrs Montagu* I, p. 49; *A Series of Letters* II, p. 146.

47 Blunt, *Mrs Montagu*, II, p. 142.

48 Roberts, *Memoirs*, III, p. 305.

49 Thomas, 'Th'instructive moral, and important thought', p. 142.

50 In the first volume of *A Series of Letters* alone there are references to reading the letters of Madame de Sévigné (pp. 49, 59, 335) and Madame de Maintenon (p. 317), and memoirs of Melle de Montpensier (p. 106) and Anne of Austria (p. 429): Climenson, *Elizabeth Montagu* II, p. 2; Doran, *A Lady*, p. 55; *A Series of Letters* I, p. 530.

51 Grant, *Memoir and Correspondence* II, p. 68; Elwin, *Lord Byron's Wife*, p. 159; L'Estrange, *Life of Mary Russell Mitford* I, pp. 293, 300, 305; II, p. 39 (she criticises Austen's 'want of elegance', loves Darcy but thinks Elizabeth 'pert' and 'worldly', but counts Austen a 'great favourite' and prefers her to Edgeworth); John A. Doyle, *Memoir and Correspondence of Susan Ferrier, 1782–1854* (1929), p. 128; Colvin, *Maria Edgeworth: Letters from England*, pp. 46, 257; Johnson, *Jane Austen: Women, Politics and the Novel*, p. 160.

52 George Holbert Tucker, 'Jane Austen's reading' in *Jane Austen the Woman: Some Biographical Insights* (1994), p. 129; Chapman, *Jane Austen's Letters*, p. 443.

53 Frank W. Bradbrook, *Jane Austen and her Predecessors* (Cambridge, 1966), p. 3; Henry Thomas Austen, 'Biographical notice of the author' in R. W. Chapman, ed., *The Novels of Jane Austen*, V (1923), p. 7. For Austen's intertextual practices, see also Doody, 'Jane Austen's reading'; Kenneth L. Moler, *Jane Austen's Art of Allusion* (Lincoln, Neb., 1968); Marilyn Butler, *Jane Austen and the War of Ideas* (Oxford, 1975); Johnson, *Jane Austen: Women, Politics and the Novel*; Jocelyn Harris, *Jane Austen's Art of Memory* (Cambridge, 1989), and 'Jane Austen and the burden of the (male) past: the case reexamined' in

Devoney Looser, ed., *Jane Austen and the Discourses of Feminism* (Basingstoke, 1995).

54 Doody, 'Jane Austen's Reading', p. 349; Johnson, *Jane Austen: Women, Politics and the Novel*, p. 32; see above, p. 00; Bradbrook, *Austen and her Predecessors*, p. 27.

55 Doody, 'Jane Austen's reading', p. 356.

56 For Pope, see Harris, *Art of Memory*, esp. pp. 20, 63, 140–1, 204; for Johnson, see Peter L. De Rose, *Jane Austen and Samuel Johnson* (Washington, DC, 1980), and Claudia Johnson, '"The Operations of Time and the Changes of the Human Mind": Jane Austen and Dr Johnson again', *Modern Language Quarterly* 44 (1983), pp. 23–8.

57 Harris, 'Jane Austen and the burden of the (male) past', p. 94.

58 *Coelebs* XI, pp. 396–7; Henry Austen, 'Biographical notice', p. 7; James Edward Austen-Leigh, *Memoir of Jane Austen*, p. 89; *Sense and Sensibility*, ch. 10; *Mansfield Park*, pp. 6, 45.

59 Park Honan, *Jane Austen: Her Life* (1987), p. 337; Tucker, 'Jane Austen's reading', pp. 147–8.

60 Johnson, *Jane Austen: Women, Politics and the Novel*, p. xx.

61 *Northanger Abbey*, p. 58.

62 'Love and Friendship' in R. W. Chapman, ed., *Minor Works* (Oxford, 1954; hereafter abbrev. *MW*), p. 81.

63 Brunton is referred to in *Letters*, pp. 344, 423; *Camilla* in *Letters*, pp. 9, 13, 14; *Evelina* pp. 180, 388, 438; *Cecilia* p. 254; Sarah Harriet Burney in *Letters*, p. 180; Edgeworth *Letters*, p. 405; Lennox, *Letters*, p. 173; Morgan, *Letters*, p. 251; Radcliffe in *Northanger Abbey*, *passim*, and *Letters*, p. 377; Roche's *Children of the Abbey* is alluded to in *Emma*, p. 29 and *Clermont* in *Northanger Abbey*, p. 40; Smith, see below, pp. 00; West, *Letters*, pp. 405, 466; Hawkins, *Letters*, p. 422; Hannah More, see below, p. 150; Edward Copeland, 'Money talks: Jane Austen and *The Lady's Magazine*' in Grey, *Jane Austen's Beginnings*, pp. 160, 169, 168.

64 Alexander Dyce, cit. Tucker, p. 134; Harris, 'Jane Austen and the burden of the (male) past', p. 92.

65 *Persuasion*, p. 234; Moler, *Jane Austen's Art of Allusion*, pp. 90, 81; R. Brimley Johnson, *Jane Austen: Her Life, Her Work, Her Family, and Her Critics* (1930), pp. 133–4; Doody, 'Jane Austen's reading', p. 358; *Northanger Abbey*, pp. 69, 62.

66 *Northanger Abbey*, p. 58.

67 Doody, 'Jane Austen's reading', p. 359; Elizabeth Bohls, *Woman Travel Writers and the Language of Aesthetics, 1716–1818* (Cambridge, 1995), p. 1; *MW*, pp. 144, 146; Bradbrook finds the influence of Smith in *Northanger Abbey* (*Austen and Her Predecessors*, p. 102), Moler in *Sense and Sensibility* (*Jane Austen's Art of Allusion*, p. 55) and *Persuasion* (p. 194), as well as the juvenilia (p. 161).

68 Gary Kelly, *English Fiction of the Romantic Period 1789–1830* (1989), p. 114.

69 Johnson, *Jane Austen: Women, Politics and the Novel*, pp. 134, 138; Harris, *Art of Memory*, pp. 169–87.

70 Lee Erikson, 'The Economy of Novel Reading: Jane Austen and the

Circulating Library', *Studies in English Literature* 30 (1990), p. 584; *Persuasion*, p. 130.

71 Bradbrook, *Austen and Her Predecessors*, pp. 29, 30.

72 Adela Pinch, 'Lost in a book: Jane Austen's *Persuasion*', *Studies in Romanticism* 32 (1993), pp. 111–12.

73 Stewart, *Dear Reader*, p. 107; Harris, 'Jane Austen and the burden of the (male) past', p. 96.

74 Bradbrook, *Austen and Her Predecessors*, p. 30; Harris, 'Jane Austen and the burden of the (male) past', p. 96.

75 See above, p. 33.

76 Roger Gard, *Jane Austen's Novels: the Art of Clarity* (New Haven, 1992), p. 17; Butler, *Jane Austen and the War of Ideas*; Margaret Kirkham, *Jane Austen, Feminism and Fiction* (1983); Gilbert and Gubar, *Madwoman in the Attic*.

77 Kelly, 'Women novelists and the French revolution debate', p. 384.

78 Michael Worton and Judith Still, eds., *Intertextuality: Theories and Practice* (Manchester, 1990), p. 6.

79 Moler, *Jane Austen's Art of Allusion*, pp. 75–106; Bradbrook, *Austen and Her Predecessors*, pp. 87–8; Johnson, *Jane Austen: Women, Politics and the Novel*, p. 48; Brian Southam, *Jane Austen's 'Sir Charles Grandison'* (Oxford, 1980), p. 18. Harris (*Sir Charles Grandison*), p. xl, thinks this play 'unlikely' to be Austen's, but its strategies are generally consistent with her intertextual practices.

80 Doody, 'Jane Austen's reading', p. 350; Tucker, 'Jane Austen's reading', p. 132; Antoinette Burton, ' "Invention is what delights me": Jane Austen's remaking of "English" history' in Looser, *Jane Austen and the Discourses of Feminism*, p. 46.

81 Johnson, *Jane Austen: Women, Politics and the Novel*, pp. 22, 13.

82 J. M. S. Tompkins, 'Elinor and Marianne: a note on Jane Austen', *Review of English Studies* (1940), pp. 33–43.

83 Johnson, *Jane Austen: Women, Politics and the Novel*, p. 61.

84 Ibid., p. 142.

85 Honan, *Jane Austen: Her Life*, p. 388; Mary Waldron, 'The frailties of Fanny: *Mansfield Park* and the evangelical movement', *Eighteenth-Century Fiction* 6 (1994), pp. 281, 273, 265, 281, 267, and edition of *Coelebs* (Bristol, 1995), esp. p. xxviii; Johnson, *Jane Austen: Women, Politics and the Novel*, p. 96.

86 Bradbrook, *Austen and her Predecessors*, p. 34; Honan, *Jane Austen: Her Life*, p. 329; Mellor, 'Why women didn't like Romanticism', p. 278; and see Kirkham, *Jane Austen: Feminism and Fiction*, pp. 33–52.

87 Johnson, *Jane Austen: Women, Politics and the Novel*, pp. 49, 153; jacket blurb.

5 WHERE AND HOW SHOULD WOMEN READ?

1 Chartier, *Frenchness in the History of the Book*, pp. 28, 30, 29.

2 James Raven, 'From promotion to proscription: arrangements for reading and eighteenth-century libraries' in Raven, Small and Tadmor, eds., *Practice and Representation of Reading*, p. 188; *Pride and Prejudice*, p. 343.

3 E.g. 'Letters from Miss Heartfree' 7 (1776), p. 141; 'Letters from Miss Beauchamp to Miss Granby' 7 (1776), p. 592; 'A Series of Letters' 11 (1780), p. 65; 'The Fortunate Sequel' 11 (1780), p. 228; 'Female Correspondence' 12 (1781), p. 26.

4 *The Diary of Samuel Pepys*, ed. Robert Latham and William Matthews, vol. IX, pp. 21–2, 57–8.

5 A. N. L. Munby, *Sale Catalogues of Libraries of Eminent Persons*, vols. VII (1973) and V (1972); see above, p. 65.

6 J. E. Austen-Leigh, *Memoir of Jane Austen*, p. 102.

7 Halsband, *Letters* III, p. 8.

8 *The Absentee* (orig. 1812; Oxford, 1988), p. 126.

9 Eliza Parsons, *The Mysterious Warning* (orig. 1796; repr. 1968), p. 87; *The Castle of Wolfenbach* (orig. 1793; repr. 1968), p. 27; *Lady's Magazine* 35 (1804), p. 222.

10 Shelley, *The Last Man* (orig. 1826; repr. 1985), p. 339; *Lady's Magazine* 39 (1808), p. 494.

11 Hett, *Memoirs of Susan Sibbald*, p. 176; Hays, *Emma Courtney*, p. 21; Mrs Godfrey Clark, ed., *Gleanings from an Old Portfolio* I, pp. 29–30; Raven, 'From promotion to proscription', p. 186.

12 Eliza Fenwick, *Secresy* (orig. 1795; repr. 1989), pp. 20, 61, 75–7.

13 *Lady's Magazine* 13 (1782), p. 17; 41 (1810), p. 31 and 40 (1809), p. 508; 10 (1779), p. 298.

14 *The Works of Mrs Amelia Opie* (Philadelphia, 1843), I, pp. 13, 34, 38.

15 See above, p. 94.

16 Inchbald, *A Simple Story* (orig. 1791; repr. 1989).

17 'Closet' is used by Harriet Byron (*Sir Charles Grandison* VII, p. 270); by Frances Thynne Seymour (Helen Sard Hughes, *The Gentle Hertford: Her Life and Letters*, New York, 1940, p. 247), and by Mary Delany (Llanover, *Autobiography and Correspondence of Mrs Delany* I, p 15); 'book-room' by Frances Burney (see above, p. 136) and Frances Boscawen (Llanover, n.s. III, p. 353). Lennox's *The Female Quixote* distinguishes between a male 'Library' and a female 'Closet' (repr. 1989, p. 7).

18 Gonda, *Reading Daughters' Fictions*, p. 112; Colvin, *Maria Edgeworth: Letters from England*, pp. 256–60.

19 Ruth Perry, 'Bluestockings in Utopia' in Tobin, ed., *History, Gender and Eighteenth-Century Literature*, p. 164.

20 Lady Lonsdale, letter to Lady Louisa Stuart (Clark, *Gleanings from an Old Portfolio*, II, p. 159); Anne Lister (Whitbread, *I Know my Own Heart*, p. 196); see also Holroyd (Adeane, *Early Married Life*, p. 280), Seward, *Letters* IV, pp. 99–100; Elizabeth Mavor, *The Ladies of Llangollen* (Harmondsworth, 1973), p. 70.

21 Raven, 'From promotion to proscription', p 175.

22 Desmond Hawkins, *The Grove Diaries*, pp. 152, 150, 136.

23 Raven, *Judging New Wealth*, pp. 129–30; Paul Kaufman, *Libraries and their Users* (1969), pp. 102–13.

24 Kaufman, *Libraries*, pp. 29, 210, 214.

25 Ibid., pp. 83, 130, 94, 100.
26 Whitbread, *I Know my Own Heart*, pp. 1, 2, 34–5, 45–6, 59, 83, 85, 143.
27 De Acton, *Essays on the Art* II, pp. 265–6.
28 Kaufman, *Libraries*, pp. 41–3.
29 Grant, *Letters from the Mountains* II, p. 268, *Memoirs and Correspondence* I, p. 217; *Betsy Sheridan's Journal*, p. 56.
30 Kaufman, *Libraries*, p. 183; John Brewer, *The Pleasures of the Imagination: English Culture in the Eighteenth Century* (1997), pp. 184–6.
31 Benger, *Memoirs* I, p. 170; *Lady's Magazine* II (1781), p. 191.
32 Blakey, *Minerva Press*, pp. 116–17.
33 Kaufman, *Libraries*, pp. 190–1.
34 *A Picture of London* (1804), cit. Kaufman, *Libraries*, p. 192.
35 *Thraliana*, p. 1090.
36 Kaufman, *Libraries*, p. 192.
37 Raven, *Judging New Wealth*, p. 54.
38 Smith, *Marchmont* II, p. 225.
39 Turner, *Living by the Pen*, pp. 144–5.
40 Raven, 'From promotion to proscription', pp. 176, 186, 179.
41 *Diaries of Mrs Anne Milnes Lumb of Silcoates, near Wakefield, in 1755 and 1757*, ed. Charles Milnes Gaskell (1884), p. 10.
42 Varma, *Evergreen Tree*, p. 6; D'Israeli, *Curiosities of Literature* II, pp. 217–18; R. B. Sheridan, *The Rivals* I.ii, p. 39 in R. Crompton Rhodes, ed., *Plays and Poems of Richard Brinsley Sheridan* (Oxford, 1928); *Christian Lady's Magazine*, cit. Varma, *Evergreen Tree*, p. 6; Hawkins, *Countess and Gertrude* II, p. 162; Clara Reeve, *Progress of Romance* II, p. 77.
43 Raven, 'From promotion to proscription', p. 182.
44 Thackeray, *Roundabout Papers*, Oxford Thackeray, ed. George Saintsbury (Edinburgh 1903), vol. XVII, p. 418.
45 See above, pp. 9–10.
46 Paul Kaufman, *The Community Library: a Chapter in English Social History*, *Transactions of the American Philosophical Society* 57, pt. 7, (1967), pp. 50–2.
47 Robert Bisset, *Douglas: or, the Highlander* (1800), II, p. 290; Christopher North, *Noctes Ambrosianae* (orig. 1822–35; repr. Edinburgh, 1868), I, p. 288.
48 Kaufman, *Community Library*, suppt. 2, pp. 59–60.
49 *Lady's Magazine* 20 (1789), p. 177; *Rivals* I, ii, p. 52; Courtney Melmoth, *Family Secrets*, cit. Kaufman, *Community Library*, p. 59.
50 'Beauty in search of knowledge', *Eighteenth-Century Fiction* 6 (1993/4), p. 282; Smith, *Conversations, Introducing Poetry*, p. 113; *Rural Walks* I, p. 13.
51 George H. Nettleton, 'The books of Lydia Languish's circulating library', *Journal of English and German Philology* 5 (1903–5), pp. 492–500.
52 See above, p. 144; *Nocturnal Visit* III, p. 171; *Lady's Magazine* 38 (1807), p. 26.
53 Smith, *Marchmont* II, pp. 224–5; Elizabeth and Richard Griffith, *Series of Genuine Letters*, (1786), V, p. 15.

54 Smith, *Letters of a Solitary Wanderer* I, p. vi.
55 See above, p. 115.
56 Irwin, *English Library*, p. 236; Kaufman, *Libraries*, p. 224.
57 Varma, *Evergreen Tree*, p. 4; Kaufman, *Libraries*, p. 143.
58 Kaufman, *Community Library*, pp. 11–14.
59 Raven, 'From promotion to proscription', p. 180.
60 *Lady's Magazine* 20 (1789), p. 177.
61 Combe, *The Devil upon Two Sticks in England* (1790), II, p. 83.
62 Taylor, *Early Opposition*, p. 8.
63 Eaves and Kimpel, *Richardson*, p. 287; *Thraliana* pp. 534, 547, quoting *Cadenus and Vanessa*, lines 371–2.
64 Edgeworth, *Castle Rackrent*, pp. 65–6.
65 Ferris, *Achievement of Literary Authority*, p. 40; Hawkins, *Rosanne* III, p. 43; Green, *Mental Improvement*, pp. 38, 41, 42.
66 *The Sylph* 5, 6 Oct. 1795, pp. 35–8.
67 More, *Stories for the Middle Ranks*, pp. 103–4; Lamb, 'Detached Thoughts on Books and Reading', pp. 196–7.
68 Hunter, *Before Novels*, pp. 40, 42.
69 Kett, *Emily* I, p. 222; II, p. 94.
70 See above, pp. 133–4; LeFanu, *Betsy Sheridan's Journal*, p. 88.
71 Hughes, *Gentle Hertford*, p. 7; Llanover, *Autobiography and Correspondence of Mrs Delany* I, p. 13.
72 Thomas Day, *Sandford and Merton* (orig. 1783; repr., n.d.), p. 309.
73 Llanover, *Autobiography and Correspondence of Mrs Delany* III, pp. 533–4; n.s. II, p. 141; Blower, *Maria* II, p. 95; Smith, *Rambles Farther* II, pp. 83–4.
74 Seward, *Letters* I, p. 128; Naomi Tadmor, ' "In the even my wife read to me": women, reading and household life in the eighteenth century' in Raven, Hill and Tadmor, eds., *Practice and Representation of Reading*, p. 165.
75 Llanover, *Autobiography and Correspondence of Mrs Delany* III, pp. 137, 162; Boas, *Harriet Shelley*, e.g. p. 29; Feldman and Scott-Kilvert, *Journals of Mary Shelley* I, pp. 26, 27, 37, 49, 51, etc.; Stocking, *Journals of Claire Clairmont*, pp. 33, 47, 49, etc.
76 Wardle, *Collected Letters of Mary Wollstonecraft*, p. 241.
77 Llanover, *Autobiography and Correspondence of Mrs Delany* I, p. 94.
78 Chartier, *Frenchness in the History of the Book*, p. 18.
79 Alberto Manguel, *A History of Reading* (1996), p. 123; Chartier, *Frenchness in the History of the Book*, p. 18.
80 Roberts, *Memoirs and Correspondence* III, p. 389.
81 Manguel, *History of Reading*, p. 123.
82 Eaves and Kimpel, *Richardson*, p. 361.
83 Tadmor, 'In the even my wife read to me', p. 168; *Thraliana*, p. 534; Eaves and Kimpel, *Richardson*, p. 287.

6 PREPARING FOR EQUALITY: CLASS, GENDER, READING

1 Roberts, *Memoirs* II, p. 225.
2 Ibid., II, p. 189; Blunt, *Mrs Montagu* II, pp. 252, 254.
3 Lewis, *Journals and Correspondence of Miss Berry* II, p. 262.
4 Chartier, *Frenchness in the History of the Book*, p. 23.
5 Smith, *Old Manor-House*, pp. 293, 372–3, 166–7, 470–1, 478–9; Schiebinger, *Nature's Body*, p. 193.
6 Ellis, *Politics of Sensibility*, p. 59.
7 *The Interesting Narrative of the Life of Olaudah Equiano or Gustavus Vasa the African* (orig. 1789) in Paul Edwards, ed., *Equiano's Travels* (1967), pp. 54, 62, 69, 74.
8 Francis D. Adams and Barry Sanders, *Three Black Writers in Eighteenth-Century England* (Belmont, 1971), pp. 17, 19; *The Letters of the Late Ignatius Sancho* (orig. 1782) in Paul Edwards and David Dabydeen, eds., *Black Writers in Britain 1760–1890* (Edinburgh 1991), p. 31.
9 John Shields, ed., *The Collected Works of Phillis Wheatley* (New York, 1988); pp. vii, 15, 163, 90–1, 9–12, 101–13; and see notes, esp. pp. 278, 285–6, 295, 303.
10 *The History of Mary Prince*, pp. 73–4, 82; Rebecca Jackson's autobiography was written 1830–2: see Henry Louis Gates Jr, *The Signifying Monkey: a Theory of African-American Literary Criticism* (New York, 1988), pp. 241–2.
11 *A Narrative*, pp. 16–17; Gates, *Signifying Monkey*, pp. 130–1.
12 Edwards and Dabydeen, *Black Writers in Britain*, p. 31.
13 Chartier, *Frenchness in the History of the Book*, p. 10.
14 Wollstonecraft, *Wrongs of Woman*, pp. 110–11; Brewer, *Pleasures of Imagination*, p. 192; Raven, *Judging New Wealth*, p. 69.
15 [Humphrey Repton], *Variety: a Collection of Essays* (1788), pp. 50–1, 57–8; Lewis, *Journals and Correspondence of Miss Berry* II, p. 262; Leavis, *Fiction and the Reading Public*, p. 153; Coleridge, *Lay Sermons*, ed. R. J. White (1972), p. 36; North, *Noctes Ambrosianae* III, pp. 342–3.
16 Bernard Mandeville, *The Fable of the Bees*, ed. Philip Harth (Harmondsworth, 1989), pp. 278, 303.
17 Munby, *Sale Catalogues of Libraries of Eminent Persons* V, p. 499.
18 *Lady's Magazine* 35 (1804), pp. 37–8; Altick, *English Common Reader*, p. 9; James Currie, 'Prefatory Remarks on the Character and Condition of the Scottish Peasantry' in *The Works of Robert Burns* (Edinburgh, 1800), I, pp. 3–4.
19 Roberts, *Memoirs* III, p. 362; Hett, *Memoirs of Susan Sibbald*, pp. 166–7, 200, 178.
20 Roberts, *Memoirs* II, p. 435.
21 McKillop, 'Charlotte Smith's letters', p. 252; Jan Fergus, 'Provincial servants' reading', p. 222.
22 Edward Hall, ed., *Miss Weeton: Journal of a Governess 1807–11* (1936) and *Miss Weeton: Journal of a Governess 1811–25* (1939).
23 Richard Greene, *Mary Leapor: a Study in Eighteenth-Century Women's Poetry* (Oxford, 1993), p. 17; see above, p. 12.
24 *Lady's Magazine* e.g. 11 (1780), p. 566; 13 (1782), pp. 6, 284; Raven, *Judging New Wealth*, p. 238.

25 Chartier, 'General introduction: print culture' in *The Culture of Print: Power and the Uses of Print in Early Modern Europe* (Cambridge, 1989), p. 4.

26 Fergus, 'Provincial servants' reading', p. 223; Greene, *Mary Leapor*, p. 11; Flora Fraser, *The Unruly Queen: the Life of Queen Caroline* (1996), p. 99.

27 Arthur Aspinall, ed., *The Letters of the Princess Charlotte, 1811–1817* (1949), pp. 1, 9, 26, 35, 88, 108, 4, 24, 26.

28 Kilgour, *Rise of the Gothic Novel*, p. 72.

29 Wollstonecraft, *Wrongs of Woman*, p. 148; cf. Hays, *Emma Courtney*, p. 31.

30 Altick, *English Common Reader*, p. 417.

31 Carl Philip Moritz, *Journeys of a German in England* (orig. 1783), ed. Reginald Nettel (1983), pp. 42–4.

32 *Idler*, pp. 90–1.

33 Lamb, *Rosamund Gray* (orig. 1798; repr. Oxford, 1991); for *Julia de Roubigné*, see e.g. Smith, *Ethelinde* v, pp. 115–16; Maturin, *The Wild Irish Boy* III, p. 297.

34 Raven, *Judging New Wealth*, p. 57; Altick, *English Common Reader*, pp. 39, 38; Hannah More, 'Prefatory Letter' to Yearsley's *Poems, on Several Occasions* (1785), p. ix; Yearsley, 'Clifton Hill' line 79 (in *Poems, on Several Occasions*).

35 Edmund Blunden, *Sketches in the Life of John Clare* (1931), p. 46.

36 *The Autobiography of the Working Class*, ed. John Burnett, David Vincent and David Mayall, vol. I, (Brighton, 1984) for 1790 to 1900 includes 783 male autobiographies and only 74 female, and of these women only a handful were born before 1820.

37 Margaret Spufford, *Small Books and Pleasant Histories: Popular Fiction and its Readership in Seventeenth-Century England* (Cambridge, 1981), p. 4.

38 Yearsley, *Poems, on Various Subjects* (1787), 'To Mr. ****, An Unlettered Poet, On Genius Unimproved', p. 81.

39 *Thraliana*, p. 697.

40 Jane Marcet, *Conversations on Political Economy* (2nd edn, 1817), p. 107; *Critical Review* 33 (1772), p. 327; Lackington, *Memoirs of the Forty-Five First Years of the Life of James Lackington . . . Written by Himself* (1792), p. 257.

41 Ivy Pinchbeck, *Women Workers and the Industrial Revolution, 1750–1850* (orig. 1930; repr. 1977), p. 7; More, *Stories for the Middle Ranks* in *Works* (1818), IV, p. 87.

42 'The Poetical Petition of the Books of a Circulating Library in Bath', cit. Kaufman, *Libraries*, p. 189; Ian Watt, *The Rise of the Novel: Studies in Defoe, Richardson and Fielding* (1957), p. 148.

43 Fergus, 'Provincial servants' reading', p. 203.

44 Ibid., pp. 222, 209.

45 Anthony Heasel, *The Servant's Book of Knowledge* (1773), cit. Irwin, *English Library*, p. 255; Hett, *Memoirs of Susan Sibbald*, p. 178; *Thraliana*, p. 355.

46 *Idler* 46, 3 March 1759, pp. 144–5; Hall, *Miss Weeton: Journal of a Governess 1807–11*, p. 5.

47 See below, p. 188.

48 Stone, *Broken Lives*, p. 240.

49 *Gentleman's Magazine* 54 (1784), p. 80; Greene, *Mary Leapor*, pp. 10, 93–4; for

Yearsley, see below, p. 191; for Little, see 'Given to a Lady Who Asked me to Write a Poem' in Lonsdale, *Eighteenth-Century Women Poets*, p. 455.

50 Christian Milne, 'To a Lady who Said it was Sinful to Read Novels', in *Simple Poems on Simple Subjects* (Aberdeen, 1805), p. 48; Elizabeth Hands, 'A Poem, On the Supposition of an Advertisement appearing in a Morning paper, of the Publication of a Volume of Poems, by a Servant-Maid', and 'A Poem, on the Supposition of the Book having been Published and Read' in Lonsdale, *Eighteenth-century Women Poets*, pp. 425–9.

51 *Gentleman's Magazine* 54 (1784), p. 80; Moira Ferguson, *Eighteenth-Century Women Poets: Nation, Class and Gender* (Albany, 1995), p. 1; Landry, *Muses of Resistance*, p. 58; Mary Waldron, *Lactilla, Milkwoman of Clifton: The Life and Writings of Ann Yearsley, 1753–1806* (Athens, Georgia, 1996), p. 14.

52 Landry, *Muses of Resistance*, p. 35; Elizabeth Hands, 'A Poem, on the Supposition of an Advertisement', lines 31, 34; 'A Poem, on the Supposition of the Book having been Published', lines 43–51 in Lonsdale, *Eighteenth-Century Women Poets*, pp. 426, 428.

53 See above, p. 178; Landry, *Muses of Resistance*, p. 129; Greene, *Mary Leapor*, pp. 168–71; Mary Collier, 'An Epistolary Answer to an Exciseman, Who doubted her being the Author of the *Washerwoman's Labour*' (orig. 1762), p. 31 in Ferguson, *Eighteenth-Century Women Poets*, p. 15; Landry, *Muses of Resistance*, p. 129; Lonsdale, *Eighteenth-Century Women Poets*, p. 454; Ferguson, *Eighteenth-Century Women Poets*, pp. 14, 17.

54 *Lady's Magazine* 38 (1805), pp. 477–9; Landry, *Muses of Resistance*, pp. 85, 138; Greene, *Mary Leapor*, p. 11; Fergus, 'Provincial servants' reading', p. 223; Ferguson, *Eighteenth-Century Women Poets*, p. 92.

55 Landry, *Muses of Resistance*, p. 101.

56 Ferguson, *Eighteenth-Century Women Poets*, p. 47.

57 Landry, *Muses of Resistance*, p. 129.

58 More, prefatory letter to Yearsley, *Poems, on Several Occasions* (1785), p. viii; Greene, *Mary Leapor*, p. 9.

59 Ferguson, *Eighteenth-Century Women Poets*, p. 47.

60 Waldron, *Lactilla*, pp. 13–26.

61 Ibid., pp. 27–47.

62 Greene, *Mary Leapor*, pp. 65, 10, 93–4.

63 Ibid., p. 14.

64 Greene, *Mary Leapor*, pp. 166, 210–13, 13; Landry, *Muses of Resistance*, p. 95.

65 Letter [from Bridget Freemantle] to John ***** Esq., prefaced to Leapor's *Poems, upon Several Occasions* (1748–51), II, pp. xx–xxii.

66 Landry, *Muses of Resistance*, p. 110.

67 Greene, *Mary Leapor*, p. 117.

68 *Thraliana*, p. 826.

69 Kathryn Kirkpatrick, 'Sermons and strictures: conduct-book proprietary and property relations in eighteenth-century England' (Tobin, *History Gender and Eighteenth-Century Literature*), p. 217.

70 Aspinall, *Letters of Princess Charlotte*, p. 38.

71 *Stories for the Middle Ranks*, p. 378.

72 *Stories for the Middle Ranks*, p. 376; Roberts, *Memoirs* III, p. 135; *Stories for the Middle Ranks*, pp. 337; Roberts, *Memoirs* III, pp. 134–5.

73 Roberts, *Memoirs* II, pp. 424–5; III, p. 474; II, p. 429.

74 Ibid., IV, pp. 174, 138.

75 Ibid., IV, pp. 138, 76.

76 Ibid., IV, pp. 137–8, 175.

77 Sutherland, 'More's counter-revolutionary feminism', pp. 38, 36, 42, 35; see also Mitzi Myers, 'Reform or ruin: "A Revolution in Female Manners"', *Studies in Eighteenth-Century Culture* 11 (1982), pp. 199–216.

78 Roberts, *Memoirs* IV, pp. 249, 256; II, p. 202; *Stories for the Middle Ranks*, p. 354.

79 *Coriolanus* I.i.95–154.

80 Sutherland, 'More's counter-revolutionary feminism', p. 42.

81 Roberts, *Memoirs* IV, pp. 255–6; 'Two Wealthy Farmers', pp. 102–3, 264–8.

82 Roberts, *Memoirs* IV, pp. 175–6.

7 A DANGEROUS RECREATION: WOMEN AND NOVEL-READING

1 Pearson, 'Books, my greatest joy', pp. 9–11; William Godwin, 'Of history and romance' (orig. 1797) in Maurice Hindle, ed., *Caleb Williams* (Harmondsworth, 1988), p. 368.

2 Ferris, *Achievement of Literary Authority*, pp. 32, 33, 31; Johnson, *Rambler* 4, p. 21.

3 Ros Ballaster, 'Romancing the novel: gender and genre in early theories of narrative' in Dale Spender, ed., *Living by the Pen: Early British Women Writers* (New York, 1992), p. 189; Gary Kelly, 'Unbecoming a heroine: novel reading, romanticism and Barrett's *The Heroine*', *Nineteenth-Century Literature* 45 (1990–1), p. 226; Godwin, 'Of history and romance', p. 369.

4 Clery, *Rise of Supernatural Fiction*, pp. 88, 101.

5 Sandham, *Twin Sisters*, p. 144.

6 Ferris, *Achievement of Literary Authority*, p. 35.

7 William Charles Macready in Brian Southam, *Jane Austen: the Critical Heritage* (1968), p. 118; John Scott, *London Magazine* 1 (1820), p. 11; *Lady's Magazine* 11 (1780), p. 693; 4 (1773), pp. 293, 531; 11 (1780), p. 275; 18 (1787), p. 596; 22 (1791), pp. 59–61.

8 *Wanderer*, p. 8; *Evelina*, p. 7.

9 Opie, *The Father and Daughter* (1801; repr. 1995), pp. vii, vi, 6–8, 170; *Belinda*, Advertisement.

10 Jessamyn Jackson, 'Why novels make bad mothers,' *Novel* 27 (1994), p. 161.

11 Grant, *Memoirs* II, p. 84; A. F. Wedd, ed., *The Fate of the Fenwicks: Letters to Mary Hays (1798–1828)* (1927), p. 233.

12 Kelly, 'Unbecoming a heroine', p. 225.

13 Carole A. Senf, *The Vampire in Nineteenth-Century English Literature* (Bowling Green, 1988), p. 38.

14 George Colman, *Polly Honeycombe, A Dramatick Novel* (orig. 1760) in Richard

W. Bevis, ed., *18th-Century Drama: Afterpieces* (1970), p. 136, line 18; Smith, *Rambles Farther* I, p. 63; Reeve, *Progress of Romance* I, p. 111.

15 Reeve, *Progress of Romance* I, p. 111; Thomas Holcroft, *Alwyn; or, the Gentleman Comedian* (1780), I, pp. vi–vii.

16 Horace Walpole, *The Castle of Otranto* (orig. 1764) in E. F. Bleiler, ed., *Three Gothic Novels* (New York, 1966), p. 21; Godwin, 'Of history and romance', pp. 368–9.

17 Jackson, 'Why novels make bad mothers', p. 161.

18 Mackenzie, 'On Novel Writing' (1785), cit. Ellis, *Politics*, p. 205; Johnson, *Rambler*, p. 252; Lennox, *Female Quixote*, p. 377; Edgeworth, 'Angelina, or L'Amie Inconnue' in *Moral Tales*.

19 Anna Maria Porter, 'Delusions of the Heart', *Lady's Magazine* 26 (1795), pp. 520–1.

20 Wollstonecraft, *Analytical Review* 7 (1790), pp. 98–9.

21 *Lady's Magazine* 13 (1782), p. 13; Philogamus, *The Present State of Matrimony* (1739) in Jones, *Women in the Eighteenth Century*, p. 79.

22 Reeve, *Progress of Romance* I, pp. 96–7; *Lady's Magazine* 12 (1781), p. 13; Reeve, *Progress of Romance* I, p. 68.

23 Ballaster, 'Romancing the novel', p. 190.

24 Lennox, *Harriot Stuart* I, pp. 11, 29; *Euphemia* I, p. 186

25 Reeve, *Progress of Romance* II, p. 6.

26 Ballaster, 'Romancing the novel', p. 194.

27 Levin, 'The Cure of Arabella's Mind', pp. 278, 273, 275.

28 David Marshall, 'Writing masters and "masculine exercises" in *The Female Quixote*', *Eighteenth-Century Fiction* 5 (1993), p. 120.

29 Doody, 'Introduction', pp. xxi.

30 Debra Malina, 'Rereading the patriarchal text: *The Female Quixote, Northanger Abbey*, and the trace of the absent mother', *Eighteenth-Century Fiction* 8 (1996), pp. 274, 292; Greene, *Mary Leapor*, p. 46.

31 Doody, 'Introduction' pp. xxvii.

32 Christine Roulston, 'Histories of nothing: romance and femininity in Charlotte Lennox's *The Female Quixote*', *Women's Writing* 2 (1995), p. 34.

33 Dale Spender, *Man Made Language* (1980); Roulston, 'Histories of nothing', p. 34; Dalziel, *Female Quixote*, p. 394, lists other ambiguous words like 'favour', 'infidelity' and 'squire'.

34 Pilkington, *Memoirs*, p. 213; Graves, 'The Heroines; or, Modern Memoirs' (orig. 1751), cit. James L. Clifford, introduction to Paul-Gabriel Boucé, ed., *The Adventures of Peregrine Pickle* (1983), p. xviii).

35 Greene, *Mary Leapor*, pp. 46; Roulston, 'Histories of nothing', p. 38.

36 Roulston, 'Histories of nothing', pp. 25–6.

37 Doody, 'Introduction', pp. xxx.

38 Roulston, 'Histories of nothing', pp. 39, 37–8.

39 *Female Quixote*, pp. 82, 392, xvii, 82.

40 Laurie Langbauer, 'Romance revised: Charlotte Lennox's *The Female Quixote*', *Novel* 18 (1984), p. 30.

41 Leland E. Warren, 'Of the conversation of women: *The Female Quixote* and the dream of perfection', *Studies in Eighteenth-Century Culture* 2 (1982), p. 379; Dalziel, back cover; Deborah Ross, 'Mirror, mirror: the didactic dilemma of *The Female Quixote*' *Studies in English Literature* 27 (1987), p. 456; Doody, 'Introduction', p. xxx.

42 Langbauer, 'Romance revised', pp. 41–2; Patricia Meyer Spacks, 'The subtle sophistry of desire: Dr Johnson and *The Female Quixote*', *Modern Philology* 85 (1987–8), p. 534.

43 Tabitha Gilman Tenney, *Female Quixotism* (orig. 1801), ed. Jean Nienkamp and Andrea Collins (New York, 1992).

44 Langbauer, 'Romance revised', p. 44.

45 Paul Lewis, 'Gothic and mock-gothic: the repudiation of fantasy in Barrett's *Heroine*', *English Language Notes* 11 (1983–4), p. 45; Claudia Johnson, *Jane Austen*, p. 133; Kelly, 'Unbecoming a heroine', p. 227.

46 Kelly, 'Unbecoming a heroine', p. 241.

47 Jacqueline Howard, *Reading Gothic Fiction: a Bakhtinian Approach* (Oxford, 1994), p. 151.

48 *The Children of the Abbey* appears six times in the footnotes; Morgan's *Ida of Athens* seventeen times, *The Wild Irish Girl* six times, *The Novice of St Dominick* four times, *St Clair* twice; there are also allusions to *The Missionary* (e.g. III, p. 142).

49 Jackson, 'Why novels make bad mothers', p. 163.

50 Pope, *Essay on Criticism*, line 73.

51 Robert Kiely, *The Romantic Novel in England* (Cambridge, Mass., 1972), pp. 121, 134–5; Anne Henry Ehrenpreis, introduction to *Northanger Abbey*, p. 8.

52 Kiely, *Romantic Novel*, p. 126.

53 Gregory, *Legacy*, pp. 87–8.

54 Gilbert and Gubar, *Madwoman in the Attic*, p. 135; Johnson, *Jane Austen*, pp. 35; see also Judith Wilt, *Ghosts of the Gothic: Austen, Eliot, and Lawrence* (Princeton, NJ, 1980), esp. pp. 45–7, 126–51.

55 Maria Edgeworth in Hare, *Life and Letters* I, p. 247).

56 Linda Hutcheon, *A Theory of Parody: the Teachings of Twentieth-Century Art Forms* (New York, 1985), p. 79.

57 Janet Todd, ed., *Dictionary of British and American Women Writers* (1984), p. 139; *Monthly Review*, Feb. 1811 and May 1812 (68), p. 109, cit. Montagu Summers, *A Gothic Bibliography*, n.d., p. 51.

58 See above, pp. 83.

59 Cruse, *Englishman and his Books*, p. 226.

60 James Beattie, 'On Fable and Romance' (1783) in Williams, *Novel and Romance*, p. 327.

CONCLUSION

1 Kett, *Emily* I, p. 17.

Select bibliography

Unless otherwise stated, the place of publication is London.

PRIMARY TEXTS

Anon., *The Polite Lady, or, a course of female education. In a series of letters* (J. Newbury, 1760).

Anon., *Hortensia: or, the Distressed Wife. A Novel. By a Lady* (Robinson and Roberts, 1769), 2 vols.

Anon., *Fatal Obedience; or, the History of Mr Freeland* (F. and J. Noble, 1780), 2 vols.

Anon., *Hartley House, Calcutta* (orig. 1789; Pluto Press, 1989).

Anon., *Laura Valmont, a Novel. Written by a Lady* (Charles Dilly, 1791).

Anon., *The Evils of Adultery and Prostitution* (T. Vernor, 1792).

Anon., *The Use of Circulating Libraries Considered* (orig. 1797) in Devendra P. Varma, ed., *The Evergreen Tree of Diabolical Knowledge* (Consortium Press, Washington, DC, 1972).

Acton, Eugenia de, *Essays on the Art of Being Happy, addressed to a young mother* (Lane, Newman and Co., 1803), 2 vols.

Adams, Francis D. and Barry Sanders, *Three Black Writers in Eighteenth-Century England* (Wadsworth, Belmont, 1971).

Adeane, J. H., ed., *The Girlhood of Maria Josepha Holroyd [Lady Stanley of Alderly]* (Longmans, Green and Co., 1896).

   The Early Married Life of Maria Josepha Lady Stanley (Longmans, Green and Co, 1899).

Anley, Charlotte, *Miriam; or, the Power of Truth* (orig. John Hatchard and Sons, 1826; 6th edn, 1839).

Aspinall, Arthur, ed., *The Letters of the Princess Charlotte, 1811–1817* (Home and Van Thal, 1949).

Aspinall-Oglander, Cecil, *Admiral's Wife: Being the Life and Letters of the Hon. Mrs Edward Boscawen from 1719 to 1761* (Longman's Green and Co., 1940).

   Admiral's Widow: Being the Life and Letters of the Hon. Mrs Edward Boscawen from 1761 to 1805 (Hogarth Press, 1942).

Austen, Jane, *Pride and Prejudice* (orig. 1813), ed. Tony Tanner (Penguin, Harmondsworth, 1972).

Mansfield Park (orig. 1814), ed. Tony Tanner (Penguin, Harmondsworth, 1966).

Emma (orig. 1816), ed. Ronald Blythe (Penguin, Harmondsworth, 1966).

Northanger Abbey (orig. 1817), ed. Anne Ehrenpreis (Penguin, Harmondsworth, 1972).

Persuasion (orig. 1817), ed. Pat Rogers (Everyman, 1994).

Minor Works, ed. R. W. Chapman (Oxford University Press, 1954).

Jane Austen's Letters, ed. R. W. Chapman (Oxford University Press, 1969).

Austen-Leigh, J. E., *Memoir of Jane Austen*, ed. R. W. Chapman (Oxford University Press, Oxford, 1926).

Bage, Robert, *Barham Downs* (orig. 1784; Ballantyne's Novelists' Library 9, Hurst, Robinson and Co., 1824).

Hermsprong; or, Man as he is not (orig. 1796), ed. Peter Faulkner (Oxford University Press, 1985).

Barrett, Eaton Stannard, *Woman, a Poem* (John Murray, 1810).

The Heroine, or Adventures of Cherubina (orig. 1813), as *The Heroine, or Adventures of a Fair Romance Reader* (3rd edn, Henry Colburn, 1815), 2 vols.

Barry, Edward, *Essays* (Smart and Cowslade, Reading, 1806).

Beckford, William, *Modern Novel Writing; or , the Elegant Enthusiast* (G. G. and J. Robinson, 1796).

Behn, Aphra, *Love Letters between a Nobleman and his Sister* (orig. 1687; Virago, 1987).

Benger, Elizabeth, *Memoirs of the Late Mrs Elizabeth Hamilton* (Longman, Hurst, Rees, Orme and Brown, 1818), 2 vols.

Bennett, Agnes Maria, *The Beggar Girl and her Benefactors* (Minerva, 1799), 5 vols.

Bennett, Betty T., ed., *The Letters of Mary Wollstonecraft Shelley* (Johns Hopkins University Press, Baltimore, 1980).

Bennett, Betty, and Charles Robinson, *The Mary Shelley Reader* (Oxford University Press, 1990).

Bennett, John, *Letters to a Young Lady* (W. Eyres, Warrington, 1798), 2 vols.

Berkenhout, John, *A Volume of Letters from Dr Berkenhout to his Son at the University* (J. Archdeacon, Cambridge, 1790).

Bessborough, Earl of, ed., *Georgiana: Extracts from the Correspondence of Georgiana, Duchess of Devonshire* (John Murray, 1955).

Bisset, Robert, *Douglas; or, the Highlander* (Anti-Jacobin Press by T. Crowder, 1800), 4 vols.

Bloom, Edward A., and Lillian D. Bloom, eds., *The Piozzi Letters*, vols. I–III (University of Delaware Press and Associated University Presses, Newark and London, 1989–93).

Blower, Elizabeth, *George Bateman: A Novel* (J. Dodsley, 1782), 3 vols.

Maria. A Novel (J. Dodsley, 1785), 2 vols.

Features from Life; or, A Summer Visit (J. Dodsley, 1788), 2 vols.

Blunt, Reginald, ed., *Mrs Montagu, 'Queen of the Blues'. Her Letters and Friendships from 1762 to 1800* (Constable, 1923), 2 vols.

Boaden, James, ed., *Memoirs of Mrs Inchbald* (R. Bentley, 1833), 2 vols.

Boswell, James, *Life of Johnson* (orig. 1791), ed. Pat Rogers (Oxford University Press, Oxford, 1980).

Boswell's London Journal, 1762–1763, ed. Frederick A. Pottle (orig. 1950; Edinburgh University Press, Edinburgh, 1991).

Brightwell, Cecilia Lucy, *Memorials of the Life of Amelia Opie* (AMS Press, New York, 1975)

Broadhurst, Thomas, *Advice to Young Ladies on the Improvement of the Mind and Conduct in Life* (Bath, 1810).

Brooke, Frances, *The History of Emily Montague* (orig. 1769; New Canadian Library 27, Aylesbury and Slough, 1961)

The Excursion (orig. 1777), ed. Paula R. Backscheider and Hope D. Cotton (University Press of Kentucky, Lexington, 1997).

Brunton, Mary, *Self-Control* (orig. 1810; Pandora, 1986).

Discipline (orig. 1814; Pandora 1986).

Emmeline, with some other Pieces (orig 1819; Routledge and Thoemmes Press, 1992).

Burney, Frances, *Evelina; or the History of a young Lady's Entrance into the World* (orig. 1778), ed. Edward A. Bloom with Lillian D. Bloom (Oxford University Press, Oxford, 1982).

Cecilia; or, Memoirs of an Heiress (orig. 1782; Virago, 1986).

Camilla; or, A Picture of Youth (orig. 1796), ed. Edward A. Bloom and Lillian D. Bloom (Oxford University Press, Oxford, 1986).

The Wanderer (orig. 1814), ed. Margaret Anne Doody, Robert L. Mack and Peter Sabor (Oxford University Press, Oxford, 1991).

Memoirs of Dr Burney (E. Moxon, 1832), 3 vols..

The Early Diary of Frances Burney 1768–1778, ed. Annie Raine Ellis (George Bell and Sons, 1889), 2 vols. (abbrev. *ED*).

Diary and Letters of Madame D'Arblay, ed. Charlotte Barrett (orig. 1842–6; Swan Sonnenschein, 1893), 4 vols. (abbrev. *DAL*).

The Journals and Letters of Fanny Burney (Madame D'Arblay), ed. Joyce Hemlow *et al.* (Clarendon Press, Oxford, 1972–84), 12 vols. (abbrev. *JAL*).

The Early Journals and Letters of Fanny Burney, ed. Lars E. Troide *et al.* (Clarendon Press, Oxford, 1986–). (abbrev. Troide).

The Complete Plays of Frances Burney, ed. Peter Sabor (Pickering, 1995), 2 vols.

Carroll, John, ed., *Selected Letters of Samuel Richardson* (Clarendon Press, Oxford, 1964).

Chapone, Hester (Mulso), *Works* (1775).

Chesterfield, Philip Dormer Stanhope, 4th Earl of, *Letters of the Earl of Chesterfield to his Son* (orig. 1774), ed. Charles Strachey (Everyman, 1901).

Chorley, Henry F., *Memorials of Mrs Hemans* (Saunders and Otley, 1836), 2 vols.

Clark, Mrs Godfrey, ed., *Gleanings from an Old Portfolio* (privately printed for D. Douglas, Edinburgh, 1898), 3 vols.

Cleland, John, *Memoirs of a Woman of Pleasure* (orig. 1748–9), ed. Peter Sabor (Oxford University Press, Oxford, 1986).

Climenson, Emily J., *Passages from the Diaries of Mrs Philip Libbe Powys of Hardwick*

House, *Oxon. A.D. 1756 to 1808* (Longmans, Green and Co., 1899).

Elizabeth Montagu, the Queen of the Blue-Stockings. Her Correspondence from 1720 to 1761 (John Murray, 1906), 2 vols.

Coleridge, Samuel Taylor, *Lay Sermons*, ed. R. J. White (Routledge Kegan Paul, 1972).

Collier, Jane, *An Essay on the Art of Ingeniously Tormenting* (A. Millar, 1753).

Colman, George, *Polly Honeycombe, A Dramatick Novel* (orig. 1760) in Richard W. Bevis, ed., *Eighteenth-Century Drama: Afterpieces* (Oxford University Press, 1970).

Colvin, Christina, *Maria Edgeworth: Letters from England 1813–1844* (Clarendon Press, Oxford, 1971).

Maria Edgeworth in France and Switzerland: Selections from the Edgeworth Family Letters (Clarendon Press, Oxford, 1979)

Combe, William, *The Devil upon Two Sticks in England* (Topographic Press, J. Walker, 1790), 4 vols.

Dacre, Charlotte, *Confessions of the Nun of St Omer* (orig. 1805; Arno Press, New York, 1972), 3 vols.

Hours of Solitude: a collection of original poems (D. N. Shury, 1805), 2 vols.

Zofloya; or, the Moor (orig. 1806; Arno Press, New York, 1974), 3 vols.

The Libertine (T. Cadell and W. Davies, 1807), 2 vols.

The Passions (orig. 1811; Arno Press, New York, 1974), 4 vols.

Darwin, Erasmus, *A Plan for the Conduct of Female Education in Boarding Schools* (Derby, J. Drewry for J. Johnson, 1797).

Day, Thomas, *Sandford and Merton* (orig. 1783; repr. Routledge, n.d.).

D'Israeli, Isaac, *Curiosities of Literature* (George Routledge and Sons, London, 1865), 3 vols.

A Dissertation on Anecdotes (C. and G. Kearsley, 1793).

Vaurien; or, Sketches of the Times (T. Cadell, 1797), 2 vols.

Doran, Dr, *A Lady of the Last Century* (Richard Bentley, 1873).

Doyle, John A., ed., *Memoir and Correspondence of Susan Ferrier* (Eveleigh Nash and Grayson, 1929).

Duncombe, John, *The Feminiad, a Poem* (orig. 1754), ed. Jocelyn Harris (Augustan Reprint society, no. 207, William Andrews Clark Memorial Library, University of California, Los Angeles, 1981).

Edgeworth, Maria, *Letters for Literary Ladies* (orig. 1795; Everyman 1993).

The Parent's Assistant (orig. 1796–1800; Routledge, 'A New Edition', n.d.)

Castle Rackrent (orig. 1800; Oxford University Press, Oxford, 1980).

Belinda (orig. 1801; Everyman, 1993).

Early Lessons (orig. 1801–3, J. Johnson; vols. I–II, 12th edn of 1833; vols. III–IV, 6th edn, 1829), 4 vols.

Moral Tales for Young People (orig. 1801; Ward Lock, n.d.)

Popular Tales (orig. 1804) in *Tales and Novels by Maria Edgeworth*, vol. II (Henry G. Bohn; and Simpkin, Marshall and Co., 1870).

Leonora (orig. 1806) in *The Novels of Maria Edgeworth in Twelve Volumes* (Dent, 1893), vol. III.

Ennui (orig. 1809) in Marilyn Butler, ed., *Castle Rackrent and Ennui* (Penguin, Harmondsworth, 1992).

Tales of Fashionable Life (orig. 1809–12) in *Tales and Novels by Maria Edgeworth* vols. v–vi (Henry G. Bohn; and Simpkin, Marshall and Co., 1870).

The Absentee (orig. 1812; Oxford University Press, Oxford, 1988).

Patronage (orig. 1814; Pandora, 1986).

Harrington in *Harrington and Ormond, Tales* (2nd edn, R. Hunter and Baldwin, Cradock, and Joy, 1817), vol. I.

Ormond (orig. 1817; Alan Sutton, Gloucester, 1990).

Memoirs of Richard Lovell Edgeworth (orig. 1820; Irish University Press, Shannon, 1969), 2 vols.

Harry and Lucy Concluded; being the Last Part of Early Lessons (R. Hunter, Baldwin, Cradock, and Joy, 1825), 4 vols.

Helen (orig. 1834; Pandora, 1987).

Orlandino (William and Robert Chambers, Edinburgh, 1848).

Edgeworth, Maria and Richard Lovell, *Practical Education* (J. Johnson, 1798), 2 vols.

Edgeworth, Richard Lovell, *Poetry Explained for the Use of Young People* (J. Johnson, 1802).

Edwards, Paul, and David Dabydeen, *Black Writers in Britain 1760–1890* (Edinburgh University Press, Edinburgh, 1991).

Eland, G., ed., *Purefoy Letters 1735–1753* (Sidgwick and Jackson, 1931), 2 vols.

Equiano, Olaudah, *The Interesting Narrative of the Life of Olaudah Equiano or Gustavus Vasa the African* (orig. 1789) in Paul Edwards, ed., *Equiano's Travels* (Heinemann, 1967).

Feldman, Paula R., and Diana Scott-Kilvert, eds., *The Journals of Mary Shelley 1814–1844* (Clarendon Press, Oxford, 1987), 2 vols.

Fenwick, Eliza, *Secresy; or, the Ruin on the Rock* (orig. 1795; Pandora, 1989).

Ferrier, Susan, *Marriage* (orig. 1818), ed. Rosemary Ashton (Virago, 1986).

The Inheritance (orig. 1824; Three Rivers Books, Bampton, 1984).

Destiny (orig. 1831) in *The Works of Susan Ferrier*, Holyrood edn, vol. III (Eveleigh, Nash and Grayson, 1929).

Fielding, Henry, *Joseph Andrews and Shamela*, ed. Douglas Brooks-Davies (Oxford University Press, Oxford, 1980).

Tom Jones (orig. 1749; Penguin, Harmondsworth, 1966).

Amelia (orig. 1751), ed. A. R. Humphries (Everyman, 1974), 2 vols.

Fielding, Sarah, *The Adventures of David Simple* (orig. 1744–53), ed. Malcolm Kelsall (Oxford University Press, Oxford, 1987).

The Governess, or Little Female Academy (orig. 1749; Juvenile Library (Oxford University Press, 1968).

Folger Collective on Early Women Critics, *Women Critics 1660–1820* (Indiana University Press, Bloomington and Indianapolis, 1995).

Fordyce, James, *Sermons to Young Women* (orig. 1765; 3rd edn, A. Millar, T. Cadell, J. Dodsley and J. Payne, 1766), 2 vols.

Fremantle, Anne, ed., *The Wynne Diaries* (Oxford University Press, 1935), 3 vols.

Gaskell, Charles Milnes, ed., *Diaries of Mrs Anne Lumb of Silcoates, near Wakefield, in 1755 and 1757* (privately printed, 1884).

Godwin, William, 'Of History and Romance' in Maurice Hindle, ed., *Caleb Williams* (Penguin, Harmondsworth, 1988).

Italian Letters; or, the History of the Count de St Julien, ed. Burton R. Pollin (University of Nebraska Press, Lincoln, 1965).

Goldsmith, Oliver, *The Citizen of the World* (orig. 1760) in Arthur Friedman, ed., *Collected Works of Oliver Goldsmith* (Oxford University Press, Oxford, 1966), vol. ii.

The Vicar of Wakefield (orig. 1766; Oxford University Press, Oxford, 1981).

Gould, Robert, *The Works of Mr Robert Gould* (W. Lewis, 1709), 2 vols.

Grant, Anne, *Letters from the Mountains: Being the Real Correspondence of a Lady between the Years 1773 and 1807* (orig. 1807; 4th edn, Longman, Hurst, Rees and Orme, 1809), 3 vols.

Memoirs of an American Lady; with Sketches and Scenery in America (Longman, Hurst, Rees and Orme, 1808), 2 vols.

Grant, J. P., ed., *Memoirs and Correspondence of Mrs Grant of Laggan* (Longman, Brown, Green and Longmans, 1844), 3 vols.

Graves, Richard, *Eugenius, or Anecdotes of the Golden Vale* (J. Dodsley, 1785), 2 vols.

Gray, Mrs Edwin, *Papers and Diaries of a York Family 1764–1839* (Sheldon Press, 1927).

Green, Sarah, *Mental Improvement for a Young Lady, on her Entrance into the World; Addressed to a Favourite Niece* (Minerva, 1793).

Romance Readers and Romance Writers (T. Hookham Jr and E. T. Hookham, 1810), 3 vols.

Scotch Novel Reading; or, Modern Quackery (A. K. Newman, 1824), 3 vols.

Greg, Mrs Eustace, *Reynolds-Rathbone Diaries and Letters, 1753–1839* (privately printed, 1905).

Gregory, John, *A Father's Legacy to his Daughters* (orig. 1774; 'A New Edition', Cadell and Davies et al., 1814).

Griffith, Richard and Elizabeth, *A Series of Genuine Letters between Henry and Frances* (W. Johnston, 1757), 2 vols.

A Series of Genuine Letters between Henry and Frances (J. Bew, 1786), 6 vols.

Gronniosaw, James Albert Ukawsaw, *A Narrative of the Most Remarkable Particulars in the Life of James Albert Ukawsaw Gronniosaw* (W. Gye, Bath, 1770).

Gwynn, Albinia, *The Rencontre; or, Transition of a Moment* (Minerva Press, 1784), 2 vols.

Hall, Edward, ed., *Miss Weeton: Journal of a Governess 1807–1811* (Oxford University Press, 1936).

Miss Weeton: Journal of a Governess 1811–1825 (Oxford University Press, 1939).

Halsband, Robert, ed., *The Complete Letters of Lady Mary Wortley Montagu* (Clarendon Press, Oxford, 1965–7), 3 vols.

Hamilton, Elizabeth, *Translation of the Letters of a Hindoo Rajah; written Previous to, and During a Period of Residence in England* (G. G. and J. Robinson, 1796), 2 vols.

Memoirs of Modern Philosophers (orig. Bath, R. Crutwell for G. G. and J. Robinson, 1800; 2nd edn), 3 vols.

Letters on the Elementary Principles of Education (2nd edn, Bath, R. Crutwell for G. G. and J. Robinson, 1801), 2 vols.

The Cottagers of Glenburnie (2nd edn, Edinburgh, James Ballantyne, 1808).

Hamilton, Mary, *Munster Village* (orig. 1778; Pandora, 1987).

Hare, Augustus J. C., *The Life and Letters of Maria Edgeworth* (Edward Arnold, 1894), 2 vols.

Hawkins, Sir John, *The Life of Samuel Johnson* (orig. 1787), ed. Bertram H. Davis (Jonathan Cape, 1961).

Hawkins, Laetitia-Matilda, *The Countess and Gertrude; or, Modes of Discipline* (F. C. and J. Rivington, 1811), 4 vols.

Rosanne; or, A Father's Labour Lost (F. C. and J. Rivington, 1814), 3 vols.

Hayley, William, *The Triumphs of Temper: a Poem. In Six Cantos* (J. Dodsley, 1781).

Hays, Mary, *Memoirs of Emma Courtney* (orig. 1796; Pandora, 1987).

The Victim of Prejudice (orig. 1799; Broadview Press, Ontario, 1994).

Female Biography; or, Memoirs of Illustrious and Celebrated Women (Richard Phillips, 1803), 6 vols.

Haywood, Eliza, *The Invisible Spy* (T. Gardner, 1755), 4 vols.

Helme, Elizabeth, *St Margaret's Cave; or, the Nun's Story* (Earle and Hemet, 1801), 4 vols.

The Pilgrim of the Cross; or, the Chronicles of Christabelle de Mowbray (P. Norbury, Brentford, 1805), 4 vols.

St Clair of the Isles; or, the Outlaws of Barra (Longman and Rees, 1803), 4 vols.

Hemans, Felicia, *The Works of Mrs Hemans* (William Blackwood and Sons, Edinburgh, 1839), 7 vols.

Herbert, Dorothea, *Retrospections of Dorothea Herbert, 1770–1789* (Gerald Howe, 1929)

Hett, Frances Paget, ed., *The Memoirs of Susan Sibbald (1783–1812)* (John Lane, Bodley Head, 1926)

Hill, George Birkbeck, *Johnsonian Miscellanies* (orig. 1897; Constable, 1966), 2 vols.

Holcroft, Thomas, *Alwyn; or, the Gentleman Comedian* (Fielding and Walker, 1780), 2 vols.

Anna St Ives (orig. 1792; Oxford University Press, 1970).

The Adventures of Hugh Trevor (orig. 1794–7; Oxford University Press, 1978).

Honoria, *The Female Mentor; or, Select Conversations* (orig. 1793; 2nd edn, T. Cadell, 1798), 2 vols.

Hughes, Helen Sard, *The Gentle Hertford: Her Life and Letters* (Macmillan, New York, 1940).

Hume, David, 'Of Essay Writing', *Essays Moral, Political and Literary* (Oxford University Press, 1963).

Ilchester, Earl of, ed., *The Journal of Elizabeth Lady Holland (1791–1811)* (Longmans, Green and Co., 1908), 2 vols.

Inchbald, Elizabeth, *A Simple Story* (orig. 1791; Pandora, 1989).
    Nature and Art (G. G. and J. Robinson, 1796), 2 vols.
Jenner, Charles, *The Placid Man or, Memoirs of Sir Charles Beville* (J. Wilkie, 1770), 2 vols.
Johnson, R. Brimley, ed., *The Letters of Mary Russell Mitford* (John Lane, Bodley Head, 1925)
    Bluestocking Letters (Bodley Head, 1926)
Johnson, Samuel, *Life of Savage* (orig. 1743) in *Samuel Johnson, Lives of the Poets* (Everyman, 1975).
    The History of Rasselas, Prince of Abyssinia (orig. 1759) in *The History of Rasselas and The History of Dinarbas* (Everyman, 1994).
    The Idler and The Adventurer, ed. W. J. Bate, John M. Bullitt and L. F. Powell, Yale Johnson edition (Yale University Press, New Haven and London, 1963) vol. II.
    The Rambler, ed. W. J. Bate and Albrecht B. Strauss, Yale Johnson edition (Yale University Press, New Haven and London, 1969) vols. III–IV.
Jones, Frederick L., ed., *Mary Shelley's Journal* (University of Oklahoma Press, Norman, 1947).
    Maria Gisborne and Edward E. Williams, Shelley's Friends: their Journals and Letters (University of Oklahoma Press, Norman, 1951).
Jones, Vivien, ed., *Women in the Eighteenth Century: Constructions of Femininity* (Routledge, 1990).
    The Young Lady's Pocket Library, or Parental Monitor (Thoemmes Press, Bristol, 1995).
Keir, Susan, *Interesting Memoirs. By a Lady* (A. Straker and T. Cadell, 2nd edn, 1785), 2 vols.
Kelly, Isabella, *The Abbey of St Asaph* (Minerva, 1795), 3 vols.
Kett, Henry, *Emily: a Moral Tale* (Rivington, 1809), 2 vols.
King, Sophia, *Waldorf; or, the Dangers of Philosophy, A Philosophical Tale* (G. G. and J. Robinson, 1798), 2 vols.
Knight, Ellis Cornelia, *Dinarbas; a Tale: Being a continuation of Rasselas* (orig. 1790) in *The History of Rasselas and The History of Dinarbas* (Everyman, 1994).
Knox, Vicesimus, *Essays, Moral and Literary* (orig. 1779) in *Works of Vicesimus Knox* (J. Mawman, 1824), vols. I–II.
Lackington, James, *Memoirs of the Forty-Five First Years of the Life of James Lackington . . . Written by Himself* (Lackington, 1792).
Lady's Magazine vols. 1–49 (1770–1818).
Lamb, Lady Caroline, *Glenarvon* (2nd edn, H. Colburn, 1816), 2 vols.
Lamb, Charles, *Rosamund Gray* (orig. 1798; Woodstock Books, Oxford, 1991)
    Essays of Elia and Last Essays of Elia, ed. Jonathan Bate (Oxford University Press, Oxford, 1987).
Lamb, Charles and Mary, *Mrs Leicester's School: or, the History of Several Young Ladies, Related by Themselves* (orig. 1808) in E. V. Lucas, ed., *The Works of Charles and Mary Lamb* (Methuen and Co., 1903), vol. III.
Leapor, Mary, *Poems upon Several Occasions* (J. Roberts, 1748–51), 2 vols.

Lefanu, Alicia, *Memoirs of the Life and Writings of Mrs Frances Sheridan* (G. and W. B. Whittaker, 1824).

LeFanu, William, ed., *Betsy Sheridan's Journal: Letters from Sheridan's Sister* (Oxford University Press, Oxford, 1986).

Lennox, Charlotte, *The Life of Harriot Stuart. Written by Herself* (J. Payne and J. Bouquet, 1750), 2 vols.

The Female Quixote (orig. 1752), ed. Margaret Dalziel (Oxford University Press, Oxford, 1989).

Henrietta (A. Millar, 1758), 2 vols.

Euphemia (T. Cadell and J. Evans, 1790), 4 vols.

L'Estrange, A. G., ed., *The Life of Mary Russell Mitford . . . Related in a Selection from her Letters to her Friends* (R. Bentley, 1870), 3 vols.

Levy, M. J., ed., *Perdita: the Memoirs of Mary Robinson (1758–1800)* (Peter Owen, 1994).

Lewis, Matthew, *The Monk* (orig. 1796), ed. Louis Peck (Grove Press, New York, 1952).

Lewis, Lady Theresa, *Extracts from the Journals and Correspondence of Miss Berry* (Longmans, Green and Co., 1865), 3 vols.

Llanover, Lady, ed., *The Autobiography and Correspondence of Mary Granville, Mrs Delany* (Richard Bentley, 1861), first series 3 vols., second series 3 vols.

Lockhart, John Gibson, *The Life of Sir Walter Scott* (T. A. Constable, Edinburgh, 1902–3), 10 vols.

Lonsdale, Roger, ed., *Eighteenth-Century Women Poets: an Oxford Anthology* (Oxford University Press, Oxford, 1989).

Lovell, Ernest J., Jr, ed., *His Very Self and Voice: Collected Conversations of Lord Byron* (Macmillan, New York), 1954.

Medwin's Conversations of Lord Byron (Princeton University Press, Princeton, 1966).

Lady Blessington's 'Conversations of Lord Byron' (Princeton University Press, Princeton, 1969).

Luard, C. G., ed., *The Journal of Clarissa Trant* (Bodley Head, 1925).

Lucas, Charles, *The Infernal Quixote: a Tale of the Day* (Minerva Press, 1801), 4 vols.

MacDonald, Edgar E., ed., *The Education of the Heart: the Correspondence of Rachel Mordecai Lazarus and Maria Edgeworth* (University of North Carolina Press, Chapel Hill, 1977).

Macaulay, Catharine, *Letters on Education* (orig. 1790; Woodstock Press, Oxford, 1994).

Mackenzie, Henry, *The Man of Feeling* (orig. 1771; Oxford University Press, 1970).

Julia de Roubigné (W. Strahan and T. Cadell, 1777), 2 vols.

Mandeville, Bernard, *The Fable of the Bees* (orig. 1723), ed. Philip Harth (Penguin, Harmondsworth, 1989).

Mangin, Edward, *Piozziana: or, Recollections of the Late Mrs Piozzi: With Remarks. By a Friend* (E. Moxon, 1833).

Manley, Delarivier, *The New Atalantis* (orig. 1709), ed. Ros Ballaster (Penguin, Harmondsworth, 1992).

Marcet, Jane, *Conversations on Political Economy* (orig. 1816; 2nd edn, Longman, Hurst, Rees, Orme and Browne, 1817).

Marchand, Leslie A., ed., *Byron's Letters and Journals* (John Murray, 1973–81), 11 vols.

Marrs, Edwin W., Jr, *The Letters of Charles and Mary Lamb* (Cornell University Press, Ithaca and London, 1976), 3 vols.

Maturin, Charles Robert, *The Fatal Revenge; or, the Family of Montorio* (orig. 1807; Arno Press, New York, 1974), 3 vols.

   The Wild Irish Boy (orig. 1808; Arno Press, New York, 1977), 3 vols.

   The Milesian Chief (orig. 1812; Garland, New York, 1979), 4 vols.

   Women; or, Pour et Contre (James Ballantyne, Edinburgh, 1818), 3 vols.

   The Albigenses (orig. 1824; Arno Press, New York, 1974), 4 vols.

Mayne, Ethel Colburn, *The Life and Letters of Anne Isabella, Lady Noel Byron* (Constable and Co., 1929).

McKillop, Alan Dugald, 'Charlotte Smith's letters', *Huntington Library Quarterly* 15 (1952), pp. 237–55.

Meeke, Mary, *Count St Blancard; or, the Prejudiced Judge* (W. Lane, 1795), 3 vols.

Minifie, Susannah and Margaret, *The Histories of Lady Frances S- and Lady Caroline S-* (R. and J. Dodsley, 1763), 4 vols.

Mitchell, L. G., ed., *The Purefoy Letters 1735–1753* (Sidgwick and Jackson, 1973).

Montagu, Matthew, ed., *The Letters of Mrs Elizabeth Montagu* (T. Cadell and W. Davies, 1809), 4 vols.

More, Hannah, *Village Politics. Addressed to all the Mechanics, Journeymen, and Day Labourers in Great Britain by Will Chip, a Country Carpenter* (F. and C. Rivington, 2nd edn, 1792).

   Strictures on the Modern System of Female Education (T. Cadell Jr and W. Davies, 1799), 2 vols.

   Hints Towards Forming the Character of a Young Princess (orig. 1805) in *Works* (H. Fisher, R. Fisher and P. Jackson, 1834) vol. iv.

   Coelebs in Search of a Wife (orig. 1808), vols. xi and xii of *The Works of Hannah More* (T. Cadell and W. Davies, 1818).

   Works (T. Cadell and W. Davies, 1818), 19 vols.

Morgan, Sidney Owenson, *St Clair; or, the Heiress of Desmond* (E. Harding, S. Highley and J. Archer, 1803).

   The Wild Irish Girl (orig. 1806; Pandora, 1986).

   Woman; or, Ida of Athens (Longman, 1809), 4 vols.

   The Missionary; an Indian Tale (J. J. Stockdale, 2nd edn, 1811), 3 vols.

   Lady Morgan's Memoirs: Autobiography, Diaries and Correspondence (W. H. Allen and Co., 1862), 2 vols.

Moritz, Carl Philip, *Journeys of a German in England* (orig. 1783), ed. Reginald Nettel (Cape, 1983).

Morley, Edith J., ed., *Henry Crabb Robinson on Books and their Writers* (J. M. Dent and Sons, 1938).

Morley, Edith J., 'Sarah Harriet Burney, 1770–1844', *Modern Philology* 39 (1941), pp. 132–58.

Munby, A. N. L., ed., *Sale Catalogues of Libraries of Eminent Persons* (Mansell with Sotheby Parke-Bernet), vols. v (1972) and vii (1973).

'North, Christopher' (i.e. John Wilson), *Noctes Ambrosianae* (orig. 1822–35; repr. William Blackwood and Sons, Edinburgh, 1868), 4 vols.

Opie, Amelia, *The Father and Daughter* (orig. 1801; Routledge/Thoemmes, 1995).
　Adeline Mowbray, or the Mother and Daughter (orig. 1804; Pandora, 1986)
　The Warrior's Return, and Other Poems (Longman, Hurst, Rees and Orme, 1808)
　The Works of Mrs Amelia Opie (orig. 1843; AMS, 1974), 3 vols.

Parsons, Eliza, *The History of Miss Meredith* (T. Hookham, 1790), 2 vols.
　The Errors of Education (Minerva Press, 1791), 3 vols.
　The Castle of Wolfenbach; a German Story (orig. 1793; Folio Press, 1968)
　The Mysterious Warning (orig. 1796; Folio Press, 1968).

Partington, Wilfred, *The Private Letter-Books of Sir Walter Scott* (Hodder and Stoughton, 1930).

Peacock, Thomas Love, *Nightmare Abbey* (orig. 1818; Penguin, Harmondsworth, 1986).

Pennington, Montagu, ed., *A Series of Letters between Mrs Elizabeth Carter and Miss Catherine Talbot, from the Year 1740 to 1770: to which are added, Letters from Mrs Elizabeth Carter to Mrs Vesey, between the Years 1763 and 1787* (F. C. and J. Rivington, 1808), 2 vols.
　Letters from Mrs Elizabeth Carter to Mrs Montagu between the Years 1755 and 1800. Chiefly upon Literary and Moral Subjects (F. C. and J. Rivington, 1817), 3 vols.
　Memoirs of the Life of Mrs Elizabeth Carter (F. C. and J. Rivington, 1807).

Pennington, Lady Sarah, *An Unfortunate Mother's Advice to her Absent Daughters* (S. Chandler and W. Bristow, 1761; also, with additional items in bibliography, 3rd edn, 1761, and 8th edn, Taylor and Hessey, 1817).

Pepys, Samuel, *The Diary of Samuel Pepys*, ed. Robert Latham and William Matthews (G. Bell and Sons, 1970–83).

Phillips, Teresia Constantia, *An Apology for the Conduct of Mrs Teresia Constantia Phillips* (printed for the author, 1748–9), 3 vols.

Pilkington, Laetitia, *Memoirs of Laetitia Pilkington*, (orig. 1748–54), ed. A. C. Elias Jr (University of Georgia Press, Athens and London, 1997), 2 vols.

Polwhele, Richard, *The Unsex'd Females: a Poem* (Cadell and Davies, 1798).

Pope, Alexander, *Pope: Poetical Works*, ed. Herbert Davis (Oxford University Press, Oxford, 1978).

Porter, Jane, *Thaddeus of Warsaw* (orig. 1803; 2nd edn, A. Strahan, 1804), 4 vols.

Pratt, Samuel Jackson, *Shenstone-Green; or, the New Paradise Lost* (R. Baldwin, 1779), 3 vols.

Prince, Mary, *The History of Mary Prince, a West Indian Slave, Related by Herself* (orig. 1831), ed. Moira Ferguson (Pandora, 1987).

Radcliffe, Ann, *A Sicilian Romance* (T. Hookham, 1790), 2 vols.
　The Romance of the Forest (orig. 1791), ed. Chloe Chard (Oxford University Press, Oxford, 1986).
　The Mysteries of Udolpho (orig. 1794), ed. Bonamy Dobrée (Oxford University Press, Oxford, 1980).

The Italian (orig. 1797), ed. Frederick Gerber (Oxford University Press, Oxford, 1981).

Radcliffe, Mary Anne, *The Female Advocate* (orig. 1799; Woodstock Books, Oxford, 1994).

Manfroné; Or the One-Handed Monk (orig. 1809; Arno Press, New York, 1972), 4 vols.

Raysor, Thomas Middleton, ed., *Samuel Taylor Coleridge: Shakespeare Criticism* (J. M. Dent, 1960), 2 vols.

Reeve, Clara, *The Old English Baron* (orig. 1777), as *The Champion of Virtue. A Gothic Story* (Oxford University Press, 1977).

The Progress of Romance (for the author by W. Keymer, Colchester, 1785), 2 vols.

Repton, Humphrey, *Variety: a Collection of Essays* (T. Cadell, 1788).

Richardson, Samuel, *Pamela* (orig. 1740–1; Everyman, 1974), 2 vols.

Clarissa (orig. 1747–8; Penguin, Harmondsworth, 1985).

Sir Charles Grandison (orig. 1753–4), ed. Jocelyn Harris (Oxford University Press, Oxford, 1986).

Roberts, Arthur, ed., *Letters of Hannah More to Zachary Macaulay* (John Nisbet and Co., 1860).

Roberts, William, *Memoirs of the Life and Correspondence of Mrs Hannah More* (R. B. Seeley and W. Burnside 1834), 4 vols.

Robinson, Mary, *Vancenza; or, the Dangers of Credulity* (Bell, 1792), 2 vols.

Angelina (T. Hookham and J. Carpenter, 1796), 3 vols.

Walsingham; or, the Pupil of Nature (orig. 1797; Routledge and Thoemmes Press, 1992), 4 vols.

The Natural Daughter (T. N. Longman and O. Rees, 1799), 2 vols.

Roche, Regina Maria, *The Children of the Abbey* (W. Lane, 1796) 4 vols.

Clermont: a Tale (orig. 1798; Folio Press, 1968).

Sandham, Elizabeth, *The Twin Sisters; or, The Advantages of Religion* (orig. 1788 as *The Twin Sisters; or, the Effects of Education*; 12th edn, J. Harris and Sons, 1819).

Schaw, Janet, *Journals of a Lady of Quality . . . in the Years 1774–1776*, ed. Evangeline Walker Andrews and Charles Mclean Andrews (2nd edn, Yale University Press, New Haven, 1934).

Scott, Sarah, *The History of Cornelia* (orig. 1750; Routledge and Thoemmes Press, 1992).

Millenium Hall (orig. 1762), ed. Gary Kelly (Broadview Press, Ontario, 1995).

Scott, Sir Walter, *Waverley* (orig. 1814; Penguin, Harmondsworth, 1972).

Selincourt, Ernest de, ed., *The Letters of William and Dorothy Wordsworth* (2nd edn, Clarendon Press, Oxford, 1967), 3 vols.

Seward, Anna, *Letters of Anna Seward* (George Ramsay and Co., Edinburgh, 1811), 6 vols.

Shakespeare, William, *Much Ado about Nothing*, Arden Shakespeare, ed. A. R. Humphreys (Methuen, 1981).

Twelfth Night, Arden Shakespeare, ed. J. M. Lothian and T. W. Craik (Methuen, 1975).

Coriolanus, Arden Shakespeare, ed. Philip Brockbank (Methuen, 1976).

Shelley, Mary and Percy Bysshe, *History of a Six Weeks Tour* (orig. 1817; Woodstock, Oxford, 1992).

Shelley, Mary, *Frankenstein* (orig. 1818), ed. Marilyn Butler (Oxford University Press, Oxford, 1994).

The Last Man (orig. 1826; Hogarth Press, 1985).

Lodore (orig. 1835; Pickering, 1996).

Falkner (orig. 1837; Pickering, 1996).

Matilda (written 1819) in Janet Todd, ed., *Wollstonecraft's 'Maria' and Shelley's 'Matilda'* (Penguin, Harmondsworth, 1993).

Sheridan, Frances, *Memoirs of Miss Sidney Biddulph* (orig. 1761–7; Pandora, 1987).

Sheridan, Richard Brinsley, *Plays and Poems of Richard Brinsley Sheridan*, ed. R. Crompton Rhodes (Oxford University Press, Oxford, 1928).

Sibbitt, Adam, *Thoughts on the Frequency of Divorces in Modern Times* (T. Cadell Jr. and W. Davies, 1800).

Silliman, Benjamin, *Letters of Shahcoolen* (orig. 1802), ed. Ben Harris McClary, Scholars' Facsimiles and Reprints, Gainesville, Florida, 1962).

Sleath, Eleanor, *The Orphan of the Rhine* (orig. 1798; Folio Press, 1968).

The Nocturnal Minstrel; or, the Spirit of the Wood (Minerva, 1810).

Smith, Charlotte, *The Romance of Real Life* (T. Cadell, 1787), 3 vols.

Emmeline: the Orphan of the Castle (orig. 1788: Pandora, 1987).

Ethelinde; or the Recluse of the Lake (T. Cadell, 1789), 5 vols.

Desmond (G. G. and J. Robinson, 1792), 3 vols.

The Old Manor House (orig. 1793; Oxford University Press, 1989).

The Banished Man. A Novel (T. Cadell Jr and W. Davies, 1794), 4 vols.

The Wanderings of Warwick (J. Bell, 1794).

Montalbert (S. Low for E. Hooker, 1795), 3 vols.

Rural Walks: in Dialogues intended for the Use of Young Persons (orig. 1795; 4th edn, T. Cadell Jr and W. Davies, 1800), 2 vols.

Marchmont (S. Low, 1796), 4 vols.

Rambles Farther: a Continuation of Rural Walks (T. Cadell Jr and W. Davies, 1796), 2 vols.

The Young Philosopher (T. Cadell Jr and W. Davies, 1798), 4 vols.

The Letters of a Solitary Wanderer (Sampson Low, 1800), 3 vols.

Conversations, Introducing Poetry: Chiefly in Subjects of Natural History for the Use of Children and Young Persons (orig. 1804; T. Nelson and Sons, 1863).

Smith, Nowell C., ed., *Wordsworth's Literary Criticism* (revd. Howard Mills, Bristol Classical Press, Bristol, 1980).

Smollett, Tobias, *The Adventures of Roderick Random* (orig. 1748), ed. Paul-Gabriel Boucé (Oxford University Press, Oxford, 1979).

Humphrey Clinker (orig. 1771), ed. Paul-Gabriel Boucé (Oxford University Press, Oxford, 1984).

Southam, Brian, *Jane Austen: the Critical Heritage* (Routledge Kegan Paul, 1968).

ed., *Jane Austen's 'Sir Charles Grandison'* (Clarendon Press, Oxford, 1980).

Sterne, Lawrence, *The Life and Opinions of Tristram Shandy* (orig. 1759–67; Everyman, 1967).

Stocking, Marion Kingston, with David Mackenzie Stocking, *The Journals of Claire Clairmont* (Harvard University Press, Cambridge, Mass., 1968).

Taylor, Eliza, *Education; or, Elizabeth, Her Lover and Husband. A Tale for 1817* (Minerva, 1817), 3 vols.

Tenney, Tabitha Gilman, *Female Quixotism* (orig. 1801), ed. Jean Nienkamp and Andrea Collins (Oxford University Press, New York and Oxford, 1992).

Thackeray, William Makepeace, *Roundabout Papers* (orig. 1863) Oxford Thackeray, ed. George Saintsbury (Oxford University Press, 1908), vol. XVII.

Thomson, James, *The Denial; or, the Happy Retreat* (J. Sewell, 1790), 3 vols.

Thrale, Hester Lynch, (later Piozzi), *Anecdotes of Samuel Johnson* (orig. 1786; Alan Sutton, Gloucester, 1984).

Observations and Reflections Made in the Course of a Journey through France, Italy and Germany (orig. 1789; University of Michigan Press, Ann Arbor, 1967).

Thraliana: the Diary of Mrs Hester Lynch Thrale (later Mrs Piozzi) 1776–1809, ed. Katharine C. Balderston (Clarendon Press, Oxford, 1942), 2 vols.

Todd, Janet and Marilyn Butler, eds., *The Works of Mary Wollstonecraft* (Pickering and Chatto, 1989), 7 vols.

Walpole, Horace, *The Castle of Otranto* (orig. 1764) in E. F. Bleiler, ed., *Three Gothic Novels* (Dover Press, New York, 1966).

Wardle, Ralph M., ed., *Collected Letters of Mary Wollstonecraft* (Cornell University Press, Ithaca and London, 1979).

Watts, Isaac, *The Improvement of the Mind* (J. Buckland, T. Longman etc., 1782), 2 vols.

Wedd, A. F., ed., *The Love-Letters of Mary Hays (1779–1780)* (Methuen, 1925).

The Fate of the Fenwicks: Letters to Mary Hays (1798–1828) (Methuen, 1927).

West, Jane, *The Advantages of Education; or the History of Maria Williams* (W. Lane, 1793), 2 vols.

A Gossip's Story, and a Legendary Tale (T. N. Longman and O. Rees, 1796), 2 vols.

A Tale of the Times (T. N. Longman and O. Rees, 1799), 3 vols.

The Infidel Father (A. Strahan for T. N. Longman and O. Rees, 1802), 3 vols.

Letters to a Young Lady (Longman, Hurst, Rees and Orme, 1806), 3 vols.

Wheatley, Phillis, *The Collected Works of Phillis Wheatley*, ed. John Shields (Oxford University Press, New York, 1988).

Whitbread, Helena, ed., *I Know My Own Heart: the Diaries of Anne Lister 1791–1840* (Virago, 1988).

No Priest but Love: the Journals of Anne Lister from 1824–1826 (Smith Settle, Otley, 1992).

White, James, *The Adventures of King Richard Cœur-de-Lion* (T. and J. Evans, 1791), 3 vols.

Williams, Helen Maria, *Julia, a Novel* (orig. 1790; Routledge and Thoemmes Press, 1995).

Wollstonecraft, Mary, *Thoughts on the Education of Daughters* (orig. 1787) in Janet Todd and Marilyn Butler eds., *The Works of Mary Wollstonecraft* (Pickering and Chatto, 1989).
Original Stories from Real Life (J. Johnson, 1788).
A Vindication of the Rights of Woman (orig. 1792), ed. Ashley Tauchert (Everyman, 1995).
The Wrongs of Woman (orig. 1798) in Gary Kelly, ed., *Mary and the Wrongs of Woman* (World's Classics, 1980).
Woodfin, Mrs A., *Northern Memoirs; or, the History of a Scotch Family* (F. and J. Noble, 1756), 2 vols.
Yearsley, Ann, *Poems, on Several Occasions. By Ann Yearsley, a Milkwoman of Bristol* (T. Cadell, 1785).
Poems, on Various Subjects (printed for the Author, 1787).
A Catalogue of the Books, Tracts, &c contained in Ann Yearsley's Public Library, No. 4, Crescent, Hotwells (Bristol, 1793).
The Royal Captives: a Fragment of Secret History. Copied from an old Manuscript (J. Stockdale, Dublin, 1795), 2 vols.
The Rural Lyre: a Volume of Poems (G. G. and J. Robinson, 1796).

SECONDARY TEXTS

Aaron, Jane, ' "On Needlework": protest and contradiction in Mary Lamb's essay', *Prose Studies* (1987), pp. 159–77.
Altick, Robert D., *The English Common Reader: a Social History of the Mass Reading Public 1800–1900* (University of Chicago Press, Chicago, 1957).
Armstrong, Nancy, *Desire and Domestic Fiction: a Political History* (Oxford University Press, Oxford, 1987).
'The rise of the domestic woman' in Nancy Armstrong and Leonard Tennenhouse, eds., *The Ideology of Conduct: Essays in Literature and the History of Sexuality* (Methuen, 1987), pp. 96–141.
Ballaster, Ros, 'Romancing the novel: gender and genre in early theories of narrative' in Dale Spender, ed., *Living by the Pen: Early British Women Writers* (Athene, Teachers College Press, Columbia University, New York, 1992), pp. 188–200.
Barry, Jonathan, 'Literacy and literature in popular culture: reading and writing in historical perspective' in Tim Harris, ed., *Popular Culture in England, c. 1500–1850* (Macmillan, Basingstoke, 1995), pp. 69–94.
Basker, James G., 'Radical affinities: Mary Wollstonecraft and Samuel Johnson' in Alvaro Ribeiro and James G. Basker, eds., *Tradition in Transition: Women Writers, Marginal Texts, and the Eighteenth-Century Canon* (Clarendon Press, Oxford, 1996), pp. 41–55.
'Dancing dogs, women preachers and the myth of Johnson's misogyny', *Age of Johnson* 3 (1990), pp. 63–90.
Bennett, Betty and Charles Robinson, *The Mary Shelley Reader* (Oxford University Press, London, 1990).

Blakey, Dorothy, *The Minerva Press, 1790–1820* (Oxford University Press for the Bibliographical Society, Oxford, 1935).

Bloom, Harold, *The Anxiety of Influence: a Theory of Poetry* (Oxford University Press, 1973).

Blumberg, Jane, *Mary Shelley's Early Novels* (Macmillan, Basingstoke, 1993).

Blyth, Henry, *Caro: the Fatal Passion* (Hart Davis, 1972).

Boas, Louise Schutz, *Harriet Shelley: Five Long Years* (Oxford University Press, 1962).

Bohls, Elizabeth A., *Women Travel Writers and the Language of Aesthetics, 1716–1818* (Cambridge University Press, Cambridge, 1995).

Bottoms, Janet, 'In the absence of Mrs Leicester: Mary Lamb's place in the development of a literature of childhood' in Mary Hilton, Morag Styles and Victor Watson eds., *Opening the Nursery Door: Reading, Writing and Childhood 1600–1900* (Routledge, 1997), pp. 117–32.

Bowers, Toni, *The Politics of Motherhood: British Writing and Culture 1680–1760* (Cambridge University Press, Cambridge, 1996).

Bowstead, Diana, 'Charlotte Smith's *Desmond*: the epistolary novel as ideological argument' in Mary Anne Schofield and Cecilia Macheski, eds., *Fetter'd or Free? British Women Novelists 1670–1815* (Ohio University Press, Ohio, 1986), pp. 237–63.

Bradbrook, F. W., *Jane Austen and her Predecessors* (Cambridge University Press, Cambridge, 1966).

Brewer, John, *The Pleasures of the Imagination: English Culture in the Eighteenth Century* (HarperCollins, 1997).

'Reconstructing the reader: prescriptions, texts and strategies in Anna Larpent's reading' in Raven, Small and Tadmor, eds., *Practice and Representation of Reading*, pp. 226–45.

Brophy, Elizabeth Bergen, *Women's Lives and the Eighteenth-Century English Novel* (University of South Florida Press, Tampa, 1991).

Brown, Alice, *The Eighteenth-Century Feminist Mind* (Harvester Press, Brighton, 1987).

Burton, Antoinette, ' "Invention is what delights me": Jane Austen's remaking of "English" history' in Devoney Looser, ed., *Jane Austen and the Discourses of Feminism* (Macmillan, Basingstoke, 1995), pp. 35–50.

Butler, Marilyn, *Jane Austen and the War of Ideas* (Clarendon Press, Oxford, 1975).

Maria Edgeworth: a Literary Biography (Clarendon Press, Oxford, 1972).

'The woman at the window: Ann Radcliffe in the novels of Mary Wollstonecraft and Jane Austen' in Janet Todd, ed., *Gender and Literary Voice* (Holmes and Meier, New York, 1980), pp. 128–48.

Campbell, Gina, 'How to read like a Gentleman: Burney's instructions to her critics in *Evelina*', *English Literary History* 57 (1990), pp. 557–83.

Campbell, Mary, *Lady Morgan: the Life and Times of Sydney Owenson* (Pandora, 1988).

Chambers, Ross, *Room for Maneuver: Reading (the) Oppositonal (in) Narrative* (University of Chicago Press, Chicago, 1991).

Chartier, Roger, *Frenchness in the History of the Book: from the History of Publishing to the History of Reading* (American Antiquarian Society, Worcester, Mass., 1988).
  The Culture of Print: Power and the Uses of Print in Early Modern Europe (Cambridge University Press, Cambridge, 1989).
Clery, E. J., *The Rise of Supernatural Fiction, 1762–1800* (Cambridge University Press, Cambridge, 1995).
Clifford, James L., *Hester Lynch Piozzi (Mrs Thrale)* (2nd edn, Clarendon Press, Oxford, 1968).
Colley, Linda, *Britons: Forging the Nation 1707–1837* (orig. 1992; Pimlico, London, 1994).
Copeland, Edward, *Women Writing about Money: Women's Fiction in England 1790–1820* (Cambridge University Press, Cambridge, 1995).
Cruse, Amy, *The Englishman and his Books in the Early Nineteenth Century* (Harrap, London, 1930).
Cutting-Gray, Joanne, *Woman as 'Nobody' and the Novels of Fanny Burney* (University of Florida Press, Gainesville, 1992).
Dällenbach, Lucian, *The Mirror in the Text*, trans. Jeremy Whitely with Emma Hughes (Polity Press, Cambridge, 1989).
Davidoff, Leonore, and Catherine Hall, *Family Fortunes: Men and Women of the English Middle Class 1780–1850* (orig. 1987; Routledge, 1992).
DeMaria, Robert, Jr, *The Life of Samuel Johnson* (Oxford University Press, Oxford, 1993).
Derrida, Jacques, *Positions*, trans. Alan Bass (University of Chicago Press, Chicago, 1981).
Doody, Margaret Anne, 'Jane Austen's Reading' in J. David Grey, ed., *The Jane Austen Handbook* (Athlone Press, 1986), pp. 347–63.
  Frances Burney: the Life in the Works (Cambridge University Press, Cambridge, 1988).
  'Introduction', Charlotte Lennox, *The Female Quixote*, ed. Margaret Dalziel (Oxford Univeristy Press, Oxford, 1989).
Duncan Eaves, T. C., and Ben D. Kimpel, *Samuel Richardson: a Biography* (Clarendon Press, Oxford, 1971).
Dunne, Tom, 'Fiction as 'the best history of nations': Lady Morgan's Irish novels' in Dunne ed., *The Writer as Witness: Literature as Historical Evidence*, Historical Studies xvi (Cork UniversityPress, Cork, 1987), pp. 133–59.
Ellis, Markman, *The Politics of Sensibility: Race, Gender and Commerce in the Sentimental Novel* (Cambridge University Press, Cambridge, 1996).
Elwin, Malcolm, *Lord Byron's Wife* (Macdonald, 1962).
Epstein, Julia, and Kristina Straub, eds., *Body Guards: the Cultural Politics of Gender Ambiguity* (Routledge, 1991).
Erikson, Lee, 'The economy of novel reading: Jane Austen and the circulating library', *Studies in English Literature* 30 (1990), pp. 573–90.
Fergus, Jan, 'Provincial servants' reading in the late eighteenth century' in Raven, Hill and Tadmor, eds., *Practice and Representation of Reading* pp. 202–25.

Ferguson, Moira, *Eighteenth-Century Women Poets: Nation, Class and Gender* (SUNY, Albany, 1995).

Ferris, Ina, *The Achievement of Literary Authority: Gender, History and the Waverley Novels* (Cornell University Press, Ithaca, 1991).

Fetterley, Judith, *The Resisting Reader: a Feminist Approach to American Fiction* (Indiana University Press, Bloomington, 1978).

Fish, Audrey A., Anne K. Mellor and Esther Schor, eds., *The Other Mary Shelley: Beyond Frankenstein* (Oxford University Press, New York and Oxford, 1993).

Flint, Kate, *The Woman Reader, 1837–1914* (Oxford University Press, Oxford, 1993).

Flyn, Elizabeth A., and Patrocinio Schweickart, *Gender and Reading: Essays on Readers, Texts and Contexts* (Johns Hopkins University Press, Baltimore, 1986).

Foucault, Michel, *The History of Sexuality: an Introduction*, trans. Robert Hadley (Vintage, New York, 1980).

Franklin, Caroline, *Byron's Heroines* (Clarendon Press, Oxford, 1992).

Freund, Elizabeth, *The Return of the Reader: Reader-Response Criticism* (Methuen, London, 1987).

Gallagher, Catherine, *Nobody's Story: the Vanishing Acts of Women Writers in the Marketplace 1670–1820* (Clarendon Press, Oxford, 1994).

Galloway, W. F., 'The conservative attitude toward fiction, 1770–1830', *PMLA* 55 (1940), pp. 1041–59.

Garber, Marjorie, *Vested Interests: Cross-Dressing and Cultural Anxiety* (Routledge, 1992).

Gilbert, Sandra, and Susan Gubar, *The Madwoman in the Attic: the Woman Writer and the Nineteenth-Century Literary Imagination* (Yale University Press, New Haven, 1979).

Gittings, Robert, and Jo Manton, *Claire Clairmont and the Shelleys* (Oxford University Press, 1992).

Gonda, Caroline, *Reading Daughters' Fictions 1709–1834: Novels and Society from Manley to Edgeworth* (Cambridge University Press, Cambridge, 1996).

Green, Katherine Sobba, *The Courtship Novel 1740–1820: a Feminized Genre* (University Press of Kentucky, Lexington, 1991).

Greene, Richard, *Mary Leapor: a Study in Eighteenth-Century Women's Poetry* (Clarendon Press, Oxford, 1993).

Greer, Germaine, *Slipshod Sibyls: Recognition, Rejection and the Woman Poet* (Viking, London, 1995).

Grundy, Isobel, 'Samuel Johnson as patron of women', *Age of Johnson* 1 (1987), pp. 59–77.

Harris, Jocelyn, *Jane Austen's Art of Memory* (Cambridge University Press, Cambridge, 1989).

'Jane Austen and the burden of the (male) past: the case reexamined' in Devoney Looser, ed., *Jane Austen and the Discourses of Feminism* (Macmillan, Basingstoke, 1995), pp. 87–100.

Haslam, Richard, 'Lady Morgan's novels from 1806 to 1833: cultural aesthetics and national identity', *Eire-Ireland*, 22: 4(1987), pp. 11–25.

Hawkins, Desmond, *Shelley's First Love: the Love Story of Percy Bysshe Shelley and Harriet Grove* (Archon Books, 1992).
Hemlow, Joyce, 'Fanny Burney and the courtesy books', *PMLA* 45 (1950), pp. 732–61.
, *The History of Fanny Burney* (Clarendon Press, Oxford, 1958).
Hilbish, Florence May Anna, *Charlotte Smith, Poet and Novelist (1749–1806)* (University of Philadelphia, 1941).
Hill, Bridget, *The Republican Virago: the Life and Times of Catherine Macaulay, Historian* (Clarendon Press, Oxford, 1992).
Hofkosh, Sonia, 'The writer's ravishment: women and the romantic author – the example of Byron' in Mellor, *Romanticism and Feminism*, pp. 93–114.
Homans, Margaret, *Bearing the Word: Language and Female Experience in Nineteenth-Century Women's Writing* (University of Chicago Press, Chicago, 1986).
'Keats reading women, women reading Keats', *Studies in Romanticism* 29 (1990), pp. 341–70.
Honan, Park, *Jane Austen: her Life* (Weidenfeld and Nicholson, 1987).
Houston, R. A., *Literacy in Early Modern Europe: Culture and Education 1500–1800* (Longman, 1988).
Howard, Jacqueline, *Reading Gothic Fiction: a Bakhtinian Approach* (Clarendon Press, Oxford, 1994).
Howard, Susan K., 'Identifying the criminal in Charlotte Lennox's *The Life of Harriot Stuart*', *Eighteenth-Century Fiction* 5 (1993), pp. 137–52.
Hutcheon, Linda, *A Theory of Parody* (Methuen, New York, 1985).
Irwin, Raymond, *The English Library: Sources and History* (George Allen and Unwin, 1966).
Jackson, Jessamyn, 'Why novels make bad mothers', *Novel* 27 (1994), pp. 161–74.
Janes, Regina M., 'On the reception of Mary Wollstonecraft's *A Vindication of the Rights of Woman*', *Journal of the History of Ideas* 39 (1978), pp. 293–302.
Johnson, Claudia, *Jane Austen: Women, Politics and the Novel* (University of Chicago Press, Chicago, 1988).
Jones, Ann H., *Ideas and Innovations: Best Sellers of Jane Austen's Age* (AMS Press, New York, 1986).
Jones, Chris, *Radical Sensibility: Literature and Ideas in the 1790s* (Routledge, 1993).
Jones, Kathleen, *A Passionate Sisterhood: the Sisters, Wives and Daughters of the Lake Poets* (Constable, 1997).
Jones, Vivien, *Women in the Eighteenth Century: Constructions of Femininity* (Routledge, 1990).
Kaufman, Paul, *The Community Library: a Chapter in English Social History*, *Transactions of the American Philosophical Society*, 57, pt. 7 (1967).
Libraries and their Users (Library Association, 1969).
Kelly, Gary, ' "This pestiferous reading": the social basis of reaction against the novel in late eighteenth- and early nineteenth-century Britain', *Man and Nature* 4 (Edmonton, 1985), pp. 183–94.
English Fiction of the Romantic Period 1789–1830 (Longmans, 1989).
'Unbecoming a heroine: novel reading, romanticism and Barrett's *The*

Heroine', *Nineteenth-Century Literature* 45 (1990–1), pp. 220–41.

'Women novelists and the French revolution debate: novelizing the revolution/revolutionizing the novel', *Eighteenth-Century Fiction* 6 (1994), pp. 369–88.

Women, Writing and Revolution 1790–1827 (Clarendon Press, Oxford, 1993).

Keymer, Tom, *Richardson's Clarissa* and the Eighteenth-Century Reader (Cambridge University Press, Cambridge, 1992).

Kiely, Robert, *The Romantic Novel in England* (Harvard University Press, Cambridge, Mass., 1972).

Kilgour, Maggie, *The Rise of the Gothic Novel* (Routledge, 1995).

Kirkham, Margaret, *Jane Austen, Feminism and Fiction* (Harvester Press, Brighton, 1983).

Klancher, Jon P., *The Making of English Reading Audiences, 1790–1832* (University of Wisconsin Press, Madison, 1987).

Knights, Elspeth, 'A "licensuous" daughter: Mehetabel Wesley 1697–1750', *Women's Writing* 4 (1997), pp. 15–38.

Kowaleski-Wallace, Elizabeth, *Their Father's Daughters: Hannah More, Maria Edgeworth and Patriarchal Complicity* (Oxford University Press, New York, 1991).

Landry, Donna, *The Muses of Resistance: Labouring-Class Women's Poetry in Britain, 1739–96* (Cambridge University Press, Cambridge, 1990).

Langbauer, Laurie, 'Romance revised: Charlotte Lennox's *The Female Quixote*', *Novel* 18 (1984), pp. 29–49.

Leavis, Q. D., *Fiction and the Reading Public* (orig. 1932; repr. Penguin, Harmondsworth, 1979).

Levin, Kate, ' "The Cure of Arabella's Mind": Charlotte Lennox and the disciplining of the female reader', *Women's Writing* 2 (1995), pp. 271–90.

Lewis, Paul, 'Gothic and mock-gothic: the repudiation of fantasy in Barrett's *Heroine*', *English Language Notes* 21 (1983–4), pp. 44–52.

London, April, 'Jane West and the politics of reading' in Alvaro Ribeiro and James G. Basker, eds., *Tradition in Transition: Women Writers, Marginal Texts, and the Eighteenth-Century Canon* (Clarendon Press, Oxford, 1996), pp. 56–74.

Looser, Devoney, ed., *Jane Austen and the Discourses of Feminism* (Macmillan, Basingstoke, 1995).

MacDonald, Susan Peck, 'Jane Austen and the tradition of the absent mother' in Cathy N. Davidson and E. M. Broner, eds., *The Lost Tradition: Mothers and Daughters in Literature* (Frederick Ungar, New York, 1980), pp. 58–69.

Macfadyen, Heather, 'Lady Delacour's library: Maria Edgeworth's *Belinda* and fashionable reading', *Nineteenth-Century Literature* 48 (1993), pp. 423–39.

Magee, William H., 'The happy marriage: the influence of Charlotte Smith on Jane Austen', *Studies in the Novel* 7 (1975), pp. 120–32.

Manguel, Alberto, *A History of Reading* (Harper Collins, 1996).

Marchand, Leslie A., *Byron: a Portrait* (orig. 1971; repr. Pimlico, 1993).

Marks, Elaine, and Isabelle de Courtivron, eds., *New French Feminisms* (Harvester Press, Brighton, 1981).

Marshall, David, 'Writing masters and "masculine exercises" in *The Female Quixote*', *Eighteenth-Century Fiction* 5 (1993), pp. 105–35.

Mavor, Elizabeth, *The Ladies of Llangollen* (Penguin, Harmondsworth, 1973).

McKee, John B., *Literary Irony and the Literary Audience: Studies in the Victimization of the Reader in Augustan Fiction* (Rodopi NV, Amsterdam, 1974).

Mellor, Anne K., *Romanticism and Feminism* (Indiana University Press, Bloomington, 1988).

Romanticism and Gender (Routledge, 1993).

'Why women didn't like romanticism: the views of Jane Austen and Mary Shelley' in Gene W. Ruoff, ed., *The Romantics and Us: Essays on Literature and Culture* (Rutgers University Press, New Brunswick and London, 1990), pp. 274–87.

Melman, Billie, *Women's Orients: English Women and the Middle East, 1718–1918* (orig. 1992; 2nd edn, Macmillan, 1995).

Messenger, Ann, *His and Hers: Essays in Restoration and Eighteenth-Century Literature* (University Press of Kentucky, Lexington, 1986).

Mieczikowski, Cynthia J., 'The parodic mode and the patriarchal imperative: reading the female reader(s) in Tabitha Tenney's *Female Quixotism*', *Early American Literature* 25 (1990), pp. 34–45.

Mills, Sara, *Discourses of Difference: an Analysis of Women's Travel Writing and Colonialism* (Routledge, 1991).

Feminist Stylistics (Routledge, London, 1995).

Mudge, Bradford Keyes, *Sara Coleridge, a Victorian Daughter: her Life and Essays* (Yale University Press, New Haven, 1989).

Myers, Mitzi, 'Sensibility and the "Walk of Reason": Mary Wollstonecraft's literary reviews as cultural critique' in Syndy McMillan Conger, ed., *Sensibility in Transformation: Creative Resistance to Sentiment from the Augustans to the Romantics* (AUP, Toronto and London 1990), pp. 120–44.

Myers, Sylvia Harcstark, *The Bluestocking Circle: Women, Friendship, and the Life of the Mind in Eighteenth-Century England* (Clarendon Press, Oxford, 1990).

Nettleton, George H., 'The books of Lydia Languish's circulating library', *Journal of English and Germanic Philology*, 5 (1903–5), pp. 492–500.

Nussbaum, Felicity, and Laura Brown, eds., *The New 18th Century: Theory, Politics, English Literature* (Methuen, 1987).

Orr, Clarissa Campbell, ed., *Wollstonecraft's Daughters: Womanhood in England and France 1780–1820* (Manchester University Press, Manchester, 1996).

Phillips, Patricia, *The Scientific Lady: a Social History of Women's Scientific Interests 1520–1918* (Weidenfeld and Nicolson, 1990).

Pinch, Adela, 'Lost in a book: Jane Austen's *Persuasion*', *Studies in Romanticism* 32 (1993), pp. 97–117.

Poovey, Mary, *The Proper Lady and the Woman Writer: Ideology as Style in the Works of Mary Wollstonecraft, Mary Shelley and Jane Austen* (University of Chicago Press, Chicago, 1984).

Porter, Roy, *English Society in the Eighteenth Century*, Pelican Social History of Britain (Penguin, Harmondsworth, 1982).

Porter, Roy, and Lesley Hall, *The Facts of Life: the Creation of Sexual Knowledge in Britain, 1650–1950* (Yale University Press, New Haven, 1995).

Raven, James, *Judging New Wealth: Popular Publishing and Responses to Commerce in England, 1750–1800* (Clarendon Press, Oxford, 1992).

'From promotion to proscription: arrangements for reading and eighteenth-century libraries' in Raven, Hill and Tadmor, eds., *Practice and Representation of Reading*, pp. 175–201.

Helen Small and Naomi Tadmor, eds., *The Practice and Representation of Reading in England* (Cambridge University Press, Cambridge, 1996).

Ray, William, *Literary Meaning: from Phenomenology to Deconstruction* (Basil Blackwell, Oxford, 1984).

'Reading women: cultural authority, gender and the novel: the case of Rousseau', *Eighteenth-Century Studies* 27 (1994), pp. 421–47.

Rees, Joan, *Shelley's Jane Williams* (William Kimber, 1985).

Rendall, Jane, 'Writing history for British women: Elizabeth Hamilton and the *Memoirs of Agrippina*' in Clarissa Campbell Orr, ed., *Wollstonecraft's Daughters: Womanhood in England and France 1780–1820* (Manchester University Press, Manchester, 1996), pp. 79–93.

Ribeiro, Alvaro, and James G. Basker, eds., *Tradition in Transition: Women Writers, Marginal Texts, and the Eighteenth-Century Canon* (Clarendon Press, Oxford, 1996).

Richardson, Alan, *Literature, Education, and Romanticism: Reading as Social Practice 1780–1832* (Cambridge University Press, Cambridge, 1994).

'Romanticism and the colonization of the feminine' in Mellor, *Romanticism and Feminism*, pp. 13–25.

Richter, David H., 'Reception of the gothic novel in the 1790s' in Robert W. Uphaus, ed., *The Idea of the Novel in the Eighteenth Century* (East Lansing, 1988), pp. 117–37.

Rivers, Isobel, ed., *Books and their Readers in 18th-Century England* (Leicester University Press, Leicester, 1982).

Ross, Deborah, 'Mirror, mirror: the didactic dilemma of *The Female Quixote*', *Studies in English Literature* 27 (1987), pp. 455–73.

Ross, Marlon, *The Contours of Masculine Desire: Romanticism and the Rise of Women's Poetry* (Oxford University Press, Oxford, 1989).

Roulston, Christine, 'Histories of nothing: romance and femininity in Charlotte Lennox's *The Female Quixote*', *Women's Writing* 2 (1995), pp. 25–42.

Sale, William M., Jr, *Samuel Richardson: Master Printer*, Cornell Studies in English 37 (Cornell University Press, Ithaca, 1950).

Sales, Roger, 'Pierce Egan and the representation of London' in Philip W. Martin and Robin Jarvis, eds., *Reviewing Romanticism* (Macmillan, 1992).

Sapiro, Virginia, *A Vindication of Political Virtue: the Political Theory of Mary Wollstonecraft* (University of Chicago Press, Chicago, 1992).

Schiebinger, Londa, *The Mind Has No Sex? Women in the Origins of Modern Science* (Harvard University Press, Cambridge, Mass., 1989).

Nature's Body: Sexual Politics and the Making of Modern Science (Pandora, 1994).

Schofield, Mary Anne, and Cecilia Macheski, eds., *Fetter'd or Free? British Women Novelists 1670–1815* (Ohio University Press, Athens, Ohio, 1986).

Schweickart, Patrocinio P., and Elizabeth A. Flynn, eds., *Gender and Reading: Essays on Readers, Texts and Contexts* (Johns Hopkins University Press, Baltimore, 1986).

Scott, Joan Wallach, *Gender and the Politics of History* (Columbia University Press, New York, 1988).

Shippen, Eliza Pearl, *Eugenia de Acton (1749–1827)* (University of Pennsylvania, Philadelphia, 1945).

Shteir, Ann B., 'Linnaeus's daughters: women and British botany' in Barbara J. Harris and JoAnn K. McNamara, eds., *Women and the Structure of Society* (Duke University Press, Durham NC, 1984) pp. 67–73.

'Botanical dialogues: Maria Jacson and Women's popular science writing in England', *Eighteenth-Century Studies* 23 (1989–90), pp. 301–17.

Cultivating Women, Cultivating Science: Flora's Daughters and Botany in England 1760–1860 (Johns Hopkins University Press, Baltimore, 1996).

Simons, Judy, *Diaries and Journals of Literary Women from Fanny Burney to Virginia Woolf* (Macmillan, 1990).

Small, Helen, *Love's Madness: Medicine, the Novel, and Female Insanity, 1800–1865* (Oxford University Press, Oxford, 1996).

Small, Miriam Rossiter, *Charlotte Ramsay Lennox: an Eighteenth-Century Lady of Letters* (orig. 1935; new edn, n.p., 1969).

Smith, Olivia, *The Politics of Language (1791–1819)* (Clarendon Press, Oxford, 1984).

Spacks, Patricia Meyer, 'The subtle sophistry of desire: Dr Johnson and *The Female Quixote*', *Modern Philology* 85 (1987–8), pp. 532–42.

Spencer, Jane, *The Rise of the Woman Novelist: from Aphra Behn to Jane Austen* (Basil Blackwell, Oxford, 1986).

Spufford, Margaret, *Small Books and Pleasant Histories: Popular Fiction and its Readership in Seventeenth-Century England* (Cambridge University Press, Cambridge, 1981).

Staves, Susan, 'Fatal marriages? Restoration plays embedded in eighteenth-century novels' in Douglas Lane Patey and Timothy Keegan, eds., *Augustan Studies: Essays in Honor of Irvin Ehrenpreis* (University of Delaware Press, Newark, 1985), pp. 95–107.

Stewart, Garrett, *Dear Reader: the Conscripted Audience in Nineteenth-Century British Fiction* (Johns Hopkins University Press, Baltimore, 1996).

Stone, Lawrence, *The Family, Sex and Marriage in England 1500–1800* (Harper and Row, New York, 1977).

Broken Lives: Separation and Divorce in England 1660–1857 (Oxford University Press, Oxford, 1993)

Stuart, Dorothy Margaret, *Dearest Bess: the Life and Times of Lady Elizabeth Foster, afterwards Duchess of Devonshire* (Methuen, 1955).

Sutherland, Kathryn, 'Hannah More's counter-revolutionary feminism' in

Kelvin Everest, ed., *Revolution in Writing: British Literary Responses to the French Revolution* (Open University Press, Milton Keynes, 1991), pp. 27–63.

Tadmor, Naomi, ' "In the even my wife read to me": women, reading and household life in the eighteenth century' in Raven, Hill and Tadmor, eds., *Practice and Representation of Reading*, pp. 162–74.

Taylor, Gary, *Reinventing Shakespeare: a Cultural History from the Restoration to the Present Day* (Hogarth Press, 1990).

Taylor, John Tinnon, *Early Opposition to the English Novel: the Popular Reaction from 1760 to 1830* (King's Crown Press, New York, 1943).

Thomas, Claudia, ' "Th'instructive moral, and important thought": Elizabeth Carter reads Pope, Johnson and Epictetus', *Age of Johnson* 4 (1991), pp. 137–69.

Tillyard, Stella, *Aristocrats: Caroline, Emily, Louisa and Sarah Lennox, 1740–1832* (Vintage, 1995).

Tobin, Beth Fowkes, ed., *History, Gender, and Eighteenth-Century Literature* (University of Georgia Press, Athens, 1994).

Todd, Janet, *Women's Friendship in Literature* (Columbia University Press, New York, 1980).

Todd, Janet, ed., *Dictionary of British and American Women Writers 1660–1800* (Rowan and Allanheld, Totowa, NJ, 1985).

Tompkins, J. M. S., *The Popular Novel in England, 1770–1800* (orig. 1932; Methuen, 1962).

Trouille, Mary Seidman, *Sexual Politics in the Enlightenment: Women Writers Read Rousseau* (State University of New York Press, Albany, 1997).

Turner, Cheryl, *Living by the Pen: Women Writers in the Eighteenth Century* (Routledge, 1992).

Ty, Eleanor, *Unsex'd Revolutionaries: Five Women Novelists of the 1790s* (University of Toronto Press, Toronto, 1993).

Uphaus, Robert W., ed., *The Idea of the Novel in the Eighteenth Century* (Colleagues Press, East Lansing, 1988).

Walker, Ralph S., 'Charles Burney's theft of books at Cambridge', *Transactions of the Cambridge Bibliographical Society* 3 (1959–63), pp. 313–26.

Warren, Leland E., 'Of the conversation of women: *The Female Quixote* and the dream of perfection', *Studies in Eighteenth-Century Culture* 2 (1982), pp. 367–80.

Watson, Nicola J., *Revolution and the Form of the British Novel 1790–1825* (Clarendon Press, Oxford, 1994).

Watt, Ian, *The Rise of the Novel: Studies in Defoe, Richardson and Fielding* (orig. 1957; Pelican, Harmondsworth, 1972).

Wiles, Roy McKeen, 'The relish for reading in provincial England two centuries ago' in Paul J. Korshin, ed., *The Widening Circle: Essays on the Circulation of Literature in Eighteenth-century Europe* (University of Pennsylvania Press, Philadelphia, 1976), pp. 85–115.

Williams, Carolyn D., 'Poetry, pudding, and Epictetus: the consistency of Elizabeth Carter' in Alvaro Ribeiro and James G. Basker, eds., *Tradition in*

Transition: Women Writers, Marginal Texts, and the Eighteenth-Century Canon (Clarendon Press, Oxford, 1996), pp. 3–24.

Williams, Ioan, *Novel and Romance 1700–1800: a Documentary Record* (Routledge and Kegan Paul, 1970).

Wittreich, Joseph, *Feminist Milton* (Cornell University Press, Ithaca, 1987).

Wolfson, Susan J., 'Explaining to her sisters: Mary Lamb's *Tales from Shakespeare*' in Marianne Novy ed., *Women's Re-visions of Shakespeare* (University of Illinois Press, Urbana and Chicago, 1990), pp. 16–40.

Wolstoneholme, Susan, *Gothic (Re)Visions: Writing Women as Readers* (SUNY, Albany, New York, 1993).

Wrigley, E. A., and R. Schofield, *The Population of England 1541–1871: a Reconstruction* (Edward Arnold, London, 1981).

Wunsheimer, Joel, 'Fiction and the force of example' in Robert W. Uphaus, ed., *The Idea of the Novel in the Eighteenth Century* (East Lansing, 1988), pp. 1–19.

Index

Aaron, Jane   244 n. 53
Acton, Eugenia de   24, 61, 63, 83, 161
  Essays on the Art of Being Happy 227 n. 11; 236
    nn. 67, 76; 240 n. 137; 252 n. 27
Adams, Francis D. and Sanders, Barry   254
    n. 8
Adeane, J. H.   225 n. 76; 226 n. 90; 231 n. 7;
    239 n. 114; 241 n. 3; 251 n. 20
Addison, Joseph   97, 153, 188, 246 n. 12
  Cato 174
  The Guardian 129, 130
Aikin, Anna Letitia, *see* Barbauld
Akenside, Mark   58, 135, 178
  Pleasures of the Imagination 130
Alfieri's *Myrrha* 245 n. 77
Allen's library   169
Altick, Robert   236 n. 77; 254 n. 18; 255 nn.
    30, 34
Anacreon   103
Anley, Charlotte, *Miriam* 44, 231 n. 10
Anne of Austria   248 n. 50
Anquetil's History of Greece   233 n. 36
Anson, George, *A Voyage round the World* 55
Arabian Nights 23, 246 n. 12
Ariosto, Ludovico   106, 119
Armstrong, Nancy   2, 46, 221 nn. 6, 7; 225 n.
    69; 232 nn. 18, 20, 23
Arnold, Samuel James, *The Creole* 137
Aspinall, Arthur   255 n. 27; 256 n. 70
Aspinall-Oglander, Cecil   222 n. 12
Astell, Mary   226 n. 80
astronomy   66
Austen family   14, 163
Austen, Henry Thomas, 'Biographical notice
    of the author' 248 n. 53; 249 n. 58
Austen, Jane   17, 21, 22, 46, 71, 113, 122, 128,
    142–51, 153, 168, 181, 224 n. 51; 226 n. 85;
    232 n. 17; 234 n. 40; 240 nn. 123, 135; 243
    n. 34; 248–50 nn. 51–87
  'Catherine, or the Bower' 46, 146, 150
  Emma 146–7, 150, 159, 249 n. 63

'The History of England' 146, 149
Lady Susan 48, 232 n. 25
Letters 232 n. 25; 249 n. 63
'Love and Friendship' 146, 249 n. 62
Mansfield Park 46, 51, 55, 56–7, 66–7, 72,
    143, 144, 146, 150, 159, 233 n. 32; 235 n.
    52; 236 n. 73; 237 n. 90; 239 n. 113; 249 n.
    58; 250 n. 85
Northanger Abbey 24, 50–1, 53, 96, 100, 103,
    128, 144, 145, 146, 147, 198, 207, 209–13,
    214, 215, 217, 226 n. 92; 227 nn. 104, 13;
    232 n. 25; 233 n. 32; 241 n. 144; 247 n. 15;
    249 nn. 61, 63, 65, 66; 258 n. 30;
    259 n. 51
Persuasion 127, 143, 146, 147–8, 159, 247 n.
    14; 249 nn. 65, 67; 250 nn. 70, 72
Pride and Prejudice 48, 143, 144, 145, 149–50,
    152, 154, 158, 166, 225 n. 70; 232 n. 25;
    248 n. 51; 251 n. 2
Sanditon 17, 145, 148, 164
Sense and Sensibility 144, 145, 147, 150, 181,
    249 nn. 58, 67
Sir Charles Grandison 149, 250 n. 79
Austen-Leigh, J. E., *Memoir of Jane Austen* 239
    n. 109; 249 n. 58; 251 n. 6
Autobiography of the Working Class 255 n. 36

Bacon, Francis   1, 93, 165
Bage, Robert, *Barham Downs* 165
Baillie, Joanna   33, 40–1, 54, 55, 141
  A Series of Plays 234 n. 42
Balderston, Katharine C.   227 n. 6
Ballaster, Ros   200, 257 n. 3; 258 nn. 23, 26
Barash, Carol   239 n. 110
Barbauld, Anna Letitia   2, 5,7, 88, 135, 136,
    241 n. 143; 247 n. 34
Barber, Mary   26, 246 n. 11
Baronetage   147
Barrett, Charlotte   231 n. 12
Barrett, Eaton Stannard
  The Heroine 68, 144, 198, 206–9, 210, 211,

Barrett (*cont.*)
212, 213, 215, 217, 218, 238 n. 100; 242 n.
14; 247 n. 13; 257 n. 3
Woman, a Poem 225 n. 73
Barry, Edward 111, 245 n. 60
Barry, Jonathan 10, 224 nn. 50, 52; 226 n. 78
Basker, James 229 nn. 46, 52, 54, 60
Bath circulating libraries 162, 164, 168, 169
Beattie, James 189, 259 n. 60
Beauclerk, Lady Diana 31
Beckford, William, *Vathek* 38
Behn, Aphra 22, 23, 122, 200
Love Letters between a Nobleman and his Sister
246 n. 1
Bellamy, George Anne 162
Belle Assemblée, La 65, 80, 127, 224 n. 44; 237
n. 85; 241 n. 144
Benger, Miss 233 n. 28; 240 nn. 124, 127; 252
n. 31
Bennett, Agnes Maria 230 n. 64
The Beggar Girl and her Benefactors 98, 128,
158, 208, 247 n. 15
Bennett, John, *Letters to a Young Lady* 49, 232
n. 22; 240 n. 136
Berkenhout, John 68, 238 n. 101
Berry, Mary 5, 44, 112, 176–7, 179, 223 n. 23;
225 n. 67; 231 n. 12; 254 nn. 3, 15
Bessborough, Earl of 222 n. 12
Bewell, Alan 238 n. 97
Bible 25, 43–6, 62, 90, 178, 184, 188, 193–4,
228 n. 21
Biddell, Jane Ransom 34
Birmingham libraries 160, 161, 162
Bisset, Robert
Douglas 164, 252 n. 47
Modern Literature 80
Blair, Hugh, *Sermons* 46, 143, 146
Blake, William 20
Blakey, Dorothy 230 n. 64; 239 n. 112; 252 n.
32
Bleich, David 226 n. 97
Blessington, Lady 230 n. 76; 231 n. 85
Bligh, Captain 135
Bloom, Harold 18, 148, 226 n. 87
Blower, Elizabeth 128
George Bateman 24, 46, 62, 95, 127–8, 171,
227 n. 13; 236 n. 72; 247 nn. 14, 15
Maria 24, 110, 154, 172, 173, 227 n. 13; 253
n. 73
Bluestockings 65, 96, 138, 139
Blumberg, Jane 230 n. 70
Blunden, Edmund 255 n. 35
Blunt, Reginald 235 nn. 49, 50, 51; 239 n.
108; 240 n. 136; 248 nn. 36, 47; 254 n. 2
Blyth, Henry 231 n. 84

Boas, Louise Schultz 242 n. 12; 243 n. 24, 28,
30; 253 n. 75
Boccaccio, Giovanni 106
Bohls, Elizabeth 249 n. 67
Boileau, Nicolas 130
Bolingbroke, Henry St John 77, 78, 140
Bonhote, Elizabeth 230 n. 64
Boscawen, Frances 3, 65, 172, 222 n. 12; 251
n. 17
Boswell, James 30, 31, 32, 55, 77, 223 n. 21
Life of Johnson 31, 229 nn. 45, 46, 48, 53, 56;
234 n. 46
London Journal 229 n. 50; 240 n. 123
Tour of the Hebrides 183
botany 67–8
Boteler divorce 112
Bowdler, Henrietta 62
Bowers, Toni 222 n. 8; 228 n. 21
Bowstead, Diana 241 n. 147
Bradbrook, F. W. 248 n. 53; 249 nn. 54, 67;
250 nn. 71, 74, 79, 86
Bradshaigh, Lady Dorothy 26, 27, 28
Brant, Clare and Purkiss, Diane 246 n. 2
Brereton, Jane 141
Brewer, John 162, 223 n. 28; 225 n. 61; 240 n.
136; 252 n. 30; 254 n. 14
Brightwell, Cecilia Lucy 221 n. 6
Bristol Library Association 160, 161
Bristol circulating libraries 162, 167
British and Foreign Bible Society 12
Broadhurst, Thomas, *Advice to Young Ladies*
225 n. 68
Brooke, Frances
The Excursion 59, 60, 235 n. 62; 236 n. 63;
241 n. 144
History of Emily Montague 60, 159, 235 n. 56;
236 nn. 63, 75
Lady Julia Mandeville 188, 197
Brophy, Brigid 239 n. 121
Brophy, Elizabeth Bergen 19, 226 nn. 96,
101; 245 n. 68
Brown, Laura 235 n. 48
Brunton, Mary 12, 24, 144, 168, 197, 249 n.
63
Discipline 171
Emmeline 225 nn. 59, 69; 227 n. 12; 241 n.
144
Self-control 84, 109, 144, 166, 171, 227 n. 15
Buckingham, Duke of, *The Rehearsal* 61, 137,
246 n. 12
Bunyan, John, *Pilgrim's Progress* 184, 188
Bürger's 'Lenore' 135
Burke, Edmund 11, 12
Burney family 14, 52
Burney, Charles 128, 130–1

Burney, Charles Jr 132, 247 n. 30
Burney, Frances 11–12, 13, 16, 32, 39, 44, 45,
   46, 52, 54, 63, 67, 70, 73, 78, 94, 100, 103,
   106, 122, 123, 127–37, 139, 140, 143, 144–5,
   146, 147, 151, 171, 197, 206, 213, 231 n. 12;
   232 nn. 14, 16; 233 n. 36; 234 n. 42; 238
   nn. 92, 104, 105; 240 n. 126; 243 n. 33; 244
   n. 47; 247 nn. 20, 22, 24, 27, 29, 31, 33, 34,
   35; 251 n. 17
   Camilla 17, 21, 58, 84, 128, 130, 136, 145,
      163, 211, 235 nn. 56, 59; 247 nn. 16, 22,
      34; 249 n. 63
   Cecilia 18, 85, 109, 129–30, 145, 158, 208,
      209, 211, 247 nn. 16, 19; 249 n. 63
   Evelina 15, 21, 60, 70, 85, 128, 129, 141, 145,
      148, 168, 197, 208, 236 n. 66; 239 n. 114;
      247 n. 16; 249 n. 63; 257 n. 8
   Memoirs of Dr Burney 247 n. 26
   The Wanderer 39, 40, 80, 81, 130, 136, 151,
      197, 247 nn. 23, 25; 257 n. 8
   The Witlings 128
   The Woman-Hater 48, 109, 128, 232 n. 25;
      247 n. 17
Burney, Sarah Harriet 52, 71, 106, 144, 234
   n. 36; 244 n. 48; 249 n. 63
Burns, Robert 33, 59, 148, 168, 184, 187, 214,
   254 n. 18
Burton, Antoinette 250 n. 80
Butler, Marilyn 148, 243 n. 34; 247 n. 16; 248
   n. 53; 250 n. 75
Byron, Anne Isabella Millbank, Lady 34, 38,
   46, 143, 226 n. 103; 232 n. 17; 248 n. 51
Byron, John, *Narrative* 55
Byron, George Gordon, Lord 13, 16, 19, 20,
   21, 22, 33, 34, 36–41, 59, 87, 136, 143, 148,
   161, 181, 215, 230 nn. 70, 75, 76, 77, 78;
   231 nn. 79–90

Cadell, Thomas 229 n. 43
Cameron, Kenneth Neill 243 n. 27
Campbell, Mary 234 n. 44
Campbell, Thomas 39, 148
Canning, George 206
Caroline, Queen 255 n. 26
Carroll, John 227 n. 11; 228 nn. 22, 23, 24,
   27, 29, 31, 32, 33, 34, 37; 246 n. 3
Catherine the Great 233 n. 36
Carter, Elizabeth 24, 26, 27, 29, 30, 31, 49,
   66, 69, 71, 72, 91, 100, 122, 136, 137–42,
   151, 228 n. 28; 233 n. 28; 234 n. 41, 42;
   237 n. 90; 243 n. 33; 247 n. 34; 248 nn. 40,
   41, 42, 46, 50
Cavendish, Margaret 97
Centlivre, Susanna 26, 39
Cervantes, Miguel de 206, *see also Don Quixote*

Chambers, Ross 224 n. 46
Chandler, Mary 60
Chapman, R. W. 226 n. 84; 232 n. 25
Chapone, Hester Mulso 27, 30, 57, 66, 71, 83
   Letters on the Improvement of the Mind 48, 233 n.
      31; 235 n. 53; 237 n. 88; 239 nn. 108, 110
Charlotte, Princess 181, 192, 255 n. 27; 256 n.
   70
Charlotte, Queen 67, 134
Charlton, Mary 230 n. 64
Chartier, Roger 8, 152, 177, 223 n. 35; 250 n.
   1; 253 nn. 78, 79; 254 nn. 4, 13; 255 n. 25
Chateaubriand, François René, 'Atala' 76
Chatelet, Madame de 141
Chatterton, Thomas 168, 190
Chaucer, Geoffrey 143, 190
Chauncy, William Henry 191
Chesterfield, Philip Dormer Stanhope, Earl
   of 69, 147, 238 n. 102; 240 n. 136
Chorley, Henry F. 230 ns 66, 69, 72
Churchill, Charles 135
Cibber, Colley 125
Cicero 132, 139
Clairmont, Claire 34, 92, 93, 98, 106, 243 n.
   25; 244 n. 47; 253 n. 75
Clare, John 184–5, 187, 188, 255 n. 35
Clark, Mrs Godfrey 228 n. 18; 251 nn. 11, 20
Clarke, Samuel 140
Clarke, Mrs 38
Clavering (Essex) reading club 161
Clayton, Mrs 139
Cleland, John, *Memoirs of a Woman of Pleasure*
   112, 245 n. 63
Clery, E. J. 196, 221 n. 6, 224 n. 49; 240 n.
   137; 257 n.4
Clifford, James L 242 n. 11
Climenson, Emily 237 n. 88; 248 nn. 45, 50
Cobbett, William 184
Cockburn, Catherine, *see* Trotter, Catherine
Coleridge, Hartley 69
Coleridge, Samuel Taylor 22, 34, 39, 99,
   143, 168, 179, 227 n. 6; 254 n. 15
Coleridge, Sara 34, 230 n. 70; 238 n. 103
Colley, Linda 224 n. 54
Collier, Jane, *The Art of Ingeniously Tormenting*
   130
Collier, Mary 187, 188, 256 n. 53
   The Woman's Labour 189
Collins, William 58, 102, 130
Colman, George, *Polly Honeycombe* 257 n. 14
Colvin, Christina 226 n. 85; 227 n. 104; 247
   n. 16; 248 n. 51
Combe, William, *The Devil upon Two Sticks in
   England* 165, 253 n. 61
Complete Servant Maid, The 186

conduct books 46–9
Congreve, William 40, 61, 190, 246 n. 12
 Love for Love 60
Constant, Benjamin, *Adolphe* 38
Cooper, James Fenimore 198
Cook, Captain James 133
Cooper, Maria Susannah, *The Exemplary Mother* 186, 187
Cooper, Richard 190
Copeland, Edward 221 n 1; 225 n. 74; 249 n. 63
Cowley, Abraham 5, 246 n. 11
Cowper, Judith 59–60
Cowper, William 58, 89, 143–4, 168
 'John Gilpin' 91
 The Task 91
Cox, Joseph Mason 244 n. 46
Crabbe, George 40, 144
Crébillon's *The Sofa* 38
Critical Review 255 n. 40
Crittenden, Walter M. 242 nn. 11, 19
Cruse, Amy 224 n. 51; 259 n. 59
Curll, Edmund 126
Cuthbertson, Catherine, *The Romance of the Pyrenees* 94, 154
Cutting-Gray, Joanne 247 n. 18

Dacier, Anne 69, 124
Dacre, Charlotte 16, 88, 89, 100, 105, 116–21, 242 n. 7; 245 n. 80
 The Confessions of the Nun of St Omer 117–18, 120, 245 n. 81
 The Libertine 119, 120, 245 n. 81
 The Passions 118–19, 240 n. 124; 245 n. 81
 Zofloya, or the Moor 120, 245 nn. 80, 81
Dallas, R. C 230 n. 75
Dällenbach, Lucien 10, 224 n. 48
Dalziel, Margaret 258 n. 33; 259 n. 41
Dante 116
d'Arblay, Alexandre 135–6
D'Arblay, Frances *see* Burney
Darlington circulating library 169
Darwin, Erasmus 68, 85
 Plan for the Conduct of Female Education 241 n. 145
Davidoff, Leonore and Hall, Catherine, *Family Fortunes* 34, 221 n. 7; 230 n. 67; 237 n. 80; 238 n. 91
Davidson, Cathy N. and Broner, E. M. 245 n. 70
Day, Thomas, *Sandford and Merton* 172, 253 n. 72
Defoe, Daniel
 Moll Flanders 124
 Robinson Crusoe 136, 186

Delany, Dr 172
Delany, Mary 61, 65, 66, 67, 139, 172, 173, 222 n. 20; 236 n, 69; 237 nn. 84, 90; 238 n. 95; 242 n. 9; 248 n. 44; 251 n. 17; 253 nn. 71, 73, 75, 77
DeMaria, Robert Jr 229 nn. 43, 49, 54
Derrida, Jacques 6, 223 n. 25
De Selincourt, Ernest 222 n. 19
Devonshire, Georgiana Cavendish, Duchess of 3, 222 n. 12
Diderot, Denis 3
Didion, Joan 226 n. 79
D'Israeli, Isaac 4, 5, 83–4
 Curiosities of Literature 222 n. 14, 223 nn. 21, 22; 241 n. 141; 252 n. 42
 A Dissertation on Anecdotes 223 n. 21
 Vaurien 78
Disraeli, Benjamin 137
Dixon, Sarah 141
Doddridge, Philip, *The Rise and Progress of Religion in the Soul* 195
Donoghue, Emma 13, 225 n. 64
Don Quixote 136, 208, 246 n. 12
Doody, Margaret Anne 204, 224 n. 51; 225 n. 72; 226 n. 86; 232 n. 17; 234 n. 40; 235 n. 52; 247 nn. 17, 22, 23, 34; 248 nn. 36, 53; 249 nn. 54, 55, 65, 67; 250 n. 80; 258 nn. 29, 31, 37; 259 n. 41
Doran, Dr 248 nn. 45, 50
Doyle, John A 248 n. 51
drama 60–4
Dryden, John 25, 58, 127, 189, 228 n. 21; 246 n. 11
 Fables 188
 Oedipus (with Lee) 61
DuBosq, Jacques 225 n. 69
Duncombe, John, *The Feminiad* 26, 228 n. 25
Dyce, Alexander 249 n. 64

Eaves, T. C. Duncan and Kimpel, Ben D. 226 n. 102; 228 nn. 22, 35, 38; 252 n. 63; 253 nn. 82, 83
Echlin, Lady 28
Edgeworth family 14
Edgeworth, Elizabeth 46
Edgeworth, Maria 20, 21, 41, 53, 54, 64, 65, 67, 74, 77, 96, 100, 128, 143, 144, 159, 206, 227 n. 105; 232 n. 17; 243 n. 33; 247 n. 16; 249 n. 63; 251 n. 18; 259 n. 55
 The Absentee 39, 154, 251 n. 8
 'Angelina; or, L'Amie Inconnue' 199, 258 n. 18
 Belinda 2, 38, 39, 45, 48, 60, 80–1, 94, 108, 151, 197, 211, 222 n. 10; 232 n. 13; 236 n. 63; 242 n. 16; 257 n. 9

Castle Rackrent 73, 169–70, 234 nn. 40, 42; 239 n. 115; 253 n. 64
Early Lessons 234 n. 41; 238 n. 94
'Emilie de Coulanges' 63, 236 n. 74
Ennui 39
'The Good French Governess' 226 n. 102; 234 n. 43
Harrington 60, 236 n. 66; 247 n. 16
Harry and Lucy Concluded 65, 237 n. 81
Helen 32, 51, 155, 159, 233 n. 32; 251 n. 18
Leonora 17, 72, 73, 98, 239 nn. 113, 115
Letters for Literary Ladies 2, 222 n. 11; 225 n. 67; 226 n. 92; 237 nn. 81, 89; 238 nn. 92, 100
'Mademoiselle Panache' 5, 18, 72, 165
The Modern Griselda 39
Moral Tales 222–3 n. 20; 226 n. 103
Ormond 20, 24, 227 nn. 103, 13
'The Orphans' 51
Parent's Assistant, The 233 n. 32; 238 n. 94
Patronage 39, 40, 63, 72, 137, 159, 236 n. 74; 239 n. 113; 247 n. 16
'The Rabbit' 238 n. 94
'Simple Susan' 238 n. 94
Tales of Fashionable Life 98, 209, 231–2 n. 12
'Vivian' 44, 45
Edgeworth, Richard Lovell 14, 41, 64
Edgeworth, Richard Lovell and Maria, *Practical Education* 231 n. 5; 234 n. 41; 238 n. 107; 241 n. 140
Edinburgh circulating libraries 164
Edinburgh Review 245 n. 60
Edwards, Paul 254 nn. 7, 8, 12
Edwards, Philip 234 nn. 45, 46; 235 n. 48
Egan, Pierce 226 n. 101
Ehrenpreis, Anne Henry 259 n. 51
Elias, A. C. Jr 222 n. 19
Ellis, Markman 221–2 n. 8; 225 nn. 60, 69, 71; 240 n. 136; 245 n. 58; 254 n. 6; 258 n. 18
Ellison, Monroe 222 n. 20
Elphinstone, Margaret Mercer 181
Elwin, Malcolm 226 n. 102; 231 n. 88; 232 n. 17; 248 n. 51
Emily Herbert see Inchbald, Elizabeth
Epictetus 72, 91, 138, 169
Epstein, Julia and Straub, Kristina 224 n. 43
Equiano, Olaudah 177, 254 n. 7
Erikson, Lee 250 n. 70
Eusebius 172
Evans, Sarah 162
Evils of Adultery and Prostitution 111, 245 n. 60

Fabricant, Carol 235 n. 48
Falconer, William 135

Farquhar, George 61, 246 n. 12
The Beaux-Stratagem 62
The Constant Couple 62
The Recruiting Officer 62, 236 n. 71
Sir Harry Wildair 62
Fatal Connexion, The 166
Fatal Obedience 2, 95, 110, 222 n. 10
Favret, Mary A. 230 nn. 63, 70
Fénélon's *Treatise on the Education of Daughters* 245 n. 67
Fenwick, Eliza 197–8, 257 n. 11
Secresy 155, 251 n. 12
Fergus, Jan 10, 186, 224 n. 49, 254 n. 21; 255 nn. 26, 43, 44; 265 n. 54
Ferguson, Moira 256 nn. 51, 53, 54, 56, 59
Ferrier, Susan 16, 34, 143, 248 n. 51
Destiny 48, 59, 232 n. 26; 235 n. 58
The Inheritance 24, 52, 227 n. 15; 230 n. 68
Marriage 8, 44, 48, 59, 62, 72, 73, 171, 223 n. 34; 231 n. 9; 235 nn. 59, 60; 236 n. 72; 239 nn. 113, 115
Ferris, Ina 8, 116, 170, 197, 222 n. 17, 223 n. 35; 245 n. 78; 253 n. 65; 257 nn. 2, 6
Fetterley, Judith 10, 224 n. 46
Fielding, Henry 21, 23–4, 94, 197, 199
Amelia 23, 61, 62, 131, 236 n. 69
Joseph Andrews 23, 98, 140, 227 nn. 8, 9
Shamela 23, 227 nn. 8, 9
Tom Jones 13, 23, 24, 61, 62, 85, 110, 140, 167, 185, 211, 225 n. 62; 227 n. 9; 236 n. 69
Fielding, Sarah 4, 26, 54, 97, 140
The Adventures of David Simple 93, 185, 222 n. 19
The Governess 7, 221 n. 5
Finch, Anne, Countess of Winchilsea 35
Finch, Lady Isabella 153, 158
fire 169
Fish, Audrey A. 230 n. 70
Fletcher, John, *The Captain* 245 n. 77
Flint, Kate 8, 16, 221 n. 3; 223 n. 35; 226 n. 77; 227 n. 105
Fontenelle's *Entretiens sur la pluralité des mondes* 65
Fordyce, James 25, 43, 46, 48, 49, 55, 83, 199
Sermons to Young Women 46, 110, 227 n. 17; 231 n. 6; 233 n. 33; 234 n. 47; 240 n. 137; 245 n. 60
Foucault, Michel 9, 223 n. 39
Fox's *Book of Martyrs* 188
Franklin, Caroline 230 n. 76; 245 n. 69
Fraser, Flora 255 n. 26
Freemantle, Bridget 190, 191
French 71–2, 74–7, 91
Freud, Sigmund 16

Freund, Elizabeth 10, 224 n. 46
Froissart, Jean 12

Gallagher, Catherine 247 n. 21
Galloway, W. F. 240 n. 138
Galt, John 214
Garber, Marjorie 224 n. 42
Gard, Roger 250 n. 76
Gates, Henry Louis Jr 254 nn. 10, 11
Gaudentio di Lucca 5, 222–3 n. 20
Gay, John 127, 190, 246 n. 11
Genlis, Stéphanie de 71, 135, 183
Alphonsine 146
Gentleman's Magazine 12, 187, 255 n. 49; 256 n. 51
German 71, 72–7, 91
Gessner, Johann 135
The Death of Abel 135, 188
Gibbon, Edward 5, 16, 32, 52, 165, 223 n. 21
Gilbert, Sandra and Gubar, Susan, *The Madwoman in the Attic* 22, 148, 227 n. 1; 250 n. 76; 259 n. 54
Gillray, James 74
Gisborne, Thomas 48, 83, 240 nn. 137, 138
An Enquiry into the Duties of the Female Sex 232 n. 27
Gittings, Robert and Manton, Jo 242 nn. 9, 12
Glanville, Lady 107
Glasse, Hannah 32, 39
Gloucester, Duchess of 180
Godwin, William 19, 25, 43, 78, 79, 80–2, 149, 199, 222 n. 18
Caleb Williams 39, 181
Italian Letters 227 n. 17
'Of History and Romance' 257 nn. 1, 3; 258 n. 16
Goethe, Johann Wolfgang von 8, 118
Sorrows of Young Werther 5, 73–4, 76, 111, 135, 146, 167, 169, 190, 242 n. 7
Goldsmith, Oliver 83, 135, 149, 188
The Citizen of the World 240 n. 139
The Vicar of Wakefield 24, 39, 52, 136, 137, 188, 227 n. 11
Gonda, Caroline 110, 221 n. 7; 224 n. 41; 233 n. 28; 244 n. 57; 251 n. 18
Gould, Robert 246 n. 7
Grant, Anne 29, 34, 73, 81, 87, 92, 143, 162, 163, 197, 222 n. 9; 230 n. 69
Letters from the Mountains 228 nn. 18, 39, 41; 233 n. 31; 239 n. 115; 240 n. 133; 241 n. 1; 252 n. 29
Grant, J. P. 222 n. 9; 229 n. 62; 241 n. 1; 242 nn. 9, 10; 248 n. 51; 252 n. 59; 257 n. 11
Graves, Richard 203, 258 n. 34

Eugenius, or Anecdotes of the Golden Vale 94
Gray, Mrs Edwin 225 n. 65
Gray, Faith 14
Gray, Margaret 14
Gray, Thomas 102, 188
Greek 69–71, 94
Green, Katharine Sobba 228 n. 39; 232 n. 20
Green, Sarah 8, 44, 46, 50, 55, 60, 61, 62, 83, 170, 213
Mental Improvement for a Young Lady 96, 213, 231 n. 10; 232 n. 19; 233 nn. 29, 34; 234 n. 46; 236 n. 65, 67; 239 n. 109; 240 n. 137; 247 n. 13; 253 n. 65
Romance Readers and Romance Writers 213
Scotch Novel Reading 8, 198, 213–18
Greene, Richard 190, 254 n. 23; 255 nn. 26, 49; 256 nn. 53, 54, 58, 62, 63, 64, 67; 258 nn. 30, 35
Greer, Germaine 230 n. 72
Gregory, John 43, 44, 45, 46, 47, 48, 49, 50, 83
Father's Legacy to his Daughters 46, 47, 74, 89, 210–11, 222 n. 17; 231 nn. 6, 10; 232 nn. 13, 22, 24, 25; 233 n. 30; 240 n. 137; 242 n. 6; 259 n. 53
Greville, Frances 190
Grey, J. David 232 n. 25; 249 n. 63
Grey, Lady Jane 51, 124
Grierson, Constantia Crawley 124
Griffith, Elizabeth 11, 166
The Delicate Distress 166
Griffith, Elizabeth and Richard, *A Series of Genuine Letters between Henry and Frances* 52, 222 n. 13; 224 n. 56; 225 n. 76; 252 n. 53
Griffiths, John 162
Gronniosaw, James Albert Ukawsaw 178, 254 n. 11
Grove, Charlotte 24, 160, 163, 228 n. 18
Grove, Harriet 98–9, 160, 163, 228 n. 18
Grundy, Isobel 30, 226 n. 79; 229 n. 52
Guardian, The 129
Guicciardini, Francesco 103
Guiccioli, Teresa 34, 38
Gunning, Elizabeth, *The Orphans of Snowdon* 242 n. 7
Guthrie's *General History of England* 233 n. 36

Halifax Library 161
Hall, Lesley 223 n. 39, 224 n. 45
Halsband, Robert 222 n. 16; 229 n. 42; 235 n. 49; 237 n. 84; 238 n. 104; 241 n. 1; 242 n. 9; 251 n. 7
Hamilton, Elizabeth 49, 53, 54, 77, 83, 233 n. 28; 234 n. 42; 240 nn. 124, 127
The Cottagers of Glenburnie 7, 51, 162, 183,

223 n. 30; 233 n. 32
Letters on the Elementary Principles of Education
80, 234 n. 41; 240 nn. 132, 137
Memoirs of Modern Philosophers 44, 78, 79, 81,
98–9, 149–50, 157–8, 171–2, 180, 231 n. 12
Translation of the Letters of a Hindoo Rajah 55,
72, 234 nn. 41, 44; 240 n. 138
Hamilton, Lady Mary, *Munster Village* 159
Hamilton, Mary 172
Hands, Elizabeth 187, 188, 256 n. 52
Hare, Augustus J. C. 232 n. 17; 247 n. 16; 259
n. 55
Harris, Jocelyn 148, 248–9 n. 53; 249 nn. 56,
57, 64, 69; 250 nn. 73, 79
Harrison, James 12
Hartley House, Calcutta 236 n. 75
Hawkesworth, John 31, 234 n. 46
Hawkins, Desmond 228 n. 18; 243 n. 24; 251
n. 22
Hawkins, Sir John, *Life of Samuel Johnson* 225
n. 66; 229 nn. 44, 56
Hawkins, Laetitia-Matilda 5, 42, 59, 144, 249
n. 63
   The Countess and Gertrude 15, 33, 44, 46, 49,
51, 55, 56, 66, 73, 83, 158, 171, 222 n. 19;
225 nn. 62, 70; 227 n. 14; 231 n. 9; 232 n.
12, 27; 233 n. 32; 234 n. 45; 235 n. 59; 238
nn. 90, 98, 100, 102; 239 n. 114; 241 n.
139; 252 n. 42
   Rosanne 44, 222 n. 17, 18; 231 nn. 4, 9; 244
n. 50; 253 n. 65
Hayden, Ruth 238 n. 95
Hayes, Philippa 180, 181
Hayley, William
   Marcella 172
   The Triumphs of Temper 73, 128, 239 n. 114;
247 n. 15
Hayman, Ann 181
Hays, Mary 32, 74, 87, 99, 241 n. 2
   Emma Courtney 5, 13, 53, 66, 75, 155, 156,
222 n. 19; 225 n. 62; 234 n. 41; 237 n. 90;
251 n. 11; 255 n. 29
   Female Biography 51, 54, 151
   Letters and Essays 239 nn. 115, 118
   The Victim of Prejudice 66, 114, 237 n. 90
Haywood, Eliza 23, 26, 65, 140
   The History of Jemmy and Jenny Jessamy 242
n. 7
   The Invisible Spy 186, 237 n. 84
Hegel, Georg Wilhelm Friedrich 67
Helme, Elizabeth
   St Margaret's Cave 92
   *Travels from the Cape of Good-Hope into the
Interior Parts of Africa* 72
Helvétius, Claude Arien 77

Hemans, Felicia 33, 34, 35, 40, 106, 230 nn.
66, 69, 72
Hemlow, Joyce 131, 232 nn. 14, 19, 22, 25;
233 n. 36; 247 n. 28
Henson, Eithne 229 n. 46
Hereford circulating library 169
Hertford, Countess of 65, 92, 172, 251 n. 17;
253 n. 71
Hertfordshire, lack of evidence for circulating
libraries 163
Hervey, James, 'Meditations among the
Tombs' 88
Hett, Frances Pagett 222 n. 19; 225 n. 59; 243
n. 32; 251 n. 11; 254 n. 19; 255 n. 45
Highmore, Susanna 27, 28
Hilbish, Florence 239 n. 114
Hill, Bridget 50, 233 n. 29
Hill, Dr 32
Hill, George Birkbeck 229 n. 57
Hirsch, Pam 240 n. 130
history 49–55
Hitchener, Elizabeth 98
Hobbes, Thomas 78
Hobhouse, John Cam 37
   Miscellany 40
Hofkosh, Sonia 231 n. 82
Hogg, James 179, 214
Hogg, Thomas Jefferson 93
Holcroft, Thomas 184, 258 n. 15
Holroyd, Maria Josepha 18, 43, 73, 87, 225
n. 76; 226 n. 90; 251 n. 20
Holyhead circulating library 163
Homans, Margaret 113, 230 n. 74; 245 nn.
71, 73, 75
Homer 71, 102, 178
   Odyssey 139, 190
Honan, Park 249 n. 59; 250 n. 85
Honoria, *The Female Mentor* 241 n. 139
Hooker, Richard 138
Hooke's Roman History 233 n. 29
Horace 70, 102, 103, 231 n. 83; 246 n. 11
Hortensia; or, the Distressed Wife 7, 60, 67, 236
n. 66; 238 n. 94
Horwitz, Barbara 232 n. 25
Howard, Jacqueline 259 n. 47
Howell, Mrs 230 n. 64
Hume, David 5, 49, 54, 77, 78, 171, 172, 223
n. 21; 233 n. 29; 234 n. 43
Hunt, Leigh 168, 245 n. 62
Hunter, J. Paul 170–1, 221 n. 4, 224 n. 53;
225 n. 60; 231 n. 12; 234 n. 44; 235 n. 52;
253 n. 68
Hutcheon, Linda 213, 259 n. 56
Hutcheson's *Essay on the Passions* 247 n. 12
Hutchinson, Lucy 52

Illustrious Chambermaid, The 242 n. 7
Inchbald, Elizabeth 197
  Emily Herbert 242 n. 7
  Lovers' Vows 72
  Nature and Art 15, 87, 197, 225 n. 70
  A Simple Story 114, 157, 158–9, 197, 251 n. 16
informative reading 49
Innerpeffray library 160
Innocent Adultery, The 166
Irigaray, Luce 9, 223 n. 37
Irwin, Raymond 245 n. 62; 253 n. 56; 255 n. 45
Iser, Wolfgang 10, 17, 226 n. 81

Jacson, Maria 67, 237 n. 83
Jackson, Jessamyn 207, 257 n. 10; 258 n. 17; 259 n. 49
Jackson, Rebecca 178, 254 n. 10
Janes, Regina M 240 n. 131
Jauss, Hans Robert 101
Jennens, Susanna 190, 191
Jenner, Charles, *The Placid Man* 241 n. 143
Johnson, Claudia 32, 151, 229 n. 60; 240 nn. 123, 135; 248 nn. 51, 53; 249 nn. 54, 56, 60, 69; 250 nn. 79, 81, 83, 84, 85, 87; 259 n. 54
Johnson, R. Brimley 248 n. 39; 249 n. 65
Johnson, Samuel 1, 6, 14, 19, 21, 24, 29–33, 39, 42, 70, 93, 132, 136, 137, 143, 179, 183, 186, 197, 199, 202, 204, 205, 206, 221 n. 1; 229 n. 43; 249 n. 56
  Adventurer 229 nn. 50, 58, 59
  Dictionary 30
  The Idler 183, 186, 229 n. 59; 255 nn. 32, 46
  Life of Savage 53
  Lives of the Poets 31–2, 188
  Rambler 6, 30, 42, 229 nn. 51, 55; 231 n. 1; 257 n. 2; 258 n. 18
  Rasselas 32, 92, 208, 229 n. 59
Jones, Ann H. 223 n. 32; 246 n. 87
Jones, Mary 141
Jones, Vivien 232 nn. 21, 23; 245 n. 67; 258 n. 21
Jones, Sir William 13
Jonson, Ben 61
Josephus 188
Juvenal 13

Kaims, Henry Home, Lord, *Elements of Criticism* 49, 92
Kaufman, Paul 162, 163, 168, 251 n. 23; 252 nn. 24, 25, 28, 30, 33, 34, 36, 46, 48, 49; 253 nn. 56, 57, 58; 255 n. 42
Keats, John 19, 36, 37, 168, 230 n. 74
Keir, Susan, *Interesting Memoirs* 7, 62, 63, 236

  nn. 72, 75
Keith of Ravelstone, Mrs 22
Kelly, Gary 221 n. 2; 246 n. 83; 249 n. 68; 250 n. 77; 257 nn. 3, 12; 259 nn. 45, 46
Kelly, Hugh, *Memoirs of a Magdalen* 110
Kelly, Isabella 100, 230 n. 64
  The Abbey of St Asaph 94
Kelsall, Malcolm 222 n. 19
Kett, Henry, *Emily* 15, 46, 49, 51, 55, 57, 58, 63, 65, 66, 67, 112, 165, 233 nn. 31, 33, 34, 35; 234 n. 45; 235 nn. 53, 58; 236 n. 77; 237 n. 90; 253 n. 69; 259 n. 1
Keymer, Tom 227 n. 16; 228 nn. 20, 23, 25, 26, 30, 32, 35, 36
Kibworth (Leics) reading club 161
Kiely, Robert 259 nn. 51, 52
Kilgour, Maggie 221 n. 8, 222 n. 18; 226 n. 81; 242 n. 17; 243 nn. 31, 36, 37; 246 n. 82; 255 n. 28
King, Sophia 117
  Waldorf 43, 78, 79
Kirkham, Margaret 148, 250 n. 76
Klancher, Jon P. 226 n. 81
Knights, Elspeth 228 n. 24
Knox, Vicesimus 52, 55, 71, 77, 78, 83, 86, 153
  Essays, Moral and Literary 232 n. 13; 233 n. 35; 234 n. 46; 238 n. 107; 240 nn. 124, 139; 241 n. 151
Kotzebue, August von 72, 242 n. 7
Kowaleski-Wallace, Elizabeth 244 n. 45; 245 nn. 66, 74
Kristeva, Julia 9, 113, 223 n. 37

Lacan, Jacques 114
Lackington, James 185, 255 n. 40
Laclos, Choderlos de, *Les liaisons dangereuses* 135
Ladies of Llangollen 13, 97, 159, 251 n. 20
Lady's Magazine 2, 5, 6, 7, 12, 14, 18, 19, 24, 29, 43, 44, 46, 48, 50, 53, 55, 59, 60, 65, 66, 69, 70–1, 80, 96–7, 100, 108, 113, 128, 137, 144, 152–3, 155, 159–60, 161, 162, 166, 168, 173, 181, 196, 197, 199, 221 n. 2; 222 n. 10; 222 n. 17; 223 nn. 22, 24, 30, 31; 225 nn. 67, 77; 226 n. 84; 227 n. 12; 228 n. 40; 231 nn. 5, 7, 8, 9; 232 nn. 13, 16, 27; 233 nn. 29, 30, 31, 35; 234 nn. 37, 42, 44; p. 235 nn. 53, 57, 59; 236 nn. 64, 67, 68; 237 nn. 84, 85, 88; 238 n. 102; 240 nn. 131, 137; 241 n. 143; 242 nn. 13, 19; 243 n. 20; 244 nn. 40, 43, 50, 55; 245 n. 68; 247 n. 14; 248 n. 37; 249 n. 63; 251 nn. 3, 9, 10, 13; 252 nn. 31, 49, 52; 253 n. 60; 254 nn. 18, 24; 256 n. 54; 257 n. 7; 258 nn. 21, 22

Lady's Monthly Museum 79, 84, 108, 164, 227 n. 12; 241 n. 143; 244 n. 55

Lamb, Lady Caroline 38, 40, 231 n. 84
  Glenarvon 38, 84, 156, 241 n. 145

Lamb, Charles 19, 170
  'Detached Thoughts on Books and Reading' 253 n. 67
  'Mackery End, in Hertfordshire' 244 n. 51
  Rosamund Gray 184, 255 n. 33

Lamb, Charles and Mary, 226 n. 96
  Mrs Leicester's School 45, 107–8, 114, 115, 244 n. 52
  Tales from Shakespeare 237 n. 78

Lamb, Mary 62

Landry, Donna 59, 235 n. 61; 236 nn. 62, 69; 256 nn. 51, 52, 53, 54, 55, 57, 64, 66

Lane, William 33

Langbauer, Laurie 258 n. 40; 259 nn. 42, 44

Larpent, Anna 7, 12, 13, 82, 163, 169, 223 n. 28

Latin 64, 69–71, 188

Lawrence, James, *The Empire of the Nairs* 99

Leapor, Mary 26, 61, 181, 187, 188, 190–2, 254 n. 23; 255 nn. 26, 49; 265 nn. 53, 54, 62, 63, 64, 67
  Crumble-Hall 60, 191
  Poems on Several Occasions 191, 256 n. 58

Leavis, Q. D. 230 n. 67; 254 n. 15

Lee, Nathaniel
  Oedipus (with Dryden) 61
  Theodosius 61

Lee, Sophia, *The Recess* 54

Leeds Library Society 160

Lefanu, Alicia 42, 222 n. 19; 231 nn. 1, 2, 3; 253 n. 70

LeFanu, William 231 n. 3

L'Enclos, Ninon de 106

Leicester circulating library 169

Lennox, Caroline 52

Lennox, Charlotte 8, 23, 26, 97, 144, 199, 207, 244 n. 56; 249 n. 63
  Euphemia 108 9, 113, 117, 171, 201, 203, 247 n. 14; 258 n. 24
  The Female Quixote 8, 30, 113, 144, 146, 197, 198, 199, 201–6, 208, 209, 210, 212, 215, 216, 217, 218; 251 n. 17; 258 nn. 18, 28, 30, 32, 33, 39, 40, 41; 259 n. 42
  Henrietta 23, 110, 140, 169, 227 n. 10; 245 n. 59
  The Lady's Museum 231 n. 8
  Life of Harriot Stuart 46, 110, 113, 158, 201, 202–3, 258 n. 24
  Poems on Several Occasions 201

Le Sage, Alain René, *Gil Blas* 183

L'Estrange, A. G. 225 n. 61; 227 n. 5; 248 n. 51

Levin, Kate 201, 205, 244 n. 56; 258 n. 27

Lew, Joseph 235 n. 52

Lewis, Mary 162

Lewis, Matthew, *The Monk* 45, 104, 111, 117, 211, 232 n. 15

Lewis, Paul 259 n. 45

Lewis, Theresa 223 n. 23; 231 n. 12; 254 nn. 3, 15

libraries, circulating 162–9, 184

libraries, private 152–60

libraries, public 160–2

Lillo, George, *The London Merchant* 60

Linnaeus (Carl von Linné) 68

Lister, Anne 13, 73, 82, 105, 161, 221 n. 5; 225 n. 64; 251 n. 20

literacy rates 11–12

Little, Janet 187, 256 n. 49

Liverpool libraries 160, 161

Livy 139

Llanover, Lady 222 n. 20; 236 n. 69; 237 nn. 84, 90; 242 n. 9; 248 n. 44; 253 nn. 71, 73, 75, 77

Lloyd, Mrs 162

Locke, John 25, 77, 98, 140, 143, 190

Lockhart, John Gibson 227 n. 4

London circulating libraries 162, 163

London Library Society 160

London Magazine 257 n. 7

Longinus 139

Lonsdale, Roger 227 n. 3; 248 n. 37; 256 nn. 49, 50, 52, 53

Looser, Devoney 249 n. 53; 250 n. 80

Lovell, Ernest J. 230 nn. 75, 76, 77

Lowther, Lady 35

Luard, C. G. 225 n. 62

Lucan 139

Lucas, Charles, *The Infernal Quixote* 79

Lucy, George 180

Lumb, Anne Milnes 163, 252 n. 41

Macartney, Lord, *Journal of the Embassy to China* 55, 56–7

Macaulay, Catherine 5, 9, 19, 24, 31, 32, 44, 64, 97, 142, 233 n. 29
  Letters on Education 18, 223 n. 38, 227 n. 10; 228 n. 18; 231 n. 11

Macaulay, Thomas Babbington 168

Macauley, Elizabeth 62

MacCarthy, B. G. 227 n. 104

MacDonald, Susan Peck 245 n. 70

Mackenzie, Anna Maria 230 n. 64

Mackenzie, Henry 258 n. 18
  Julia de Roubigné 95, 184, 255 n. 33

Mackenzie, Henry (*cont.*)
The Man of Feeling 82, 106, 166, 186, 197, 240 n. 136
Macready, William Charles 257 n. 7
Maintenon, Madame de 248 n. 50
Malina, Debra 258 n. 30
Mandeville, Bernard de 3, 179, 192, 193
The Fable of the Bees 254 n. 16
Mangin, Edward, *Piozziana* 243 n. 33
Manguel, Alberto 173, 253 nn. 79, 81
Manley, Delarivier 23, 111–12, 122, 245 n. 61; 246 n. 1
Marcet, Jane 237 n. 83
Conversations on Political Economy 255 n. 40
Marchand, Leslie A 230 nn. 70, 76; 231 nn. 79, 83, 84, 85, 89, 90
Marie Antoinette 1
Marks, Elaine and de Courtivron, Isabelle 223, n. 37
Marmontel 94
Marrs, Edwin J. 226 n. 95
Marshall, David 258 n. 28
Marshall, James 168
Martin, Philip and Jarvis, Robin 226 n. 101
Masters, Mary 32, 141
Maturin, Charles Robert
The Milesian Chief 51, 94, 233 n. 32; 242 n. 16
The Wild Irish Boy 72, 79, 239 n. 113; 255 n. 33
Women 58, 63, 94, 235 n. 58; 236 n. 74; 242 n. 16
Mavor, Elizabeth 251 n. 20
Maxwell, Caroline 62
McGann, Jerome 230 n. 70
McKee, John B. 226 n. 80
Medici, Lorenzo di 119
Medwin, Thomas 38, 230 n. 77; 231 nn. 80, 84
Meeke, Mary 230 n. 64
Mell, Donald C. 236 n. 62
Mellor, Anne K. 33, 225 n. 75; 229 nn. 61, 62; 230 nn. 63, 70; 231 n. 82; 250 n. 86
Melman, Billie 234–5 n. 47; 235 n. 49
Melmoth, Courtney, *see* Pratt, Samuel Jackson
Memoirs of the Count Grammont 37
Messenger, Ann 236 n. 63
Michasiw, Kim Ian 245 n. 80; 246 n. 86
Middleton divorce 187
Milne, Christian 187, 256 n. 50
Mills, Sara 8, 223 n. 36; 234–5, n. 47
Milton, John 20, 58, 59, 68, 89, 101, 102, 127, 136, 143, 155, 172, 177, 178, 181, 183, 188, 189, 206, 211, 246 nn. 9, 11; 247 n. 34
Comus 116

Paradise Lost 5, 15, 25, 186, 189, 228 n. 21; 238 n. 101
Minerva Press 10, 16, 33, 162
Minifie, Margaret and Susannah, *The Histories of Lady Frances S- and Lady Caroline S-* 235 n. 55; 238 n. 102
mise-en-abyme 10
Mistakes of the Heart 166
Mitford, Mary Russell 12–13, 22, 143, 225 n. 61; 227 n. 5; 248 n. 51
Moler, Kenneth L 248 n. 53; 249 nn. 65, 67; 250 n. 79
Montaigne, Michel de 93
Montagu, Duke of 177
Montagu, Elizabeth 29, 31, 32, 56, 63, 96, 135, 136, 138, 139, 140, 141, 142, 176, 228 n. 41; 233 n. 31; 235 nn. 49, 50, 51; 237 n. 88; 239 n. 108; 240 n. 136; 248 nn. 40, 41, 42, 45, 46, 47, 50; 254 n. 2
Montagu, Mary Wortley 5, 29, 56, 65, 70, 92, 142, 153, 158, 183, 222 n. 16; 229 n. 42
Monthly Mirror 245 n. 60
Monthly Review 259 n. 67
Montpensier, Mademoiselle de 248 n. 50
Moore, John
Mordaunt 3
Zeluco 20
Moore, Thomas 39, 40, 108, 172, 179
Life of Byron 33, 148
More, Hannah 3, 12, 17, 24, 29, 39, 43, 44, 48, 50, 52, 55, 57, 63, 66, 70, 71, 72, 73, 77, 79, 83, 84, 96, 107, 137, 141, 144, 151, 170, 173–4, 176, 179, 180, 181, 183, 185, 189–90, 192–5, 206, 222 n. 13; 223 n. 30; 225 n. 60; 226 n. 84; 227 n. 11; 228 n. 41; 249 n. 63; 255 n. 34; 256 n. 58
Cheap Repository Tracts 192, 193
Coelebs in Search of a Wife 15, 44, 58, 67, 69, 88–92, 117, 137, 143–4, 146, 149, 150, 162, 173, 174, 196, 209, 223 n. 30; 225 n. 72; 231 n. 9; 232 n. 16; 233 n. 29; 234 n. 38; 235 nn. 54, 58; 238 nn. 94, 104, 107; 239 n. 113; 248 n. 37; 249 n. 58; 250 n. 85
Hints towards Forming the Character of a Young Princess 192; 233 nn. 29, 34; 234 n. 46; 235 n. 48; 236 n. 76; 241 n. 142
Moriana 241 n. 142
'Mr Fantom' 240 n. 128
The Search after Happiness 248 n. 37
Stories for the Middle Ranks 192, 240 n. 128; 253 n. 67; 255 n. 41; 256 nn. 71, 72; 257 n. 78
Strictures on the Modern System of Female Education 232 nn. 16, 20; 232 n. 20; 233 nn. 29, 31; 234 n. 38; 239 nn. 111, 113, 115;

240 nn. 123, 127, 137; 241 n. 142
'The Sunday School' 193
'The Two Wealthy Farmers' 185–6, 195, 256 n. 81
Thoughts on the Importance of the Manners of the Great 192
Village Politics 194
Morgan, Sydney Owenson 40, 144, 145, 207, 234 n. 44; 249 n. 63
Ida of Athens 259 n. 48
Lady Morgan's Memoirs 239 n. 120
The Life and Times of Salvator Rosa 54
The Missionary 99, 137, 243 n. 29; 259 n. 48
The Novice of St Dominick 98, 259 n. 48
O'Donnel 209
The Princess, or the Beguine 54
St Clair; or, the Heiress of Desmond 75, 239 n. 118; 241 n. 152; 259 n. 48
The Wild Irish Girl 75–7, 239 n. 121; 259 n. 48
Moritz, Carl Philip 183, 255 n. 31
Morley, Edith J. 234 n. 36; 244 n. 48
Mudge, Bradford Keyes 230 n. 70; 235 n. 53; 238 n. 103
Munby, A. N. L. 251 n. 5, 254 n. 17
Murdoch, John, *Tears of Sensibility* 242 n. 7
Murray, Hugh 240 n. 138
Murray, John 36, 40
Musgrave, Agnes 230 n. 64
Myers, Mitzi 257 n. 77
Myers, Sylvia Harcstark 229 n. 52; 247 n. 32

Neckar, Madame, *see* Staël, Germaine de
Nettleton, George H. 252 n. 51
Newton, Sir Isaac 4, 165
Newton, Richard 2, 221 n. 5
Newton Abbot circulating library 169
North, Christopher, *Noctes Ambrosianae* 164, 179, 252 n. 47; 254 n. 15
Norton, Rictor 224 n. 43
Novelist's Magazine 12
novels 82–6, 196–218
Nussbaum, Felicity 235 n. 48; 246 n. 2

Oedipus 245 n. 77
Oliver, Mrs 29
Opie, Amelia 221 n. 6; 251 n. 14
Adeline Mowbray 81–2, 99, 114, 149–50, 240 n. 134
The Father and Daughter 197, 257 n. 9
Madeline 156
Orr, Clarissa Campbell 234 n. 42
Osborne, Thomas 29
Otway, Thomas 40, 190
The Orphan 60, 94
Venice Preserv'd 62

Ovid 71, 103, 178, 231 n. 83
Owenson, Sydney, *see* Morgan, Sydney Owenson
Oxford, Lady 38

Paine, Thomas 7, 12, 78, 99, 130, 193
The Rights of Man 181
Park, Mungo 183
Parker, Roszika 231 n. 4
Parsons, Eliza 120, 128, 230 n. 64
The Errors of Education 51, 222 n. 17; 233 n. 32; 241 n. 139
The Castle of Wolfenbach 154, 251 n. 9
The History of Miss Meredith 247 n. 16
The Mysterious Warning 154, 251 n. 9
Partington, Wilfred 239 n. 114; 244 n. 49
Pascoe, Judith 238 nn. 95, 100
Peacock, Thomas Love 93
Nightmare Abbey 19, 226 n. 93
Pearson, Jacqueline 244 nn. 46, 55; 257 n. 1
Pedder, Mrs 182, 183
Pennington, Montagu 139, 140, 141, 142, 228 n. 28; 234 nn. 41, 42; 237 n. 90; 243 n. 33; 248 nn. 40, 41, 42
Pennington, Lady Sarah 15, 45, 50, 58, 83, *An Unfortunate Mother's Advice to her Absent Daughters* 232 n. 16; 233 n. 29; 235 n. 57; 240 n. 137
Penzance women's reading group 161
Pepys, Samuel 153, 251 n. 4
Pepys, Sir William Weller 3, 180
Perry, Ruth 251 n. 19
Petrarch, Francesco 102, 119
Petronius 103
Philips, Ambrose, *The Distrest Mother* 61, 246 n. 12
Philips, Katherine 124, 142, 246 n. 11
Phillips, Patricia 237 nn. 84, 86
Phillips, Teresia Constantia 7, 123, 138, 142, 223 n. 27
philosophy and metaphysics 77–82
Pickwick Papers 137
Pilkington, Laetitia 5, 7, 112, 122–7, 142, 151, 203–4, 222 n. 19, 223 n. 27
Memoirs 246 nn. 3, 4, 5, 6, 8, 9, 10, 11, 12; 247 n. 12; 258 n. 34
Pinch, Adela 250 n. 72
Pinchbeck, Ivy 255 n. 41
Pindar 139
Pindar, Peter 87
Piozzi, Hester, *see* Thrale, Hester
Pitt, William 206
Plumptre, Anne 181
Plutarch 5, 52, 54, 139, 171, 233–4 n. 36

poetry 57–64, 101–2
Polidori, John, *The Vampyre* 198
Polite Lady, The 233 n. 29
Polwhele, Richard, *The Unsex'd Females* 68, 238 nn. 99, 101
Ponsonby, Sarah 13, *see also* Ladies of Llangollen
Pope, Alexander 18, 40, 58, 59–60, 62, 84, 127, 130, 135, 136, 137, 139, 143, 155, 177, 178, 188, 189, 190, 191, 206, 209, 211, 236 n. 63; 246 n. 11; 247 n. 34; 249 n. 56
  'On the Art of Sinking in Poetry' 236 n. 63
  'Eloisa to Abelard' 134, 189
  'Epistle to a Lady' 236 n. 63; 241 n. 141
  'Epistle to Dr Arbuthnot' 235 n. 62
  Essay on Criticism 259 n. 50
  Essay on Man 58
  The Rape of the Lock 60, 147, 236 n. 63
Porter, Anna Maria 258 n. 19
Porter, Jane, *Thaddeus of Warsaw* 63, 71, 84, 239 n. 109
Porter, Roy 9, 223 nn. 39, 40, 224 nn. 45, 51, 52, 53
Pratt, Samuel Jackson 167
  Family Secrets 164–5, 167, 245 n. 62; 252 n. 49
  Shenstone-Green 58, 235 n. 56
Prince, Mary 178, 254 n. 10
Prior, Matthew 127, 189, 211, 246 n. 11

Quintilian 139

Racine, Jean 130
Ramsay, Alan 180, 214, 246 n. 11
Radcliffe, Ann 16, 21, 59, 62, 88, 100–5, 106, 117, 119, 120, 121, 127, 141, 144, 146, 180, 207, 211–12, 243 nn. 34, 38, 38, 40; 249 n. 63
  The Italian 101, 103, 104, 207, 243 n. 37
  The Mysteries of Udolpho 100, 101, 102, 102, 104–5, 163, 207, 211, 235 n. 59; 243 n. 37; 244 n. 41
  The Romance of the Forest 59, 66, 100, 101, 102, 103, 104, 207, 235 n. 58; 236 n. 72; 238 n. 90; 243 n. 39
  A Sicilian Romance 101, 102, 141, 207, 243 n. 37
Radcliffe, Mary Anne, *The Female Advocate* 224 n. 44
Raven, James 8, 11, 12, 181, 184, 223 nn. 28, 35; 224 nn. 41, 49, 51, 52, 55, 57; 225 nn. 58, 60; 227 n. 2; 250 n. 2; 251 nn. 11, 21, 23; 252 nn. 37, 43; 253 nn. 59, 74; 254 nn. 14; 24; 255 nn. 34

Ray, William 223 n. 24; 239 n. 117
Raynal, Abbé 138
Raysor, Thomas Middleton 227 n. 6
Rees, Joan 242 n. 9
Reeve, Clara, *The Progress of Romance* 15, 200, 201, 232 n. 19; 240 n. 138; 252 n. 42; 257 n. 14; 258 nn. 15, 22, 25
Rendall, Jane 234 n. 42
Repository, The 233 n. 29
Repton, Humphrey 172, 179, 254 n. 15
Resolute Lady; or, the Fortunate Footman, The 242 n. 7
Reward of Constancy, The 166
Reynolds, Sir Joshua 5
Ricardo, David 159
Richardson, Alan 221 n. 4; 224 n. 52; 225 n. 60; 229 n. 61
Richardson, Charlotte 188
Richardson, Samuel 21, 24–29, 43, 123, 125, 137, 140, 143, 145, 148, 197, 199, 204, 205, 213, 227 n. 11; 228 n. 24
  Clarissa 17, 27–9, 85, 107, 110, 136, 148, 167, 169, 172, 175, 181, 186, 187, 197, 199, 204, 227 n. 16; 228 nn. 20, 21, 24, 25, 26, 30, 32, 35, 36
  Pamela 25, 61, 92, 127, 167, 185, 236 n. 69; 242 nn. 7, 10; 246 n. 12
  Sir Charles Grandison 20, 26–7, 59, 61, 71, 83, 85, 98, 145, 149, 152, 163, 174, 180, 187, 208, 212, 228 n. 21; 235 n. 58; 236 nn. 69, 75; 239 n. 109; 251 n. 17
Richter, David H. 101, 243 n. 35
Roberts, William 222 n. 13; 225 n. 60; 226 n. 83; 227 n. 11; 228 n. 41; 235 n. 54; 237 nn. 79, 90; 240 nn. 124, 138; 244 n. 50; 248 n. 48; 253 n. 80; 254 nn. 1, 2, 19, 20; 256–7 n. 72; 257 nn. 73–6, 78, 81, 82
Robertson, William 93, 165, 233 n. 29; 234 n. 36
Robinson, Mary 7, 151
  Memoirs 87–8, 223 n. 27; 243 n. 4
  The Natural Daughter 92, 114, 115, 167–8, 207, 242 n. 10
  Vancenza 70
  Walsingham 167, 170
Roche, Regina Maria 100, 121, 144, 230 n. 64
  Clermont 58, 235 n. 56; 236 n. 75; 244 n. 41; 249 n. 63
  The Children of the Abbey 7, 94, 98, 146, 156–7, 171, 181, 207, 208, 223 n. 29; 244 n. 40; 249 n. 63; 259 n. 48
  The Nocturnal Visit 95, 110, 120, 154, 155, 166, 243 n. 40; 244 nn. 41, 43; 245 n. 59; 252 n. 52

Rogers, Samuel 37, 39, 136, 247 n. 34
Roland, Manon 84, 87
Rollin's Ancient History 233 n. 29
romance and the novel 198–200
Rosa Matilda, *see* Dacre, Charlotte
Ross, Deborah 259 n. 41
Ross, Marlon 229 n. 61; 230 n. 65; 231 n. 81
Roulston, Christine 258 nn. 32, 33, 35, 36, 38
Rousseau, G. S. 223 n. 40; 237 nn. 82, 87; 238 n. 92
Rousseau, J. J. 3, 8, 43, 77, 79, 95, 130, 139, 140, 239 n. 118
    Confessions 140
    Julie, ou la Nouvelle Eloise 73, 74–7, 119, 135, 167, 209
Rowbotham, Sheila 234 n. 39
Rowe, Elizabeth 26, 130, 142
Rowe, Nicholas 190
    Jane Shore 61
    The Royal Convert 60
Rowley, William 237 n. 87
Ruffhead, Owen 18
Rundell, Mrs, *Domestic Cookery* 39
Ruoff, Gene W. 229 n. 62
Ruskin, John 34
Rutland, lack of evidence for circulating libraries 163

Sade, Marquis de, *Justine* 38
Sale, William M 228 n. 24
Sales, Roger 226 n. 100
Salisbury circulating libraries 162
Salisbury Reading Society 160
Sancho, Ignatius 177, 178, 254 n. 8
Sandham, Elizabeth, *The Twin Sisters* 44, 45, 196, 231 n. 9; 232 n. 16; 257 n. 5
Sapiro, Virginia 237 n. 78; 239 n. 118
Savage, Richard 246 n. 11
Schaffer, Kay 235 n. 47
Schaw, Janet 92, 242 n. 10
Schiebinger, Londa 67, 237 n. 80; 238 nn. 93, 94, 98; 239 n. 112; 254 n. 5
Schellenberg, Betty A. 96, 242 n. 18
Schofield, Mary Anne 241 n. 146
Schofield, Mary Anne and Macheski, Cecilia 241 n. 147
Schor, Esther 230 n. 70
Schweickart, Patrocinio and Flynn, Elizabeth A. 226 n. 98
scientific reading 64–68
Scott, Joan Wallach 233 n. 31
Scott, John 257 n. 7
Scott, Sarah 93, 96, 139
    History of Cornelia 110, 111–12, 113, 245 n. 59

Millenium Hall 69, 97, 159, 194, 197, 238 n. 102
Scott, Sir Walter 35, 40, 98, 99, 137, 143, 148, 168, 174, 198, 213–18, 227 n. 4; 239 n. 114
    Rob Roy 216
    Waverley 35, 197, 198, 206, 213, 230 n. 73
Scudery, Madame 38
Senf, Carole A. 257 n. 13
Sevigné, Marie de 71, 133, 248 n. 50
Seward, Anna 14, 17, 39, 48, 53, 56, 100, 232 n. 27; 234 nn. 36, 41; 235 n. 49; 238 n. 100; 239 n. 113; 241 n. 152; 243 n. 33; 251 n. 20; 253 n. 74
Seymour, Frances Thynne, *see* Hertford, Countess of
Shaftesbury 78
Shakespeare, William 58, 62–4, 101, 102, 106, 130, 136, 137, 143, 148, 155, 188, 190
    As You Like It 116, 246 n. 10
    Coriolanus 194, 257 n. 79
    Hamlet 127, 137, 174, 246 n. 10
    Henry IV 127, 246 n. 10
    Henry V 246 n. 10
    Henry VI 174
    Henry VIII 246 n. 10
    Julius Caesar 127, 246 n. 10
    King John 64
    King Lear 174, 246 n. 10
    Macbeth 62, 127, 174, 246 n. 10
    Measure for Measure 127, 246 n. 10
    Merchant of Venice 60, 63, 246 nn. 9, 10
    Merry Wives of Windsor 246 n. 10
    A Midsummer Night's Dream 147, 246 n. 10
    Much Ado about Nothing 81, 240 n. 133
    Othello 60, 127, 246 n. 10
    Richard III 246 n. 10
    Romeo and Juliet 63, 147
    The Tempest 116, 190, 246 n. 10
    Timon of Athens 246 n. 10
    Troilus and Cressida 172
    Twelfth Night 63, 148, 236 n. 75
    The Winter's Tale 246 n. 10
Sharrock, Catherine 226 n 79
Shelley, Elizabeth 118
Shelley, Harriet Westbrook 93, 99, 242 n. 12; 253 n. 75
Shelley, Mary 12, 34–5, 65, 71, 93, 181, 222 n. 15; 230 n. 70; 237 n. 84; 242 n. 12; 243 n. 25; 253 n. 75
    Falkner 51, 59, 93, 153, 233 n. 32; 235 nn. 58, 60
    Frankenstein 5, 100, 220, 222 n. 15
    The Last Man 154, 251 n. 10
    Lodore 69, 172, 238 n. 103
    Matilda 115, 245 n. 76

Shelley, Mary and Percy Bysshe, *History of a Six Weeks Tour* 243 n. 26
Shelley, Percy Bysshe 20, 34, 92, 98–100, 118, 168
   Zastrozzi 118
Shelley, Percy Bysshe and Elizabeth, *Original Poetry by Victor and Cazire* 246 n. 84
Sheridan, Betsy 162, 171, 231 n. 3; 233 n. 28; 252 n. 29; 253 n. 70
Sheridan, Frances 5, 42, 222 n. 19; 231 nn. 1, 2, 3
   History of Sidney Biddulph 70, 110, 238 n. 106; 245 n. 59
Sheridan, Richard Brinsley
   The Rivals 48, 165–6, 252 nn. 42, 49
   The School for Scandal 61
   The Stranger 242 n. 7
Sherlock's Sermons 143
Shrewsbury School library 160
Shrimpton, Theophilus 164
Shteir, Ann B. 64, 68, 224 n. 42; 237 nn. 80, 81, 82, 83, 86; 238 nn. 92, 93, 94, 96, 97, 98, 103
Shuckford, Dr 138
Sibbald, Susan 5, 12, 100, 155, 180, 186, 222 n. 19; 225 n. 59; 243 n. 32; 251 n. 11; 254 n. 19
Sibbit, Adam, *Thoughts on the Frequency of Divorces* 111, 245 n. 60
Siddons, Sarah 234 n. 36
Silliman, Benjamin, *Letters of Shahcoolen* 236 n. 64; 240 nn. 129, 130
Simons, Judy 221 n. 5
Sleath, Eleanor 121
   The Orphan of the Rhine 196–7, 244 n. 40
Small, Helen 117, 223 n. 28; 224 n. 49; 245 n. 80; 246 nn. 85, 87
Smith, Adam 108
Smith, Charlotte 16, 52, 58, 59, 67, 73, 85–6, 141, 144, 146, 163, 165, 166, 172, 180, 207, 238 n. 95; 239 n. 114; 249 nn. 63, 67; 254 n. 21
   Celestine 137
   Conversations, Introducing Poetry 85, 235 n. 58; 241 n. 146; 252 n. 50
   Desmond 29, 85, 113, 141, 234 n. 38; 236 n. 65; 241 nn. 147, 149
   Emmeline 73, 93, 137, 146, 154, 166, 239 n. 115; 241 nn. 146, 149; 242 n. 10
   Ethelinde 29, 95, 137, 166, 241 nn. 146, 147, 150; 255 n. 33
   Letters of a Solitary Wanderer 93, 241 n. 149; 253 n. 54
   Marchmont 114–15, 116, 117, 154, 252 nn. 38, 53

Montalbert 95, 113, 241 n. 147
The Old Manor House 113, 154, 177, 241 nn. 146, 147; 254 n. 5
Rambles Farther 51, 233 n. 32; 235 nn. 58, 59; 253 n. 73; 257 n. 14
Romance of Real Life, The 241 n. 150
Rural Walks 85, 235 nn. 58, 59; 238 n. 96; 241 nn. 146, 148; 252 n. 50
Young Philosopher, The 241 nn. 146, 147
Smith, Sidney 240 n. 137
Smollett, Tobias 78, 166, 197, 199
   History of England 12
   Humphrey Clinker 23, 227 n. 7
   Peregrine Pickle 172, 185, 258 n. 34
   Roderick Random 3, 77, 140, 185, 240 n. 125
Sortes Virgilianae 94–5
Southam, Brian 250 n. 79; 257 n. 7
Southerne, Thomas 40
   The Fatal Marriage 61, 62
Southey, Robert 39, 89, 98, 99, 168
   Life of Nelson 174
Spacks, Patricia Meyer 259 n. 42
Spectator 22, 25, 97, 129, 136, 154, 188, 243 n. 20
Spencer, Jane 224 n. 41
Spender, Dale 257 n. 3; 258 n. 33
Spenser, Edmund 154, 167, 189
   The Faerie Queene 106
Spufford, Margaret 255 n. 37
Staël, Germaine de 37, 40, 135
   Corinne 38
   Delphine 18
Stanley, Lady, *see* Holroyd, Maria Josepha
Stanyan, Temple, *Grecian History* 205
Staves, Susan 61, 236 nn. 69, 70; 242 n. 15
Steele, Richard 246 n. 12
   The Tender Husband 61
Sternberg, Janet 226 n. 79
Sterne, Laurence 25, 139, 199, 206
   A Sentimental Journey 98, 136, 138, 139, 166
   Tristram Shandy 136, 208, 228 n. 19
Stewart, Garrett 224 n. 46; 226 n. 81; 242 n. 16; 250 n. 73
Stock, Ellen, *see* Weeton, Ellen
Stone, Lawrence 112, 245 n. 64; 255 n. 48
St Pierre's *Paul et Virginie* 76
Streatfield, Sophie 70
Stuart, Lady Louisa 106, 155, 228 n. 18; 239 n. 114; 251 n. 20
Stukeley, William, *Avebury* 160
Summers, Montagu 259 n. 57
Sutherland, Kathryn 233 n. 31; 242 nn. 5, 8; 257 nn. 77, 80
Swift, Jonathan 25, 58, 127, 169, 188, 228 n. 21; 246 n. 11

Cadenus and Vanessa 253 n. 63
Gulliver's Travels 107, 136, 244 n. 50
Tale of a Tub 184
Sylph, The 245 n. 67; 253 n. 66
Sympathy of Souls 242 n. 7

Tacitus 139
Tadmor, Naomi 223 n. 28; 224 n. 49; 253 nn. 74, 83
Talbot, Catherine 20, 26, 30, 53, 54, 138, 140, 142, 174, 228 n. 28; 234 n. 41; 248 n. 41
Tasso, Torquato 101, 103, 119
Taunton women's reading group 161
Tatler, The 129, 136
Taylor, Ann and Jane 67
Taylor, Eliza, *Education: or Elizabeth, her Lover and Husband* 15, 128, 225 n. 71; 247 n. 14
Taylor, John Tinnon 241 nn. 141, 143; 253 n. 62
Taylor, Mrs, *Practical Hints to Young Females* 187
Tears of Sensibility 166
Tennenhouse, Leonard 232 n. 20
Tenney, Tabitha Gilman, *Female Quixotism* 205–6, 259 n. 43
Terence 139
Thaxted reading club 161
Thackeray, William Makepeace 252 n. 44
Theobald, Lewis 236 n. 73
Thomas, Claudia 248 nn. 37, 43, 49
Thompson, Ann and Roberts, Sasha 236 nn. 73, 74, 78
Thomson, James 58, 102, 136, 165, 188, 189, 190, 247 n. 34
Seasons 58, 59, 177
Thomson, James, *The Denial* 59, 181, 235 n. 58
Thrale, Hester 22, 30, 31, 45, 63, 66, 93, 100, 130, 136, 153, 162, 169, 175, 179, 186, 192
Anecdotes of Samuel Johnson 229 nn. 45, 47, 48
Thraliana 227 n. 6; 229 n, 46; 237 n, 90; 242 n. 16; 243 n. 33; 252 n. 35; 253 nn. 63, 83; 255 nn. 39, 45; 256 n. 68
Thucydides 54, 70, 139
Tibullus 103
Tillyard, Stella 233 n. 35
Tindall 78
Tobin, Beth Fowkes 235 n. 52; 251 n. 19; 256 n. 69
Todd, Janet 227 n. 105; 243 nn. 23, 34; 245 n. 76; 259 n. 57
Tompkins, J. M. S. 234 n. 43; 243 n. 21; 250 n. 82

Tonna, Charlotte 63–4
Too Civil by Half 242 n. 7
Too Friendly by Half 242 n. 7
translations 69–70
Trant, Clarissa 12, 13, 73, 225 n. 61; 239 n. 115
Trelawney, Edward 92
Trimmer, Sarah 7, 45
Trouille, Mary Seidmann 239 nn. 110, 116, 118, 119
Troide, Lars E. 234 n. 42
trope of the talking book 178
Trotter, Catherine 142
Trumbach, Randolph 223 n. 40; 224 n. 43
Tucker, George Holbert 248 n. 52; 249 n. 59, 64; 250 n. 80
Turner, Cheryl 224 n. 57; 227 n. 2; 252 n. 39
Turner, Thomas 172, 174
Twentyman, Miss 161
Ty, Eleanor 224 n. 47; 237 n. 90

Uphaus, Robert W 243 n. 35
Use of Circulating Libraries Considered 169, 223 n. 26

Vane, Lady 123, 142
Varma, Devendra P. 223 n. 26; 245 n. 62; 252 n. 42; 253 n. 57
Vesey, Elizabeth 65, 66, 138, 139, 153
Virgil 71, 178
Voltaire 40, 52, 63, 77, 79, 119, 135, 138, 139, 190, 233 n. 36
Candide 135, 139, 247 n. 33
Volney's *Les ruines* 99
Voyage à Plombières 13
voyages and travels 55–7

Wakefield, Priscilla 237 n. 83
Waldron, Mary 150, 250 n. 85; 256 nn. 51, 60, 61
Walker, George, *The Vagabond* 74, 78, 240 n. 130
Waller, Edmund 246 n. 11
Walpole, Horace, *The Castle of Otranto* 189, 258 n. 16
Walton, Izaak, *The Complete Angler* 184
Warren, Leland E 258 n. 41
Watson, Nicola J 230 nn. 63, 73; 239 nn. 116, 119; 240, n. 122; 243 n. 23
Watt, Ian 186, 255 n. 42
Watts, Isaac 163
The Improvement of the Mind 222 n. 16
Webster, Frances 38
Wedd, A. F. 241 n. 2; 257 n. 11

Weeton, Ellen (later Stock)   180–3, 186, 254 n. 22; 255 n. 46

Weeton, Thomas Jr   182

Wesley, John   56

Wesley, Mehetabel   26, 228 n. 24

West, Jane   24, 52, 59, 61, 65–6, 83, 141, 144, 151, 249 n. 63
  The Advantages of Education   50, 51, 58, 67, 196, 233 nn. 29, 33; 238 nn. 94, 95; 241 n. 139; 248 n. 37
  A Gossip's Story   149, 150
  The Infidel Father   3, 248 n. 37
  Letters to a Young Lady   234 n. 38; 236 n. 67; 237 n. 86; 240 n. 127; 248 n. 37
  A Tale of the Times   32, 74, 141, 158, 227 n. 12; 235 n. 59

Westmeath, Marchioness of   112

Wheatley, Phillis   177–8, 254 n. 9

Whitbread, Helena   221 n. 5; 225 n. 64; 239 n. 114; 240 n. 136; 252 n. 26

White, James, *The Adventures of King Richard Caeur-de-Lion*   245 n. 62

Whitehead, William   18, 136, 247 n. 34

Whitehaven circulating library   169

Whole Duty of Man, The   23, 30, 112

Wilberforce, William   193

Williams, Anna   32, 141

Williams, Carolyn D.   138, 239 n. 112; 248 n. 38

Williams, Helen Maria   142
  Julia   15, 58, 59, 62, 73–4, 225 nn. 71, 72; 236 nn. 71, 72

Williams, Ioan   226 nn. 88, 89; 232 n. 13; 233 n. 31; 234 n. 46; 259 n. 60

Williams, Jane   92

Wilson, Carol Shiner and Haefner, Joel   238 n. 95

Wilson, Penelope   238 n. 102

Wilson, Sarah, *A Visit to Grove Cottage*   67

Wilt, Judith   259 n. 54

Wiseman, Susan   226 n. 80

Wither, George, *Emblems*   184

Withering, William, *Botanical Arrangement*   67, 68

Wittreich, Joseph   226 n. 99

Wolfson, Susan J   230 n. 70; 237 n. 78

Wollaston's *Religion of Nature Delineated*   247 n. 12

Wollstonecraft, Mary   5, 16, 25, 32, 43, 44–5, 54, 56, 57, 61, 63, 64, 65, 68, 73, 74, 79–82, 84, 93, 98, 99, 100, 130, 141, 148, 151, 173, 179, 182, 194, 233 n. 33; 237 n. 78; 239 n. 118; 240 n. 130; 242 n. 11; 243 nn. 33, 34; 253 n. 76; 258 n. 20
  The Female Reader   15, 43, 46, 232 n. 19; 242 n. 12
  'Hints'   226 n. 82; 235 nn. 50, 53
  Original Stories from Real Life   173
  Thoughts on the Education of Daughters   46, 80, 221 n. 5; 231 n. 11; 232 n. 22; 236 n. 68
  Vindication of the Rights of Woman   46, 48, 99, 151, 162, 226 n. 83; 228 n. 18; 232 n. 19, 24, 27; 234 n. 42; 235 nn. 50, 53; 238 n. 101; 241 n. 142; 255 n. 29
  The Wrongs of Woman; or, Maria   74–5, 97, 118, 207, 221 n. 2; 239 n. 118; 242 n. 10; 245 n. 76; 254 n. 14

Wolstoneholme, Susan   243 n. 31; 244 n. 44

Wordsworth, Dorothy   5, 34, 112, 222 n. 19

Wordsworth, William   8, 33, 34, 35, 39, 59, 148, 168, 222 n. 19; 230 n. 71
  Lyrical Ballads   247 n. 34

Worton, Michael and Still, Judith   250 n. 78

Wraxall's *Memoirs*   135

Wyatt, Jean   245 n. 72

Wycherley, William   61

Xenophon   139, 246 n. 12

Yearsley, Ann   71, 164, 184, 185, 187, 188–92, 256 n. 49
  'Clifton Hill'   189, 255 n. 34
  Poems, on Several Occasions   189, 255 n. 34; 256 n. 58
  Poems on Various Subjects   190, 255 n. 38
  The Royal Captives   191–2, 221 n. 2

Yeovil, Book Society of   160

Young, Edward   25, 58, 127, 136, 178, 188, 189, 204, 228 n. 21; 246 n. 11; 247 n. 34
  Night Thoughts   58, 177, 189